PREFACE

The purpose of this book is to provide a concise introduction to the criminal law of Scotland. This work is intended to meet the needs of law students, but it is hoped that it will be of use to those engaged in the practice of the criminal law.

It is inevitable that in a book of this nature there will be omissions. We hope, however, that we have managed to deal with the most important aspects of criminal law, covering those offences which most commonly arise in the criminal courts. While we have generally confined ourselves to stating the current law of Scotland, at many points we have drawn attention to the position in other jurisdictions. In particular, we have attempted to refer to the many important developments which have occurred in other Commonwealth countries where, over the last two decades or so, criminal law has undergone a significant programme of judicially-led reform.

Any book on the criminal law of Scotland stands in the shadow of Sheriff Gordon's magnum opus, *The Criminal Law of Scotland*. The debt that criminal law studies in Scotland owe to this work is as apparent in this book as it is elsewhere. We have also been much assisted by the most useful casebook compiled by Mr Christopher Gane and Sheriff Charles Stoddart.

We are grateful for assistance which we received from a number of quarters, in particular, from the staff of Butterworths Law Publishers, and from Alexander Gerver, who compiled the index. Responsibility for any errors and omissions rests solely with the authors.

Alexander McCall Smith
David Sheldon

Scots Criminal Law

R A A McCall Smith, LLB, PhD
Reader in Law, University of Edinburgh

David Sheldon, LLB, Solicitor
Lecturer in Law, University of Edinburgh

Edinburgh
Butterworths
1992

United Kingdom

Butterworth & Co (Publishers) Ltd, 4 Hill Street,
EDINBURGH EH2 3JZ, 88 Kingsway,
LONDON WC2B 6AB

Australia

Butterworths Pty Ltd, SYDNEY, MELBOURNE,
BRISBANE, ADELAIDE, PERTH, CANBERRA and
HOBART

Belgium

Butterworth & Co (Publishers) Ltd, BRUSSELS

Canada

Butterworths Canada Ltd, TORONTO and
VANCOUVER

Ireland

Butterworth (Ireland) Ltd, DUBLIN

Malaysia

Malayan Law Journal Sdn Bhd, KUALA LUMPUR

New Zealand

Butterworths of New Zealand Ltd, WELLINGTON
and AUCKLAND

Puerto Rico

Equity de Puerto Rico, Inc, HATO REY

Singapore

Butterworth & Co (Asia) Pte Ltd, SINGAPORE

USA

Butterworth Legal Publishers, ST PAUL, Minnesota;
SEATTLE, Washington; BOSTON, Massachusetts;
AUSTIN, Texas and D & S Publishers,
CLEARWATER, Florida

A CIP Catalogue record for this book is available from the British Library.

ISBN 0 406 25269 6

Typeset by BP Integraphics Ltd, Bath, Avon
Printed and bound in Great Britain by Thomson Litho Ltd, East Kilbride, Scotland

Contents

IV. PROPERTY OFFENCES

V. OFFENCES AGAINST THE STATE AND ADMINISTRATION OF JUSTICE

Table of statutes

Table of cases

List of abbreviations

A Crim R	Australian Criminal Reports
AC	Law Reports, Appeal Cases (House of Lords and Privy Council) 1890–
ALJR	Australian Law Journal Reports
All ER	All England Law Reports 1936–
ALR	Australian Law Reports
Ark	Arkley's Justiciary Reports 1846–48
Broun	Broun's Justiciary Reports 1842–45
CCC	Canadian Criminal Cases
CLR	Commonwealth Law Reports (Australian)
Car&P	Carrington and Payne's Reports (England) 1823–41
Coup	Couper's Justiciary Reports 1868–85
Cox CC	Cox's Criminal Cases (England) 1843–1941
CR	Criminal Reports (Canada)
Crim App Rep	Criminal Appeal Reports (England) 1908–
Crim LR	Criminal Law Review
D&A	Deas and Anderson's Decisions (Court of Session) 1829–32
DLR	Dominion Law Reports (Canada)
Dears&B	Dearsly and Bell 169 English Reports 1856–58
EHRR	European Human Rights Reports 1979–
ER	English Reports 1220–1865
F	Federal Reporter (USA) 1880–1924
F&F	Foster and Finlayson 171–3 English Reports 1856–67
F(J)	Justiciary Cases in Fraser's Session Cases 1898–1906
GWD	Green's Weekly Digest 1986–

HKLR	Hong Kong Law Reports
Irv	Irvine's Justiciary Reports 1851–68
JC	Justiciary Cases 1917–
KB	Law Reports, King's Bench Division (England) 1900–52
Macq	Macqueen's House of Lords Reports 1851–65
MedLR	Medical Law Reports
Mo	Missouri Reports (USA)
NBR	New Brunswick Reports
NE	North Eastern Reporter (USA)
NYS	New York State Reports
NZLR	New Zealand Law Reports 1883–
P&NGLR	Papua and New Guinea Law Reports
QB	Law Reports, Queen's Bench Division (England) 1891–1901, 1952–
R(J)	Justiciary Cases in Rettie's Session Cases 1873–98
RTR	Road Traffic Reports 1970–
SA	South African Law Reports 1947–
SASR	South Australian State Reports
SCCR	Scottish Criminal Case Reports 1981–
SCCR Supp	Scottish Criminal Case Reports Supplement (1950–80)
SCR	Supreme Court Reports (Canada)
SLR	Scottish Law Reporter 1865–1925
SLT	Scots Law Times 1893–1908, and 1909–
So	Southern Reporter (USA)
SR	Southern Rhodesia Reports
SR(NSW)	State Reports (New South Wales)
St Tr	State Trials 1163–1820
Swin	Swinton's Justiciary Reports 1835–41
Tas SR	Tasmanian State Reports
VLR	Victorian Law Reports (Australia)
VR	Victorian Reports 1870–72, and 1957–
WLR	Weekly Law Reports (England) 1953–
WR	Weekly Reporter (England) 1852–1906
White	White's Justiciary Reports 1885–93

Journals

Br J Crim	British Journal of Criminology
Brit Med J	British Medical Journal
Camb LJ	Cambridge Law Journal
Can Bar Rev	Canadian Bar Review
Col L Rev	Columbia Law Review
Crim L J	Criminal Law Journal (Australia)
Crim LQ	Criminal Law Quarterly
Crim LR	Criminal Law Review
Int Comp LQ	International and Comparative Law Quarterly
J Crim L	Journal of Criminal Law
JLS	Journal of the Law Society
JR	Juridical Review
LQR	Law Quarterly Review
Med Sci Law	Medicine, Science and the Law
NILQ	Northern Ireland Law Quarterly
NLJ	New Law Journal
SALJ	South African Law Journal

Textbooks

Alison: Archibald Alison *Principles and Practice of the Criminal Law of Scotland* (2 vols, 1832 and 1833)

Burnett: J Burnett *A Treatise on Various Branches of the Criminal Law of Scotland* (1811)

Gane and Stoddart: CHW Gane and CN Stoddart *A Casebook on Scottish Criminal Law* (2nd edn, 1988, Greens)

Gordon: GH Gordon *The Criminal Law of Scotland* (2nd edn, 1978, supplement 1992, Greens)

Hume: David Hume *Commentaries on the Law of Scotland Respecting the Description and Punishment of Crimes* (2 vols, 1797) (reprinted 1986, Butterworths)

Macdonald: George Macdonald *Practical Treatise on the Criminal Law of Scotland* (1867) (5th edn, 1948, by J Walker and DJ Stevenson)

Mackenzie: George Mackenzie *Laws and Customs of Scotland in Matters Criminal* (1678–99)

Smith and Hogan: JC Smith and Brian Hogan *Criminal Law* (6th edn, 1991, Butterworths)

Wheatley: John Wheatley *Road Traffic Law in Scotland* (1989, Butterworths)

I. GENERAL PRINCIPLES

1. The sources of Scots criminal law

The criminal law of Scotland is a combination of common and statutory law. Many crimes are still based on common law, this being the case both with serious crimes (such as murder or rape) as well as with the less serious crimes (such as minor assault or breach of the peace). Common law has tended to be a more important source of criminal law in Scotland than it has been in England; there is no equivalent in Scotland, for example, of the Theft Acts 1968 and 1978, nor is there any draft criminal code. Scotland, therefore, remains one of the very few jurisdictions in which an uncodified system of criminal justice is applied. There is a growing number of statutory offences, however, some of which touch upon areas previously exclusively governed by the common law.[1] Some new statutory offences are of course completely novel, particularly where the criminal law addresses a problem thrown up by changed social habits or by advances in technology. The Misuse of Drugs Act 1971, along with its predecessor Acts, deals with a problem which criminal lawyers of the nineteenth century simply would not have recognised. Similarly, the Human Organ Transplants Act 1989 creates offences which had no equivalent in the common law.

The common law of crime is based on custom, as embodied in the decisions of the criminal courts. Romano-canonical sources were important in the development of Scots criminal law, with the criminal courts making frequent references to texts of Roman law and to the works of jurists in the European civilian tradition. By the end of the eighteenth century, however, such sources were of secondary importance, domestic Scottish authorities being considered more pertinent. The earlier influence of Roman law was sufficient to place pre-eighteenth century Scots law in a reasonably close intellectual relationship with its continental counterparts, but

---

[1] Examples include the Sexual Offences (Scotland) Act 1976 and the Civic Government (Scotland) Act 1982.

this proximity was irretrievably shattered by the movement to criminal law codification which occurred in the nineteenth century. As a result of this, Scots criminal law cannot easily be classified in comparative terms. It is not a typical system of the Anglo-American tradition (where codification is increasingly the norm); nor has it much in common with the codified criminal law systems of civil law countries in Europe and elsewhere. In some respects it is close to English criminal law, particularly where United Kingdom statutes are involved, but there are nonetheless substantial differences between the criminal law of the two jurisdictions, and superficial similarities may be misleading. The Scots law of murder, for example, differs markedly from its English law counterpart in the way in which the *mens rea* requirement is defined. The end result may be very similar in each case, but the process by which a conclusion is reached may be very different. For practical purposes the starting point for any investigation of modern Scots criminal law must be the work of the late eighteenth-century jurist, David Hume.[1] Hume's *Commentaries on the Law of Scotland Respecting the Description and Punishment of Crimes* was first published between 1797 and 1800, although the commonly-used edition is that which appeared in 1844.[2] The particular importance of Hume's treatise lies in the fact that it was written at the end of a period of considerable development in the criminal law and represents a systematisation of an area of the law which had not benefited from the same degree of conceptual organisation as had civil law. Hume was not the first legal writer to turn his attention to the criminal law of Scotland: Sir George Mackenzie's *Laws and Customs of Scotland in Matters Criminal*, which appeared between 1678 and 1699, and William Forbes' *Institutes of the Law of Scotland*, published in 1730, both set out to provide a complete account of the criminal law, but both, for different reasons, had outlived their usefulness by the late eighteenth century.

The authority enjoyed by Hume's work was considerable, both during the nineteenth and twentieth centuries, and it is still not uncommon for it to be cited before the courts today. It is important to bear in mind that although Hume is considered an institutional writer, his work is no more than a statement of the law as it was at the time of his writing, and his views do not have the weight of statute. The courts are therefore prepared to depart from his

---

[1] For an account of Hume's legal career, see DM Walker *The Scottish Jurists* (1985, Edinburgh) p 316 et seq.
[2] A reprint of this edition was published in 1986: Law Society of Scotland, Edinburgh.

interpretation of the law, as was the case in *HM Adv v Stallard*[1], in which the High Court held that social conditions had so changed as to make Hume's views on the subject of the marital exemption in rape unacceptable. Yet the authority which the *Commentary* still enjoys is undoubted, particularly when an issue arises for which there is no modern precedent and which requires court to address a fundamental issue of principle.

Subsequent writers on the criminal law are occasionally cited before the courts, although there is none with the authority of Hume. Archibald Alison's *Principles and Practice of the Criminal Law of Scotland*, published between 1832–33, is referred to from time to time, but is not considered a work of major significance. There has been great reliance on George Macdonald's *Practical Treatise on the Criminal Law of Scotland*, which ran to many editions from the time of its first publication in 1867. The edition currently used by the courts is the fifth edition, which appeared in 1948. In spite of its limitations, this work has had an undoubted status as the *vade mecum* of practitioners for over a century, and is still extensively referred to. Sir Thomas Smith's *Short Commentary on the Law of Scotland*, which was published in 1962, was primarily concerned with civil law, but dealt with criminal matters as well, and played a major part in reawakening interest in theoretical aspects of Scots criminal law. But the real credit for this must go to Sheriff Gordon's magisterial work, *The Criminal Law of Scotland*.[2] This book, which is in the highest traditions of criminal law scholarship, is in daily use in Scottish criminal law practice and also enjoys a considerable reputation in the supreme courts of other jurisdictions.

The real source of the law, of course, is not the textbook but the decisions of the courts. The common law of crimes is located in the judgments of the High Court and, to a lesser extent, those of sheriff courts. There is a wealth of criminal law decisions to quarry, but in practice it is unusual for a modern court to go back to decisions which were made earlier than the nineteenth century. On most issues, where relevant Scottish precedents are to be found, these will occur in twentieth-century reports, although it may sometimes be necessary to refer to decisions made in the late nineteenth century. This is not to say that older authorities are discountenanced; much will depend on the subject matter. On a question of statutory liability, for example, the relevant decisions will

---

[1] 1989 SCCR 248, 1989 SLT 469.
[2] 2nd edn, 1978. 2nd cumulative supplement, 1992.

inevitably be modern, the reason for this being that the issue of strict liability has only been discussed by the courts since an appreciable body of statutory criminal law came into existence during the twentieth century.

The influence of English sources on Scots law generally has been the subject of some controversy. Scots criminal law is not subject to appeal to the House of Lords, and has not therefore been interpreted by English judges. Criminal law has also been, by its very nature, more local in character, and the mercantile influences which tend to uniformity in commercial law, do not operate in this area. At the same time, there has undoubtedly been a degree of English law influence, both terminological and substantive, a matter upon which Hume himself expressed concern. Scots lawyers use the terms *mens rea* and *actus reus*, as do their counterparts in systems based on English law, and the old Scots equivalent of *mens rea*, dole, seems largely to have disappeared. In matters of substance there have been instances in which the courts have imported English legal decisions into Scots law, occasionally somewhat controversially, as in the case of *Meek and Others v HM Adv*[1], where Scots law was said to be the same as English law in respect of error in rape, a positon which conflicted with a well-established body of Scottish decisions on the requirements of error.

The comparative self-sufficiency of Scots law in relation to criminal law sources does not preclude the need to refer to cases from other jursidictions. The ingenuity of criminal defenders – or their counsel – means that novel points will always arise. Such issues may be settled on the basis of pure principle, or on the basis of authority, and a precedent-based system invariably looks to the latter. A small jurisdiction will have a relatively limited range of criminal decisions to which reference might be made, and in these circumstances the decisions of other jurisdictions will be useful. Most frequent reference is made to English decisions, for reasons of convenience, but there is no reason why the decisions of other Commonwealth jurisdictions should not carry weight. This is particularly the case with Canadian and Australian decisions, where a great deal of judicial attention has been paid to the principled development of the criminal law. Examination of the decisions of other jurisdictions may also assist to identify areas where one's own laws are defective or in need of reform. Even a cursory examination of the criminal jurisprudence of, say, the Supreme Court of Canada or the High Court of Australia, will reveal a

---

[1] 1982 SCCR 613, 1983 SLT 280.

number of areas where Scots law appears to have shown little inclination for reform. For example, the courts in both these jurisdictions have made major efforts to address the problem of strict liability and to ameliorate its most strikingly unfair features; there has been no movement in this respect either in Scots or English law. At the same time, irrespective of any criticism that might be made in such respects, in the area of evidence and procedure, Scots law enjoys a deservedly high reputation. In particular, the 110-day rule, which requires that the trial should commence within this period where a person accused of a crime is held in custody, is a valuable and much admired safeguard against dilatory justice. Similarly, the rule of evidence requiring corroboration prevents unsound conviction, expecially where confessions are involved.

THE ROLE OF CRIMINAL STATUTES

Although Scots criminal law may be predominantly of a common law nature, statutes nevertheless play an increasingly major part in the criminal law. There has been some debate as to the precise place of minor statutory offences in the scheme of the criminal law: are such breaches of the law to be considered crimes (in the true sense of the word) or are they merely 'non-criminal offences' ? There certainly exists a moral distinction in the minds of most people between those acts which are intrinsically and profoundly wrong – such as murder – and those acts which are either trivial or technical breaches of the law – such as parking offences. This distinction is certainly mirrored in the sentencing patterns of the courts, but it is not necessarily reflected in the way in which crimes are classified or described in the law. There is a tendencey to describe minor infringements of the law as 'offences' rather than as crimes, but the term 'offence' is also used in relation to serious breaches. Nor will the seriousness of an infringement be determined by whether or not it is punished by common law or statute. Many statutory offences involve morally-reprehensible conduct, and may anyway be based on earlier common law crimes. This is the case, for example, with some of the offences specified in the Sexual Offences (Scotland) Act 1976.

On balance, it is preferable to describe as crimes only those infringements of the criminal law which attract moral opprobrium. This would mean that the stigma which goes with conviction of a crime is reserved for those who really deserve it. The term 'offence' will probably continue to be used indiscriminately, but it only acquires real moral force in the appropriate context, when it is linked with a morally-reprehensible act (such as assault, theft, murder and the like).

For a considerable period there was a marked tendency in English-speaking jurisdictions to interpret penal statutes restrictively, that is, in favour of the accused. The origins of this are to be found in judicial attempts during the nineteenth century to limit the draconian effects of laws which provided for the death penalty for even comparatively minor infringements of the criminal law. This principle was on occasion applied in a way which was most favourable to the accused, but this approach has now largely been abandoned in favour of a more liberal theory of interpretation[1]. Penal statutes are now interpreted according to the same canons of construction as are applied to other statutes, but if, at the end, there remains an element of doubt as to whether the conduct of the accused falls within the scope of the statute, this doubt will be resolved in favour of the accused. In every case the question will be whether the conduct of the accused can reasonably be said to have infringed the law according to the ordinary meaning of the language used in the statute. The courts will not speculate on what the intention of the legislature must have been: the test is what the legislature actually said in the statute. For example, in cases involving the possession of minute quantities of controlled drugs, arguments that the intention of the legislature must have been to penalise possession of usable quantities have not prevented the conviction of those possessing minute quantities of the drugs in question.[2]

THE DECLARATORY POWER

A further source of criminal law is the declaratory power of the High Court. This is the power vested in the High Court to declare conduct to be a crime, even if it has not previously been considered to be criminal. This power is exercised retrospectively; it is therefore possible that a person may act on sound legal advice that what he is doing is not criminal, only to discover subsequently that he is to be penalised. The extent to which this infringes the principle of legality is self-evident, and will be discussed further below.

[1] For discussion, see FAR Bennion, *Statutory Interpretation* (2nd edn, 1992) p 381.
[2] For example, *Bocking v Roberts* (1973) 3 All ER 962.

The *locus classicus* of the declaratory power in the nineteenth century is the case of *Bernard Greenhuff*[1]. Greenhuff had been convicted of running a gaming house in which cards were played, a form of conduct which clearly offended at least some moral sensibilities at the time. There was one strong dissenting opinion in this case, but for the majority of the judges there was no question but that this was conduct which implied the greatest social danger and which therefore justified the invocation of the declaratory power. It was accepted, though, that this power should be used sparingly. As one of the judges, Lord Mackenzie, put it, 'In order to bring any act within the jurisdiction of this court, as a crime . . . the act must either in itself be so grossly immoral and mischievous on the face of it, that no man can fairly be ignorant of its nature, or it must have been settled by a course of experience, and become notorious, that such is its nature'.[2] In no other nineteenth-century case is the declaratory power used so openly. The bounds of criminal liability were, of course, extended, but this tended to be achieved through the technique of bringing novel forms of criminal conduct within the categories of existing offences. An example of this process was afforded by the decision in *William Fraser*[3] in which the accused was convicted of fraud in respect of his obtaining sexual intercourse with a woman on the basis of pretending to be her husband.[4] Bringing the facts of conduct within the ambit of existing criminal offences is an unexceptional procedure, and necessary if the criminal law is to avoid an undesirable status. This was emphasised in the controversial case of *HM Adv v Khaliq*[5] in which Lord Justice-General Emslie quoted with approval the dictum of Lord Cockburn in his dissenting judgment in *Greenhuff*: 'An old crime may certainly be committed in a new way; and a case, though never occurring before on its facts, may fall within the spirit of a previous decision, or within an established general principle.'[6] There are nevertheless limits to this process. In particular, it should not result in unforeseeable criminal liability. If it does, it is subject to precisely the same criticisms as is the declaratory power.

The existence of the declaratory power has been reasserted in the twentieth century, most unambiguously in the case of *Grant v*

---

1 (1838) 2 Swin 236.
2 At 268.
3 (1847) Ark 280.
4 See also *Holmes and Lockyer* (1869) 1 Couper 221. There is a discussion of this, and other nineteenth-century cases in *Gordon*, para 1–24.
5 1983 SCCR 483, 1984 JC 23.
6 1984 JC 23 at 32.

Allan[1] (in which the court nevertheless declined to use the power). In a number of modern cases the courts have in effect created new crimes, but have not done so on the basis of the declaratory power. Two cases in particular demonstrate this: *Strathern v Seaforth*[2] and *McLaughlan v Boyd*[3]. In *Strathern* the crime of the clandestine taking and using of another's property was created, the grounds for this being the adverse social consequences of failing to punish such conduct; in *McLaughlan*, which is a case which has left a very much more significant mark on the law, the crime of shameless indecency was recognised by the court. In the latter case, Lord Justice-General Clyde pointed out that it would be a mistake

'... to imagine that the criminal common law of Scotland countenances any precise and exact categorisation of the forms of conduct which amount to crime. It has been pointed out many times in this Court that such is not the nature or quality of the criminal law of Scotland. I need only refer to the well-known passage of Baron Hume's institutional work, in which the broad definition of crime – a doleful or wilful offence against society in the matter of "violence, dishonesty, falsehood, indecency, irreligion" is laid down'.[4]

This would appear to set remarkably broad boundaries for the criminal law. Although it is clear that precise definition is an unrealistic goal in criminal law and that some offences must be broadly stated (as is the case with theft or assault), it is quite another thing to use broad moral categories, such as dishonesty or falsehood, as the basis of criminalisation. No objection may be had to this passage from *Hume* if it is taken as indicating some of the common moral features which happen to occur in many criminal offences, but it is a different proposition to say that all forms of dishonesty, indecency etc are potentially criminal. Yet this is what the decision in *McLaughlan* does, and the proposition is repeated in the more recent case of *HM Adv v R*.[5]

The clearest modern recognition of the declaratory power is to be found in the judgment of Lord Justice-Clerk Ross in *Grant v Allan*[6], a case which illustrates the occasional fineness of the distinction between immoral and criminal conduct. The accused, who was employed by a commercial firm, abstracted computerised information relating to clients of the firm and then offered this for sale

[1] 1987 SCCR 402, 1988 SLT 11.
[2] 1926 JC 100, 1926 SLT 445.
[3] 1934 JC 19, 1933 SLT 629.
[4] 1934 JC 19 at 22.
[5] 1988 SCCR 254, 1988 SLT 623.
[6] 1987 SCCR 402, 1988 SLT 11.

to a commercial competitor. He was charged with the theft of this information, but objections to the relevancy of the charge were sustained. The court declined to exercise the declaratory power in this case, citing in support of this position Lord Reid's observations in *Shaw v DPP*[1] to the effect that the place to decide on the punishment of immoral acts is Parliament. The judgment makes it clear, nonetheless, that the power is there if the court wishes to exercise it.

It is significant that there is no twentieth-century case in which the courts have exercised the declaratory power openly, and this raises the question as to which circumstances it is likely to be used in. In the realm of sexual conduct, an area in which one might well expect to encounter moral disapproval of previously unpunished conduct, the breadth of the offence of shameless indecency makes any resort to the declaratory power unnecessary.In respect of other offences against the person, as has been shown in the decision in *Khaliq*,[2] the offence of causing real injury is capable of dealing with a range of hazardous activities, and the offence of assault is similarly capable of wide interpretation.

In the area of property offences, the concepts of theft and fraud are similarly sufficiently broad to encompass most forms of conduct which the courts might wish to punish. Finally, there is breach of the peace, a common law offence which has been so widely interpreted by the courts as to enable it to be used in relation to virtually any form of anti-social conduct, provided that such conduct can be witnessed by others. The circumstances in which the declaratory power is likely to be needed in the future are therefore not altogether clear and the question arises as to why the courts should continue to assert its existence.

There are powerful arguments against the continued existence of the declaratory power. There is no doubt that in the formative period of the criminal law, a law-making power on the part of the courts was necessary, especially in the absence of a tradition of legislative activity in this area. That time is long since passed, and there is no reason why Parliament cannot address the relatively few new forms of criminality which will require to be considered. This is particularly so now that Scotland has a permanent law reform body, the Scottish Law Commission, which can address in-depth controversial areas of criminal law and make recommendations to the legislature.

The declaratory power offends the basic legal principle that there should be no criminal offence without clear prior prohibition –

---

[1] [1962] AC 220 at 275.
[2] 1983 SCCR 483, 1984 JC 23.

nullum crimen sine lege. One aspect of this objection is that the retroactive application of a sanction is unjust in that it punishes one for unavoidable ignorance. If a legal prohibition does not exist at the time at which the act is committed, then there could not have been any opportunity of knowing the law. Moreover, there is a sense in which the legal system is barred from retroactive declarations of criminality: it must be implicit in any acceptable system of rules that that which is not prohibited is permissible. If the criminal law does not explicity prohibit certain forms of conduct, then such conduct may properly be taken to be permitted. It is not open to the courts subsequently to withdraw this implied permission to act once an action has been performed.

The principle of non-retroactivity of criminal law finds expression in numerous statements of rights,[1] and is embodied in Article 7(1) of the European Convention on Human Rights, which states:

'No one shall be held guilty of any criminal offence on account of any act or omission which did not constitute a criminal offence under national or international law at the time it was committed. Nor shall a heavier penalty be imposed than one that was applicable at the time the criminal offence was committed.'

If there is any argument in favour of it, it must be that it prevents serious wrong-doing, in the sense of grossly immoral conduct, from going unpunished, and thereby preserves public confidence in the willingness and ability of the courts to punish wrongdoers. It also satisfies the retributive principle; the immoral actor cannot be said to deserve (in the moral sense) his punishment. Yet the value of the principle of legality outweighs both of these considerations, both of which are open to capricious abuse. Finally, the declaratory power so starkly conflicts with the legal principles which lie at the heart of criminal jurisprudence in the western tradition that its continued existence can only be considered anomalous in a modern legal system.

THE CLASSIFICATION OF CRIMES

There is no officially-endorsed classification of crimes in Scots criminal law. *Hume* follows no particular overall system, while

---

[1] It was recognised by the drafters of the French Declaration of the Rights of Man of 1789 and appears in Art 1, s 9(3) of the United States Constitution. For further discussion, see Popple J, 'The right to protection from retroactive criminal law' (1989) 13 Crim L J 251.

Macdonald's principal distinction is between those offences which may attract a capital or prison sentence and those offences which are 'not truly crimes' (welfare or regulatory offences). The latter are inevitably statutory, but it is unhelpful to make a firm distinction between statutory and common law offences in that the subject matter of each category may overlap. There are certain statutory offences which deal with topics traditionally dealt with by the common law. Similarly the mental requirement in statutory and common law offences may be the same: not all statutory offences are offences of strict liability. For this reason, any classification may include offences of either type within the same category.

The following classification takes into account the nature of the interest which the criminal law seeks to protect:

(1) Crimes against the person. The highest value which the law seeks to protect is that of human life. Crimes against the person range from minor assaults to murder.

(2) Crimes against property. This is a broad category, including not only those crimes in which the property of others is wrongfully appropriated by another, but also those crimes which entail the wrongful destruction of property.

(3) Crimes against the state. The interests protected by this category of crimes are state interest in security and good government.

(4) Public order and public morality crimes. No single personal interest may be compromised by such crimes, but the community as a whole may be said to be harmed by criminal activity of this nature.

(5) Regulatory offences. These offences (rarely called crimes) are those which infringe laws required for the administration of a complex modern society. They include pollution and factory regulations, road traffic law, and other similar material. The breach of such regulations may be minor, or it may have profound adverse consequences (as in a serious pollution offence, which may have a major effect on the property of others and on the environment in general).

The classification of crimes according to the interests protected is the scheme which has been favoured, in one form or another, by both civilian jurists and those in the Anglo-American tradition. Roman law tended to classify crimes more on the basis on which harm was perpetrated than on the basis of the harmed interest, but by the time of jurists such as Voet and Matthaeus, the focus had shifted to interests. The classifications of English law have ranged from the terse, tripartite system of JF Stephen's *History of the*

Criminal Law of England[1] (offences against the persons of individuals; offences against the property of individuals; and offences against public rights) to the ten-part scheme of *Russell on Crime*.[2] Most modern penal codes in the continental tradition favour a classification not dissimilar to that proposed above, although it is not unusual to find categories of offence which have no direct counterpart in the English-speaking world. An example is the category of 'crimes against the family', found as a separate category in the Italian and related codes.[3]

THE TERRITORIAL SCOPE OF CRIMINAL LAW

Scots criminal law observes the territorial principle. This means that the courts are principally concerned with crimes which are committed within Scotland; criminal acts committed elsewhere are not normally the concern of the Scottish courts. Difficult issues may arise, however, in the following circumstances: where an act is committed in Scotland which takes effect outwith Scotland; or where an act is committed in Scotland but takes effect elsewhere.

An act performed in Scotland which has criminal consequences in another country may in certain cirumstances be triable in Scotland. If the act itself amounts to a criminal offence according to the law of Scotland, then that criminal offence will of course be triable in Scotland. If the act performed in Scotland does not of itself amount to an offence, then the Scots courts would still have jurisdiction, provided that the 'main act' element of the offence has been performed in Scotland.

The term 'main act' appears in *Hume* in a discussion of cross-border crimes.

'If one compose and print a libel in England and circulate it here, or if one forge a deed abroad and utter it here, certainly the proper Courts for the trial of such a case are those of this country, since it is here that the main act is done which completes the crime ... it may plausibly be argued that he shall be subjected to the same course of trial who shall write an incendiary letter in England, and put it in a course of conveyance, thence by means of which it is received by the person to whom it is addressed in Scotland'.[4]

---

[1] 1883.
[2] JWC Turner (ed) (12th edn, 1964).
[3] Codice Penale, Arts 556–574 (Italy).
[4] II, 54.

The meaning of 'main act' seems clear enough in the context of the first two examples; the accused performs within Scotland those acts which constitute the definitional elements of the offence. Hume goes further than this, stating that a person who acts outwith Scotland, but whose act takes effect within Scotland, may still be triable before a Scottish court. In such a case, of course, no 'main act' is done within Scotland, unless 'main act' is taken as being synonymous with 'main effect'. Certainly Hume accepts that there will be jurisdiction where a crime takes effect, as the passage quoted above demonstrates. In *John Thomas Witherington*[1] it was held that the High Court had jurisdiction in a case where a fraudulent order for goods was written in England and posted to Scotland, where it was acted upon. The ratio of this decision is the fact that the effect of the fraud was felt in Scotland; it was there that the victim acted upon the representation and there that the damage occurred. Hume's 'main act' passage was referred to, but it is clear that the court was more concerned with the issue of where the crime is completed. This would appear to be a 'taking effect' theory rather than a 'main act' theory.

The 'main act' theory is supported by *Macdonald*,[2] and was specifically approved by the Court of Criminal Appeal in *Laird v HM Adv*.[3] In *Laird* the accused had been convicted of fraud in respect of a scheme which they had concocted in Scotland but which involved the making of fraudulent representations in England. The exchange of the goods which formed the basis of the fraudulent scheme, together with the payment of the purchase price, took place in England, both of which facts which were taken into account in holding that the 'main act' was located in Scotland. There is no confusion in this case of notions of 'main act' and 'main effect', but the court nonetheless appeared to take a broad view of what amounts to a 'main act'. Indeed, one of the judgments in *Laird* goes so far as to suggest that the taking of an initial step in Scotland would be sufficient to establish jurisdiction for the Scottish courts.

The root of the problem for Scots law here is that the term 'main act' is used loosely by Hume, and later by Macdonald, both of whom seem to consider it to be equivalent to, or at least not exclusive of, 'main effect'. The main act theory provides a theory of

---

[1] (1881) 4 Couper 475, (1881) 8 R(J) 41.
[2] *Macdonald* p 191. For discussion, see *Gordon* para 3–43, and PW Ferguson, 'Jurisdiction and criminal law in Scotland and England' 1987 (32) Juridical Review 179.
[3] 1984 SCCR 469, 1985 JC 37.

jurisdiction which is not incompatible with the principle of territoriality, but it cannot be combined with a main effect theory without implying concurrent jurisdiction. The main act may be committed in country **A** and the main effect felt in country **B**. If both theories are applied, then jurisdiction may be exercised by the courts in both **A** and **B**, which offends the principle of territoriality.

There is ample Scottish authority for the proposition that jurisdiction lies where the criminal act has its effect. This is the tenor of Hume's approach, and this finds judicial support in *HM Adv v Allan*,[1] *HM Adv v Bradbury*,[2] and *Witherington*.[3] In the English courts, where the issue has received close judicial attention, there has been a consistent application of the rule that jurisdiction is to be exercised where the crime takes effect.[4] This approach may place certain limitations on the ability of the courts to punish acts which cause harmful consequences abroad, but it at least avoids difficulties that may arise out of the differences which exist between substantive systems of criminal law. A person may perform in Scotland an act which takes effect abroad, but the effect abroad might not amount to a crime in the law of Scotland. Is he then to be charged with an offence which forms no part of Scots law ? This would be unacceptable. It could be argued, however, that the main act theory applies only in relation to those crimes which are crimes under Scots law. This certainly deals with the objection, but the theory is still open to the charge that it potentially busies the Scottish courts with crimes which are primarily the concern of another jurisdiction. It may be that a conscientious state has this obligation, but if this is so, it is an obligation which has in the past received only very cautious recognition, and any extension of the obligation should arguably be achieved through the statutory development of extra-territorial jurisdiction. This has been achieved in the case of terrorist, drug and aviation offences, and it may be that international fraud is an appropriate case for similar treatment.[5]

---

[1] (1873) 2 Couper 402.
[2] (1972) 2 Couper 311.
[3] (1881) 4 Couper 475.
[4] *R v Treacy* [1971] AC 537, (1973) 1 All ER 940; *R v Doot* [1973] AC 807.
[5] For drug trafficking, see W Gilmore, 'Combatting international drugs trafficking: the 1988 UN Convention against illicit traffic in narcotic drugs and psychotropic substances' (Commonwealth Secretariat, 1991, London). Under the Criminal Justice (International Co-operation) Act 1990, the Scottish courts have jurisdiction in respect of drugs being smuggled on foreign vessels on the High Seas.

CRIMINAL LAW AND MORALITY: THE LIMITS OF INTERVENTION

One of the most important issues in criminal law theory is that of the proper scope of the criminal law. The positivist would argue that the boundaries of the criminal law are determined by those acts which are actually punishable by the courts. That action is criminal, then, which breaches a provision of the criminal law, whether statutory or common law in origin. All other acts, no matter how immoral they may be, are not criminal. This points to a fundamental fact which any analysis of criminal law must acknowledge: criminal law and morality are two quite distinct concepts. The rules of criminal law may reflect the morality of the society which they regulate, but this coincidence is not a necessary one. A society may be governed by certain criminal law rules which many people may find abhorrent, but this moral objection does not diminish the legal validity of the rules. Such laws may properly be called unjust or immoral, but unless a natural law position is adopted, they are still appropriately described as laws.

The acceptance of a possible dichotomy between criminal law and moral rules does not necessarily preclude the use of moral principles as a basis for the development of criminal law. Rules of morality are the foundation of criminal law; many crimes exist because of the moral conviction of legislators or the courts that the conduct in question is morally wrong. Yet the moral wrongfulness of an act is not, by itself, a sufficient ground for the criminalisation of that conduct. Some acts may be considered immoral but do not necessarily deserve to be treated as criminal – a breach of a promise, the telling of a lie, or the sexual or emotional exploitation of another are all examples of immoral conduct, but they are not usually punished by the criminal law.

The characteristic which attracts the attention of the criminal law is harm to a specific interest which is recognised as being of such weight as to merit criminal law protection. Some of these interests are social in nature – such as the interest which society has in protecting public order – others are private – such as the interest which the individual has in his physical integrity or property. Faced with these numerous and varied interests, the draftsman of the criminal law must decide what principle is to govern the selection of some interest for criminal law protection and the rejection of others. For example, everybody has an interest in his reputation, but should the criminal law make it an offence to defame another? The answer in Scots law is that it is not; in other legal systems certain forms of defamation are treated as criminal. Or should it be a crime to display pornography openly? This may be criminal in Scotland, but in certain other jurisdictions the interest which the community at large has in being protected from possible offence of this nature is not given legal recognition.

A principle which attracts considerable support amongst legal and social philosophers holds that the criminal law should be invoked only in those cases where conduct causes or threatens a real degree of harm to the welfare of others. This limitation was expressed by John Stuart Mill in the nineteenth century,[1] and has been echoed in the works of a number of twentieth-century writers. It was the philosophy which underpinned the Report of the Wolfenden Committee[2] (which recommended the liberalisation of the law in relation to prostitution and homosexual offences) and to a very great extent it represents the consensus in modern criminal jurisprudence. According to this approach, private consensual acts are not the concern of the criminal law, provided that there is no substantial harm caused to the participants. The possession and enjoyment of pornography should therefore fall outwith the scope of the criminal law, as should all sexual acts conducted in private between consenting adults.

The attraction of such a philosophy of criminal law is that it maximises individual freedom, which is seen to be a good. At the same time it is open to the criticism that the libertarian position frequently overestimates the extent to which acts are private. In his celebrated debate with HLA Hart, the English judge, Lord Devlin, argued that many private acts are, in fact, capable of causing harm to the 'fabric of society'.[3] Indeed, it was Devlin's belief that any act of immorality weakened society in some way, even if there was no apparent individual victim. This argument has found little support, although it is certainly possible to argue that mere knowledge of the fact that certain forms of conduct are being perpetuated may combine to a process of 'moral blunting' or 'moral brutalisation', the ultimate effect of which may be felt by society in general or by individual victims. The mere knowledge that women are being subjected to insult and degradation in pornography causes understandable distress to many women (and men), and this distress may exist irrespective of the consensual status of the participants. It may also be felt that this mere knowledge could somehow embolden potential abusers of women to translate fantasy into reality, or just

---

[1] *On Liberty* (1859).
[2] Report of the Committee on Homosexual Offences and Prostitution (Cmnd 247).
[3] *The Enforcement of Morals* (1965) ch 1.

not to bother about women's feelings; this could perhaps provide an additional argument in favour of the criminalisation of pornography.

The danger with such arguments lies in the fact that they readily lead one into a position in which virtually any form of immoral conduct becomes a candidate for criminalisation. Such a position would be intolerable because of the restriction of freedom it would involve and also because of the extent to which it would damage respect for the criminal law. The criminal sanction is an extreme one, to be used as sparingly as possible. For most forms of day-to-day immorality, moral disapproval and informal social sanctions must suffice, and only when crucial state or individual interests are at stake should the criminal law intervene. Such techniques may be shown to fail, of course, and in such cases criminal sanctions may properly be used, provided that the harm threatened is sufficiently grave. Race relations legislation is a useful example here. The distress caused by racial insult, and the social dislocation which racial tension causes, are such that what might normally be a matter of moral censure or exhortation becomes, quite properly, a matter for concern on the part of the criminal law.

2. Principles of liability

Before a person can be convicted of a criminal offence, it must be established (1) that he committed a criminal act or omission and (2) that his conduct was accompanied by a 'guilty' state of mind. This is usually expressed as the requirement that there be an *actus reus* (a wrongful act) and *mens rea* (a wrongful state of mind). There is an important exception to this proposition, however, in the case of certain offences created by statute. These may be offences of strict liability, which do not require *mens rea* on the part of the accused. They are discussed separately below.

The following example illustrates the dual requirement. **X**, while shooting on a shooting range, sees what he takes to be the target appearing. In fact, it is a hiker who has ignored the warning notices. **X** fires and the hiker is fatally wounded. **X** has committed the *actus reus* of a criminal offence (he has shot the victim) but there is no *mens rea* (because of **X**'s excusable error). There is therefore no criminal liability.

THE *ACTUS REUS* REQUIREMENT

The criminal law does not punish mere intentions: there must be an overt action or an omission to act before liability is attributed. Acts may consist of a single event or of a series of events. The striking of another is an example of a single event, which amounts, in fact, to the *actus reus* of assault. Other acts may be more complex, involving one or more actions on the part of the actor, followed by certain consequences. The act of defrauding another may consist of the writing of a misleading statement, the issuing of the statement to another, and the recipient's acting upon the statement. The act of murder consists of the physical harming of the victim followed by a necessary consequence: the victim's death. Single event crimes have been referred to as 'conduct crimes'; crimes requiring more than one event have been referred to as 'result crimes'. This division of crimes is of practical importance, in that it may be necessary to prove *mens rea* in relation to both circumstances and consequences, and therefore each element in such crimes must be clearly identified.

The voluntary act requirement

When the *actus reus* takes the form of an act rather than an omission, this act must be voluntary. The meaning of the term 'voluntary' is very specific here, and must be distinguished from the concept of voluntary action as being that which one positively wishes to do. A reluctant conscript may join the armed services involuntarily; a taxpayer may pay his taxes involuntarily – in both of these cases the actor would rather not do what he does. In the context of the criminal law, however, the term voluntary refers to action which is performed under the control of the actor. Involuntary acts are therefore those which the actor does not know he is performing or acts which he cannot stop himself from performing. Awareness or control may be absent where:

(i) The criminal state of affairs results from external events beyond the control of the actor.

The classic example of this is where an external force is responsible for what happens. This external force may take the form of a natural phenomenon (for example, a gust of wind) or of human intervention. In *Hogg v Macpherson*[1] the accused's car collided with a lamp standard as a result of a heavy gale, and there was therefore no liability. Similarly, in *Hugh Mitchell*,[2] where a man attacked a woman carrying a child, forcing her to squeeze the child, responsibility for the death rested with the man and not the woman. If, therefore, **A** seizes **B** and, taking hold of his hand, forces him to strike **C**, **B** cannot be said to have assaulted **C** – there was no voluntary act on his part.

There is a curious category of cases which would appear to be an exception to this fundamental requirement of a voluntary act. This is the category of the so-called 'status offences', in which the gravamen of the charge is not what the accused is alleged to have done but what he was at a particular time. The best-known of these cases

---

[1] 1928 JC 15, 1928 SLT 35.
[2] (1856) 2 Irv 488.

is *R v Larsonneur*,[1] in which the accused, a Frenchwoman, was arrested by the Irish police and taken to Britain, where she was of the offence of being an alien 'found' in the United Kingdom without permission. In *Winzar v Chief Constable of Kent*[2] the accused had been brought to hospital, where he was found to be drunk. The police were called, and they removed him to their car, which was parked on the road. The accused was then convicted of being drunk on the highway. In both of these cases, the offence was based on the status of the accused at a particular time, rather than anything they were alleged to have done. It might be argued that there was some degree of culpability in the case of *Winzar* in that he had allowed himself to become intoxicated, but he could only be called to account for the eventual public drunkenness if it could be shown that he could have foreseen the possibility of being removed and put in a public place; in the absence of such foreseeability a person in his position is surely blameless.

(ii) The criminal state of affairs results from a reflex action on the part of the accused.

There are some movements which may be performed in a state of consciousness but which are nevertheless not under the control of the actor. These movements – commonly known as reflex actions – are not actions in the full sense of the word (not being willed by the actor) and they should not therefore attract criminal liability. A person whose arm jerks in a sudden, uncontrolled movement, causing him to knock over a person standing next to him, should not be convicted of assault; he has not chosen to strike his victim, nor could he have stopped himself from doing so.[3] In the Australian case of *Ryan v The Queen*[4] the appellant had armed himself with a rifle and set about robbing a petrol station. In the course of the robbery, the proprietor of the petrol station had moved suddenly, allegedly causing Ryan's finger to tighten on the trigger of the rifle. It was argued on the appellant's behalf that the act of pulling the

---

[1] (1933) 29 Cox CC 673.
[2] Times, March 28, 1983; discussed by CMV Clarkson and HM Keating *Criminal Law: Text and Materials* (1990) p 122.
[3] In *Jessop v Johnstone* 1991 SCCR 238 a boy struck a teacher with a rolled-up jotter. The teacher responded by punching him, a response which the sheriff accepted as being a reflex action. The High Court did consider it to be such, but Lord Justice-Clerk Ross observed: 'We appreciate that there may be cases where a person instinctively reacts to violence in a reflex way, such as if a person suddenly and without warning struck and turns round sharply so that he comes into contact with his assailant...' (at 240).
[4] (1969) 121 CLR 205, [1966–67] ALJR 488.

trigger was not a voluntary act and that it could not therefore give rise to criminal liability. This was rejected, as the court took the view that the overall act of killing the proprietor consisted of a number of parts – including the pointing of the weapon – and since these other parts were voluntary then the killing itself could be taken to be a voluntary act.

Involuntariness was raised more successfully, however, in *Hill v Baxter*[1] where the accused was acquitted of a driving offence on the grounds that he had lost control of his car when a swarm of bees had entered it by a window and he had instinctively moved his arms to protect himself.

(iii) The criminal state of affairs has been produced by the action performed during unconsciousness.

Acts performed in a state of unconsciousness, or during a state of grossly impaired consciousness, are known as automatic acts, the person performing them being, temporarily, an automaton. This can arise in a number of ways, amongst which are: through somnambulism; as a result of concussion caused by physical insult to the brain; through the presence of abnormal sugar levels in the blood; or during or shortly after an epileptic seizure. More controversially, it is apparent that a state of dissociation can develop as a result of extreme psychological stress and that this may result in action which has many of the features of automatism.

Somnambulism. Somnambulism, or sleep-walking, occurs during slow-wave sleep, when the body is capable of fairly complex movement. Somnambulistic violence is rare, but there is fairly general agreement among psychiatrists that it is quite possible for a sleeping person to commit assault or even homicide in a state of complete unconsciousness and to have no waking recollection of what has been done.In such a case, there is clearly no voluntary act and therefore it could be argued that there can be no *actus reus*.

There are comparatively few decisions on this point, although one of the earlier reports is a Scottish one, the case of *Simon Fraser*.[2] Fraser had killed his 18-month-old son and claimed that he had done this during his sleep. The jury was directed that if this was so, then he was not responsible for what happened, a view which they were prepared to accept. In the event, Fraser agreed to sleep alone in future, a precaution which is mirrored in modern

[1] [1958] 1 QB 277, [1958] 1 All ER 193.
[2] (1878) 4 Coup 70.

medical advice to those who have been troubled by aggressive behaviour during sleep. Later cases have been inconsistent. The Supreme Court of Victoria was prepared to allow the complete acquittal of a somnambulistic mother who killed her teenage daughter during a dream that a hostile soldier was on her daughter's bed,[1] and a similarly receptive view to a somnambulistic interpretation of an apparently motiveless killing was taken by the Supreme Court of Ontario in *R v Parks*.[2] A remarkable aspect of Parks is the fact that the accused claimed to have driven a number of miles along a motorway – while still asleep – before carrying out a vicious somnambulistic attack on his parents-in-law, with whom he had had a good relationship. The court clearly had difficulty in accepting that such a complicated course of conduct could be committed somnambulistically, but ruled that an acquittal on the grounds of non-insane automatism was a proper verdict in such a case. The contrary view was reached by the English Court of Appeal in *R v Burgess*[3] in which it was held that somnambulistic automatism was a form of insanity and should therefore be treated as insane automatism. The implications of this are discussed below.

Other forms of automatism. Somnambulistic automatism may come before the courts fairly rarely, but this is not so with certain other forms of automatism, notably automatism induced by epilepsy or diabetes. Although there is no particular association of epilepsy with violence, epileptics may occasionally commit violent acts in the post-ictal stage (that is, in the immediate aftermath of a seizure). These acts are clearly beyond their control, and, if the voluntary act requirement were to be applied, there would be no *actus reus*. Until the recent decision in *HM Adv v Ross*,[4] which recognised a defence of non-insane automatism, the effect of the decision in *HM Adv v Cunningham*[5] was to deny the possibility of acquittal on the grounds of automatism, while leaving open the possibility in such cases of a defence of insanity. In *Cunningham* the accused, who was charged with certain driving offences, claimed that he was acting in a state of temporary dissociation resulting from an epileptic fuge or 'other pathological condition'. The court ruled that any 'mental or

[1] *R v Cogdon* (1950, unreported) Supreme Court, Victoria, discussed by N Morris, 'Somnambulistic homicide' (1951) 5 Res Judicatae 29. On somnambulism, see I Oswald and J Evans 'Serious violence during sleep walking' (1985) 147 Brit Jnl Psychiatry 688. On automatism in general, see P Fenwick 'Automatism' in R Bluglass and P Bowden (eds) *Principles and Practice of Forensic Psychiatry* (1990) p 161.
[2] 1990 78 CR (3d) 1.
[3] [1991] 2 All ER 769.
[4] 1991 SCCR 823, 1991 SLT 564.
[5] 1963 JC 80, 1963 SLT 345.

pathological condition short of insanity – any question of diminished responsibility owing to any cause, which does not involve insanity' was relevant only to the question of mitigating circumstances and sentence. The court in *Cunningham* expressly disapproved the earlier decision of Lord Murray in *HM Adv v Ritchie*[1], in which it had been accepted that if a person is not 'master of his own actions' (through the operation of some temporary overcoming factor, in this case toxic fumes), the presumption of responsibility may be overcome and a special defence succeed. *Cunningham*'s rejection of this placed persons who act automatically in an absurd position. They could assert their non-responsibility, but only through the defence of insanity, which involved the prospect of compulsory hospitalisation. Even if an epileptic could be described as insane in terms of the Scots law on the subject – which requires a total and non-temporary alienation of reason – the question remained as to what was the point of sending or admitting an epileptic or a diabetic to a psychiatric hospital? The only justification can be that of public safety, and such considerations should be applied only where there are clear grounds to suggest that there is a possibility of a recurrence of the violent behaviour in question.

The reaction to the decision in *Cunningham* was overwhelmingly negative, and indeed in a number of cases lower courts appeared to have ignored the decision and acquitted in cases involving automatism. In *Farrell v Stirling*[2] the accused, a diabetic, was charged with an offence under the Road Traffic Act 1972, and claimed to have been suffering from hyperglaecemia at the time of the offence. The sheriff sought to distinguish *Cunningham* and held that the movements of the accused's hands, body and legs were involuntary and 'wholly uncontrolled by any conscious effort of will on his part'. This approach was not endorsed, however, in *Carmichael v Boyle*[3] when the High Court upheld a Crown stated case appeal from a sheriff court which had acquitted a diabetic who had committed assault in a state of hyperglaecemia. The High Court emphasised that *Cunningham* unambiguously excluded any defence of automatism in such a case and that this must remain the position until the legislature decided otherwise or until a larger court overruled the decision.

The opportunity arose in *Ross (Robert) v HM Adv*.[4] In this case the accused had been convicted of attempted murder and assault in

---

1 1926 JC 45, 1926 SLT 308.
2 1975 SLT (Sh Ct) 71.
3 1985 SCCR 58, 1985 SLT 399.
4 1991 SCCR 823, 1991 SLT 564.

respect of a frenzied knife attack which he carried out on a number of strangers in a public place. The accused contended that the can of lager which he had been drinking had, without his knowledge, been adulterated with Temazepam and LSD, and that he had therefore been acting as an automaton and should be acquitted. This defence was successful, the court overturning *Cunningham*'s rejection of non-insane automatism on the grounds that in such a case there was no question of *mens rea*:

'In principle it would seem that in all cases where a person lacks the evil intention which is essential to guilt of a crime he must be acquitted ... So if a person cannot form any intention at all because he is asleep or unconscious at the time, it would seem impossible to hold that he had *mens rea* and was guilty in the criminal sense of anything he did when he was in that state. The same result would seem to follow if, for example, he was able to form intention to the extent that he was controlling what he did in the physical sense, but had no conception whatever at the time that what he was doing was wrong. His intention, such as it was, would lack the necessary evil ingredient to convict him of a crime. Insanity provides the clearest example of this situation, but I do not see way there should be no room for the view that the lack of evil intention in cases other than insanity, to which special considerations apply, should not also result in an acquittal. Indeed, since it is for the Crown to prove *mens rea* as well as the *actus reus* of an offence, it would seem logical to say that in all cases where there is an absence of *mens rea* an acquittal must result.'[1]

In his survey of the cases, Lord Justice-General Hope noted that *Cunningham*, although hitherto binding, was contradicted by the decision in *Ritchie* and by dicta of Lord McCluskey in *HM Adv v Raiker*[2], and that it was also fundamentally out of step with English and Commonwealth decisions. *Cunningham* was seen as a policy-influenced decision, based on a fear that 'laxity or confusion' would result if the court were to admit such a defence; a fear which the Lord Justice-General saw as misplaced.

The decision in *Ross* is limited to those cases where automatic behaviour is not self-induced, and where the factor which produces it is not the result of 'continuing disorder of the mind or body which might lead to the recurrence of the disturbance of ... mental faculties'.[3] Where automatism is so produced, *Cunningham* stands, and the only defence will be that of insanity. As a result of this, Scots law is now essentially the same as English law on this point and automatism may be divided into non-insane and

---

[1] At 829 per Lord Justice-General Hope.
[2] 1989 SCCR 149.
[3] At 829.

insane categories, the implications being the same in both jurisdictions. The court spent some time on two further points. It was argued by the Crown that, by analogy with the defence of insanity, the burden of proof of non-insane automatism should rest on the accused. This was rejected, the court pointing out that non-insane automatism does not involve the rebuttal of any presumption of insanity; the issue at stake is one of responsibility. A further contention of the prosecution – that the defence should be a special one, requiring written notice – was considered by the court, but opinion was reserved. The implications of the decision in *Ross* soon came to be tested.

In *Sorley v HM Adv*[1] the appellant had been convicted of a breach of the peace which he alleged was committed only because the can of lager given to him by another contained three sleeping tablets and two LSD tablets inserted without his knowledge. The court stressed that the defence of automatism required that three elements be present: (1) that the automatic state should result from an external factor which was not self-induced; (2) that this factor must be one which the accused was not bound to foresee, and (3) that it should have resulted in a total alienation of reason causing a complete loss of self-control. In the case under consideration, the court held that although there was an admission by the person who had given the appellant the can of lager that he placed the drugs in it, there was no other evidence of the fact that the accused was suffering from a total alienation of reason. For this, clear evidence was required, and this would usually involve the giving of opinions by experts, which may help to corroborate the evidence of those who observed the accused's conduct at the time. It is evident, then, that the courts will need considerable convincing of a total alienation of reason, and that nothing short of expert medical evidence will satisfy them.

Automatism in other systems. In English law, and many of its related legal systems, two forms of automatism defence are recognised. Non-insane automatism (which results in acquittal) occurs where the factor which produces the automatism emanates from an external source; insane automatism (which has the same result as the insanity defence) occurs where the automatism results from a disease of the mind. Examples of the former will be automatism resulting from concussion, the inhalation of fumes, or the injection

[1] 1992 SCCR 396.

of an excessive quantity of insulin;[1] examples of the latter will include automatic states resulting from an epileptic seizure[2] or, in the case of diabetics, hyperglaecemia resulting from a failure to inject insulin,[3] and, since the decision in *R v Burgess*,[4] somnambulism. Although there have been criticisms of the range of conditions falling into the latter group – is a diabetic really insane? – the approach adopted in these systems has at least the attraction of leading to acquittal where the automatism is totally unconnected with any disease process and where there is therefore no reason for supposing that the accused is likely to pose a future threat to the public.

Omissions

In the majority of cases the *actus reus* consists of an act rather than an omission to act. The criminal law is generally reluctant to impose liability on the basis of an omission, although in certain circumstances this may happen. This reluctance is attributable in part to conceptions of causation which tend to downplay the causative potency of omissions and in part to a desire to limit the extent of criminal liability. While everybody can appreciate the causal link between positive acts and their consequences, the equivalent link between omissions and their consequences tend to be less readily acknowledged. The person who pushes another into a river may be said to have caused his victim's drowning; the person who, being able to rescue a swimmer whom he sees drowning, but who fails to take any steps to do so, is less likely to be identified as the cause of the swimmer's death. As far as the limitation of criminal liability is concerned, liability for omissions is inherently more open-ended, and even uncertain, than is liability for positive acts. In the example used above, if a general liability for failure to rescue is accepted, where does the duty to rescue begin and end ? Is a person to be liable for failing to call the police if he hears violence being perpetrated next door ? Is he liable for the violence he hears being perpetrated in the next street ? It is precisely this sort of difficulty which has resulted in the restriction of omission liability to those cases where one or more of a small number of special factors is present.

[1] *R v Quick* [1973] 1 QB 910, [1973] 3 All ER 347.
[2] *R v Sullivan* [1984] AC 156, [1983] 2 All ER 673.
[3] *R v Hennessy* [1989] 1 WLR 287, [1989] 2 All ER 9.
[4] [1991] 2 QB 92, [1991] 2 All ER 769.

Is there a duty to prevent the commission of a crime?

There is Scottish authority to the effect that a person who fails to take steps to prevent a crime does not thereby commit an offence. In *George Kerr and Ors*[1] several accused who looked over a hedge while a rape was being committed in a field were acquitted on a charge of art and part guilt of rape, a decision which demonstrates the offensive results to which the principle of non-responsibility for omissions can give rise. A similar outcome occurred in *R v Clarkson*[2] and *R v Broughham*[3]. In *Clarkson* it was held that the mere presence of the accused, a soldier, as a spectator of a barrack-room rape perpetrated by his fellow soldiers, was not enough to secure his conviction for aiding and abetting the offence – a result which, once again, will strike many as shocking.

Mere presence on the scene of a crime may result in criminal liability if there is some factor, in addition to presence, which justifies the inference of a duty to act in some way. In *Wilcox v Jeffrey*[4] the accused attended (as a journalist working for the sponsoring magazine) an illegal concert given by a visiting professor of the saxophone. It was held that his presence, in the circumstances, amounted to an encouragement of the illegality; liability therefore could only have been avoided by efforts made to stop the performance or by walking out. The question of whether the mere presence of the accused amounted to encouragement will depend on all the circumstances. Fortuitous presence will clearly not be sufficient to give rise to a duty to act, but, as pointed out by the Queensland Court of Appeal in *Beck*[5] 'a calculated presence or a presence from which opportunity is taken can project positive encouragement and support for the principal offender'. It is probably the case then in Scots law that a person who realises that his presence is lending support to another in a criminal act, is under a duty to withdraw from the scene of the crime if he wishes to avoid criminal liability.

There is a line of cases in other jurisdictions involving failure by a passenger in a car to prevent the commission of a road traffic offence by the driver. One of the earliest of these cases is *Du Cros v Lambourn*[6] in which the owner of a car was convicted of aiding and abetting offences committed by the person who was driving his car at the time;

[1] (1871) 2 Coup 334.
[2] [1971] 3 All ER 344.
[3] (1986) 43 SASR 187.
[4] [1951] 1 All ER 464.
[5] (1989) 43 A Crim R 135 at 142.
[6] 1907 1 KB 40.

the owner had failed to do anything to prevent the commission of these driving offences, and was held liable for his omission to act. It is questionable whether a mere passenger (one who is not the owner of the car) who failed to prevent reckless or dangerous driving would be held liable for an omission; certainly, in other cases of this sort the accused has been in a position of some authority over the driver.[1]

In a small number of cases, statute imposes an obligation to act in respect of the commission of a crime by another. Under section 172 of the Road Traffic Act 1988, a person who is required by the police to give information as to the identity of a driver suspected of committing certain offence under the Act commits an offence if he fails to give that information. The duty to act imposed by the Prevention of Terrorism (Temporary Provisions) Act 1989 is even more rigorous. It is an offence under section 18(1) of this Act for a person who has information relating to the commission of terrorist offences not to give such information to the authorities, even if not requested to do so.

The categories of omission liability

In spite of the fact that omissions are less likely to attract criminal liability than positive acts, there are certain circumstances in which the courts are prepared to treat an omission as criminal. These are:

(1) Where there have been prior dangerous actings on the part of the accused. A person who creates a situation of danger for another may be held liable for any injury that ensues if he fails to avert the danger he has created. In a sense, such situations do not entail pure omission liability, as there is an earlier act on the part of the accused. This act, however, may not be a wrongful one itself, and any wrongfulness must therefore be located in the omission.

Several cases are concerned with a victim who is placed in a situation of danger and then abandoned. In *McManimy and Higgins*[2] two lodging housekeepers were convicted of culpable homicide after they had removed an ill guest and left him out in the street, where he died. In *HM Adv v McPhee*[3] the exposure of an

[1] *R v Shikuri* 1939 AC 225.
[2] (1847) Ark 321.
[3] 1935 JC 46, 1935 SLT 179.

assaulted victim was similarly at issue, although in a case of this type the death of the victim can be seen as much as a consequence of the assault as of the abandonment to the elements.

The decision in *McPhail v Clark*[1] demonstrates how an innocent situation may later become dangerous through the operation of natural forces. In this case the accused had set fire to straw in a field, something which he was entitled to do, but then failed to extinguish the fire after it had spread and the smoke had begun to cause a danger to passing motorists. This failure to act, once he had become aware of the danger, was held to amount to a culpable omission and he was convicted of recklessly endangering the lives of car occupants. The English case of *Miller*[2] is to similar effect. Here a squatter had inadvertently set fire to a mattress in the house he was occupying, and rather than extinguish the flames he had merely moved to another room. The appellant's conviction of causing reckless damage was upheld by the House of Lords in a decision which can be interpreted in more than one way. In one view the ratio of *Miller* is that a prior dangerous act imposes liability to act[3] in another, liability in *Miller* is based on the 'continuing' act theory which sees the initial causing of the fire and the subsequent attitude of recklessness towards it as being part of one overall continuing act.[4] Whichever view is taken, the result is the same; the first explanation, however, has the advantage of avoiding the necessity of treating what are clearly discrete events as being a single act.

The control of dangerous things may be treated as an instance of prior act responsibility in that the acquisition of such control, or its continuance after there has been a realisation of dangerousness, amounts to a prior dangerous act. There is no Scottish authority on this point, but it is submitted that the person who willingly takes control of a dangerous thing of whatever nature (whether it be animate or inanimate) will be liable for the damage caused by that thing, provided that he is negligent in failing to prevent that damage. The degree of negligence manifested must be such as to amount to the reckless indifference referred to in *McPhail v Clark*[5] and in other cases in which criminal liability is imposed for negligent conduct.[6] On this basis, the owner of a dangerous building might be held criminally liable for injury caused by the collapse of the building if he

---

[1] 1982 SCCR 395, 1983 SLT (Sh Ct) 37.
[2] [1983] 2 AC 161, [1983] 1 All ER 978.
[3] See JC Smith [1982] Crim LR 527.
[4] See Glanville Williams [1982] Crim LR 773.
[5] 1982 SCCR 395, 1983 SLT (Sh Ct) 37.
[6] See the discussion of negligence liability at p 39 below.

has failed to take steps to prevent such injury and if this failure amounts to recklessness. The custodians of dangerous animals might be convicted of recklessly endangering the lives and safety of others if they fail to take suitable steps to prevent such danger.

(2) Where the status of the accused is such that he has a duty to act. A person who occupies a public office or a positon of responsibility of some sort may have a duty to act to prevent the occurrence of harm and may be criminally liable if he fails to do so. Liability for culpable homicide may result where death has resulted from the accused's failure to discharge the duties imposed by his position.[1] The life-guard who culpably fails to make any effort to rescue the swimmer in distress may be liable for his omission, as may the prison warder who stands by and allows an unpopular prisoner to be fatally assaulted. In other cases there may be art and part liability, as in *Bonar v Macleod*[2], where the accused, a police officer, failed to intervene to prevent the assault of a person in police custody by an officer junior to himself.

(3) Where a close relationship exists between the accused and a person who suffers harm which the accused has failed to prevent. The existence of a relationship of dependence between two persons may give rise to a duty to act to prevent harm. The Scottish courts have not addressed the issue, but are likely to infer the existence of such an obligation in the case at least of parent and minor child, and possibly in other cases. It might be that a duty is owed to a spouse to prevent harm, and the same view might today be taken of unmarried persons living together. It is not the family relationship which matters in these cases, but the fact that the parties are members of the same household. The essence of the obligation is the dependence which normally follows such a close relationship. The failure of a householder to summon medical help for a long-term lodger who is gravely ill gives rise to the same form of moral disapproval as the failure of a parent to do the same thing for a minor child living in his household.[3]

---

[1] *William Hardie* (1847) Ark 247: failure of an Inspector of Poor to deal with an application for assistance.

[2] 1983 SCCR 161.

[3] One of the few cases involving a failure to rescue family is the Australian case of *R v Russell* [1933] VLR 59. In this case, the accused failed to take steps to prevent his estranged wife from jumping into a swimming pool with his two young children. He was convicted of the manslaughter of all three, although his conviction in respect of the wife's death was based on the criminality, at that point, of suicide. If events were repeated in the same jurisdiction today, there would be no conviction

A legally recognised relationship of dependence may come into existence through the assumption of a duty. A number of cases involve a failure to provide care and attention for elderly people for whom the accused assumed responsibility. In *R v Instan*,[1] for example, the accused lived with an aged aunt whom she neglected in the last twelve days of the aunt's life, failing to call medical help to deal with the gangrene which the aunt had developed. The decision in *R v Stone and Dobinson*[2] was to similar effect. In this case the accused persons failed to look after the frail sister of one of them whom they had admitted to live in the house: they were held liable for manslaughter after she died from neglect.[3]

(4) Where an obligation is imposed by contract. A person may have an obligation to act imposed upon him by contract. Failure to perform his duties under the contract may result in the imposition of criminal liability. If **A** agrees to watch **B**'s children, and fails to do so, he may be liable for the culpable homicide of one of the children if he or she falls into a river and drowns.

MENS REA

The commission of an act prohibited by the criminal law, an *actus reus*, will not be sufficient ground to criminal liability unless a necessary mental element is present. This is the general rule, to which there is an important category of exceptions: offences of strict liability.[4] Except in cases of strict liability, the prosecution must prove that the accused acted with a culpable state of mind, now generally known as *mens rea* (a guilty mind). The objective of this requirement is the limitation of criminal liability to those cases in which the accused committed a prima facie wrongful act in a wrongful cast of mind. In theory, therefore, the *mens rea* requirement should exculpate those who are morally innocent. In practice, the outcome may be different, and it has been said that all the *mens rea*

---

on those grounds: P Brett, L Waller and CR Williams *Criminal Law* (6th edn, 1989) p 507.

[1] [1893] 1QB 450.

[2] [1977] 1 QB 354, [1977] 2 All ER 341.

[3] For criticism of the decision, see Glanville Williams, 'What should the Code do about omissions' (1987) 7 Legal Studies 92.

[4] Discussed below at p. 42

requirement achieves is the identification of those states of mind which the law regards as appropriate for conviction.[1]

Mens rea and dole

Mens rea is the modern term used most frequently in Scots law; in the older cases, and in *Hume*, the equivalent term was dole, a word possibly derived from the Latin expression dolus (evil). The classic definiton of dole is drawn from *Hume*, who describes it as 'that corrupt and evil intention which is essential (so the light of nature teaches, and so all authorities have said) to the guilt of any crime'.[2] *Hume* also speaks of the *malus animus* necessary for conviction of crime. This, he says, is 'vice or corruption of purpose which has the effect of 'fixing' an 'evil character' on a deed.[3] Both of these definitions focus on the specific state of mind of the accused in respect of the criminal act; *Hume* also seems prepared to take into account the broader mental attitude of the accused, stating that the act 'must be attended with such circumstances as indicate a corrupt and malignant disposition, a heart contemptuous of order, and regardless of social duty'.[4] In modern law, the character of the accused is irrelevant, except perhaps in determining punishment. Criminal guilt is not determined by the extent to which one's outlook on the world is malicious or anti-social, but by the intention with which one performs such acts as come under the scrutiny of the courts. The criminal law does not therefore punish a malignant disposition; it punishes malignantly conceived acts.

The differing *mens rea* requirement of individual crimes

There is no single, universal form of *mens rea* which will suffice for all crimes. Each crime has its own *mens rea* requirement, and in order to be convicted of that crime the accused must have demonstrated that particular mental state on committing the crime. Another way of approaching this is to say that the state of mind of the accused person must fit the outlines of the *actus reus*. Murder requires that the accused either intended the death of his victim

---

[1] Cf the identification of the principles underlying the doctrine of *mens rea* in A Ashworth *Principles of Criminal Law* (1991) pp 127–178.
[2] I, 21.
[3] I, 23.
[4] I, 22.

or that he acted with wicked recklessness. Theft requires that the accused should have intended to deprive the owner of his property, usually, but not always, permanently. Assault requires that the accused should have inflicted force or the threat of force with **evil intent** (that is, with the intent of causing the victim harm). The *mens rea* requirement of these three common law crimes is therefore different, although there may be elements, such as intention, which are common to all of them.

Legislation may define a *mens rea* requirement very specifically. For example, a statute may read: Any person who makes a false statement to a returning officer with the intention of causing a false return to be made, commits an offence. Here the *mens rea* requirement of the statutory offence is not met if the accused has made a false statement unknowingly and therefore without any intention of causing a false return to be made.

Mens rea and motive

In the statutory example cited above, the motive with which a person acts is relevant to determining whether *mens rea* is present. This type of case is exceptional; in general, motive does not affect *mens rea*. A motive provides the reason for which an act is performed, and in most cases this is not taken into account by a court in determining guilt. Motive may play a role in mitigating punishment, but this occurs after the essential question of criminal liability has been decided. Theft committed with a motive of giving the proceeds to the poor may strike some as an act performed with a laudable motive, especially if the property is stolen from a heartless and impersonal corporation. This motive, however, has no bearing on the *mens rea* requirement of theft, which does not look to the reasons for which property is taken. In *Palazzo v Copeland*[1] the accused had fired a gun to scare off a group of drunken and abusive youths. His appeal against a conviction for breach of the peace was rejected on the grounds that although his motive was the 'sound one' of trying to stop a breach of the peace on the part of the youths, this was irrelevant. This decision may be contrasted with the decision of the English Court of Appeal in *R v Court*.[2] The appellant here had been convicted of indecent assault, having confessed to the police an indecent motive for touching a young girl. It was

[1] 1976 JC 52.
[2] [1989] AC 28, [1988] 2 All ER 221.

observed that motive often throws a light on intention and is there-fore generally admissible in the proving of intention. If this reasoning had been applied in *Palazzo v Copeland*, the act of firing the shotgun may well have been seen as one committed without any intention of causing a breach of the peace, and it is difficult to see how conviction could be justified in such circumstances.

In practice, too, motive may play an important role in determining whether a prosecution is instituted or deciding the nature of the offence. Mercy killing provides an instance of this. A distressed rela-tive, who kills a dying person in order to relieve the victim of further suffering, generally atttracts sympathy. Here the unselfish motive of the avoidance of suffering may incline the prosecution to accept a plea of diminished responsibility, even on slender medical evidence, with a view to avoiding conviction of murder.

Motive also plays a part in determining whether certain defences of justification are available. A person who destroys property in order to prevent the occurrence of a greater harm, may be able to claim the defence of necessity. In such a case, the motive with which he acts is central to the availability of the defence. The same is true of the defence of coercion, which may be available to one who commits a criminal offence in order to avoid a threat of severe physical harm to himself. It is implicit in this defence that the motive with which he acts must be one of avoiding the harm to himself, and enquiry may be directed towards determining just that. A further example of cir-cumstances in which motive may determine the wrongfulness or otherwise of an act is that of the doctor examining a patient. If the doctor conducts an intimate examination in order to reach a diag-nosis, his therapeutic motive justifies the touching involved. If, how-ever, his motive is not therapeutic, and he conducts the examination for improper reasons, the touching becomes an indecent assault. In *Stewart v Thain*[1] the motive of a schoolmaster in chastising the naked buttocks of a boy was taken into account in determining whether the chastisement was a lawful application of discipline or a sexual as-sault. The finding of a disciplinary motive was sufficient in this case to justify the act.

The constituent elements of *mens rea*

Mens rea may be inferred if the accused person acts either (1) with the requisite intention; (2) recklessly; or (3) negligently. As has already

---

[1] 1981 JC 13, 1981 SLT (Notes) 2.

been pointed out, different offences will require different forms of *mens rea* and whichever of these three states of mind needs to be proved will depend on the way in which the *mens rea* requirement is phrased in relation to the offence in question. For murder, for example, the third of these states of mind – negligence – will not be sufficient to establish *mens rea*. The same is true of theft: one cannot steal property negligently. Assault can be committed either intentionally or, as it now appears, recklessly.[1]

Intention

The intentional commission of a crime provides us with the classic case of criminal liability. If **A** aims a blow at **B**, he intends to commit assault, and the culpability of such intentional action is beyond controversy. Yet there are many cases in which the intentionality of an act will be less evident, particularly where the focus of attention is, as in murder, not so much the act itself but a consequence which follows upon that act. Such cases have given rise to much jurisprudential debate, criminal law in this area providing rich pickings for the philosophers. The discussion has proved particularly intense in systems such as English law, which define murder entirely in terms of intention to kill or to cause grievous bodily harm. In Scots law, the definition of murder encompasses recklessness, and hence the need for close analysis of the concept of intention in this context has not been pressing. Intention, however, does feature in judicial pronouncements on *mens rea* in Scots law and therefore requires analysis.

A useful starting point may be to define intention in terms of what it is not. The antithesis of intentional action is accidental action. The difference between dropping a thing to the floor and throwing it down is clear enough; in the first case the actor does not direct any action towards the achievement of the result, whereas in the second case he performs an act which has the objective of the thing's landing on the floor. In the first case therefore the fall of the thing is unintentional, or accidental, while in the second it is intended. As a minimum, then, we can exclude from our account of intentional action those events which are properly considered to be accidents.

To act intentionally is to act with a view to bringing something about. An intended event is **wanted** by the actor, although he may

---

[1] *Roberts v Hamilton* 1989 SCCR 240, 1989 SLT 399. For general discussion, see A Ashworth, 'Recklessness in assault' (1991) 107 LQR 187.

not want it for itself but as a means to a further end. If **A** wishes to inherit his elderly relative's money and kills her for this reason, he intends her death. It may be that his real want is the money; it may even be that he very much dislikes the idea of his relative dying. If, however, he is sufficently motivated by the thought of the ultimate reward he may accept the killing of the relative as a necessary evil to be borne in order to achieve the further ambition. The fact that the death is not wanted for its own sake does not make the relative's killing any the less intentional. Something which is not wanted may therefore still be intended.

Difficulties arise in cases where a person wants **X** to occur but where consequences **Y** and **Z** also result from his bringing about of **X**. Are these consequences to be considered to have been intended by the actor? **A** may leave rat poison in his shed with the aim of killing a troublesome rat. If the rat poison is eaten by a young child, **B**, who dies as a result, is **A** to be held to have intended the death of the child ? The answer is surely no. Yet a different reply might be given in a case where **A** has set fire to his neighbour's house with a view to driving him out of the neighbourhood. **A** may believe the house to be empty, or may think that the blaze will not approach that part of the house where the neighbour is sleeping, and yet in one view the death of the neighbour may be regarded as having been intended by **A**.

The issue here is one of foresight of consequences and the effect which foresight has upon intention. In *DPP v Hyam*[1] the House of Lords endorsed the view that an appellant intended to cause death or serious bodily harm if she had acted in the knowledge that there was a high degree of probability that either of these would occur. This approach was later abandoned in favour of the view that foresight of virtually certain consequences did not necessarily amount to an intention to bring about these consequences, but may be evidence of the formation of such an intention.[2] According to this test, if I do **X** in the knowledge that it is virtually certain that **Y** will occur as a result of my doing **X**, then I have not necessarily intended **Y**. This interpretation of intention is extremely narrow and restricts the scope of intentional action to those consequences which form the central focus of an actor's plan of action. Such a narrow conception of intention has caused considerable difficulty for the English courts, and it is significant that the definition of intention

---

[1] [1975] AC 55, [1974] 2 All ER 41.
[2] *Hancock and Shankland* [1986] AC 455, [1986] 1 All ER 641.

proposed by the Law Commission is appreciably broader.[1] In Scotland, judicial explorations of these niceties have been avoided, which is not to say, though, that the Scots courts have not referred to the role of intention in the doctrine of *mens rea*. In *Sayers and Oths v HM Adv*[2] Lord Ross endorsed the definition of intention propounded by Asquith LJ in the civil case of *Cunliffe v Goodman*[3]: 'An intention ... connotes a state of affairs which the party "intending" ... does more than merely contemplate; it connotes a state of affairs which, on the contrary, he decides, so far as in him lies, to bring about, and which, in point of possibility, he has a reasonable prospect of being able to bring about, by his own act of volition.'

The use in statutes of terms such as 'wilfully' has been interpreted as requiring a particular form of intention on the part of the accused. To perform an act wilfully is to act voluntarily rather than involuntarily, but this is not the meaning attributed the term by the courts. In *Jas Kinnison*[4] it was held that 'wilfully' in a statute meant that the act should be done with the intention of doing the thing which was prohibited, an interpretation which would exclude acts done under a misapprehension of the nature of what was being done. In *Clark v HM Adv*[5], in which the appellants had been charged with the wilful neglect of their children, the defence argued that the reason for the neglect was fecklessness rather than malice and that the requirement of wilfulness was not met. This was rejected, the requirement of wilful neglect being taken as synonomous with intentional or deliberate neglect, which was present in spite of the motive which lay behind it.

Intention and knowledge

Whether or not action is intentional may depend on a person's knowledge of surrounding circumstances. Certain offences may require knowledge as to the identity of some other person or thing: a person does not act with the intention of assaulting a police officer if he is not aware of the fact that the person whom he is assaulting is a member of the police force. The intention necessary for reset is

---

[1] 'A person should be regarded as intending a particular result of his conduct if, but only if, either he actually intends that result or he has no substantial doubt that the conduct will have that result.' (Law Comm, 89, para 44).

[2] 1981 SCCR 312, 1981 JC 98.

[3] [1950] 2 KB 237 at 253; quoted with approval in *DPP v Hyam*, supra.

[4] (1870) 1 Coup 457.

[5] 1968 JC 53, 1969 SLT 161.

absent if the person does not know that the goods he is buying have been stolen.

A state of wilful blindness may be taken as the equivalent of knowledge. Wilful blindness occurs when a person deliberately refrains from finding out whether a state of affairs exists because he does not wish to inform himself of the truth. In order to be wilfully blind in relation to a fact, there must be a belief in the possibility of the existence of that fact. This is distinct from a mere suspicion, which may be a suspicion as to a remote possibility. In the New Zealand case of *Crooks*[1] it was pointed out that a jury was entitled to infer knowledge of the fact that property had been dishonestly obtained where the accused had deliberately abstained from inquiry 'because he knew what the answer was going to be', this being an actual belief in rather than a mere suspicion of a fact. Scottish decisions, however, appear to accept that wilful blindness may exist even where the accused's state of mind falls short of an actual belief in the likelihood of the existence of a fact. If **A** does not enquire about a fact because he cannot be bothered to do so, or because he negligently fails to consider the need to enquire, then he may be considered to be wilfully blind as to that fact. Strictly speaking, wilful blindness should not be the same thing as negligence or even recklessness in relation to a duty to enquire, but the broad interpretation of the concept favoured by the Scottish courts in cases such as *Smith of Maddiston Ltd v Macnab*[2] and *Latta v Herron*[3] suggests that a negligent or reckless failure to make enquiry may amount to wilful blindness. In *Latta* the test of wilful blindness is clearly objective, the court inferring from the surrounding facts that the accused 'must have wilfully blinded himself' to the fact that property was stolen.[4]

Recklessness

To act recklessly is to act without regard to the consequences of one's actions. A person who throws a burning cigarette out of a car window while driving though a dry forest is reckless with regard to the possibility of fire, if he knows that there is a risk that he will start a fire, but who does not care whether this happens or not. Such a

---

[1] [1981] 2 NZLR 53.
[2] 1975 SLT 86.
[3] (1967) SCCR Supp 18.
[4] For further discussion of the concept of wilful blindness, see D Lanham 'Wilful blindness and the criminal law' (1985) Crim L J 261; M Wasik and MP Thompson 'Turning a blind eye as constituting *mens rea*' (1981) 32 NILQ 328.

person is indifferent to the risk, and acts as he does in spite of his awareness of what might happen.

Recklessness requires that the actor should have been aware of the existence of the risk. It is difficult to see how one can be reckless in relation to a risk which has escaped one's attention. The risk must be considered and accepted as a possible consequence of one's action; failure to address a risk is not so much recklessness as negligence. If recklessness is inferred in circumstances where the actor has not thought about the existence of a risk at all, then the distinction between recklessness and negligence disappears. Yet it is important that this distinction be maintained, as there is a significant distinction between the two concepts in terms of moral culpability, and this difference affects issues of liability. Recklessness deservedly attracts criminal liability, whereas negligence will usually not be punishable.

The concept of recklessness in Scots law is an objective one. If a reasonable person in the position of the accused would have been aware of the existence of a risk, and if to proceed to act in the face of this risk would be considered to demonstrate indifference to the consequences, then recklessness exists. In *Gizzi v Tudhope*[1] the accused used guns for practice shooting in a place where any reasonable person would have expected people to be. This fact was sufficient to justify a finding of recklessness even if the accused in question had not themselves been aware of the risk of harm to others. Similarly, in *Allan v Patterson*[2] the High Court supported an objective view of recklessness, although this case was concerned with the statutory offence of reckless driving, and the court based its decision on the absence of any requirement in the legislation that there should be any enquiry into the state of knowledge of any particular driver. Further support for the objective view of recklessness is to be found in a number of decisions concerned with wicked recklessness in murder.[3] Here the accused's awareness or otherwise of a risk to life is immaterial provided that the degree of violence used in an attack meets the requisite objective standard.

Negligence

Negligence exists where there is a failure to act in accordance with an expected standard of conduct. The standard in question is usually that of the reasonably competent person, and this, again, is

---

[1] 1982 SCCR 442, 1983 SLT 214.
[2] 1980 JC 57, 1980 SLT 77.
[3] Discussed further at p 157 below.

an objective standard. Although a person who does his best may not be morally culpable if that best is not good enough, the law has found no difficulty in holding him to account for such conduct. Liability, though, is usually limited to civil liability, as negligent conduct does not normally evince that degree of culpability which is deemed necessary for criminal liability.

During the nineteenth century the courts were prepared to impose liability for negligent conduct as a means of regulating transport and industrial activity. This regulatory role, however, was to be taken over by specific legislation and the readiness of the courts to treat negligent conduct as criminal accordingly diminished. Gross negligence, however, continued to be punishable, principally in the context of culpable homicide, although prosecutions were rare. Today the causing of death through gross negligence may result in conviction for culpable homicide, or, in road traffic cases, for the statutory offence of causing death through dangerous driving. The standard of negligence required is high. In *Paton v HM Adv*[1] the degree of negligence required was defined as being 'gross, or wicked, or criminal negligence, something amounting, or at any rate analagous, to a criminal indifference to consequences'. The accused must therefore have fallen considerably below the level of competence expected and he must have failed to take precautions or to carry out steps which would have been very obviously necessary to any reasonably competent person. Even applying this standard, however, an argument may be made out for the non-punishability of negligence, however gross. As long as the negligent actor is unaware of a risk of harm to others, he is arguably morally unaccountable for that harm. Once he becomes aware of the risk of harm, he stands to be considered reckless, and this may quite properly give rise to criminal liability.

The coincidence of the *actus reus* and *mens rea*

The attribution of criminal liability normally requires that the commission of an *actus reus* be accompanied by *mens rea*. This rarely gives rise to difficulty, but in some cases the courts have accepted that an *actus reus* and *mens rea* may not coincide in the temporal sense, and that a wrongful state of mind at an earlier time may still influence an *actus reus* committed at a later stage. The classic example of this approach in Scots law is that of *Brennan v HM Adv*[2]

---

[1] 1936 JC 19, 1936 SLT 298.
[2] 1977 JC 38, 1977 SLT 151.

where the accused had manifested a wrongful state of mind (recklessness) before becoming intoxicated, and this was held to justify conviction in respect of an *actus reus* committed at a time when he would not have been capable of forming the necessary *mens rea*.

Several cases in other jurisdictions have been concerned with the coincidence of *actus reus* and *mens rea* in murder. In *Thabo Meli v R*[1], the accused had assaulted their victim and then, thinking him to be dead, had thrown him over a cliff. The victim had in fact been alive at the time at which he was thrown over the cliff and death resulted not from the original assault but from exposure suffered while lying at the bottom of the cliff. It was argued on behalf of the accused that they had not had the necessary *mens rea* at the time at which they committed the *actus reus* of murder, as they clearly did not intend to kill the victim at that stage. This argument was rejected, however, on the grounds that the whole episode required to be treated as a single event, and that at least some stage of the overall event they had the necessary *mens rea*. The same view was taken in *R v Church*[2], which involved the throwing into a river of what was mistakenly taken to be a dead body, and *R v Chsiwibo*[3], where the still-living victim was pushed into a hole in the ground in the belief that he was already dead.

[1] [1954] 1 WLR 228, [1954] 1 All ER 373.
[2] [1966] 1 QB 59.
[3] 1961 (2) SA 714.

3. Strict liability offences

Although *mens rea* will normally be required for conviction of a crime, a number of statutory offences may not require it in relation to one or more elements of the offence. These are known as strict liability offences and, to a great extent, they are limited to those day-to-day regulations which are needed for the ordering of a complex industrial society. Strict liability in this context originated in the nineteenth century and the number of offences in this category has grown markedly since then.[1] Most courts and at least some criminal law commentators accept them as a necessary evil,[2] although powerful arguments against strict liability continue to be made,[3] and the courts in some jurisdictions have succeeded in minimising the extent to which this form of criminal liability is attributed to those who are not morally culpable.[4]

The argument in favour of dispensing with a *mens rea* requirement in the case of at least some statutory offences rests on the proposition that without strict liability it would be impossible adequately to control certain forms of anti-social activity. If *mens rea* had to be proved in the case of every vehicle regulation, for example, the task of the authorities would become impossible. Similarly, in the case of industrial and pollution regulations, the difficulties of rebutting defences based on lack of knowledge or error would make successful prosecution rare and the level of protection afforded to society by such legislation would be reduced. These pragmatic arguments have considerable force, especially if discretion is shown in the decision to prosecute. Not every infringement of a strict liability provision will result in criminal proceedings; empirical evidence points to a

---

[1] For an historical survey see L H Leigh, *Strict and Vicarious Liability* (1982).
[2] In *R v Warner* [1969] 2 AC 256, [1968] 2 All ER 356, Lord Reid said of strict liability in relation to regulatory offences '...[it] may well seem unjust but it is a comparatively minor injustice' (at 272).
[3] See, for example, P Brett *An Inquiry into Criminal Guilt*, (1963) p 114 et seq.
[4] See discussion below at p 49.

tendency to avoid prosecution in unduly harsh circumstances.[1] Strict liability may not therefore always be the draconian weapon it is sometimes alleged to be.

The starting point in any enquiry as to whether a statutory offence involves strict liability is the presumption in favour of *mens rea*. This was stated by Lord Justice-Clerk Cooper in the following terms in *Duguid v Fraser*[2]:

'Our reports already contain many examples of cases in which it has been held that a *malum prohibitum* has been created by statutory enactment in such terms and under such circumstances as to impose an absolute obligation of such a kind as to entail this wider liability. In all such cases it has, I think, been the practice to insist that the Crown should show that the language, scope and intendment of the statute require that an exception should be admitted to the normal and salutary rule of our law that *mens rea* is an indispensable ingredient of a criminal or quasi-criminal act; and I venture to think that it would be misfortune if the stringency of this requirement was relaxed.'

The same presumption has been emphasised in other decisions. In the important case of *Sweet v Parsley*[3] Lord Reid stressed the moral significance of the presumption when he said:

'... there has for centuries been a presumption that Parliament did not intend to make criminals of persons who were in no way blameworthy in what they did. That means that whenever a section is silent as to *mens rea* there is a presumption that, in order to give effect to the will of Parliament, we must read in words appropriate to require *mens rea* ...'[4]

This presumption may, however, be rebutted in favour of strict liability, each case being determined according to guiding principles which the courts have identified over the years.

WHERE THE STATUTE USES WORDS IMPLYING *MENS REA*

The use of certain words may point to a legislative intention to require *mens rea*. If a statute requires that an act be done 'wilfully' this suggests that there must have been knowledge of the material

---

[1] For example, W G Carson 'White collar crime and the enforcement of factory legislation' (1970) 10 Br J Crim 383; G Richardson 'Strict liability for regulatory crime: the empirical research' [1987] Crim L R 295.

[2] 1942 JC 1, 1942 SLT 51.

[3] [1970] AC 132 (HL), 1969 1 All ER 347.

[4] [1970] AC 132 (HL) at 148.

elements of the offence and an intention to achieve the prohibited results.[1] In *R v Sheppard*[2] the court, when called upon to interpret the meaning of the phrase 'wilfully neglects' in the Children and Young Persons Act 1933, took the view that reckless conduct could be wilful. If this were to be followed in Scotland, **A** could, under the terms of a hypothetical statute, be convicted of an offence of say, 'wilfully discharging toxic waste from industrial premises' if he was aware of the fact that there was a risk that his conduct might cause the discharge but did not care whether or not this occurred. 'Knowingly' implies that there must be awareness of such facts as are material to the offence; in possession cases, for example, where the statute refers to one who 'knowingly possesses', there must be knowledge of the nature of the substance or object possessed, not just knowledge of the fact that the item is in one's possession. In *Black v H M Adv*[3], where the offence charged was that of possession of explosives, the court held that it had to be proved that the accused knew of the character of the substances stored in his house; mere knowledge that they were there was insufficient. Where mere possession, as opposed to knowing possession, is at issue, knowledge of the character of the item may not be necessary.[4] Other words sometimes used to import a *mens rea* requirement are: 'fraudulently'[5] and 'maliciously'. The word 'falsely' does not suggest that *mens rea* is required,[6] nor does the term 'corruptly'[7].

The stipulating of a *mens rea* requirement in one or more sections of a statute and not in others may be taken to suggest that *mens rea* is not required in the latter. In *Pharmaceutical Society of Great Britain v Storkwein Ltd* (1986) 83 Crim App Rep 359 (HL), the fact that the Medicines Act 1968 stipulated for *mens rea* in some sections but not in the section under consideration was taken as grounds for concluding that Parliament intended strict liability.

---

[1] *James Kinnison* (1870) 1 Couper 457. See also Lord Young's definition of 'wilfully' in *Grant v Wright* (1876) 3 Couper 282, 3 R (J) 28. As *Gordon* points out (para 8–18) there is little Scottish authority on the significance of the use of 'wilfully' in a statute. The English courts have not been entirely consistent in their interpretation of this term: compare *Eaton v Cobb* [1950] 1 All ER 1016 with *Maidstone Borough Council v Mortimer* [1980] 3 All ER 522.
[2] [1981] AC 394 [1980] 3 All ER 899.
[3] 1974 SLT 247.
[4] For example, *Winkle v Wiltshire* [1951] 1 KB 684, [1951] 1 All ER 479.
[5] *Cox and Hodges* (1982) 75 Crim App Rep 291.
[6] *R v Cummerson* [1968] 2 QB 534, [1968] 2 All ER 863.
[7] *Smith* [1960] 1 All ER 256, [1960] 2 QB 423.

WHERE THE STATUTE IS SILENT AS TO *MENS REA*

In the absence of any specific mention of a *mens rea* requirement the court may still apply the presumption in favour of *mens rea*. In deciding on the rebuttal of the presumption courts have taken into account the following factors:

(i) The regulatory nature of the statutory provision

Statutory provisions intended to regulate the day-to-day functioning of society may be considered regulatory offences, which do not require *mens rea*. The main examples of these offences are traffic offences, pollution offences, and trading offences. The common characteristic of these offences is their importance for the protection of the public – strict liability, it is felt, is justified in the interests of public safety. This rationale is explicitly endorsed in one of the best known cases of this sort, *Alphacell v Woodward*[1], in which a company was convicted of causing pollution to enter a river[2] in spite of the absence of evidence of knowledge of the pollution or negligence on the company's part. In his judgment in this case Lord Salmon said:

'It is of the utmost importance that rivers should not be polluted ... The offences created by the Act of 1951 seem to me to be prototypes of offences which "are not criminal in any real sense, but are acts which in the public interest are prohibited under a penalty" ... I can see no valid reason for reading the word "intentionally", "knowingly" or "negligently" into s 2(1)(a) ... This may be regarded as a not unfair hazard of carrying on a business which may cause pollution ... If ... it was held ... that no conviction could be obtained ... unless the prosecution could discharge the often impossible onus of proving that the pollution was caused intentionally or negligently, a great deal of pollution would go unpunished and undeterred ...'[3]

(ii) Is the offence a real crime?

'Real crimes' and regulatory offences are to be contrasted in that the former involve moral opprobrium and the possibility of a high

---

[1] [1972] AC 824, [1972] 2 All ER 475.
[2] Under s 2(1)(a) of the Rivers (Prevention of Pollution) Act 1951.
[3] At 848. For a similar justification of strict liability in terms of social interest, see *Lim Chin Aik v The Queen* [1963] AC 160, [1963] 1 All ER 223 (PC), at 174 per Lord Evershed.

penalty, and therefore require *mens rea*.[1] The distinction is not a clear one, as there are cases in which strict liability has been imposed in spite of the moral opprobrium surrounding the offence and the provision of a possible prison sentence for the offence. Conviction for unlawful possession of a firearm under the Firearms Act 1968 has the whiff of traditional criminality about it and also involves a maximum penalty of three years imprisonment; yet in *R v Hussain*[2] the accused was convicted of such an offence on the basis of strict liability.[3] More recently, in *Gammon (Hong Kong) Ltd v Attorney General for Hong Kong*[4], a Privy Council decision, the court held that the mere fact that a severe penalty was provided for in the legislation did not preclude strict liability:

'... there is nothing inconsistent with the purpose of the ordinance in imposing severe penalties for offences of strict liability. The legislature could reasonably have intended severity to be a significant deterrent, bearing in mind the risks to public safety arising from some contravention of the ordinance.'[5]

The ease with which courts have recently been prepared to accept strict liability in the case of offences involving either moral opprobrium or a severe sentence (or both) points to a weakening of the principle proposed in *Sweet v Parsley*[6], that moral opprobrium requires moral guilt. It is submitted, therefore, that this test must now be considered an unreliable one, although its usefulness in combatting the over-extension of strict liability offences is evident.

(iii) Could the accused have done otherwise?

From time to time the courts have acknowledged the pointlessness of punishing those who could have done nothing to avoid the occurrence of an *actus reus*. It was stated in *Reynolds v Austin & Son Ltd*[7] that as a '... safe general principle ... where the punishment

---

[1] The modern *locus classicus* of the 'real crime' concept is *Sweet v Parsley* [1970] AC 132, [1969] 1 All ER 347 in which the House of Lords reversed a tendency to allow strict liability convictions for drug-related offences, in this case the offence of being concerned in the management of premises used for the purpose of smoking cannabis. For a discussion of Canadian disquiet over strict liability statutes providing for imprisonment, see A Brudner 'Imprisonment and strict liability' (1990) 40 Univ Tor Law J 738.

[2] [1981] 1 WLR 416, (1981) 72 Crim App Rep 143. See also *R v Howells* [1977] QB 614, [1977] 3 All ER 417.

[3] The actual penalty imposed in this case was a relatively light fine.

[4] [1985] 1 AC 1 (PC), [1984] 2 All ER 503.

[5] [1985] 1 AC 1 (PC) at 17.

[6] [1970] AC 132 (HL), 1969 1 All ER 347.

[7] [1951] 2 KB 135, [1951] 1 All ER 606 at 612 per Lord Devlin.

of an individual will not promote the observance of the law either by that individual or by others whose conduct he may reasonably be expected to influence, then, in the absence of clear and express words, such punishment is not intended.' A similar view was expressed by the Privy Council in *Lim Chin Aik v The Queen*[1] in which the appellant had been convicted of an immigration offence in spite of the fact that there were no means by which he could ensure that he complied with the regulations in question, it being impracticable for him to make constant enquiries to see whether he had been put on a list of those who were prohibited from remaining in Singapore. The Privy Council accepted that in such circumstances strict liability was inappropriate and the appeal against conviction was allowed. Yet this principle is by no means consistently applied[2]: was there any way, for example, whereby the company convicted of polluting the river in *Alphacell v Woodward* could have done more to prevent the offence from occurring?

In practice, there will be very few cases in which an accused person will be able to claim that there was nothing more he could have done to prevent the occurrence of the *actus reus*. In food hygiene offences, for instance, samples can always be taken for analysis and more sophisticated and persistent checks on staff adherence to hygiene regulations could be insisted upon, even if these would have the effect of making businesses impossibly slow and unprofitable. In most cases, then, it will not be open to the accused to make the argument that there was no possibility of his having avoided committing the offence.

(iv) The effectiveness argument

The fact that a statutory provision can only be given effect to if *mens rea* requirements are dispensed with is another ground upon which the courts may opt for a strict liability interpretation.[3]

Defences

It is not clear which defences are available in a strict liability offence,

---

[1] [1963] AC 160, [1963] 1 All ER 223.
[2] Cf A Ashworth *Principles of Criminal Law* (1991) p 144; *Smith and Hogan* p 104.
[3] *Lim Chin Aik v The Queen*, supra; *Alphacell v Woodward* [1972] AC 824, [1972] 2 All ER 475.

although it is likely that insanity[1], automatism[2], and non-age would be accepted as defences in this context. Error, by contrast, would not, as error affects *mens rea* which is irrelevant in strict liability offences.

Necessity and self-defence should, in theory, be available as defences on the grounds that they are justificatory defences, the effect of which is to lead to the conclusion that the accused's act was not criminal. It was accepted in *Tudhope v Grubb*[3] that necessity was available as a defence to a strict liability offence under s 6(1) of the Road Traffic Act 1972, but this decision is a sheriff court decision currently unsupported by higher authority.[4] Coercion should be available as a defence, but there is no Scottish authority on the point.[5]

Acts of third parties or natural events ('acts of God') may be defences although there is scant Scottish authority on this point. In *Howman v Russell*[6] the effect of a gale on the lights of a car was not taken into account, but in *Alphacell Ltd v Woodward*[7] the court clearly considered that there would be circumstances in which a defence based on third party intervention would be available.

Impossibility has been accepted elsewhere as a defence in strict liability cases.[8] If it was physically impossible for the accused to have complied with the law, then the justification for punishment is obscure, other than that of encouraging others who might find it possible to comply.[9]

In an increasing number of statutes the possibility of a defence is being written into the statute. These provisions may require the accused to prove that he used all due diligence to avoid the occurrence in question, and they may also allow a defence of third

---

[1] *Gordon* para 8–27 expresses the view that it is 'almost inconceivable' that insanity would not be available as a defence in a strict liability offence.

[2] RS Clark 'Automatism and strict liability' (1968) 5 Victoria University of Wellington Law Rev 12.

[3] 1983 SCCR 330.

[4] In *Macleod v MacDougall* 1988 SCCR 519, 1989 SLT 151 the High Court declined to comment on the availability of the defence of necessity as a defence to a charge under the same section of the Road Traffic Act 1972.

[5] The issue has been discussed in Australia: *R v Loughnan* [1981] VR 443.

[6] 1923 JC 32, 1923 SLT 336.

[7] [1972] AC 824, [1972] 2 All ER 475 at 834, 840, 845, 847–8.

[8] *Kilbride v Lake* [1962] NZLR 590.

[9] For example in the United States: *U S v White Fuel Corporation* 498 F 2d 619 (1974). For discussion, see RS Clark 'The defence of impossibility and offences of strict liability' (1969) 11 Crim L Q 154; A Smart 'Criminal liability for failing to do the impossible' (1987) 103 LQR 532.

party intervention.[1] Alternatively, the statutory defence may simply allow acquittal if the accused satisfies the court that he did not have the necessary knowledge and could not, with reasonable care, have acquired this knowledge.[2]

THE POSSIBILITY OF REFORM

Dissatisfaction with strict liability and disquiet over the evident injustices it may entail has led the courts in Australia, New Zealand, and Canada to dilute considerably the severity of the doctrine. In Australia, a defence of reasonable mistake has been available for strict liability defences since the decision in *Proudman v Dayman*[3] in 1941. For some years there was doubt as to whether the accused bore the legal burden of establishing this defence, but this doubt has now been removed and it is clear that all that the accused has to do is to satisfy the **evidential** burden of proving honest and reasonable mistake (that is, he must produce sufficient evidence to make the defence a 'live issue').[4] In Canada and New Zealand a similar defence of due diligence has been developed, whereby an accused person who has taken reasonable steps to prevent an occurrence will be able to avoid liability on the grounds that he did everything that could reasonably be expected of him to avoid the offence being committed.[5] This moves strict liability in the direction of liability for negligence, a position which satisfies expectations of efficiency while at the same time avoiding the injustice of convicting those who could not have avoided the occurrence in question.

VICARIOUS LIABILITY

Vicarious liability for crime offends the normal principle that a person is not to be held accountable for the actions of another. The

---

[1] Eg Food Act 1984, s 100.

[2] Fertilisers and Feeding Stuffs Act 1926, s 7(1); Trade Descriptions Act 1968, s 24.

[3] (1941) 67 Crim LR 536.

[4] *He Kaw Teh v R* (1985) 60 ALR 449. For discussion, see P Brett, L Waller and CR Williams *Criminal Law* (6th edn, 1989) p 702 (for the New Zealand position on this issue, see *R v Strawbridge* [1970] NZLR 909 at 916).

[5] *City of Sault Ste Marie* (1978) 40 CCC 2d 353 (Canada); *Millar v Ministry of Transport* [1986] 1 NZLR 660 (NZ). For discussion, see G Orchard 'The defence of absence of fault in Australia and Canada' in P Smith (ed) *Criminal Law: Essays in Honour of JC Smith* (1987) p 114.

attribution of vicarious liability, however, is accepted in limited circumstances, particularly in offences relating to sale to the public and in licensing cases. As is the case with strict liability regulatory offences, these offences do not involve 'true criminality', a fact which goes some way towards justifying the notion of vicarious liability. Vicarious liability may be expressly provided for in a statute or it may be inferred from the nature of the statutory provision. If a statutory provision regulates an activity which normally involves employees, then the courts are likely to impose vicarious liability. For example, if a statute provides that it is an offence for a trader to sell any item without an appropriate licence, then the fact that sales are frequently conducted by employees justifies an inference of vicarious liability.[1] *Mens rea* on the part of the accused is not required, and therefore it makes no difference if an employer had no knowledge of the fact that his employee was, for example, carrying out a prohibited transaction. If the offence itself is described as requiring *mens rea*, then it is not clear whether the intent of the employee can be attributed to the employer. For example, if a statute makes it an offence 'knowingly to sell' a particular item, can an employer be convicted provided that his employee had the necessary knowledge ? There is English authority suggesting that an employer is liable in such a case,[2] and this would probably be followed in Scotland.[3]

Vicarious liability requires that the offence should have been committed by the employee acting within the scope of his employment,[4] but an act will not be removed from the scope of employment merely because it breaches general instructions given by the employer. In order to avoid vicarious liability in such a case, an employer must give highly specific instructions, the breach of which effectively puts the employee outside the scope of his employment.[5] The fact that an employer exercised all due diligence in the hiring, training and supervision of staff will not be a defence to vicarious liability, except where a statute specifically allows for this.

CAUSING AND PERMITTING OFFENCES

A statute may make it an offence to 'cause or permit' a prohibited occurrence. After a period of inconsistency in the interpretion of

---

[1] *Bean v Sinclair* 1930 JC 31.
[2] *Mousell Bros Ltd v L and NW Railway* [1917] 2 KB 836.
[3] For discussion, see *Gordon* para 8–52.
[4] *City and Suburban Dairies v Mackenna* 1918 JC 105.
[5] *Duffy v Tennant* 1952 JC 15.

such provisions, it is now clear that in certain circumstances no *mens rea* is required where the charge is one of causing something to happen;[1] permitting, by contrast, requires knowledge on the part of the accused that the prohibited act is taking place. In some cases, knowledge of the illegality will be inferred where the accused manifested wilful blindness to the possibility of the illegality.[2]

---

[1] *Lockhart v National Coal Board* 1981 SLT 161. Cf *Smith of Maddiston Ltd v Macnab* 1975 SLT 86. Whether 'causing' requires knowledge may eventually depend on the context of the provision and the presence elsewhere in the statute of qualifying words.

[2] *Smith of Maddiston Ltd v Macnab* 1975 SLT 86.

4. Corporate criminal liability

A great deal of crime is committed in the context of companies or corporations, which are the dominant forces in modern commercial life. Prosecution authorities may still proceed against individuals within companies, and always charge them personally with the crimes they have committed, but to do so may obscure the real actor behind the criminal conduct – the company itself. This is open to the obvious objection that the real culprits, those who sought to profit by the crime, may escape prosecution, while the minor official bears the brunt of the blame. It may also be difficult to identify within a company those who have actually committed a criminal offence. This will be particularly so where a company is a large multinational one, with complex and possibly impenetrable corporate structures. It is clearly simpler in such a case to prosecute the company.

Opposition to the idea of corporate liability for crime has in the past focused on the alleged inherent impossibility of a company committing a crime.[1] How can a company, which is a metaphysical entity, form a criminal intention and perpetrate an offence? The intention and the perpetration are both referable to human actors, and it is they who should be punished. This view, of course, ignores the reality of corporate action. It is widely accepted that corporations act in the real world, and the law acknowledges this by allowing companies to enter into contracts and by requiring them to answer for their negligence. If no conceptual difficulties occur in this context, then why should a company not be capable of criminal conduct? It is only if one subscribes to the teleological view that criminal conduct lies quite outside the range of competence of a corporation that one must reject the possibility of corporate crime.[2] Yet a corporation can be used as a criminal instrument. It is

---

[1] For discussion, see P French *Collective and Corporate Responsibility* (1984) p 31 et seq.

[2] For criticism of this approach, see LCB Gower *Modern Company Law* (4th edn, 1979) p 169.

possible to imagine the whole point and ethos of a company being criminal, as where the company is set up with the specific purpose of perpetrating fraud.

A further, pragmatic objection founds on the pointlessness of convicting companies of criminal offences. According to this argument, individuals can be punished for their crimes but companies cannot. A company has no conscience to shame and no physical person to detain. A company cannot be sent to prison,[1] nor can it feel the consequences of a fine. When a company is fined it is the shareholders, and indirectly the employees, who feel the consequences of the penalty. The company itself does not suffer.

These objections are based on an unrealistic notion of corporate identity. Companies do respond to threats and sanctions. A company will tailor its actions according to the consequences, as demonstrated by the assiduity with which companies will avoid bad publicity. Companies are in many respects similar to human actors, with a sense of identity, a sense of purpose, and a responsiveness to surrounding circumstances. It is true that these objectives and corporate 'state of mind' may be experienced and expressed collectively, but this does not diminish their reality. Collective interest may exist quite independently of the interests of those who make up the collectivity.

WHO MAY BE LIABLE?

Procedures exist for the prosecution, on indictment, of any 'body corporate'[2] and, on summary complaint, any 'company, association, incorporation, or body of trustees'[3]. In the latter case, any partner, manager or 'person in charge' may be dealt with 'as if he was the person offending'.

---

[1] Although this fact appeared to have escaped the attention of Parliament when it enacted the Companies Act 1967, s 68(5) of which provided: 'An insurance company which contravenes . . . shall be guilty of an offence and liable on conviction on indictment to imprisonment for a term not exceeding two years'.

[2] Criminal Procedure (Scotland) Act 1975, s 74. A body corporate includes a partnership: *Mackay Bros v Gibb* 1969 JC 26, 1969 SLT 216; *Douglas v Phoenix Motors* 1970 SLT (Sh Ct) 57.

[3] Criminal Procedure (Scotland) Act 1975, s 333.

STATUTORY OFFENCES

(1) Strict liability offences

Little difficulty has been experienced by the courts in holding a company liable for statutory offences of strict liability. The basis of this is that the company is vicariously liable for the acts of its employees, the general presumption against vicarious liability in the criminal law being rebutted either by the wording of the statute or by the implication that without vicarious liability the statute could not be applied.[1] The act of the employee must, of course, occur within the context of his employment in order for the company to be held liable on those grounds.[2] A company should not be held criminally responsible for the acts of employees who are pursuing their own private ends,[3] but it will not always be a defence for a company simply to argue that the act was committed in defiance of instructions;[4] the company must show that the instructions were express and specific.[5] The fact that the employee acted for the benefit of a person other than the company, will probably take the act out of the scope of the employee's employment and the company will therefore not be liable.[6]

(2) Statutory offences requiring *mens rea*

Where the statutory offence requires *mens rea*, as is the case with the 'permitting' offences, the question is whether the knowledge of an individual employee or director can be imputed to the company. The Scottish courts have been prepared to make this imputation: in *Clydebank Co-operative Society v Binnie*[7] the knowledge of the company's transport manager that an unlicensed vehicle was being used in the business was 'brought home' to the

---

[1] *Gair v Brewster* 1916 JC 36, 1916 1 SLT 380; *Duguid v Fraser* 1942 JC 1, 1942 SLT 51.

[2] See discussion of vicarious liability, supra, p 49.

[3] *Heriot v Auld* 1918 JC 16, 1917 2 SLT 178; *City and Suburban Dairies v McKenna* 1918 JC 105, 1918 2 SLT 155.

[4] *Linton v Stirling* (1893) 1 Adam 61, (1893) 20 R (J) 71; *Simpson v Gifford* 1954 SLT 39.

[5] See *Gordon* para 8–59.

[6] This was the approach of the court in the Canadian case of *Canadian Dredge and Dock Co Ltd v The Queen* (1985) CCC (3d) 1.

[7] 1937 JC 17, 1937 SLT 114.

company. Other decisions are to the same effect: in *Mackay Brothers & Co v Gibb*[1] the court held that the firm had knowledge of the fact that vehicle types were in an illegal condition, this knowledge being brought home to it by the knowledge of the firm's garage controller. In *Brown v W Burns Tractors Ltd*[2] a clerical assistant was aware of the fact that company drivers were driving illegally and this knowledge was attributed to the company.

Who must have knowledge within the company? Will the fact that any employee knew what was happening justify the conclusion that the company knew? Differing views have been expressed on this issue. In *Mackay Bros* the Lord Justice-Clerk suggested that the knowledge of any employee would suffice; Lord Wheatley and Lord Milligan, however, thought that there must be knowledge on the part of an employee in respect of those matters delegated to him. In *Brown* the clerical assistant who knew what was happening was the person to whom day-to-day responsibility for the relevant matters had been delegated by the company. The tendency, then, is to require that the knowledge be possessed by one who is responsible for the relevant area of the company's operations.[3] Knowledge on the part of an employee who is in no position to change working practices will not suffice. The fact that a filing clerk happens to observe another junior employee perpetrating an offence in the works yard, and is the only person (other than the perpetrator) who knows of the offence, will not mean that the company can be held to be permitting the conduct in question.

(3) Common law offences

There is now no doubt that a company may be convicted of a common law offence in Scots law, although it is clear that there are some offences, such as murder or shameless indecency[4], which a

---

1 1969 JC 26, 1969 SLT 216.
2 1986 SCCR 146.
3 *Reader's Digest Assoc v Pirie* 1973 JC 42, 1973 SLT 170.
4 *Dean v John Menzies (Holdings) Ltd* 1981 JC 23, 1981 SLT 50. In this case Lord Stott firmly excluded the possibility of corporate liability for murder, but the issue continues to be discussed elsewhere: see Helverson 'Can a corporation commit murder' (1986) 64 Wash Univ Law Quartly 967. In *H M Coroner for East Kent; ex parte Spooner* (1987) Crim App Rep 10, the Court of Criminal Appeal in England was prepared to accept that a corporate body could be guilty of manslaughter (culpable homicide).

company lacks the capacity to commit.[1] The basis on which Scots law attributes corporate liability for common law crime remains unresolved. In *Dean v John Menzies (Holdings) Ltd* it was accepted that such liability could exist, although the majority declined to identify the juristic basis of it and excluded its operation in a case of shameless indecency. The dissenting judgment of Lord Cameron in this case, however, and Lord Ross's judgment in *Purcell Meats (Scotland) Ltd v McLeod*[2] both point to an acceptance of the 'controlling mind' fiction, which was first advanced by Lord Denning in *H L Bolton Engineering Co v T J Graham & Sons Ltd*[3] and further developed in the later case of *Tesco Supermarkets v Nattrass*[4].

In *Bolton*, Lord Denning used the metaphor of the human body when he said:

'A company may in many ways be likened to a human body. It has a brain and nerve centre which controls what it does. It has also hands which hold the tools and act in accordance with directions from the centre. Some of the people in the company are mere servants and agents who are nothing more than hands who do the work and cannot be said to represent the mind or will. Others are directors and managers who represent the directing mind and will of the company and control what it does. The state of mind of those managers is the state of mind of the company and is treated by the law as such.'[5]

In *Tesco Supermarkets* an attempt was made by the House of Lords to answer the question as to who may be considered to be the controlling mind of the company, but no single criterion emerged. Various approaches were favoured, varying from the fairly formal test as to who is designated by the articles of association to exercise power on behalf of the company,[6] to the functional view of Viscount Dilhorne, who was of the opinion that the directing mind of the company was to be found in those persons who have actual control of the company's affairs and who are not subordinate to another in the exercise of this control.

---

[1] There may be cases in which even a statutory offence may require individual human agency. In *Docherty v Stakis Hotels Ltd* 1991 SCCR 6 a company was-charged with an offence under the Food Hygiene (Scotland) Regulations 1959, which placed a duty on the 'owner or other person having the management and control of a food business'. It was held that the company could not be considered as having management and control for the purposes of the regulations: '... such a corporate cannot for the purposes of this regulation have management control. A limited company can only act through its employees or servants.' (At 14.)
[2] 1986 SCCR 672, 1987 SLT 528.
[3] [1957] 1 QB 159, [1956] 3 All ER 624.
[4] [1972] AC 153, [1971] 2 All ER 127.
[5] [1956] 3 All ER 624 at 630.
[6] See the judgments in this case of Lord Pearson and Lord Diplock.

The allegation of vagueness is still levelled at the controlling mind test in spite of efforts to clarify matters on the part of the House of Lords.[1] It is certainly difficult to identify a directing mind, and none of the criteria suggested in *Tesco* really seem to draw a clear line between those who make up the directing mind and those who are no more than employees. There is also the objection that the ratio in *Tesco* allows a company to escape liability if its day-to-day managers are subject to a board-level veto;[2] this is inconsistent with the earlier Scottish authority discussed above, the tendency of which is to ask whether there was a de facto delegation of responsibility. It has also been pointed out that the *Tesco* principle is too restrictive, and makes it difficult to convict companies where the offences are committed at the level of middle rather than top management.[3] The Scots courts have not experienced this difficulty before, and therefore it is questionable whether they would wish to accept this implication of the *Tesco* decision. Much of the usefulness of corporate criminal liability lies in its ability to ensure compliance with regulations intended to control commercial and industrial life. The real blameworthiness of offending companies may lie, therefore, in the fact that their system of internal control is insufficient to supervise properly the activities of employees. This fault can realistically be pursued by the prosecution of the company, and it is perhaps here that prosecution resources are best directed.

---

[1] Eg by Lord Maxwell in *Dean v John Menzies* 1981 JC 23, 1981 SLT 50.

[2] This is an aspect of the *Tesco* decision which has been played down in a number of subsequent cases: *R v Andrew's Weatherfoil Ltd* [1972] 1 All ER 65, [1972] 1 WLR 118.

[3] B Fisse *Howard's Criminal Law* (5th edn, 1990) p 603.

5. Causation

Criminal liability for a result depends upon the accused person having caused that result. This requires the making of a satisfactory link between the act of the accused and the event in question; in the absence of such a link the criminal result is not attributable to the accused – it is not his responsibility. In most cases, causation will not be an issue, as the link between actor and result will be self-evident. In some cases, though, the liability of the accused for a result may be placed in question by causal doubts. For example, in *R v Smith*[1] the appellant stabbed the deceased, a soldier, who was then carried to the casualty station by a fellow soldier, who dropped him twice on the way. At the casualty station, the victim was administered oxygen, which was an inappropriate and dangerous treatment in the case of a lung injury, and he died. Had the victim not been incorrectly treated, his chances of recovery were estimated to be as high as 75 per cent, and on these grounds the appellant argued that his act of stabbing was not the cause of death.

The accused's appeal against conviction was unsuccessful, but what would have been the result had the victim been transported to the casualty station by ambulance, which had fortuitously crashed, causing him fatal head injuries? Or, alternatively, what would have been the result if, after the initial stabbing by Smith, the victim had been shot in the heart by another, dying immediately after the shooting? Or, to compound the complication, who would have caused death if the victim, after being stabbed by Smith, shot by another, dropped twice by his rescuer, was connected to an artificial respirator in hospital, which was then switched off by a nurse who had formed the (correct) impression that the victim was not going to survive more than a few hours?[2]

Although few cases will involve as many possible causes as the last

---

[1] [1959] 2 QB 35, [1959] 2 All ER 193.
[2] *Finlayson v HM Adv* 1979 JC 33, 1978 SLT (Notes) 60.

example, there will be circumstances in which a court has to select, from amongst a number of candidates, those events which are of special causal significance. This process of selection really amounts to an attribution of blame, and may therefore be affected by policy considerations. To identify conduct as the cause of an event entails the judgment that the person responsible for that conduct has to **answer** for a particular result, a decision which may clearly be influenced by notions of blameworthiness. Causation is therefore a moral question, and causal decisions may be affected by the angle from which one looks at a situation.

SUFFICIENT LEGAL CAUSATION

Criminal responsibility for a result requires that the act of the accused be a sufficient legal cause of the event in question. This may be stated in the following rule: **the act of the accused must have been sufficient in itself to produce the result, provided that the result was not too remote from the original act**. If this criterion is met, then the accused's act may safely be considered to be the legal cause of the result.

'Sufficient in itself'

An act will only be a cause of an event if it is *causa sine qua non*; that is, if the event would not have occurred without it. If **A** stabs **B**, who bleeds to death, the result (**B**'s death) would not have occurred but for **A**'s act of stabbing. The stabbing is therefore a *causa sine qua non*. If **A** stabs **B**, who is suffering from a terminal illness, and **B** while in hospital receiving treatment for the stab wound, dies of an unconnected illness, **A**'s stabbing is not a *causa sine qua non* as **B**'s death would have occurred without it.

An exception must be made in relation to concurrent causes. If **A** and **B** both shoot **C** at the same time, each shot being sufficiently serious to cause death, **C**'s death would have occurred without **A**'s act, yet **A** will still be held to have caused the death.[1]

---

[1] *Gordon* para 4–29, citing the authority of *HM Adv v Parker and Barrie* (1888) 2 White 79, (1888) 16 R (J) 5.

Existing conditions

An act is sufficient in itself even if it achieves its causal potency only because of an existing state of affairs. The rule that one takes one's victim as one finds him applies both in relation to the circumstances surrounding the victim at the time of an assault and in relation to the victim's personal condition (bad health, anatomical peculiarities, etc). The rule was stated by Lord Justice-Clerk Cooper in the following terms:

'It would never do for it to go forth from this court that house-breakers or robbers, or others of that character, should be entitled to lay violent hands on very old or very sick or very young people, and, if their victim died as a result, to turn around and say that they would never have died if they had not been very weak or very old or very young. That is not the law, and I think you will agree with me that it is not common sense ...'[1]

If, therefore, the accused has stabbed the victim in a vital organ, with fatal results, it will be no defence to argue that the victim's organs were abnormally positioned and that such a stabbing would not have resulted in death in a normal person. A slight wound may lead to the death of a haemophiliac, and this will be homicide even if the accused did not know of his victim's abnormal condition. Similarly, psychological or religious characteristics are irrelevant in this context. In *R v Blaue*[2] the victim, a Jehovah's Witness, declined an operation to treat a stab wound she had received at the hands of the accused, and the court observed:

'It has long been the policy of the law that those who use violence on other people must take their victim as they find them. This in our judgment means the whole man, not just the physical man. It does not lie in the mouth of the assailant to say that his victim's religious beliefs which inhibited him from accepting certain kinds of treatment were not reasonable.'[3]

---

[1] *HM Adv v Robertson and Donoghue* (Aug 1945, unreported) High Court; *Gane and Stoddart* p 183. See also *HM Adv v Rutherford* 1947 JC 1, 1947 SLT 3; *Bird v HM Adv* 1952 JC 23, 1952 SLT 446.
[2] (1975) 61 Crim App Rep 271, [1975] 3 All ER 446.
[3] At 450.

INTERRUPTION OF CAUSATION: THE *NOVUS ACTUS INTERVENIENS*

An act will not be a sufficient cause of a result if the link between it and the result is interrupted by an intervening event, a *novus actus interveniens* or *nova causa interveniens*. This intervening event must be significant enough to acquire causative potency for itself. An act which is an expected or 'regular' part of the sequence of events will not be treated as sufficient to interrupt the causal link between the original act and the result.

A *novus actus interveniens* may fall into any of the following categories:

(1) An 'act of God'

A natural event, outside human agency, may be a *nova causa interveniens*. The injured victim who is fatally struck by lightning on the way to hospital, will not be regarded as having been killed by the original assailant, even if the stab wound was potentially lethal. An 'act of God' is, however, something quite unpredictable; predictable natural events, such as a river spate or a high tide, will not amount to interrupting events.[1]

(2) An act of a third party

Third party acts may amount to a *novus actus interveniens* unless such acts are foreseeable and accepted as being 'within the risks' of the original act. The basis for recognising such an act as a *novus actus interveniens* is the general presumption that voluntary human actions are not caused and that therefore the occurrence of a voluntary human action will interrupt a causal link.[2] A simple illustration demonstrates this principle: if **A** leaves a knife on the table which is then picked up by **B** and used to kill **C**, the link between **A**'s act of leaving the knife and **C**'s death is interrupted by **B**'s intervening voluntary act.

The issue of third party intervening action arose in the unusual case of *R v Pagett*[3] in which a girl used as a human shield by the

---

[1] *Southern Water Authority v Pegrum and Pegrum* [1989] Crim LR 442.
[2] Discussed by J Feinberg in *Doing and Deserving* (1970) p 152.
[3] (1983) 76 Crim App Rep 279.

accused was fatally wounded by bullets fired by police officers. The appellant argued that the action of the police officers in firing the shots amounted to a *novus actus interveniens*, but this argument was rejected. In its decision, the Court of Appeal in England placed some weight on the view that third party action would not amount to a *novus actus interveniens* where it was either involuntary or performed in the course of official duty.[1]

It is not settled whether a criminal act on the part of another person may amount to a *novus actus interveniens* if the original act may have had fatal results anyway. A shoots B wounding him in a way which would prove fatal after thirty minutes, whatever happened, and then C happens upon the scene and takes the opportunity himself to shoot B; if B dies immediately after being shot by C (as a result of C's shot and C's shot alone), is A's act of shooting to be considered a cause of B's death? *Macdonald* takes the view that it should not, but there is no clear authority for this,[2] and it would be open to a court to espouse a contrary view. Such examples, of course, appear highly artificial and unlikely until, of course, they occur, as happened in *S v Daniels*[3]. Here A shot V, inflicting injuries which were likely in the circumstances to be fatal. B, acting independently of A, came upon the scene and shot V in the ear, as a consequence of which V died. Two of the five judges hearing A's appeal against conviction for murder, were of the view that A's act was a cause of V's death.[4]

Malregimen

Medical mishaps may substantially worsen the condition of a victim and may therefore interrupt the causal link between act and result. The action of a doctor will not normally amount to a *novus actus interveniens* provided that the doctor is not departing unduly from what is medically expected in the circumstances. In

---

[1] The Court of Appeal placed some store by the opinion expressed by HLA Hart and AM Honore in *Causation in the Law* (1st edn, 1959) p 299.

[2] *Gordon* (para 4–32) points out that the passage of *Hume* I, 181 cited by *Macdonald* in support of his proposition does not in fact provide the necessary authority, as *Hume* is dealing with a case where the original wounding is not clearly fatal.

[3] 1983 (3) SA 275.

[4] For two of the other judges, the causal issue did not need to be decided, as they took the view that A and B were acting in concert, a conclusion which would anyway justify both being convicted of V's murder. For discussion, see C R Snyman, *Criminal Law* (2nd edn, 1989) p 72.

Finlayson v HM Adv[1] the switching off by doctors of a mechanical ventilator was not treated as an interrupting cause. The decision to discontinue artificial ventilation was not treated as unwarrantable; it was, in fact, described by the court as a perfectly reasonable course of conduct, not something ultroneous or unforeseeable. In *R v Malcherek, and R v Steel*[2] the Court of Appeal in England addressed the question of brain death in two cases in which the victims were declared brain dead while respiration was still being maintained artificially. The court declined to hold that switching off of the machines constituted a *novus actus interveniens*:

'Where a medical practitioner adopting methods which are generally accepted comes bona fide and conscientiously to the conclusion that the patient is for all practical purposes dead, and that such vital functions as exist – for example, circulation – are being maintained solely by mechanical means, and therefore discontinues treatment, that does not prevent the person who inflicted the initial injury from being responsible for the victim's death.'[3]

Apart from the discussion in *Finlayson v HM Adv*[4] there is little modern Scots authority on the causal significance of intervening medical treatment. Earlier authority must be treated with some caution, given the scientific uncertainties of the times and the difficulty medical witnesses would have experienced in attributing death to a particular cause. In *James Williamson*[5] Lord Justice-Clerk Inglis accepted that the 'unskilful and unjudicious treatment' of a 'simple and early cured wound' could interrupt the causal link, and this was also accepted, more cautiously, in *Heinrich Heidmeisser*[6]. Such treatment may be a *novus actus interveniens* even if the original wound would have caused death whatever treatment was given. If the medical treatment eclipses the original wound as a cause of death, then the original wound is no longer the cause of death. Thus if **A** stabs **B** in such a way as to make **B**'s death inevitable, and **B** is then injected in hospital with the wrong drug by a doctor who has not bothered to read the label on the ampoule and dies immediately from the effect of the drug, **A**'s act is no longer the cause of death: death is caused by the injection.

A modern English case, *R v Smith*[7], has been extremely influential

---

1   1979 JC 33, 1978 SLT (Notes) 60.
2   (1981) 73 Crim App Rep 173, [1981] 2 All ER 422.
3   (1981) 73 Crim App Rep 173 at 181.
4   1978 SLT (Notes) 60, 1979 JC 33.
5   (1866) 5 Irv 326.
6   (1879) 17 SLR 266.
7   [1959] 2 QB 35, [1959] 2 All ER 193.

in a number of jurisdictions and would undoubtedly be persuasive in a Scottish decision on this matter. In *Smith*, the facts of which have been outlined above,[1] Lord Parker CJ expressed the *novus actus interveniens* principle as follows:

'Only if it can be said that the original wounding is merely the setting in which another cause operates can it be said that the death does not result from the wound. Putting it another way, only if the second cause is so overwhelming as to make the original wound merely part of the history can it be said that death does not flow from the wound . . .'[2]

The approach recommended in *Smith* has been endorsed in subsequent decisions. In *R v Evans and Gardiner (No 2)*[3] the Supreme Court of Victoria held that a failure to diagnose a common complication of an operation did not amount to a *novus actus interveniens*. More recently in *R v Cheshire*[4] the Court of Appeal in England stressed that, in order to amount to a *novus actus interveniens* the negligent treatment must be so independent of the accused's acts, and so potent in causing death, that what the accused did pales into insignificance. The original wounding does not therefore have to be the **only** cause of death; it must, however, be a significant cause of death. This test is not favourable to an assailant: only rarely will medical negligence be of such a nature as to overshadow the accused's causal contribution to the victim's death.

(3) An act of the victim himself

The victim may himself make a causal contribution to the criminal result, but this need not amount to an interruption of causation. Once again the test is whether the victim's act is of an ultroneous or unreasonable nature.

(i) The escape case

A number of cases involve victims who have caused injury to themselves in an attempt to escape from a situation of danger created by the accused. Such an attempt will not generally be a *novus actus*

---

[1] At p 58.
[2] [1959] 2 QB 35 at 43. The ruling in *Smith* might be contrasted with the less stern view expressed in *R v Jordan* (1956) 40 Crim App Rep 152, a case in which the inappropriate administration of an antibiotic to a patient with an intolerance for that antibiotic was held to be 'palpably wrong' and therefore a *novus actus interveniens*.
[3] [1976] VR 523.
[4] [1991] 3 All ER 670, [1991] 1 WLR 844.

interveniens, unless the attempt at escape is so utterly unreasonable that it could not be foreseen.[1] In *R v Roberts*[2] the appellant made sexual advances to a female passenger in his car. The passenger jumped out of the moving car and received injuries as a result; the appellant argued (unsuccessfully) that these injuries flowed from a *novus actus interveniens* on the victim's part. *R v Mackie*[3] also involved an attempt at escape, in this case by a three-year-old boy who fell downstairs, sustaining fatal injuries, while fleeing the appellant's physical ill-treatment. Once again, conduct resulting from the well-founded fear of the escapee did not amount to a *novus actus interveniens*.[4]

(ii) The victim's feckless conduct

Hume is of the view that the exacerbation of a slight injury through the 'obstinacy and intemperance' of the victim, or through his application of 'rash and hurtful applications' will interrupt causation.[5] The decision in *Joseph and Mary Norris*[6] is to like effect, the victim in this case having drunk alcohol and removed a bandage from a minor wound inflicted by the accused. Courts in other jurisdictions have been unwilling to conclude that the causal link is broken in such cases,[7] and it is submitted that a future Scottish court faced with a similar issue might be loathe to regard fecklessness on the part of the victim as an interrupting factor. It is surely foreseeable that the victim of an assault will neglect to seek treatment (which is not unusual) or will fail to comply with medical instructions. A downright refusal of medical treatment, whether on religious or other grounds, is also not unforeseeable, and was held in *R v Blaue*[8] not to amount to a *novus actus interveniens*.

---

[1] There are few cases of escape which have been found to be unreasonable. However, see *R v McEnery* 1943 SR 158 – a jump from a train to avoid assault at the hands of an unarmed drunk.

[2] (1972) 56 Crim App Rep 95.

[3] (1973) 57 Crim App Rep 453.

[4] *D P P v Daley* [1980] AC 237, (1979) 69 Crim App Rep 39 (PC): the victim's fear of being hurt must be reasonable and must be caused by the conduct of the accused. See also, *Patrick Slaven & Ors* (1885) 5 Couper 694. For discussion, see DW Elliott 'Frightening a person into injuring himself' [1974] Crim L R 15.

[5] I, 182.

[6] (1886) 1 White 292.

[7] *R v Holland* (1841) 2 M & Rob 351, 174 ER 313; *Flynn* (1867) 16 WR 319 (Ireland); *R v Mubila* 1956 (1) SA 31 (S Rhodesia).

[8] (1975) 61 Crim App Rep 271, [1975] 3 All ER 446.

(iii) The victim's suicide. Suicide by the victim of an assault may raise the question of whether the original assailant caused the victim's death. The issue is alluded to obiter in *John Robertson*[1], in which the court expressed the view that suicide following immediately upon an attack might 'come very near' to culpable homicide, but apart from this dictum there is no Scottish authority. *R v Bunn*[2] involved a murder charge in a case where the victim committed suicide three-and-a-half months after an assault, but the prosecution was abandoned on the grounds of doubts as to causation. Courts in other jurisdictions have adopted a less cautious attitude. In the American case of *Stephenson v State*[3] a homicide conviction was returned in respect of the suicide of a girl who had been raped and held captive by the accused,[4] and in *Jones*[5] a rapist was convicted of murder after his victim jumped into a river. In both these cases, of course, the suicide follows hard upon the assault; a different decision may have been reached if some time had elapsed between the original wrongful act and the commission of suicide.

The real obstacle which the prosecution will have to overcome in a suicide case is the very strong presumption that a voluntary act is usually not treated as having been itself caused by another act. It is only if the act of suicide can be considered involuntary that its presumed status as a *novus actus interveniens* can be overcome.[6] Evidence of significant depression on the victim's part may help to establish this: the act then may be viewed as nothing other than a deliberate, reasoned response to difficult circumstances.

---

[1] (1854) 1 Irv 469.
[2] *The Times*, May 11, 1989.
[3] (1933) 205 Ind 141; 179 NE 633.
[4] See discussion of the special factors in this case: *Gordon* para 4–52.
[5] 43 NE 2d 1017 (1942).
[6] The issue of causation in suicide has been extensively debated in South African courts: in *S v Grotjohn* 1970 (2) SA 355 the Appellate Division held that the victim's suicide was not a *novus actus interveniens*; see also *S v Hibbert* 1979 (4) SA 717 (contrary view: *R v Nbakwa* 1956 (2) SA 577 (Southern Rhodesia)). These cases, however, all involve encouragement to suicide rather than suicide following upon an assault.

6. Parties to crime

A criminal offence may be committed by a person acting on his own or by one who acts in concert with others. In the latter case, there may be a number of persons each of whom plays a different role in the commission of the offence, including the instigation of the crime, the provision of technical assistance for its commission (for example, the provision of firearms or keys), and actual participation in the carrying out of the crime. Each of these persons is equally responsible for the crime even if there is only one principal actor who eventually performs the *actus reus* of the crime.[1] The term used in Scots law to describe this form of guilt is 'art and part' guilt; other terms used include 'complicity in crime', 'accession to crime', or 'ancillary responsibility'.

THE JUSTIFICATION OF ART AND PART GUILT

The fact that the criminal law treats all participants in a criminal offence as equally guilty may strike some as unduly harsh, given different degrees of participation on the part of those involved. The actions of a look-out man who warns of the approach of the police may seem less reprehensible than those of the person who actually commits a robbery. Similarly, the person who provides details of another's movements in order to allow him to be set upon and killed, may in one view seem less blameworthy than the murderer who actually strikes the blows. Such intuitions, however, are open to criticism on the grounds that they fail to give adequate weight to the social danger which an accomplice represents. One who advises another to commit a crime is actually as much of a threat to society as the person who commits it: one who provides the explosives for the terrorist is as dangerous as the terrorist himself. The social

---

[1] *Hume* I, 264. *H M Adv v Lappen and Ors* 1956 SLT 109.

danger view, then, suggests that the reason why we hold accomplices responsible for crimes lies in the positive contribution they make to criminal conduct.

This view of the accomplice as a danger to society raises the question of whether the attribution art and part guilt can be justified on causal grounds. Is the accomplice causally responsible for the commission of the crime and therefore legally responsible too? This analysis has been advanced by some criminal law commentators, and has been approved in a number of cases in other jurisdictions, but has not been discussed by the Scottish courts. In some judgments causation is depicted as an essential element of accomplice liability,[1] but the theoretical objections to requiring a causal link between the accomplice's act and the eventual commission of the crime will be considerable. This is particularly so in the case where the secondary party did no more than instigate a crime. It will be effectively impossible to link the giving of advice to the actual commission of the crime, as there is no means of establishing that the action of the perpetrator resulted from the instigation rather than from a determination on his own part to go ahead with the crime. A similar difficulty is encountered in cases involving the provision of assistance, as demonstrated in the following example: **A** decides to help **B** to break into a house. He leaves a ladder by the side of the house, intending that **B** should use it to enter an upstairs window. **B**, in fact, enters by forcing the front door. In this case **A**'s act has not played a causal role in the entry to the house, but it is likely that he would still be considered art and part guilty of the burglary.[2]

FORMS OF ART AND PART LIABILITY

Art and part liability may arise where there is one of the following: (1) joint commission of a crime; (2) the commission of a crime through innocent agency; or (3) associate liability.

---

[1] Dicta to the effect that a causal link is required: *N C B v Gamble* [1959] 1 QB 11 at 20. See also *Anderson and Morris* [1966] 2 QB 110 at 120; *D P P v Merriman* [1973] AC 584 at 592 and 607; *Attorney General's Ref (No 1 of 1975)* [1975] 1 QB 773. JC Smith 'Complicity and causation' [1986] Crim L Rev 663. Cf *Howell v Doyle* [1952] VR 128 at 134 (Australia). The issue has been a controversial one in South African decisions: *S v Safatsa* 1988 (1) SA 868 (A), discussed by D Unterhalter 'The doctrine of common purpose' (1988) 105 SALJ 671.

[2] For discussion of English law on this point, see *Smith and Hogan* p 135.

(1) Joint commission

This occurs where two or more parties both perform acts which constitute an *actus reus*. An example is where **A** and **B** contemporaneously assault **C**, both striking blows. **A** and **B** have jointly committed an assault on **C** in this case. Where **A** acts as a lookout while **B** robs a bank, both **A** and **B** have jointly committed robbery of the bank.

(2) Innocent agency

Innocent agency is involved where **A** uses **B** to commit a crime, **B** being either unaware of some material factor or being innocent on other grounds, such as coercion. *R v Cogan and Leak*[1] provides an example of this. In this case, Leak forced his wife to have intercourse with Cogan, who believed that she was consenting (Leak knew that she did not consent). Leak was convicted of aiding and abetting a rape, while Cogan was acquitted, the court regarding this as an instance of the commission of a crime through innocent agency.[2]

(3) Associate liability

Art and part liability may be seen as a form of associate liability. Associate liability may be attributed to an accused who does not himself perform an *actus reus*, but who is art and part guilty because of an *actus reus* performed by another. His liability derives from that of the main perpetrator, with whose actions he has associated himself and this gives rise to a number of questions, including the following:

(a) Can there be liability where the person committing the actus reus is himself acquitted?

The acquittal of an actual perpetrator may result in a number of ways. There may be inadequate evidence against the perpetrator, or the actual perpetrator may have a defence (such as insanity or

---

[1] [1976] QB 217, [1975] 2 All ER 1059.
[2] See also *White v Ridley* (1978) 21 ALR 661: importation of drugs through the innocent agency of an airline. For general discussion, see G Orchard 'Criminal responsibility for the acts of innocent agents' [1977] NZLJ 4.

coercion[1]) which exculpates him. It is quite competent in Scotland for an accessory to be convicted of an offence in respect of which another has been acquitted, provided that he was capable of being convicted of the offence himself. In *Young v H M Adv*[2] the appellant had been charged with fraudulent offences in relation to company dealings. The directors and secretary of the company were acquitted, and it was held that the appellant could not in such circumstances be convicted as he himself, not being a director or secretary of the company, could not commit the offence in question. His liability therefore was entirely derivative upon that of his co-accused. By contrast, in *Capuano v H M Adv*[3] the appellant's conviction was upheld in the face of the acquittal of his co-accused on the grounds that the latter were not adequately identified. The distinction to be made here is that in *Capuano* the appellant was capable of committing the offence of assault himself; his fault in no sense depended on the fault of his co-accused. Stones were thrown by members of a group while he was a member; the fact that the appellant's co-accused were not satisfactorily identified as members of the group was held not to detract from the appellant's own participation in the criminal activities in question.[4]

It must be shown, however, that a prima facie criminal act was committed by some person. If, in the case of murder, it cannot be shown that a murder was committed by somebody (even a person unknown), then there can be no conviction of an accused person on art and part grounds. This does not exclude liability where the perpetrator of the act is not punishable, for reasons of excuse or for some technical legal reason, such as an evidential one. Conviction of the accessory may be achieved in such a case by the operation of the doctrine of innocent agency (discussed above). In *Cogan and Leak*[5] there was, technically, no rape because Cogan was not aware of the victim's lack of consent. This, however, did not prevent conviction, on the grounds that the offence was committed through

---

[1] In *R v Bourne* (1952) 36 Crim App Rep 125 the accused had forced his wife to have sexual connection with a dog. The Court of Appeal rejected the argument that the husband could not be guilty of aiding and abetting something which by virtue of the fact that the wife had a defence of duress, was not a criminal offence.

[2] 1932 JC 63, 1932 SLT 465.

[3] 1984 SCCR 415, 1985 SLT 196.

[4] In the Australian case of *King v The Queen* (1986) 60 ALJR 685 the appellant was convicted as an accessory to murder after the acquittal of the principal offender. The court accepted that the appellant had urged somebody to kill the deceased, and that this fact was sufficient for accessory liability, even if the identity of the actual perpetrator was unknown.

[5] [1976] QB 217, [1975] 2 All ER 1059.

innocent agency. In *Austin*[1] the accused was convicted of aiding and abetting child stealing by encouraging the father of the child to snatch the child from its mother. The latter could not be convicted of child stealing but this did not deter the court from convicting the accessory of the offence.

It can be argued that there is no theoretical problem for Scots law here. Scots law makes no distinction between principal and secondary offenders – all those involved in the crime are equally guilty.[2] This means that the innocence of the person who commits the *actus reus* is irrelevant, and all that matters is that the accused should by his actions have associated himself in some way with the commission of the crime. This approach achieves much the same result as a doctrine of innocent agency, although the doctrine of innocent agency might provide a more readily understood explanation of art and part liability in such cases.

*(b) In respect of the same act, can **A** be convicted as being art and part guilty of one offence while his co-accused is convicted of another?*

In *Melvin v H M Adv*[3] the appellant was convicted of murder while his co-accused was convicted only of culpable homicide in respect of the same incident. It was argued on behalf of the appellant that the verdict of murder was inconsistent with that returned in respect of the co-accused, as they had both acted in concert. This argument was rejected; the court held that it was open to the jury to consider the actings of art and part actors and to assess the degree of their guilt according to the extent to which their individual actings demonstrated wicked recklessness or otherwise. As Lord Stott observed:

'Where two are charged with murder the actings of the one may display such utter recklessness as to require a verdict of guilty as libelled, without it being a necessary corollary that the actings of another who is art and part in the homicide must be taken to infer the same degree of recklessness.'[4]

A similar conclusion has now been reached in English law in the House of Lords decision in *R v Howe and Oths*[5]. In his judgment in the case, Lord Mackay considered the example of **A**'s handing a

---

1 [1981] 1 All ER 374, (1981) 72 Crim App Rep 104.
2 As suggested by *Gordon* para 5–04.
3 1984 SCCR 113, 1984 SLT 365. *Melvin* is an unusual decision and it can be argued that it runs counter to the long-established view of equality of responsibility in art and part cases.
4 1984 SCCR 113 at 118.
5 [1987] AC 417, [1987] 1 All ER 771.

gun to **D**, falsely telling him that it is loaded with blank ammunition. If **D**, on **A**'s suggestion, then fires the gun at **C**, intending only to do as **A** says and frighten him, **D** might only be convicted of manslaughter. It would be absurd if **A** were not to be capable of being convicted of the more serious offence of murder.

THE VICTIM AND ART AND PART GUILT

Unwilling victims of criminal offences are clearly not art and part guilty of the offence perpetrated upon them. Willing 'victims' raise difficult questions: is the consenting victim of an assault art and part guilty of the assault, or is the girl under 16 who consents to sexual intercourse art and part guilty of an offence under the Sexual Offences (Scotland) Act 1976? As far as assault is concerned, the issue has not been decided by the courts, but in principle there is no reason why in a case such as *H M Adv v Smart*[1], where consent was held to be no defence, the victim should not be art and part liable.[2] The situation in respect of sexual offences is probably not so straightforward, and the question of art and part guilt probably depends on the purpose of the offence, that is whether it is intended to protect vulnerable persons or to prevent the commission of certain wrongful acts, irrespective of the age of the parties. Those offences which are designed to protect young or otherwise vulnerable persons probably do not entail the attribution of art and part guilt to the willing victim. There is no Scottish authority on this point, but it is likely that a Scottish court would follow the decision in *R v Tyrrell*[3] and *R v Whitehouse*[4], which have met with broad approval.[5] If this view was to be accepted, there would be no art and part liability for the willing victim in the common law offence of lewd practices.

---

[1] 1975 SLT 65.

[2] B Fisse *Howard's Criminal Law* (5th edn, 1990) p 352 takes the same view.

[3] [1894] 1 QB 710, [1891–94] All ER Rep 1215.

[4] [1977] QB 868, [1977] 3 All ER 737.

[5] See B Hogan 'Victims as parties to crime' [1962] Crim L R 683; P Gillies *The Law of Criminal Complicity* (1980) p 160; K J M Smith *A Modern Treatise on the Law of Criminal Complicity* (1991) p 239. The Law Commission Draft Criminal Code Bill (1989) states cl 27(7): 'Where the purpose of an enactment creating an offence is the protection of a class of persons no member of that class who is a victim of such an offence can be guilty of that offence as an accessory.' Compare the Australian case of *Preston* [1962] Tas SR 141: an underage girl was held to be an accomplice, not for liability purposes, but in the context of a refusal on her part to answer potentially self-incriminating questions.

The position is different in relation to incest, homosexual offences, sodomy, and shameless indecency, which all share the feature of being offences directed against morality in general rather than being offences directed against particular victims. The offence of incest is committed by both parties, although the Incest and Related Offences (Scotland) Act 1986 introduced the rule that there is no criminal liability on a girl under the age of 16 involved in an incestuous act.[1] The willing underage partner in sodomy is art and part guilty,[2] as would be an underage partner in an act of shameless indecency. In neither of these cases, however, would the young person be prosecuted, although the fact that the boy is art and part guilty may be important in determining whether his evidence is that of an accomplice and to be treated accordingly.

BILATERAL REGULATORY OFFENCES

Some statutes may make it an offence, for example, to sell or trade in certain conditions and the question then arises as to whether a purchaser or customer is art and part guilty of the offence committed by the vendor or trader. These statutes are not protective in their purpose, and the protection principle referred to above, which would exclude art and part guilt, does not therefore apply. *Gordon* suggests that there should be no liability on a purchaser in such a case, as the statutory restriction of liability to the seller indicated parliamentary intention that the purchaser should not be penalised.[3] This is not the approach adopted in other jurisdictions, where the courts have been prepared to impose accessory liability, at least where there is knowledge of the illegality. There are admittedly several cases of this sort where accomplice liability was excluded,[4] but the majority of decisions go the other way.[5] In the Australian case of *Blackmore v Linton*[6] a customer of an illegal bookmaker was

---

[1] Section 1.
[2] Cf *Tatam* (1921) 15 Crim App Rep 132: boys under 14 could not be considered accomplices to sodomy.
[3] At para 5–06.
[4] *Jenks v Turpin* (1884) 8 QB 505: no accessory liability of card players in respect of the offence of keeping a gaming house.
[5] Canadian courts have, however, discouraged liability in these circumstances: *Ex parte Barker* (1891) 30 NBR 406 (SC); *Evans v Pesce and Attorney General for Alberta* 8 CRNS 201, [1970] 3 CCC 61 (sub nom *R v Coughlan, ex parte Evans*): a police agent provocateur was held to be an accomplice to a sale of an illegal drug which he had solicited. Also *R v Dyer* (1972) 5 CCC (2d) 376, 17 CRNS 207.
[6] [1961] VR 374.

convicted as an accomplice on the grounds that 'by his action in making a bet with a bookmaker who, to his knowledge, is in the street for the purpose of betting, lends himself to that purpose and countenances and encourages the bookmaker in the violation of the law'.[1] Similarly, in *Scott v Killian*[2] it was suggested obiter that the customers of a brothel can be accomplices to the offence of receiving money in a brothel.

WHEN ART AND PART LIABILITY WILL OCCUR

(1) Doing nothing: the mere presence cases

A person who witnesses the commission of a crime does not become art and part guilty of that crime by the mere fact of being present. There is no general duty to intervene to prevent the commission of a crime, but art and part liability may result if there is some special factor of status or relationship which (i) imposes a duty to act on one person who is present at the commission of the crime; or (ii) if the mere presence of the accused amounted to active encouragement of the offence.

(i) In *Bonar v Macleod*[3] a police officer was held art and part liable for an assault committed in his presence, by a policeman who was junior to him. The duty of an employee to prevent theft of his employer's property gave rise to accomplice liability in *Ex parte Parker*[4], and in a series of cases courts have accepted that the owner of a car may be an accomplice to a driving offence committed by a person driving his car in his presence if he fails to take steps to prevent the commission of the offence.[5] The licensee of licensed premises may be art and part liable to be convicted of the offence of illegal consumption of alcohol if he remains passive in the presence of such after hours drinking on his premises.[6]

(ii) Mere presence at the scene of a crime was not sufficient for art

---

[1] At 378.
[2] (1985) 40 SASR 37.
[3] 1983 SCCR 161. See also *Forman and Ford* [1988] Crim L R 677.
[4] [1957] SR(NSW) 326.
[5] *Du Cros v Lambourne* [1907] 1 KB 40; *Harris* [1964] Crim L R 54; *Crampton v Fish* [1970] Crim L R 235; *Rabie v Faulkner* [1940] 1 KB 571; *Dennis v Plight* (1968) 11 FLR 458. The driver cases are discussed by D Lanham 'Drivers, control and accomplices' [1982] Crim L R 419.
[6] *Tuck v Robson* [1970] 1 All ER 1171, [1970] 1 WLR 741. Cf *Duxley v Gilmore* [1959] Crim LR 454.

and part guilt in *Geo Kerr and Ors*[1], but in more recent English and Commonwealth cases the courts have accepted that there might be accessory liability when mere presence amounts to encouragement. In *Allan*[2] the Court of Criminal Appeal in England accepted that mere presence at a fight could result in accomplice liability provided that the spectator knew that his presence encouraged the offender. In *Clarkson*[3], soldiers who passively witnessed a barrack-room rape were held liable to conviction as accomplices, although their conviction was quashed on the grounds that the trial judge had not informed the jury of the requirement that the accused should have **intended** their presence to encourage the offender in the carrying out of the rape.[4] Mere presence may itself be evidence of an intention to encourage, but whether it is sufficient evidence of such an intention will depend on the circumstances. The Queensland Court of Criminal Appeal has stated the matter as follows in *Beck*[5] :

'Voluntary and deliberate presence during the commission of a crime without opposition or real dissent may be evidence of wilful encouragement or aiding. It seems that all will depend on a scrutiny of the behaviour of an alleged aider and the principal offender and on the existence which might appear of bond or connection between the two actors and their actions. The fortuitous and passive presence of a mere spectator can be an irrelevance so far as an active offender is concerned. But, on the other hand, a calculated presence or a presence from which opportunity is taken can project positive encouragement and support to a principal offender. The distinction between a neutral and a guilty presence of a person at the scene of a crime will be for the jury to assess. Proof of guilt of the crime of aiding and abetting will not ordinarily be established by mere presence if no tell-tale acts are performed by the alleged aider but the intention behind and the effect of the presence of the additional person at the scene may be established by other evidence from which it is possible to say that a case of intentional encouragement or support of the principal offender is made out.'[6]

(2) Counselling and instigating an offence

To counsel an offence is to advise on the commission of an offence. There may be no encouragement that the offence be committed, as long as mutual counselling takes place. To instigate an offence is to

---

[1] (1871) 2 Couper 334.
[2] [1965] 1 QB 130, [1963] 2 All ER 897.
[3] [1971] 1 WLR 1402, [1971] 3 All ER 344.
[4] See also *Wilcox v Jeffrey* [1951] 1 All ER 464, [1951] 1 TLR 706: mere presence as a spectator at an illegal jazz performance. *Bland* [1988] Crim L R 41: no liability where the accused merely shared accommodation with a drug dealer.
[5] (1989) 43 A Crim R 135.
[6] At 142 per Macrossan, CJ.

urge or encourage its commission. It is not instigation to express a desire that a crime be committed; there must be words or action directed towards achieving that end. Nor need the instigator give directions as to how the offence is to be committed, provided the mind of the other person is turned by him to the thought of committing the crime.

There is no instigation unless the perpetrator of the crime was, in fact, influenced by the words or actions of the instigator, although an unsuccessful instigation may be charged as attempted instigation.[1] Instigation requires that the words or action were actually communicated to the perpetrator,[2] but it is not necessary that the instigation should have been directed against a particular person.[3] The withdrawal of instigation after it has been made will not affect the art and part guilt of the instigator,[4] although it is possible that he will cease to be regarded as an instigator if he has done everything in his power to stop his instigation being acted upon.[5] In *R v Croft*[6] the accused had entered into a suicide pact with the deceased. The deceased shot herself, causing a wound, and then asked for assistance. The accused left her in order to secure assistance. His conviction of murder was upheld on the grounds that he had not done anything to remove from the deceased's mind the effect of the counsel which he had previously given her.

(3) Supply of materials or information

The provider of materials or information for the purposes of committing a crime is art and part guilty of that crime. This obviously does not apply to an innocent provider – to the taxi driver, for

---

[1] *H M Adv v Tannahill and Neilson* 1943 JC 150, 1944 SLT 118; *Kay and Strain* (May 1952, unreported) High Court, Glasgow: discussed by *Gordon*, at para 6–73.

[2] *R v Krause* (1902) 66 JP 121: accused acquitted of soliciting murder as the prosecution had not proved that the letters in which he mentioned murder had been received by the person to whom they were addressed.

[3] *R v Macleod* (1970) 12 CRNS 193, 1 CCC (2d) 5 (Canada): publication of an article giving detailed instructions on the growing of cannabis plants held to amount to counselling the growing of cannabis. *R v Most* (1881) 7 QBD 244: conviction upheld in which an article urged readers in general to resort to violence.

[4] *Hume* I, 279–280.

[5] There is a suggestion to this effect in *H M Adv v Baxter* (1908) 5 Adam 609, (1908) 16 SLT 475, supported by *Gordon* para 5–24 et seq. Withdrawal of encouragement is discussed (inter alia) in *White v Ridley* (1978) 21 ALR 661. For further discussion, see the general treatment of withdrawal, above p 81.

[6] (1944) 29 Crim App Rep 169.

example, who unaware of the fact that his passenger is bent on murder, drives him to his victim's house. Some knowledge of the recipient's criminal purpose is required, although the precise extent of this knowledge may be difficult to quantify. Is it enough, for instance, that the provider entertained a suspicion that the materials may be used for the furtherance of a criminal purpose? Does the provider have to know exactly what crime the recipient has in mind, or is it sufficient if he knows that a crime of some sort will be committed?

There is no clear Scottish authority on this question, but the issue has been dealt with in a number of English and Commonwealth cases. In *R v Bainbridge*[1] the accused had obtained welding equipment for a man whom he knew would be using it for a criminal purpose. It was held that there would be no accessorial liability if there was knowledge that there was some illegal venture contemplated; there had to be knowledge of the 'type' of offence which was to be committed. The apparent helpfulness of this ruling was, however, illusory, as the notion of 'type' remained undefined. It was clear that there had to be knowledge of at least some specific features. In *Bettles*[2] knowledge of the fact that there was a 'dishonest and unlawful purpose' did not amount to knowledge of the type of offence.

Further clarification of the issue came in the decision of the House of Lords in *D P P for Northern Ireland v Maxwell*[3]. In this case the accused was convicted of being an accessory to an explosives offence, after he had directed members of a terrorist organisation to their target. He had known that the offence contemplated was one of violence, but he claimed not to know of the fact that explosives would be used. His appeal was rejected on the grounds that all that was required was that the offence actually be committed within the range of possible offences which he had foreseen. *D P P for Northern Ireland v Maxwell* does not overrule *Bainbridge*, and the type test may therefore be taken, in English law at least, as continuing to be available alongside the foresight test suggested in *Maxwell*. It would be open to a Scottish court to resort to either formulation, and it is suggested that given the 'range test' applied in other contexts, there may be a preference for the straightforward *Bainbridge* approach.

An adoption of *Bainbridge* will not, of course, dispel uncertainties. There will still be awkward cases, as illustrated in the following example. **A** gives to **B** a jemmy which he is to use for housebreaking

---

[1] [1960] 1 QB 129, [1959] 3 All ER 200.
[2] [1966] Crim LR 503.
[3] [1978] 1 WLR 1350, [1978] 3 All ER 1140.

on a target which they have both identified. Shortly before the planned housebreaking, **B** is arrested for another offence and sentenced to two years imprisonment. On his release, without any further contact with **A**, **B** carries out a housebreaking on a different target, but using the jemmy supplied by **A**. In such circumstances the type test may appear to be satisfied, while a foresight test would fail. Or can it be that a burglary committed on another target is not an offence of the same type as that committed on an originally agreed target? The elapse of time in itself makes a difference. *Hume* states that art and part guilt requires that there is assistance for an immediate crime; there will be no art and part liability in respect of crimes that are remote, in temporal terms, from the act of assistance.[1] This proposition has the authority of *Hume*, although it is difficult to see why in principle the elapse of time should make a difference. A delay in the commission of the crime is nothing to do with the person who furnishes assistance, and his liability should be capable of continuity until he has countermanded or otherwise negatived the effect of his assistance.[2]

Does the accused have to have actual knowledge of the fact that an offence is to be committed, or will some lesser mental state such as negligence or recklessness, suffice? If **A** gives **B** a knife, knowing that there is a possibility that the knife will be used for an attack on **C**, is he art and part to the subsequent attack on the grounds of recklessness? There is no Scottish authority on this point, but the view of the House of Lords in *Maxwell* was that awareness of a **probability** was sufficient to establish guilt. That view would be likely to find favour in the Scottish courts, which may also be prepared to impose liability where there is no more than a possibility of a crime being committed.[3] Wilful blindness would probably amount to actual knowledge, and thus attract art and part liability.

Negligence is another matter altogether, and it is unlikely that this state of mind could justify a holding of art and part guilt. The issue has been discussed at length by the Australian High Court in

---

[1] *Hume* I, 276; *Burnett*, p 269.

[2] The elapse of time was considered to be significant in *Attorney General v Able* [1984] QB 795, [1984] 1 All ER 277 where it was held that the publishers of a booklet detailing methods of committing suicide would not be liable for aiding and abetting a suicide under s 2(1) of the Suicide Act 1961 (which does not apply in Scotland) where 'a long period of time' has elapsed between the issuing of the booklet and the act of suicide or attempted suicide.

[3] *Mayberry* [1973] Qd R 211: accessorial liability when accused knew that offence 'might be committed'. *R v Harding* [1976] VR 129: held to be irrelevant that accused believed that murder might not take place on account of a possible change of mind by the perpetrator.

Giorgianni v The Queen[1] in which the court overturned the appellant's conviction for complicity in the offence of culpably causing death by failing to make himself aware of the dangerous state of a truck of which he was owner but not driver. The High Court took the view that nothing short of knowledge was sufficient for complicity and that even recklessness as to the possibility of an offence being committed was insufficient.[2] In Scots law negligence is almost certainly an insufficient basis for art and part guilt,[3] but a Scottish court would be unlikely to follow the *Giorgianni* decision and exclude recklessness, as to do so would be to severely limit the scope of art and part guilt.[4]

The provision of materials used for the commission of a crime may occur in the course of the provider's legitimate business, in which case the provider will not normally be art and part liable for the subsequent criminal use of the materials. It will be different, though, if he has knowledge of the illegal purpose; liability here will be determined according to the normal principles covering art and part guilt. The reckless selling of an item which might be used for criminal purposes may lead to conviction, provided there was something in the circumstances which pointed to a high degree of probability that the item sold will be used for the commission of an offence. For example, the trader who sells a weapon to a customer whom he knows to have a record of offences of violence, may be deemed to be reckless, although action is likely to be taken only against those who persist in such sales, in the face of very clear warnings.[5] The legitimacy of the provider's conduct may be a factor to be taken into account, as in *Gillick v West Norfolk and Wisbech Area Health Authority*.[6]

The giving of information used to facilitate the commission of an offence may lead to art and part liability if all that is done is to impart what *Hume* terms 'naked advice'.[7] In *H M Adv v Johnstone*[8] the accused gave a woman the name of an abortionist who was not

---

[1] (1985) 156 Crim LR 473.
[2] Two of the judges were prepared, however, to hold that wilful blindness amounts to knowledge (at 482, 495).
[3] *D Stanton & Son Ltd v Webber* (1972) Crim LR 544; *Smith v Jenner* [1968] Crim LR 99.
[4] The decision has been the subject of considerable criticism. See B Fisse *Howard's Criminal Law* (5th edn, 1990) p 333.
[5] As in *H M Adv v Khaliq* 1984 JC 23, 1983 SCCR 483.
[6] [1986] 1 AC 112 (HL), [1985] 3 All ER 402. Discussed, in its criminal aspects, by JC Smith [1986] Crim L R 166. *O'Donovan and Vereker* (1987) 29 A Crim R 292.
[7] *Hume* I, 278.
[8] 1926 JC 89, 1926 SLT 428.

known personally to her (that is, to the accused). This did not lead to art and part guilt in the offence of abortion as there was no connection between the abortionist and the provider of the information. This seems to be a very restrictive decision as it would exclude liability in a case where **A**, planning to kill **B**, asks **C** for the name of a person prepared to carry out a contract killing. **C**'s facilitation of the murder of **B** is surely culpable, as without this information, the killing may never have taken place.[1] It is submitted that the authority of *Johnstone* is weakened by the fact that it was concerned with abortion, a crime which even at that time did not necessarily attract the same degree of opprobrium as many other offences. It is difficult to see the same view being taken if the advice concerned murder or robbery.

(4) Assisting the perpetrator in the commission of the crime

Involvement in a criminal offence may result from prior agreement or may be spontaneous. Where there is agreement this may be explicit or implicit. In the case of spontaneous participation, there may be no agreement between the parties as the original perpetrator may not welcome the involvement and this may mean that he may not be considered art and part guilty of what the intromissor does. If **A** joins **B** in an assault upon **C**, and **B** does not welcome or endorse this participation, then **B** will not be art and part guilty if he detaches himself from the assault. If, however, he continues, his mental reservation as to **A**'s participation will be irrelevant: he associates himself, albeit unwillingly, with **A**'s actions.

There is a potentially difficult problem if the person who joins in an assault on another does so after the fatal blow has been struck: does such a person become guilty of the culpable homicide or murder of the victim? The issue was clarified in *McLaughlan v HM Adv*[2] in which the High Court ruled that when a person joins in an already existing criminal enterprise, there was no question of his 'homologating' what happened before he joined in; his responsibility is limited to that which occurs after he joins in. The question of cumulative effect is not dealt with in this case, and so it remains unclear what the position will be if the accused's acts combine with what has happened before he has joined in to produce the final

---

[1] Cf *Attorney General v Able* [1984] QB 795, [1984] 1 All ER 277. Cf the law in New Zealand: *Martyn* [1967] NZLR 396; *Baker* 28 NZLR 536, [1909] 1 All ER 277: accused held guilty of counselling a crime when he told a friend how to blow open safes.
[2] 1991 SCCR 733.

effect. It is submitted that in a case of homicide or assault this will be determined by the application of the rule that one takes one's victim as one finds him. If the position of an already wounded victim is exacerbated by the accused's subsequent assault, then the accused should be responsible for whatever is the outcome. A person who sees that his victim is already injured arguably demonstrates wicked recklessness in assaulting him further and may therefore be convicted of murder.[1]

WITHDRAWAL

A participant in a criminal enterprise cannot escape art and part liability merely by dissociating himself from the actions of his co-participants. Dissociation may be relevant in determining whether there is concert between the parties, but once the commission of the crime has commenced, dissociation is no defence. In *McNeil v H M Adv*[2] an attempt was made to raise a defence of dissociation on the part of a member of the crew of a ship which had been used to transport a cargo of controlled drugs to the United Kingdom. The accused alleged that he had only become aware of the nature of the cargo once at sea, and left the ship at a port before reaching Britain. On the issue of dissociation, Lord President Emslie observed:

'If a crime is merely in contemplation and preparations for it are being made, a perpetrator who then quits the enterprise cannot be held to act in concert with those who may go on to commit the crime because there will be no evidence that he played any part in its commission. If on the other hand, the perpetration of a planned crime or offence has begun, a participant cannot escape liability for the completed crime by withdrawing before it has been completed unless, perhaps, he also takes steps to prevent its completion.'[3]

This leaves open the question of whether a defence of withdrawal will be successful if the accused makes an attempt to stop the completion of the crime. The question is left undecided. Guidance is available from common law jurisdictions in which this issue has been considered, and where withdrawal has, in certain circum-

---

[1] The problem of joining in has been discussed elsewhere, notably in the South African courts: *R v Mtembu* 1950 (1) SA 670 (A); *R v Mgxwiti* 1954 (1) SA 370 (A); *R v Chenjere* 1960 (1) SA 473: Supreme Court of the Federation of Rhodesia and Nyasaland. For discussion, see R Whiting 'Joining in' 1986 SALJ 38. *S v Thomo & Ors* 1969 (1) SA 385.

[2] 1986 SCCR 288.

[3] At 318.

stances, been accepted by the courts as a defence. These decisions show, first of all, that the withdrawal should be voluntary: the abandonment of a criminal project rings insincere if it takes place in the face of imminent detection[1] or if it stems from a sense of squeamishness rather than from moral disapproval of the crime.[2] The giving of an instruction that the crime should not proceed may not be enough to relieve the accused of accessorial liability although it will, in general, be a minimum requirement of a defence of withdrawal or dissociation. Any countermand must be timely[3] and should be backed by other action directed to preventing the crime from proceeding. In *R v Becerra and Cooper*[4] Becerra knew that Cooper was carrying a knife on the burglary on which they were mutually engaged. Cooper produced the knife when they were disturbed, whereupon Becerra shouted 'Come on let's go'. Becerra argued that he had withdrawn from the common purpose by the time the stabbing occurred, but the Court of Appeal took the view that this withdrawal was ineffective. The court did not say that Becerra should have attempted to take the knife from Cooper, although it may have had in mind steps such as the shouting of a warning to the victim or the use of language more clearly indicative of an intention to withdraw.[5]

THE SCOPE OF ART AND PART LIABILITY: THE PROBLEM OF UNINTENDED CONSEQUENCES

When two or more persons act together in the pursuit of a criminal objective, they are said to be acting for a **common purpose** and

---

[1] *White v Ridley* (1978) 52 ALJR 724: abandonment of a drug importation after the suspicions of customs officials had been aroused.

[2] *R v Malcolm* [1951] NZLR 470.

[3] At 351 per Gibbs J in *White v Ridley* (1978) 21 ALR 661 'Where the accused has requested a person who is of sound and mature mind to do an act which the accused knows, but the agent does not know, is illegal, the accused will not be liable if he has given timely countermand of his request. The countermand must have been manifested by words or conduct sufficiently clear to bring it home to the mind of the agent that the accused no longer desires the agent to do what he was previously asked to do; a vague, ambiguous or perfunctory countermand would not be enough. And the accused must have done or said whatever was reasonably possible to counteract the effect of his earlier request.'

[4] (1975) 62 Crim App Rep 212.

[5] Verbal withdrawal unaccompanied by physical steps, was said by the Court of Criminal Appeal in England to be acceptable in *Fletcher and Zimnowodski* [1962] Crim LR 551; see also *Whitefield* (1984) 79 Crim App Rep 36. The issue of withdrawal in general is discussed by D Lanham 'Accomplices and withdrawal' (1987) 97 LQR 575.

each party will be art and part liable for what is done by the other in pursuit of that purpose. There is a clear modern statement of this in Lord Patrick's direction to the jury in *H M Adv v Lappen*[1]:

'. . . if a number of men form a common plan whereby some are to commit the actual seizure of the property, and some according to the plan are to keep watch, and some according to the plan are to help carry away the loot, and some according to the plan are to help dispose of the loot, then, although the actual robbery may only have been committed by one or two of them, every one is guilty of the robbery, because they joined together in a common plan to commit the robbery. But such responsibility for the acts of others under the criminal law arises if it had been proved affirmatively beyond reasonable doubt that there was such a common plan and that the accused were parties to that common plan. If it has not been proved that there was a common plan, or if it had not been proved that the accused were parties to this previously concluded common plan, then in law each is only responsible for what he himself did, and bears no responsibility whatever for what any of the other accused or any other person actually did.'

The scope of the common plan therefore determines liability: those acts which are part of the plan will be attributed to all the accused involved in the plan; those acts which fall outwith the plan will be attributed to the individual actor. The question in each case will be whether an act may be regarded as part of the plot, a matter which will be determined by the agreement, express or implied, between the parties. What is implicitly agreed will depend on the circumstances: an agreement to commit a robbery involves an agreement to use at least some degree of force; an agreement to break into a building involves implicit agreement to damage property in the course of gaining access.

On occasion a party to a joint criminal offence may depart from a previously agreed plan and do something which was not in the contemplation of his accomplices. In such a case art and part liability will depend on the foreseeability of what is done. If the act in question was foreseeable, then all parties may be art and part answerable for it; if it was unforeseen, and was committed by one of the participants for reasons of his own, then there will be no art and part liability in respect of it.[2] For example, **A** and **B** agree to break into a bank and, in the course of the break-in, **B** fires a gun at and kills a security guard. If **A** was unaware of the fact that **B** was carrying a gun and there was no agreement that violence be

---

[1] 1956 SLT 109.
[2] *H M Adv v Harris and Ors* (Sept 1950, unreported) Glasgow High Court, discussed by *Gordon*, para 5–39.

used against anyone they might encounter, then the killing is an unintended consequence as far as **A** is concerned. The question of **A**'s art and part liability for homicide will then depend on an objective test of foreseeability; that is, on the answer to the question, would the reasonable person in **A**'s position have foreseen that **B** **might have a gun which he might use during the course of the break-in.**[1] In the above case, if **A** knew that **B** had a reputation for using firearms, then the shooting might well be considered foreseeable even if nothing was said about the firearm and if the firearm was carefully concealed.[2]

ART AND PART GUILT AND STATUTORY OFFENCES

There is no bar to art and part guilt when the offence committed is a statutory offence.[3] In the past it was not possible for a person to be convicted on an art and part basis if the statutory offence was one which he was incapable himself of committing (on the grounds that he lacked special capacity).[4] Legislation has now removed this objection.[5] If the statutory offence is one of strict liability, the art and part offender will nonetheless require to have the normal *mens rea* needed for art and part guilt.[6]

---

[1] In *Walker v H M Adv* 1985 SCCR 150, 1985 JC 53 the court appeared to accept that there could be art and part liability for a stabbing if the accused knew or **should have known** of the presence of a knife. Recent English cases focus on the 'tacit agreement or understanding' of the parties rather than on an objective test of foreseeability: *Slack* [1989] 3 All ER 90, [1989] QB 775; *Wakely* [1990] Crim LR 119. (Subjective foresight leads to an acceptance of the risk that violence may be used.) Australia adopts a subjective view, requiring foresight of the possibility that the consequence in question might ensue: *Johns v The Queen* (1980) 143 CLR 108.

[2] *Gordon* (para 5–55) suggests that the notion of foreseeability will be used 'only as a last resort', when it is not possible to tell which accused struck the fatal blow. In other cases, where the role of each accused is clear, the position of each will be determined by his individual contribution to the result.

[3] *Hume* II, 239; W J Dobie 'Art and part in statutory offences' (1944) 56 JR 89. Section 31 of the Criminal Justice (Scotland) Act 1949 removed doubts as to the possibility of art and part conviction in relation to statutory offences.

[4] *Young v H M Adv* 1932 JC 63, 1932 SLT 465.

[5] Criminal Justice (Scotland) Act 1987, adding new ss 216 and 418 to the Criminal Procedure (Scotland) Act 1975.

[6] There is no Scottish authority on this, but the point is well established in English law: *Johnson v Youden* [1950] 1 KB 544, [1950] 1 All ER 300; *Smith v Jenner* [1968] Crim LR 99; *D Stanton and Son v Webber* [1972] Crim LR 544.

7. Inchoate crimes

Inchoate crimes are crimes which are not complete. There are three forms of inchoate crime: attempt, conspiracy, and incitement.

ATTEMPT

Not all criminal activity succeeds. The shot which misses its target, the bank robbery which is interrupted by the timely arrival of the police, or the fraudulent misrepresentation which fails to induce its recipient to act – all these are examples of attempted crimes. In such circumstances, no overt damage may be done to the community. The victim of attempted murder may not even be aware, at the time, of the poison in his tea cup, although the subsequent realisation of the fact that he has been the object of homicidal intentions may have a profoundly disturbing effect. In many cases, though, the actual deleterious consequences of an attempted crime may be negligible. No great harm is caused by the would-be bank robbers who are arrested by the police on their way to the bank.

There are three main issues to be considered in relation to attempts: (1) should attempted crimes be punishable in the same way as completed crimes?; (2) when does conduct amount to an attempt?; and (3) should attempts to do the impossible be punished?

(1) The punishment of attempts

A great deal of attention has been paid to the fundamental question of whether attempts should be punished to the same or a lesser extent as completed crimes, or, indeed, whether they should be punished at all. The argument for the total non-punishment of attempts is not convincing. An attempted crime constitutes a threat to social peace and a challenge to the legal order. To ignore attempted criminal activity is tantamount to condonation, and therefore a legal response to attempted crime is both justified and necessary. Yet this response must be a measured one, and should reflect the actual gravity of what has been done by the accused.

There is an argument – and a fairly convincing one at that – for the proposition that no distinction should be made in terms of punishment between attempts and completed crimes. If criminal law is concerned with the moral assessment of conduct, then it should not distinguish on the grounds of arbitrary factors, such as result. In this view, there is no moral difference between the person who fires a gun at his victim, intending to kill him, but who misses, and the person who, with the same intention, fires and succeeds in hitting the victim. Each is equally guilty from the moral point of view: all that distinguishes the two cases is what philosophers have termed 'moral luck'.[1] All that prevents the unsuccessful murderer from being a successful murderer may be a chance factor, such as a gust of wind which deflects the bullet from its course.

While this argument has its undoubted appeal, its application in criminal law is inappropriate. Criminal law is concerned with result – inevitably so – and there are clear reasons why the law should focus on what actually happens in the physical world rather than what might have happened. Realised events provide the basis of criminal law intervention, and even if this may involve a morally arbitrary choice, it nonetheless provides a practical means of limiting criminal law intervention.[2] Attempts are therefore less serious because they fail to satisfy the necessary requirements for the full criminal sanction. In addition to this, attempts are treated less seriously because they involve less real damage. An attempted murder causes less harm than a completed murder, and the same is true of an attempted robbery. A reaction to harm, rather than a reaction to interior malevolence, is a proper function of the criminal law, especially in a liberal theory of justice which seeks to

[1] B Williams 'Moral Luck' (1976) 50 Proceedings of the Aristotelean Society 115; T Nagel *Mortal Questions* (1979) p 24 et seq.
[2] The nineteenth-century jurist, Stephen, sees emphasis on result coming from the sense of public outrage that accompanies serious consequences: 'If two persons are guilty of the very same act of negligence, and one of them causes thereby a railway accident, involving the death and mutilation of many persons, whereas the other does no injury to anyone, it seems to me that it would be rather pedantic than rational to say that each had committed the same offence, and should be subjected to the same punishment. In one sense, each has committed an offence, but the one has had the bad luck to cause a horrible misfortune ...Both certainly deserve punishment, but it gratifies a natural public feeling to choose out for punishment the one who actually has caused great harm ...' *History of the Criminal Law* III, 311.

limit the extent to which the criminal law interferes in the lives of people.

(2) What conduct amounts to an attempt?

Efforts to identify a wholly satisfactory answer to this question have been conspicuously unsuccessful. A range of theories is on offer, many of them aimed at providing a theoretical structure to the sometimes inconsistent and varying approach of the courts. In many jurisdictions in the common law world, legislation defines the point at which a punishable attempt is committed; this is the case in both England and the United States, where the Criminal Attempts Act 1981[1], and the Model Penal Code,[2] require that the stage of perpetration rather than preparation be reached; continental penal codes similarly set out criteria of varying precision as to when an attempt occurs.[3] Scotland, however, has no legislation on the question, and a degree of uncertainty hangs over the question of what conduct amounts to an attempt.

The nature of the problem

The difficulties inherent in deciding when an attempt occurs are illustrated in the following hypothetical sequence:

(1) **A** decides to rob a bank.
(2) He purchases a map of the town in which the bank is situated.
(3) He visits the town and walks past the bank to view it from the outside.
(4) He enters the bank and discreetly sketches the layout on a piece of paper.
(5) He buys a gun with a view to using it on the robbery.
(6) He sets out from his house, armed with the gun, a face mask, and a bag for the money.
(7) He enters the bank wearing the mask but not yet pointing the gun or making any demands.
(8) He points the gun at the teller and asks for the money.
(9) The teller presses an alarm button. **A**, losing his nerve, runs out and returns home.

[1] Section 1(1).
[2] Other examples include the Crimes (Amendment) Act 1985 (Victoria).
[3] For example, Germany StGB s 22; France, Code Penal, s 2.

There is little doubt that at some point in the series of events, **A** may be said to have attempted to rob a bank. Yet the point at which the attempt actually occurs is not clear. If **A** were to be interrupted and arrested at point (1), thereby being unable to proceed further, would an attempt have been committed? The answer must be an unequivocal 'no'. Criminal law does not recognise 'thought crimes'. A person may form all sorts of criminal schemes in his mind, but provided he proceeds no further than that, he commits no crime. It is equally clear that by point (8) an attempted crime has been committed; yet, in between, the position may be less certain. Some may regard (6) as marking the watershed between preparatory action and attempt; others may feel that it would be premature to infer an attempt even at this point.

It is useful to distinguish an attempt from what it is not. An attempt is not a completed act; equally it is not mere preparation. It strains language to suggest that those acts which precede an attempt in themselves constitute an attempt. A prospective purchaser of an item does not attempt to purchase the item when he consults an auction catalogue or inspects the item at a viewing. It can be said, however, that an attempt is made to purchase the item once a bidding instruction is given or an actual bid is made. The acts which precede that are preparations for the actual making of the attempt; they are not sufficiently close to the completed action to be categorised as attempts.

Much has been made of the difficulty inherent in distinguishing between preparation and attempts. There may well be a grey area in which preparations and attempts blur, but this is not fatal to the whole concept of the distinction. Preparatory acts may be fundamentally different in nature from attempts, in that they are not unequivocally referable to the *actus reus* of a crime. The purchase of the map in the example above is not unequivocally referable to the commission of a robbery; entering the bank with a firearm is.

There may also be a temporal reason for the distinction. An act which precedes the commission of the final act by a considerable period may be considered mere preparation on those grounds. It simply confounds our intuitive sense of the temporal boundaries of acts to say that an act performed well before the point at which the completed act would be performed amounts to an attempt. Attempts normally occur reasonably shortly before the completed act could be anticipated.[1]

---

[1] Temporal proximity was a factor in *Davey v Lee* [1968] 1 QB 366, [1967] 2 All ER 423, and in *Jones v Brooks* (1968) 52 Crim App Rep 614. In the latter case, the

Reliance on the distinction between mere preparation and attempt allows considerable leeway in determining just when an attempt is committed. This may be a disadvantage, as it could be argued that the criminal law should reveal more clearly the boundaries between criminal and non-criminal conduct. Yet the choosing of more exact criteria may mean that one has to opt for either an earlier or later cut-off point than might be desired. For example, in the sequence above, if one were to apply a last act theory (which holds that an attempt occurs only after the actor has performed the last act necessary to achieve the result) an attempt would only be committed after he had pointed a gun at the teller and asked for the money – (8). Stage (7) would not be an attempt, under this theory, as the demand remains to be made; yet the distinction, in terms of social dangerousness, between (7) and (8) is extremely slight. Similarly, if one applies the unequivocal act theory, which holds that an attempt is committed when an act is unequivocally referable to the commission of a crime, attempt liability comes into play at stage (4), which would seem excessively early.

A potentially useful way of distinguishing between preparatory acts and attempts is to ask whether the accused was, at the point in question, 'trying to do **x**' (**x** being the crime). If the answer is yes, then he has gone beyond the point of preparation; if the answer is no, then he is merely preparing. The athlete who buys a new pair of running shoes is not trying to break the record at that precise point. Nor is he trying to break the record when he is on the track, training. He may be 'planning' to break the record, or 'hoping' to break the record, but this is not the same thing as 'trying' to break it. Once he walks up to the start line, however, we may be readier to say that he has reached the stage of 'trying'. 'Trying' would appear to involve action directed towards a desired result, and very closely linked with the possible achievement of that result. A person who tries to do something has normally embarked on a very specific course of action and has reached the stage of commitment to his objective. A person who is preparing has not necessarily reached the stage of commitment. It could be argued that this amounts to no more than substituting one vague term for another; yet the term 'to try' is perhaps more familiar in everyday usage than the term 'to attempt', and as such may be a better guide to the moral intuitions underlying the attribution of responsibility in this quarter.

court referred to 'sufficient proximity' between the act and an expressed intention to commit a crime. The New Zealand Crimes Act 1961, s 72(3) refers to 'immediate' or 'proximate' connection.

The position in Scots law

Scottish authorities are not consistent on the issue of what constitutes an attempt. Some of the cases point to a 'last act' theory, and some suggest that an attempt occurs when matters proceed beyond the point at which a person can intervene to stop what he has set in motion. This latter theory restricts liability to a very late stage in events, and is undesirable for that reason.[1] The last act theory, which enjoys more support, holds that an attempt is committed once the accused has done everything required of him to commit the crime. Attempted murder therefore exists once the parcel bomb is posted to its victim, or once the shot is fired.

The authority of *Hume* has been claimed for the last act theory, but there must be some doubt as to whether this was, in fact, his view. The relevant passage states that there is an attempted crime '...if there has been an inchoate act of execution of the meditated deed; if the man have done that act, **or part of that act**, by which he meant and expected to perpetrate his crime, and which, if not providentially interrupted or defeated, would have done so ...'[2] It has been argued[3] that this represents an endorsement of the last act theory, but the words 'or part of that act' present some difficulty. *Gordon* suggests that it is not clear what these words mean; their meaning, though, will be that any act of perpetration, rather than the last act, will suffice. This is subject, of course, to the proviso as to providential interruption or defeat, which would seem to impose liability only where the act of perpetration is a reasonably advanced one. On a strict last act theory the person arrested when beginning to pick the lock of a house does not commit burglary – he has not yet committed the last act, that of opening the door. Applying *Hume's* passage, however, the picking of the lock would certainly be attempted burglary, and rightly so.[4] *Alison*, by contrast, is unambiguously in favour of a last act approach, requiring that

---

[1] For an example, see *H M Adv v Baxter* (1908) 5 Adam 609; in *HM Adv v Mackenzies* 1913 SC(J) 107 Lord Justice-Clerk Macdonald talks of a requirement of an 'irrevocable act of commission or attempt'; in *H M Adv v Tannahill and Nelson* 1943 JC 150, 1944 SLT 118 it was stated that an attempt required 'some overt act, the consequences of which cannot be recalled by the accused' (see also *Morton v Henderson* 1956 JC 55, 1956 SLT 365).

[2] I, 27.

[3] *Gordon* para 6–38.

[4] The last act theory has not fared well in other jurisdictions: (1961) 61 Columbia L Rev 586 n88 (cases); *White* [1910] 2 KB 124. The last act theory still plays some role in determining proximity or perpetration: *D P P v Stonehouse* [1978] AC 55 at 85–87, [1977] 2 All ER 909.

the accused should have done 'all that in him lay' to effect the crime.[1]

Whatever the theoretical attractiveness of the last act theory, the weight of opinion now seems to be in favour of a preparation/perpetration test.[2] Judicial support was voiced for this approach in *HM Adv v Camerons*[3] in which a husband and wife who had conceived a plan to defraud an insurance company staged a fake robbery. The prosecution failed to prove that a claim had actually been made to the insurance company, but this did not prevent the couple's conviction for attempted fraud. In his instruction to the jury, Lord Dunedin stressed that the essence of the question was the determination of the point at which preparation ended and perpetration began. This, he said, was a question of degree which fell to be determined by the jury. The perpetration test has not received subsequent elucidation by the courts in Scotland, and the vagueness surrounding it therefore persists. The popularity of the test in other jurisdictions means that some judicial guidance is available as to when acts may be considered to progress beyond mere preparation, although in each case it will be for the jury to decide whether the accused has gone far enough. In some of the decisions the courts seem willing to categorise fairly 'advanced' acts as no more than preparatory. Travelling to the scene of an intended crime, armed to carry it out, but being arrested half a mile before reaching the destination was not sufficient to constitute an attempt in the New Zealand case of *Wilcox*.[4] Examining stolen clothes with a view to purchase has been held not to be an attempt to purchase stolen property,[5] and trailing a lorry for over a hundred miles in the hope of having the chance to steal it has similarly been held not to amount to an attempt.[6]

The following are examples of conduct which courts have held to amount to more than preparation:

(1) Breaking down a door with a view to entering premises to steal;[7]

---

[1] I, 165.

[2] See *Gordon*, for example, para 6–43 who reluctantly accepts the perpetration test as the test most likely to be endorsed in the future.

[3] 1911 SC(J) 110, 1911 2 SLT 108.

[4] [1982] 1 NZLR 191. In *Kopi-Kame* [1965–66] P&NGLR 73 the accused was arrested outside his wife's house armed with a loaded shotgun: no attempt. Another case involving travelling to the scene of the crime is *S v Magxwalisa* 1984 (2) SA 314: no attempt.

[5] *R v Croucamp* 1949 (1) SA 377.

[6] *Komaroni* (1953) 103 LJ 97.

[7] *R v Boyle and Boyle* (1986) 84 Crim App Rep 270.

(2) arranging inflammable material in a building intending to burn the building down;[1]
(3) faking death with a view to allowing one's spouse to claim under a life insurance policy;[2]
(4) assaulting a victim with the intention of committing rape.[3]

Abandonment

Scottish courts have yet to pronounce on the effect of voluntary abandonment of efforts to commit a crime, and it is not clear whether this would constitute a defence. A defence of voluntary abandonment is embodied in the American Law Institute's Model Penal Code[4] and is recognised in most European systems,[5] with the exception of English law. English law has turned its face against such a defence, principally on the grounds that the offence of attempt has already been committed and the repentance of the accused makes no difference.[6]

Arguments in favour of a defence of voluntary abandonment stress the inappropriateness of punishing one who has shown himself to be no further danger to society. It should also be borne in mind that by allowing a defence of this nature, the law encourages people to abandon criminal plans, thereby reducing the incidence of completed crime.[7] Against these factors is to be weighed the difficulty of establishing that the abandonment was, in fact, voluntary. This was alluded to in the Australian case of *R v Page*[8], where the court stressed that in almost every case there would have to be an assessment 'whether the accused desisted from sudden alarm,

---

[1] *R v Vilinsky* 1932 OPD 218 (see also *R v Taylor* 175 ER 831 (1859): striking a match in order to set fire to a haystack).

[2] *D PP v Stonehouse* [1978] AC 55, [1977] 2 All ER 909.

[3] *Williams* [1965] Qd R 86. *Quaere*: would it be attempted rape if the accused is interrupted before he seeks to effect insertion? The Queensland court appeared to accept that this could be so.

[4] Section 5.01(4): 'When the actor's conduct would otherwise constitute an attempt . . . it is an affirmative defence that he abandoned his effort to commit the crime or otherwise prevented its commission, under circumstances manifesting complete and voluntary renunciation of his criminal purpose . . .'

[5] Germany: StGB, s 24 (for discussion see R Maurach, K H Gossel and H Zipf *Strafrecht Allgemeiner Teil* 2 (1984) p 48 et seq); Switzerland, Schweizerisches Straf-gestezbuch, s 21; France, Code Penal, s 2 (for discussion, M-L Rassat *Droit Penal* (1987) p 351).

[6] *R v Taylor* 175 ER 831 (1859); *R v Page* [1933] VLR 351; *R v Lankford* [1959] Crim L R 209. Likewise, Roman Dutch law: *R v Khalpey* 1960 (2) SA 182 (R); but see criticism of C R Snyman *Criminal Law* (2nd edn, 1989) p 291.

[7] See M Wasik 'Abandoning criminal intent' [1980] Crim LR 785.

[8] [1933] VLR 351.

from a sense of wrongdoing, from failure of resolution, or from any other cause'. Even if a defence of abandonment were to be allowed, it is likely that it would be relatively easy for the prosecution to persuade jurors as to the involuntariness of the accused's desisting.

The mental element

To attempt to do something is to act with a view of bringing about a desired result. This has been taken to imply that there can be conviction for assault only where the accused intended the *actus reus*, and not where he was reckless or negligent. This raises difficult questions in relation to attempted murder. Murder can be committed recklessly, but does attempted murder require a frustrated intention to kill? If one who was only reckless can be convicted of attempted murder, then a person who at no point had any intention of killing is labelled as having tried to kill. This is seen by some as misleading and illogical.

The issue was settled for Scots law in the case of *HM Adv v Cawthorne*[1]. Cawthorne fired two shots through the door and window of a room in which he knew four people to be sheltering. The bullets did not hit anybody directly, although one of the occupants of the room was slightly grazed. Cawthorne was convicted of attempted murder and appealed against the conviction on the grounds of misdirection of the jury: the jury should have been told that attempted murder required intention to kill on the part of the accused. The appeal failed, the court being firmly of the view that the *mens rea* of murder and of attempted murder are the same. Lord Justice-General Clyde said:

'In my opinion attempted murder is just the same as murder in the eyes of our law, but for the one vital distinction, that the killing has not been brought off and the victim has escaped with his life. But there must be in each case the same *mens rea*, and that *mens rea* in each case can be proved by evidence of a deliberate intention to kill or by such recklessness as to show that the accused was regardless of the consequences of his act, whatever they may have been.'

Prior to the decision in *Cawthorne*, there was a degree of judicial disagreement as to the role of intent in attempted murder. Intent to kill had been recognised in *HM Adv v McAdam*[2], but wicked recklessness sufficed in *HM Adv v Currie*[3], a case which demonstrates precisely the sort of circumstances in which an attempted

---

[1] 1968 JC 32, 1968 SLT 330.
[2] (July 1959, unreported) Glasgow High Court.
[3] (December 1962, unreported) Glasgow High Court.

murder charge might be thought warranted: the accused, in the course of a police car chase, had swerved their car into the path of a police car which was pursuing them and had thrown objects into the path of the police vehicle. *Cawthorne* at least settles the issue, but has nonetheless caused a degree of concern. In particular it has been suggested that *Cawthorne* opens the way to charges of attempted murder in cases which are not sufficiently serious to warrant such a charge.[1] In practice, prosecution policy is to restrict attempted murder charges to those cases involving a high degree of injury or, possibly, the use of firearms.

The main argument in favour of restricting attempted murder to those cases where there was intent is that of protecting the integrity of the concept of murder. The term 'murderer' means, to the public mind, a person who has set out deliberately to take human life. The law allows murder to encompass recklessness, however, and once this is admitted, then it is difficult to see why the concept of 'attempted murder' should not similarly be extended. After all, the would-be reckless murderer and the successful reckless murderer are equally guilty morally and, from the point of view of punishment objectives, it is difficult to distinguish between them.[2]

The Scottish courts have yet to convict of attempt in respect of other crimes of recklessness, but there is no reason why they should not do so on the basis of *Cawthorne*. In *R v Khan*[3] the Court of Appeal in England upheld a conviction of attempted reckless rape, stating:

'... the intent of the defendant was precisely the same in rape and in attempted rape, and the *mens rea* was identical, namely an intention to have intercourse plus the knowledge of or recklessness as to the woman's

---

[1] This criticism, along with others, was addressed by the Scottish Law Commission in *Attempted Homicide* (Consultative Memorandum No 61, 1984).

[2] HLA Hart *Punishment and Responsibility* (1968) p 127: 'No calculation of the efficacy of deterrence or reforming measures, and nothing that would ordinarily be called retribution seems to justify this distinction. In the attempt case, for example, the variant where the intention is indirect seems equally wicked, equally harmful, and equally in need of discouragement by the law.' For further discussion, see D Stuart '*Mens rea*, negligence and attempts' [1968] Crim LR 647. English law requires an intention to kill before there can be conviction for attempted murder: *R v Whybrow* (1951) 35 Crim App Rep 141; *R v Mohan* [1976] QB 1, [1975] 2 All ER 193. Intention in this context included a foresight of a high degree of probability that death would ensue: *R v Walker and Hayles* (1989) 90 Crim App Rep 266 (C A). The Australian rule is similar: *Giorgianni v The Queen* (1985) 156 Crim LR 473 (cf the opposite view, also in an Australian High Court decision: *Alister v The Queen* (1984) 154 Crim LR 404). The Canadian courts are of the same view: *R v Ancio* (1984) 10 CCC (3d) 385.

[3] Independent, 31 Jan, 1990.

absence of consent. No question of attempting to achieve a reckless state of mind arose; the attempt related to the physical activity; the mental state of the defendant was the same.'

Statutory offences

The Scottish courts have yet to address the issue of whether *mens rea* is required where the accused is charged with attempting to commit an offence of strict liability. The following hypothetical example illustrates the problem: the legislature has created an offence of strict liability, making it an offence for a pharmacist to sell a particular drug. **A**, a pharmacist, who has inadvertently mistaken the regulated drug for an innocent one, is arrested shortly before he is going to sell the drug to a customer. Is his lack of *mens rea* a bar to conviction of an attempted breach of the regulation? The decision in *Cawthorne* suggests that there is no reason why there should not be a conviction in such a case. *Gordon* points out that the antipathy of the courts to strict liability offences might incline them to require *mens rea* here,[1] a view which has attracted some judicial support in other jurisdictions.[2] Against this view it can be argued that the justification of strict liability lies in the prevention of certain forms of conduct which could not practically be prevented if *mens rea* were to be required. This justification applies equally to attempted strict liability offences.[3]

As in the case of attempted murder, the real problem lies in the apparent illogicality of saying that a person has attempted to perform an act, when he was perhaps ignorant of those features of the act which make it a crime. For example, if **A** attempts to have sexual intercourse with a girl of 15, he may be charged with attempting to have intercourse with a girl under the age of consent. Yet, if he believed her to be 17, can he be said to have attempted to have intercourse with an underage girl? The answer to this depends on how the act is described. It can safely be said that he attempts intercourse; and from an objective point of view, he can also be said to be attempting to have intercourse with an underage girl, in that this is the act which, admittedly unknown to him, he is attempting.

In spite of his ignorance, the man who makes a mistake as to age, still commits the offence of having intercourse with a girl under the

---

[1] At para 7–89.
[2] *R v Ancio* (1984) 10 CCC (3d) 385. See, also, dicta in *Alister v The Queen* (1984) 154 CLR 404, 421–422. For support, see Glanville Williams *Criminal Law: The General Part* (2nd edn) pp 618–620; [1962] Crim L R 300.
[3] JC Smith [1962] Crim L R 143.

age of 16; the man who attempts such intercourse, can also reasonably be said to be attempting to perform an act which is punishable by law. Neither **wants** to commit the offence of having intercourse with a girl under the age of 16, and the unfairness of criminal conviction in each case is exactly the same. If the moral sense is offended by punishing an attempt in such a case, the real source of disquiet is the statutory exclusion of the defence of error in relation to the completed offence. The legislature has endorsed this exclusion, and it may therefore be not unreasonable to assume that the same principle should apply in relation to the attempted offence until a contrary legislative intention is manifest.[1]

(3) Impossible attempts

Impossibility may be factual or legal. An attempt to do the factually impossible is made when a person tries to achieve a goal by means which are physically incapable of bringing about his desired result. The classic example of this would be an attempt to poison another through the use of a substance which is, in fact, not poisonous. Legal impossibility exists where a person attempts to do something which is not criminal; that is where the intended end does not amount to a criminal offence.[2] An example of legal impossibility would be where a person, falsely believing that the making of homemade wine is an offence, sets out to make wine under the impression that in doing so he is breaking the law.

The Scottish position on attempts to do the impossible is not entirely clear. The difficulty springs from the irreconcilability of the decisions on the matter: *HM Adv v Anderson*[3] holds that attempted

---

[1] The Law Commission in England has recommended that in a case such as this knowledge of all the material facts should be required before there can be conviction of an attempt. (Law Comm No 102, para 2.15.)

[2] A great deal of confusion surrounds the notions of factual and legal impossibility. The distinction is clearly stated by Hall: 'The rules attach liability to attempts which failed because of "factual impossibility" but they exculpate where the attempt failed because of "legal impossibility". The rationale of the latter is that since the defendant would not have committed any crime even though he had done everything he intended to do, *a fortiori* he cannot be guilty of a criminal attempt if he did less than that ...In sum: (1) unless the intended end is a legally proscribed harm, causing it is not criminal, hence any conduct falling short of that is not a criminal attempt (ie the principle of legality); and (2) if the intended end is a legally proscribed harm, the failure to effect it because of a factual condition necessary to its occurrence is no defence (ie factual impossibility).' (*General Principles of Criminal Law* (2nd edn, 1960) p 586.)

[3] 1928 JC 1, 1927 SLT 651.

abortion is not committed by one who administers abortifacient drugs to a woman who is not pregnant, while *Lamont v Strathern*[1] holds that it is attempted theft to try to pick an empty pocket. It is difficult to see any meaningful distinction between the act in each case: the non-pregnancy of the woman is a question of fact, as is the emptiness of the pocket. In *Maxwell and Ors v HM Adv*[2] the court considered the question of a factual impossibility in the context of conspiracy, and took the view that it was irrelevant. The conspirators in this case had conspired to bribe members of a licensing board, but at the time of the offence the board would have been incapable of doing what the conspirators wished, as the matter was then under appeal to the sheriff. It was held that this did not affect guilt, as the whole essence of the offence of bribery was the giving of the bribe, not whether the recipient subsequently manages to arrange what the bribers wish to achieve. Although *Maxwell* does not resolve the issue of the conflict between *Anderson* and *Lamont*, it provides support for the view that factual impossibility should be no defence to a charge of attempt.[3]

The issue of legal impossibility remains unresolved. *Anderson* may be taken as a case of legal rather than factual impossibility regarding the non-pregnancy of the woman as a legal status. In this analysis Scots law recognises legal impossibility as a defence and it will not be an offence to attempt to steal one's own property, or to attempt to reset goods which have not been stolen. There are, however, strong objections to this approach, and in a number of jurisdictions this definition of illegality has been rejected on the grounds that questions of legal status are really questions of fact: whether or not goods are stolen is a question of fact, as is the issue of whether or not the umbrella one attempts to steal is one's own or another's. This view as to what constitutes legal impossibility is obviously a restrictive one, but still leaves a role for legal impossibility in that it excludes liability when what the accused has tried to do was simply not an offence known to the criminal law. This

---

[1] 1933 JC 33, 1933 SLT 118.

[2] 1980 JC 40, 1980 SLT 241.

[3] 'The argument that because of the accident of events or physical causes beyond or outwith the control or even the knowledge of the corrupting agent, the ultimate objective of the plan to corrupt or attempt to corrupt cannot be achieved, is itself enough to deprive what otherwise is a completed criminal act of its criminal quality appears on the face of it somewhat stowtling. If sound, this could place criminal responsibility at the whim of extraneous events wholly divorced from the criminally directed actions of the participants themselves', in *Maxwell* 1980 JC 40 at 44 per Lord Cameron.

accords with the remarks of Lord Aitchison in *HM Adv v Semple*[1] to the effect that the conduct in question must at least constitute a crime in the law of Scotland.

There would seem, then, to be two options open to a future court when confronted with an issue of alleged legal impossibility.

(i) The court may read *Anderson* and *Semple* as holding that when the impossibility relates to a question of legal status (whether or not goods are stolen, etc) then an attempt will not be criminal; or

(ii) the court may take *Anderson* and *Semple* as authority for the proposition that legal impossibility is a defence only where the conduct in question does not conform in its **externals** to any known criminal offence. This would exclude liability, for example, in the home winemaking case, or in a case where an accused attempts to have intercourse with a 17-year-old girl in the belief that such conduct is criminal.

The following hypothetical examples demonstrate the implications of an approach which punishes factually, but not legally impossible attempts:

(1) The accused fires a shot into an empty room, believing that his intended victim is within. This is a matter of factual impossibility, and the accused may be charged with attempted murder.[2]

(2) The accused, wanting to kill **A**, sticks pins into a doll representing **A** in the belief that this will lead to **A**'s death. It is factually impossible to bring about death in this way, but strictly speaking this is nonetheless attempted murder. It would be risible to prosecute such an attempt, although *Gordon* points out that such a person could still be dangerous, and might progress from the factually impossible means of procuring death to more objectively dangerous means.[3]

(3) The accused wishes to poison his victim. He places poison in the victim's food, but the quantity is insufficient to bring about death. This may be considered factual impossibility, in the sense that such a dose of poison is incapable of causing death, but in another view it is not so much factual impossibility as **insufficiency of means**.[4]

[1] 1937 JC 41, 1937 SLT 48, 239.
[2] As was the case, in such circumstances, in *State v Mitchell* (1902) 170 Mo 633.
[3] At para 6–50. Cf Glanville Williams *Criminal Law, The General Part* (2nd edn, 1961), p 652.
[4] *R v Collingridge* (1976) 16 SASR 117: attempt to murder wife by throwing a live wire into the bath. The current was insufficient to kill her (unless she actually touched the live wire). This was held to be attempted murder (by insufficient, rather than impossible means).

According to the decision of the House of Lords in *Haughton v Smith*[1] this would, under English common law, not amount to attempted murder. The unacceptability of such an outcome has been commented upon both by judges and criminal law writers.[2]

(4) The accused, while on holiday abroad, buys a bag of white powder which he is informed is cocaine. He hides the bag in his luggage and is apprehended on entering the United Kingdom and charged with attempting to import a controlled drug. The powder is, in fact, a harmless substance.

The accused in this case intends to commit an offence although it is impossible to commit the offence in question by importing harmless white powder. This is factual impossibility and he should be convicted of an attempt, although if a Scottish court followed *Houghton v Smith* the accused could not be convicted. In *Britten v Alpogut*[3], the accused had attempted to import cannabis into Australia whereas, in fact, he imported a legal substance. His conviction of attempting to import an illegal drug was upheld in the Supreme Court of Victoria, which held that *Houghton v Smith* was wrongly decided. In England, *Houghton v Smith* was overtaken by the Criminal Attempts Act 1981, and in *R v Shivpuri*[4] the House of Lords ruled that a defendant who imported material he falsely believed to be heroin, was rightly convicted of attempted importation of a controlled drug.

(5) The accused attempts to commit a crime which can be committed only by members of a special class of persons (for example, by company directors), of which he is not a member. This is an example of a legal impossibility and there would be no attempted crime.[5]

(6) The accused attempts to commit a crime which does not exist (for example, the accused attempts to commit the 'crime of adultery'). This is legal impossibility and cannot amount to an attempted crime.

---

[1] [1975] AC 476, 1973 3 All ER 1109.

[2] *R v Collingridge*, supra; P Brett, L Waller, and CR Williams, *Criminal Law* (1989, 6th edn), p 477 et seq. In England the Criminal Attempts Act 1981 made it clear that factual impossibility did not prevent an attempt being committed; or so Parliament thought. In *Anderton v Ryan* [1985] AC 560, [1985] 2 All ER 355 the House of Lords reintroduced the notion, only to change its mind again in *R v Shivpuri* [1987] AC 1, [1986] 2 All ER 334.

[3] [1987] VR 929. For comment, see (1987) 11 Crim L J 182.

[4] [1987] AC 1, [1986] 2 All ER 334.

[5] See *Gordon* para 6–52.

CONSPIRACY

The crime of conspiracy is committed by two or more persons who agree together to carry out a criminal purpose, whether that criminal purpose is an end in itself or a means to a further end. The crime is committed once the agreement is reached; overt acts in pursuit of the conspiracy merely provide evidence of the fact that a conspiracy has been entered into.[1] It is not a conspiracy to put forward an idea for consideration with a view to possible future agreement.[2]

The existence of a conspiracy may be proved by the actings of the accused persons; there does not have to be evidence of specific verbal or written agreement. In *West v HM Adv*[3] the conduct of the accused in loitering outside premises armed with a scissor blade and an open razor, was sufficient together with additional evidence to justify the inference that there was a conspiracy to assault and rob.

The criminal means which the accused conspired to use must be specified. It is not sufficient for the prosecution merely to allege that the accused agreed to further a criminal purpose.[4] Both conspiracy and the commission of the completed offence may be charged. Acquittal of the completed offence does not preclude conviction of conspiracy, and the acquittal of one conspirator will not preclude the conviction of others.[5]

INCITEMENT

The offence of incitement is committed by one who invites another to enter a criminal conspiracy or commit a crime. Attempted incitement may be charged if the person approached declines to join the conspiracy or commit the crime,[6] although there is no reason in

---

[1] *Crofter Hand Woven Harris Tweed v Veitch* 1942 SC (HL) 1, 1943 SLT 2 at 5 per Viscount Simon; *HM Adv v Wilson, Latta, and Rooney* (Feb 1986, unreported) High Court; *Gane and Stoddart*, p 203.
[2] *HM Adv v Smith and Ors* (May 1975, unreported) Glasgow High Court: *Gordon* para 6–56.
[3] 1985 SCCR 248.
[4] *Sayers and Ors v H M Adv* 1981 SCCR 312, 1981 JC 98.
[5] *HM Adv v Wilson, Latta, and Rooney*, supra.
[6] *HM Adv v Kay and Strain* (May 1952, unreported) Glasgow High Court: *Gordon* para 6–74; *Morton v Henderson* 1956 JC 55, 1956 SLT 365.

principle why incitement should not be charged in such a case, as the *actus reus* of the offence is complete once the invitation is made. The acceptance or otherwise of the invitation is irrelevant. It would be attempted incitement where **A** writes to **B**, urging him to commit a crime, but where the letter is intercepted and never reaches **B**.

8. Defences

ERROR

Subject to certain significant limitations, a person who acts in error may lack the *mens rea* necessary for conviction. Certain forms of error, however, are irrelevant as far as criminal liability is concerned, and a person who acts under such an error may still be convicted in respect of his mistaken actings.

Errors of Law

An error of law is to be distinguished from an error of fact, the former being generally irrelevant to the guilt of the accused. An error of law arises when the accused has reached a false conclusion as to the state of the law.[1] An error of fact, by contrast, entails a false conclusion as to a state of affairs in the physical world. If I believe that I am legally entitled to drive at 80 miles per hour on a motorway I make an error of law. If I believe that I am driving at 60 miles per hour, when in reality I am driving at 80 miles per hour, my error is an error of fact. Again, if I believe that I am entitled to shoot on sight any intruder I find on my property at night, my error is one of law. If I believe that the dark shape at which I shoot at night is a dog about to molest my sheep, whereas in reality it is a person who is crawling through the undergrowth, my error is factual rather than legal.

Errors of law may be divided into errors as to the general state of the criminal law and errors of civil law. The former do not constitute a defence to a criminal charge, whereas the latter may do so, principally in the context of offences of dishonesty.

---

[1] *Clark v Syme* 1957 JC 1, 1957 SLT 32.

Irrelevant errors of law. One of the most unbending maxims in the criminal law is *ignorantia iuris neminem excusat*: ignorance of the law is no excuse.[1] Ignorance of the law is an error of law in that the accused is unaware of the fact that his actions contravene a provision of the criminal law. Thus if **A** does not know that it is a crime to marry more than one wife, his ignorance of the law of bigamy will be no defence. A more likely example would be that of a statutory offence. If **A** does not know that Parliament has enacted legislation making it illegal to operate a vehicle without a certain form of emission control device, his ignorance of the law will be irrelevant. This will be the case even if the legislation is recent, and even if **A**, having been out of the country at the time of the enactment of the provision, could not reasonably be expected to have been aware of it.

The notion that everybody may be presumed to know the law may have been a realistic one in a simpler age, when the criminal law coincided, more or less, with the widely shared mores of society. This coincidence still exists of course, at least in respect of many common law crimes such as theft, assault, and murder, but the complexities of modern life have added a substantial corpus of criminal provisions which simply cannot be inferred through the exercise of moral intuitions or, indeed, on the basis of an ordinary understanding of society. As a result of this, ignorance of much of the criminal law is not only a possibility, it is probably also a widespread reality.

The main objection to the admission of ignorance of the law as a defence is a pragmatic one: the defence could be raised unmeritoriously and a great deal of court time wasted as a result. There are also considerations of fairness: the ignorant would be acquitted, while those who bothered to acquaint themselves with the law would be penalised. In certain contexts this could lead to unacceptable results. For example, **A** and **B** both engage in a specialist trade, which is regulated by complex rules contained in statutory instruments. **A** takes the trouble to acquaint himself with the rules, fails to comply with a provision of one of them and is punished. **B** decides deliberately to ignore all the rules and unknowingly infringes one. If an unqualified defence of ignorance of the law was available, **B** would be acquitted, although his conduct is clearly equally as culpable as **A**'s.

In a number of other jurisdictions the courts have not been deterred from introducing a defence of ignorance of the law. In

---

[1] *Hume* I, 26.

Germany such a defence has been available since 1952[1]; in Italy the Constitutional Court introduced it in 1988.[2] These developments accord with the general trend in both countries towards a requirement of fully subjective guilt before criminal conviction. English law and related systems have been reluctant to make such changes[3], and in Scotland the likelihood of any change on this matter is remote, given the tenacious adherence in Scotland to objective notions of criminal liability.

Even if the door is kept firmly closed to the reception of any ignorance of the law defence, there is one area in which reform might be effected without risking a wave of unmeritorious defences. This is the question of reliance on official advice, a category of legal error which is gradually being acknowledged in Canada and New Zealand. If a person seeks official advice as to his position and then acts upon it in good faith, it seems harsh to convict him of an offence should the advice in question prove to be misleading. The cautious acceptance of this defence elsewhere has succeeded in mitigating the effects of an otherwise uncompromising rule.[4]

There is no substantial Scottish authority in favour of the proposition that reliance on official advice is a defence. In *Roberts v Local Authority for Inverness*[5] a man who acted in accordance with official advice was held to have 'lawful authority or excuse' in terms of the statute which created the offence. This is unlikely to be generalised beyond the narrow confines of statutes with an equivalent form of wording.

Relevant errors of law. A person who mistakenly believes that he is acting under an entitlement of civil law may be acquitted on the grounds that he does not manifest the wrongful intent required for conviction of the offence.[6] Thus if **A** takes property mistakenly believing he has a legal right to do so (for example, believing that the

---

[1] 2 BGHSt 194. This rule is now embodied in s 17 of the Penal Code (StGB). The ignorance of the law must, however, be unavoidable. France and Belgium likewise accept unavoidable ignorance of the law as a defence. The South African Appellate Division accepted a defence of ignorance of the law in *S v Blom* 1977 (3) SA 513. For discussion see CR Snyman *Criminal Law* (2nd edn, 1989) p 220 et seq; R Whiting 1978 SALJ 1.

[2] Sent 364, 1988.

[3] For discussion see MP Furmston 'Ignorance of law' (1981) 1 J Legal Stud 37 (education); BR Grace 'Ignorance of the law as an excuse' (1986) 86 Col L Rev 1392.

[4] NS Kastner 'Mistake of law and the defence of officially induced error' (1986) 28 Crim Law Q 308. The advice must be that of officials, not that of the accused's lawyers: *Crichton v Victorian Dairies Ltd* [1965] VR 49.

[5] (1889) 2 White 385.

[6] *Hume* I, 73.

property is his by right of succession), he does not commit theft. His error, however, must be a reasonable one.[1] This defence is also known as the 'claim of right defence'.

Irrelevant errors of fact

Error as to the object of the crime

An error as to the object of the crime is irrelevant to the question of criminal guilt. If **A** steals a car believing that it belongs to **B**, he will still be guilty of theft if it transpires that the car belonged to **C**. Similarly if **A** shoots at and kills **B**, believing him to be **C**, he will be guilty of murder even if he had no intention of killing **B**. This is a mistake of transferred intent, which has now been clearly recognised as a feature of Scots law in the decision in *Roberts v Hamilton*[2].

Error as to the identity of the victim may be relevant when the identity of the victim forms part of the definition of the offence. For example, if **A** makes a mistake as to the identity of **B** and assaults him in ignorance of the fact that **B** is a policeman, his error as to identity will be a defence to a charge of assaulting a policeman.

Error as to method

An accused may intend to commit a crime by means **x** but as events transpire he in fact commits it by means **y**. This is an error as to mode and will, in general, be irrelevant. If **A** assaults **B** by kicking him and then stabbing him, intending to kill him by the stabbing, and if **B** then dies from the injuries received in the kicking rather than from the stab wounds, this is an error as to mode and does not affect **A**'s liability for the death of **B**. An error as to mode may be relevant, however, when the method by which a crime is committed is a 'definitional element' in that crime, that is, a particular method

---

[1] *Hume* I, 74.
[2] 1989 SLT 399, 1989 SCCR 240. Discussed further at p 143. This doctrine of transferred intent is strongly criticised by *Gordon* paras 9–12–9–13, but its acceptance by the courts is now clear. The principal objection to the doctrine is that it applies the doctrine of *versari in re illicita*, under which the accused is held liable for the unforeseen 'side effects' of illegal conduct on his part. This doctrine lies behind the rule that killing in the course of a robbery is always murder, see p 160 below. For discussion of transferred malice in English law, see A Ashworth 'Transferred malice and punishment for unforeseen consequences' in P Glazebrook (ed) *Reshaping the Criminal Law* (1978) p 77.

is required for that particular *actus reus*. If a statute provides that it is an offence to do **x** by doing **y**, a person who does **x** by doing **y** but under the erroneous belief that he is doing **x** by doing **z**, a defence may be open to him, provided, of course, the statutory offence is not one of strict liability.

Relevant errors of fact

The general principle in relation to relevant errors of fact is that the accused is judged on the facts as he thought them to be. The existence of an error as to fact may mitigate: if **A** gives **B** a pill which he takes to be a painkiller but which is in reality poison, his poisoning of **B** is unintentional. He therefore does not have the *mens rea* of murder unless, of course, he acted with a sufficient degree of recklessness. An erroneous belief may be arrived at recklessly, in which case there may be liability in those cases where recklessness is a sufficient *mens rea* for the crime in question. A man who wrongly believes that a woman consents to intercourse, and reaches this belief recklessly, cannot rely on his error to negate the *mens rea* of rape.[1]

Need the error be a reasonable one? There is scant authority on this question: two important self-defence cases refer to a requirement of reasonableness, but this is now thrown into doubt by the decision in *Meek and Ors v HM Adv*[2]. In *Owens v HM Adv*[3] Lord Normand held that a mistaken belief that the accused was being threatened would not exclude the defence of self-defence provided that such a belief was held on reasonable grounds. 'Grounds for such a belief may exist,' he said, 'although they are founded on a genuine mistake of fact'.[4] This amounts to a requirement that the reasonable person in the accused's position could have reached the conclusion that he was threatened by the victim. In *Crawford v HM Adv*[5] the court returned to the issue of reasonableness in another self-defence case. The main issue in this case was whether self-defence was justified in the circumstances, but the court expressed the clear view that 'where self-defence is supported by a mistaken belief rested on reasonable grounds, that mistaken belief must have a purely objective background and must not be purely subjective or of the nature of a hallucination'.[6]

---

[1] *Meek and Ors v HM Adv* 1982 SCCR 613, 1983 SLT 280.
[2] Ibid.
[3] 1946 JC 119, 1946 SLT 227.
[4] 1946 JC 119 at 125.
[5] 1950 JC 67, 1950 SLT 279.
[6] 1950 JC 67 at 71 per Lord Cooper.

There the matter rested until the decision in *Meek and Ors*[1] . The High Court accepted in this case that '. . . an essential element in the crime of rape is the absence of honest belief in the consent of the woman . . . The absence of reasonable grounds for such an alleged belief will, however, have a considerable bearing upon whether the jury will accept such an "honest belief" was held.'[2] If **A** therefore believes **B** to be willing to have intercourse, this belief will exclude the *mens rea* of rape **even if no reasonable man in his position would have believed similarly**. Only if he is reckless in reaching this belief will he be liable, recklessness being a sufficient *mens rea* for the crime of rape.

It is not clear whether the High Court wished to disturb the effect of the decision in *Owens* and the dictum in *Crawford*, and indeed these decisions are not discussed in the judgment in *Meek*. It is possible that the rule advanced in *Meek* will in future be limited to rape cases and that in other areas a requirement of reasonableness will be insisted upon. In principle, the rule that a genuine, though unreasonable belief, should exclude *mens rea* is preferable, on the grounds that only the subjectively guilty should be punished.[3] In practice such a rule could be kept under control by the good sense of jurors who, as Lord Emslie suggests in *Meek*, would be disinclined to believe that the accused genuinely held a mistaken belief which is grossly unreasonable.

Another way of dealing with the apparent irreconcilability of *Owens* and *Meek* is to limit the reasonableness requirement to those cases where the accused is attempting to justify his conduct, as he is in cases of self-defence, coercion, or necessity. These defences amount to an assertion on the accused's part that what he did was right, and it is not unreasonable therefore to require that this assertion of right be objectively supportable. In other circumstances, the error affects intention, and reasonableness can play no appropriate justificatory role. In such cases the accused is not saying 'What I did was right' he is merely saying 'I did not intend to do that with which I am now charged'. On this account, there is no conflict between

---

[1] 1982 SCCR 613, 1983 SLT 280.
[2] At 618 per Lord President Emslie, following *DPP v Morgan* [1976] AC 182, [1976] 61 Crim App Rep 136.
[3] There is an extensive literature on the subject of the reasonableness requirement in cases of error. Examples include: P Alldridge 'Mistake in criminal law – subjectivism reasserted in the Court of Appeal' (1984) 35 N I L Q 263; Singer 'The resurgence of *mens rea*: II – honest but unreasonable mistake of fact in self-defence' (1987) 28 Boston College Law Review 439; NJ Reville 'Self-defence: courting sober but unreasonable mistakes of fact' (1988) 52 J Cr L 84.

Owens and *Meek* and genuine but unreasonable error might have the effect of excluding *mens rea*.

INTOXICATION

Intoxication may occur as a result of the ingestion of alcohol or drugs, the legal implications of either form of intoxication being the same. In practice, the courts will be concerned almost exclusively with alcoholic intoxication, the salient effects of which are to reduce inhibitions, interfere with physical control of the body, impair awareness and, in some cases, induce amnesia.[1] Excessive drinking over a prolonged period may also result in organic brain damage of a degree sufficient to have serious behavioural implications.

The close association of alcoholic intoxication with criminal conduct is a matter borne out by the everyday experience of the courts.[2] There is a range of views on the implications of intoxication, varying from the view that intoxication should be neither an excuse nor a mitigating factor to the view that it should be a complete defence to a criminal charge. The former position may be based on the notion that the decision to become intoxicated is a voluntary one and that the consequences of this decision are quite appropriately referable to the drinker. Alternatively, even if it is accepted that some people cannot control their drinking, intoxication may still not be treated as an exculpating factor on the grounds that an impossibly high proportion of offenders would thereby be acquitted, to the clear distress of the victims of their crimes. Certainly this accords with our intuitions as to how people would respond to the information that the person who assaulted them was to be acquitted on the grounds that he was drunk at the time.

On the other hand, the inappropriateness and harshness of attributing full responsibility to the intoxicated offender may in many cases be equally apparent. *Gordon* raises the example of the

---

[1] For an account of the implications of alcoholic intoxication, see CN Mitchell 'The intoxicated offender – refuting the legal and medical myths' (1988) 11 International Journal of Law and Psychiatry 77.

[2] Recent criminological literature of note includes M McMurran and CR Hollin 'Drinking and delinquency' (1989) 29 Brit J Crim 386. In one study of a Scottish young offender institution, 63% of those questioned on admission reported that they were drunk at the time of the commission of the offence: N Heather 'Relationship between delinquency and drunkenness among Scottish young offenders' (1981) 16 Brit J of Alcohol and Alcoholism 50.

young man who drinks excessively at his first alcoholic party and who commits an indecent assault as a result.[1] To regard such a person as a deliberate criminal seems, he says, unduly harsh. This would indeed be a hard case, although it might be hoped that the relative innocence of the young man would be taken into account in sentencing, or alternatively that the Crown would have regard to it when deciding whether or not to prosecute. What, though, would be the position if the act he committed in his state of 'blind drunkenness' was to point a loaded gun at another guest and pull the trigger? Is he to be considered a murderer, or is the offence to be reduced to culpable homicide, or is he to be acquitted altogether? The more serious the offence becomes, the less appealing becomes the prospect of complete acquittal and yet, at the same time, the more draconian seems that approach which would exclude any room for mitigation in such a case. Obviously there is a world of difference between the young drunken killer and the man who shoots his victim in cold blood; yet the mandatory life sentence for murder allows little room for this difference to be acknowledged. These considerations of policy form the background against which the criminal law's response to intoxication is to be approached.

The Scots law on intoxication is, to a certain degree, unclear. Nineteenth-century cases reveal a willingness to take intoxication into account in the reduction of murder to culpable homicide, although it was not accepted as a complete defence.[2] In *Kennedy v HM Adv*[3] a full court adopted the rule of the English case of *D P P v Beard*[4] with the result that intoxication, if capable of preventing the formation of the necessary intent for murder, would reduce murder to culpable homicide. The law remained in that state until the decision in *Brennan v HM Adv*[5], in which a Full Court rejected any defence of intoxication at least in relation to murder. The decision in *Brennan* leaves a number of issues unresolved, but the following examples demonstrate the law as it stands at present:

(1) (a) **A** is given a drink which he believes to be non-alcoholic; in fact it contains a substantial amount of vodka. **A** unwittingly becomes intoxicated and commits an assault.

    A's intoxication in this case is involuntary and provided that the intoxication is of such a degree that he cannot form

---

[1] At para 12–01.
[2] *Margaret Robertson or Brown* (1886) 1 White 93. *Hume* is firm in his rejection of intoxication as a complete defence.
[3] 1944 JC 171, 1945 SLT 11.
[4] [1920] AC 479.
[5] 1977 SLT 151.

the intent necessary for assault, he should be acquitted.[1] If the alcohol merely disinhibits him then he may still be responsible for his acts, although the effect of the alcohol might possibly mitigate punishment.

(b) **A** becomes involuntarily intoxicated in circumstances identical to those in (a) above. In his state of intoxication he then launches into a vicious knife attack on **B** and kills him.

The decision in *Brennan* was entirely concerned with what the court termed 'self-induced' intoxication and the effect of this on the *mens rea* of murder. The fact that the court ruled out such intoxication as a defence may be taken as an indication that involuntary intoxication should be a defence in such a case, but the decision cannot properly be taken that far. On the strength of Lord McCluskey's dicta in *Ross*[2], involuntary intoxication (of a sufficient degree) should exclude the *mens rea* of murder and assault without distinction between them, and **A** should be acquitted.

(c) **A** becomes involuntarily intoxicated as in (a) and (b), but on this occasion rather than committing an attack on another, he gets into his car and drives away. He drives erratically, is found to be driving with an excess of alcohol in his blood, and is charged with an offence under the Road Traffic Act 1988.

This example illustrates the non-application of a defence of intoxication in relation to a strict liability offence. Liability under section 5 of the Road Traffic Act 1988 is strict and **A** would therefore have no defence. The fact, though, that he was involuntarily intoxicated may be a special reason for the court not to order endorsement or disqualification.[3]

(2) **A** takes alcohol voluntarily and in an intoxicated state he assaults **B**.

In *Brennan* the court stated that '...in crimes of basic "intent" we understand the law of England to be at one with the

---

[1] The judgment of Lord McCluskey in *Ross (Robert) v HM Adv* 1991 SCCR 823, 1991 SLT 564 provides the sole Scottish authority for the principle that involuntary intoxication may be a defence. '...one can see at once that the "evidence of *mens rea*" referred to [in *Majewski* and in *Brennan*] is wholly lacking in the case where the intoxicant has been administered to a person without his knowledge and consent.' (At 840.) English law is equally bereft of authority here, but it is clear that the rule in *D P P v Majewski* [1976] 2 All ER 142, [1977] AC 443 is not applicable in such cases and that involuntary intoxication is, therefore, a defence: *Smith and Hogan* p 218. There are several South African cases on this point: *S v Johnson* 1969 (1) SA 201 at 205, 211; *Hartyani* 1980 (3) SA 613.

[2] *Ross (Robert) v HM Adv* 1991 SCCR 823, 1991 SLT 564.

[3] Road Traffic Offenders Act 1988, ss 34(1), 44(2).

law of Scotland in refusing to admit self-induced intoxication as a defence of any kind'.[1] The English law approach thus adopted excludes intoxication as a defence in those crimes which do not require a specific intent. In English law, assault is one such crime and the court in *Brennan* was evidently of the view that assault in Scots law likewise required only basic intent. The difficulty with this view is that assault in Scots law, at least at that time, required 'evil intent' which is probably rather more than basic intent. There is also the objection that the specific/basic intent distinction is not part of Scots law. In spite of these doubts, however, the court's intention was clear: intoxication should not be a defence in a case of assault.

The recent decisions recognising recklessness as a sufficient *mens rea* for assault[2] removes potential contradictions between the decision in *Brennan* and the general law of assault. *Brennan* located the morally and legally blameworthy aspect of the accused's conduct in the recklessness inherent in becoming drunk. If recklessness is sufficient *mens rea* for assault, then the *Brennan* rule applies in assault in exactly the same way as it does in murder.

(3) **A** takes alcohol voluntarily and becomes chronically intoxicated. He then kills **B**.

This example is squarely covered by the decision in *Brennan*. **A**'s recklessness in becoming intoxicated was seen as justifying conviction in this case, the court pointing out that:

'There is nothing unethical or unfair or contrary to the general principle of our law that self-induced intoxication is not by itself a defence to any criminal charge, including in particular the charge of murder. Self-induced intoxication is itself a continuing element and therefore an integral part being the evidence of the actings of the accused who uses force against his victim. Together they add up to that criminal recklessness which it is the purpose of the criminal law to restrain . . .'[3]

(4) **A**, having become voluntarily intoxicated, takes **B**'s gold pen from **B**'s desk and slips it into his pocket. The next day he has no recollection of what happened the previous evening and the pen lies unnoticed in his coat pocket.

If *Brennan* allows a defence of intoxication in a case where the crime is one requiring more than a 'basic intent', then **A**

---

[1] At 158.
[2] *Roberts v Hamilton* 1989 SCCR 240, 1989 SLT 399; *Connor v Jessop* 1988 SCCR 624.
[3] At 158.

has a defence to a charge of theft in that he did not have the necessary *mens rea* of theft at the time at which he took the pen; that is, he did not intend to deprive **B** of his property. The sheriff would have to believe, however, that he did not form this intention and the question he may well raise is: what **did A** have in mind when he put the pen in his pocket if it was not an intention to deprive the owner of the pen of his property?

(5) **A**, intending to kill **B**, drinks alcohol to build up 'Dutch courage'. He carries through his plan, doing so in a state of intoxication.

This is an instance of *actio libera in causa* and it is clear that intoxication would be no defence here, even if *Brennan* did not exist. This is the strongest case, perhaps the only case, in which in an ideal system of criminal justice, intoxication would have no bearing at all on criminal liability.

A critique of the law

The decision in *Brennan* is essentially hostile to any defence of intoxication. To an extent, this is inevitable, as the policy arguments against recognising this defence are fairly persuasive. The drunken assault cannot be condoned, and even if the accused has acted out of character and demonstrated remorse for what he has done, this cannot amount to a complete defence. Yet it is not in this sort of case – where minor violence against persons or property may be involved – that the real harshness of the law emerges: it is in charges of murder that *Brennan* seems unduly restrictive. There are alternatives.

The most radical solution is to allow intoxication, if it is of a sufficient degree, to negate *mens rea* completely. This approach has now been adopted in Australia, where the decision in *R v O'Connor*[1] recognised that intoxication may be a complete defence if, as a result of it, the accused did not form the intention necessary for the crime. This decision goes further than those decisions, such as *D P P v Majewski*[2], which conceded that intoxication may be a defence in crimes of specific intent: *O'Connor* was concerned with assault, a crime of so-called 'basic intent'. The Australian High Court specifically rejected the distinction between 'basic' and 'specific' intent, pointing out that there was no real difference between the mental state required to perform a physical action and the mental

[1] (1981) 146 Crim L R 64; (1980) 54 ALJR 349.
[2] [1976] 2 All ER 142, [1977] AC 443.

state required to form an intention in relation to that act's consequences. The court considered the question of recklessness, but took the view that any recklessness involved in becoming intoxicated could not be 'carried forward' to be applied to a later act. Chief Justice Barwick's treatment of this point contrasts sharply with the view of recklessness expressed in *Brennan*:

'If to take alcohol or drugs with at least the risk of becoming intoxicated is in one sense a reckless thing to do, yet that variety of recklessness can scarcely be carried forward and attributed as a substitute for actual intent to do the proscribed act. The recklessness which may on occasion satisfy the requirement of *mens rea* involves an awareness of possible consequences of doing the act, ie the proscribed act charged, and at least a decision to disregard them and to act without caring for apprehended consequences. The recklessness or wantonness of the person taking alcohol or other drugs with at least the chance of becoming intoxicated is surely of quite a different order.'[1]

One obvious criticism of the decision in *O'Connor* is that it ignores the risk which intoxicated offenders pose to society and that this approach opens the floodgates to the acquittal of an excessive number of intoxicated offenders. In fact this has not happened in Australia, as juries tend to be healthily sceptical about claims that intoxication led to either involuntary action or to an inability to form the necessary intent. It is only in the extreme cases that the *O'Connor* rule will result in acquittal.[2]

Stopping considerably short of an *O'Connor*-type response is the approach currently applied in English law under *DPP v Majewski*[3]. This much criticised decision[4] holds that while intoxication does not affect crimes of basic intent, in relation to crimes of specific intent it may be relevant. Where homicide is involved, the effect of intoxication may be to reduce the offence from murder to manslaughter (culpable homicide). Scots law formerly had the latter option open to it, but this has now been removed by *Brennan*.

The solution adopted in German criminal law has a great deal to be said for it. This allows a defence of intoxication where appropriate but provides for the punishment of those who cause harm in

---

[1] At 357.
[2] For discussion, see B Fisse *Howard's Criminal Law* (5th edn, 1990) p 445. South African law espouses the same principle as that developed in *O'Connor*: *S v Chretien* 1981 (1) SA 1097. For discussion see CR Snyman *Criminal Law* (2nd edn, 1989) p 176.
[3] [1976] 2 All ER 142, [1977] AC 443.
[4] See for example A Dashwood 'Logic and the Lords in *Majewski*' [1977] Crim L R 532, 591; E Colvin 'A theory of the intoxication defence' (1981) 59 Can Bar Rev 850; A Ashworth 'Reason, logic and criminal liability' (1975) 91 LQR 102.

an intoxicated state. The offence for which the intoxicated offender is punished is not that which he does while intoxicated, but the act of becoming dangerously intoxicated in the first place. Punishment is restricted to a maximum of five years imprisonment, provided that the sentence actually awarded does not exceed the maximum sentence available for the offence for which he would have been convicted had no defence been available. The attraction of this solution, which has found favour elsewhere[1], lies in the fact that a commitment to subjective liability can be maintained while at the same time considerations of social defence and public opinion are met. The intoxicated offender is not, therefore, acquitted altogether, but those who, for example, kill while 'blind drunk' and who would not, in sobriety, be murderers are spared conviction for homicide.

INSANITY AND DIMINISHED RESPONSIBILITY

The effect of mental abnormality on criminal responsibility is one of the more controversial questions in criminal jurisprudence. At one extreme is the view that many instances of criminal behaviour are directly attributable to some psychopathology of the offender and that the proportion of criminals fully responsible for their actions is actually fairly low. Directly opposed to this is the argument that even those who are mentally abnormal are still, in the vast majority of cases, answerable for what they do. Adherents of this position tend to be sceptical when confronted with psychiatric explanations of anti-social behaviour.

Whatever role criminology may attribute to mental abnormality in the aetiology of crime, systems of criminal justice have long recognised that at least some forms of mental abnormality will exculpate an accused person. This occurs through the operation of (1) the defence of insanity, which leads to complete acquittal (although accompanied by hospital detention) and (2) the plea of diminished responsibility, the effect of which is to reduce a charge of murder to one of culpable homicide. In addition account must be taken of automatism, which may have a psychiatric explanation (fully discussed above in the context of *actus reus*), and the plea in bar of trial, which prevents criminal trial on the grounds of the inability of the accused to understand the proceedings and to instruct counsel.

---

[1] Such a system was suggested by Barwick CJ in his judgment in *O'Connor* at 358.

Mental abnormality and crime

The criminal law presupposes rationality and individual moral responsibility. The rational person acts in accordance with a view of the world which is shared by other rational agents, and behaves in a way which enables him to achieve those goals which he has identified as desirable. Such a person is usually capable of controlling himself, conforming to social norms, and of understanding the reason for such restrictions as may be placed on his behaviour.

A mentally-disturbed person may not be capable of acting rationally in accordance with the criteria outlined above. This may be because of some limitation of his understanding (a defect in his cognitive capacities) or it may arise from a volitional disability. In the latter case the person is quite capable of understanding the world about him, but cannot help himself from acting in a particular way. In either case the moral responsibility of the mentally-abnormal person may be affected. Defects in cognition have an exculpatory effect because one should not be held accountable for what one does not know; defects in volition may have a similar effect on the grounds that one is not to blame for that which he cannot help himself from doing. On either of these bases – ignorance or unfreedom – can the non-responsibility of the mentally-abnormal person be either mitigated or completely denied.

Mental abnormality does not give rise to a blanket exculpation: some mentally-disturbed persons will not be so affected by their condition as to be considered non-responsible. For this reason psychiatric evidence will need to focus on the clinical features of the condition from which such a person suffers, and it is then for the jury to determine whether this satisfies the tests for responsibility which the law has set in this area. The decision as to responsibility is therefore one which psychiatry itself may decline to make, and indeed may resent being asked to make at all.[1] What psychiatric expertise provides is an insight into the way the mind of a mentally-disturbed person may be affected by his psychiatric condition.

The main psychiatric categories and their possible bearing on criminal behaviour

Psychiatric conditions range from the relatively benign (mild neuroses) to the florid and debilitating (functional psychoses). While the former are unlikely to affect responsibility to an appreci-

---

[1] D Chiswick 'Use and abuse of psychiatric testimony' (1985) 290 Brit Med J 975.

able extent, the latter may well be so disabling as to justify exculpation.

(i) Functional psychoses. The main conditions in this category are affective disorders and the various forms of schizophrenia. Affective disorders are severe depressive illnesses which may involve delusions and a high degree of incapacity. Mania or hypomania also fall into the category of affective disorders. Mania involves inappropriate behaviour of an arrogant, over-elated sort which can have criminal implications, especially in relation to offences against property.

Schizophrenic illnesses are a relatively intractable and severe group of illnesses characterised by thought disorder. In most cases the schizophrenic will experience delusions of a disturbing nature, and these may in some circumstances lead him to act violently against imagined persecutors or in pursuit of some command which he believes he is receiving. Even in less severe cases, the anxiety and tension experienced by the schizophrenic may have an impact on behaviour towards others, and could therefore explain certain forms of criminal conduct.

(ii) Neurotic conditions. Neurotic conditions are disorders of a non-psychotic nature in which mood is affected and a person may behave in an abnormally anxious, obsessive, or ill-adapted way. The category is a broad one, but some of the more common neuroses include obsessive compulsive neuroses, anxiety disorders, and neurotic depression. The last of these is of some forensic significance; violence directed against children within the home is frequently associated with neurotic depression in the perpetrator.[1]

(iii) Personality disorders (particularly psychopathy). Psychiatry recognises a number of disorders of the personality, a hallmark of which is a defect in the ability of the person to relate to others in a socially-acceptable manner or to relate his conduct to the needs and expectations of others. A widely used diagnostic manual, the *DSM-111-R*[2], places these disorders in three main clusters: cluster A includes, amongst others, paranoid personality

---

[1] A Sims 'The phenomenology of neurosis' in R Bluglass and P Bowden *Principles and Practice of Forensic Psychiatry* (1990) pp 369, 377.

[2] American Psychiatric Association, *DSM-III-R: Diagnostic and Statistical Manual of Mental Disorders* (3rd edn, 1987, Washington).

disorder; cluster B, of greater interest here, includes antisocial personality disorder (psychopathy); and cluster C includes obsessive compulsive personality disorders and avoidant or dependent personality disorders.

The personality disorder which has attracted greatest forensic attention is psychopathy.[1] This form of personality disorder, also known as antisocial personality disorder, or sociopathy, is characterised by immature, selfish and profoundly antisocial behaviour. The psychopath is typically incapable of sympathising with others, he may be emotionally unmoved by the effects which his self-centred actions have, and he may be given to childish outbursts of inconsiderate or violent behaviour. In short, the psychopath is one in whom the normal moral restraints appear to be absent.

The aetiology of psychopathy is controversial. It is not a condition which 'comes upon' a person, as may a mental illness such as schizophrenia. This is how the psychopath is and always has been: it is his nature to be antisocial. A variety of causative factors have been put forward, ranging from genetic predisposition and organic brain peculiarities, to environmental factors in childhood. There is widespread agreement, however, that whatever might explain the phenomenon of the psychopathic personality, psychiatric treatment provides little prospect of cure. Indeed it was the conclusion of one government committee on mentally abnormal offenders, the Butler Committee, that the best place in which to manage psychopathic offenders is in prison.

The issue of the psychopath's responsibility for his actions is discussed below.

(iv) Mental illness of organic origin. Somatic (physical) illness may occur in the brain itself or elsewhere in the system and still affect the functioning of the brain. These conditions are therefore based on physical abnormalities or changes in the body. Conditions of this sort include dementia, which is a progressive deterioration of the brain accompanied by intellectual and emotional impairment, brain tumours, and epilepsy. All of these conditions may have forensic implications, as a person suffering from a disease in this category may behave in a grossly abnormal, possibly violent, fashion.

---

[1] Psychopathy is defined in s 1(2) of the Mental Health (Scotland) Act 1984 as a 'persistent disorder or disability of mind (whether or not including significant impairment of intelligence) which results in abnormally aggressive or seriously irresponsible conduct on the part of the person concerned'.

The connection between mental abnormality and crime

The diagnosis of a psychiatric condition does not necessarily provide an explanation as to why a person has committed a criminal offence: the vast majority of mentally-ill persons never commit an offence. Yet in some cases the fact that a mentally-abnormal person has committed an offence seems very clearly attributable to the mental illness itself. A person suffering from Othello Syndrome, a form of pathological jealousy leading the sufferer to become convinced that his partner is conducting an affair, who then kills his partner or the suspected lover, clearly acts because of the particular delusional beliefs. Similarly, in the case of a paranoid schizophrenic who acts on an alleged command from God to kill prostitutes, the conclusion is likely to be drawn that the schizophrenic illness is responsible for such behaviour.

These are extreme cases: there are many other forms of crime in which the insights of psychiatry may play an important explanatory role without necessarily providing grounds for exculpation. Sexual offences are an example: the psychological profile of those who engage in certain forms of sexual offence, such as paedophiliac offences or offences involving, say, sado-masochistic or necrophiliac elements, is likely to deviate substantially from the norm. This is so, also, with certain forms of fire-raising and, indeed, with some types of shop-lifting. Such offenders may continue to be morally-responsible agents, although an understanding of the psychopathological background of the offence may help explain why they commit the offences in question.

The criminal law's response to mental abnormality

(a) Informal measures. The mentally-disturbed offender who commits a minor offence may be informally dealt with by the police, or fiscal, with health service involvement. The support of psychiatric services in the disposition of such cases without resort to court appearances saves the time of the criminal courts and provides a more humane means of dealing with those who do not pose any considerable threat to society.

(b) The plea in bar of trial. An accused who for reasons of mental abnormality does not have the ability to understand legal proceedings and instruct his defence may resort to a plea in bar of trial. This may be raised, at any stage of the proceedings, by the prosecution, defence, or indeed by the court itself. The plea may be based on mental disturbance or on some other disability, such as mental retardation. Deaf-mutism has been rejected as grounds for the plea[1], as has hysterical amnesia[2]. The latter condition should, it might be argued, be accepted as the basis of such a plea as it is difficult to see how a person who is amnesic in respect of the period during which a crime is committed can adequately defend himself.[3] Such an argument has generally not found much favour, partly on the grounds that it would present too tempting a possibility for those who wish to avoid punishment and are prepared to face detention in a psychiatric hospital, and partly because amnesia is sometimes seen as of limited significance to the trial itself. In the American case of *United States v Watson*[4] the Military Court of Appeals ruled that amnesia in relation to the crime did not prevent the accused from understanding the nature of the proceedings, from asking questions, and from appreciating the elements of the offence with which he was charged. In *Wilson v United States*[5] the court listed a number of factors to be taken into account in determining the extent to which amnesia could affect fitness to stand trial, one of which is the extent to which extrinsic evidence could be used to reconstruct the circumstances of the crime.

A significant aspect to the plea in bar of trial is that it does not involve any determination of the facts forming the basis of the charge. It is therefore possible that an accused person who is found unfit at the time of the trial may be detained in a psychiatric hospital for a considerable period without there ever having been any satisfactory investigation of whether he actually did what he is alleged to have done.[6] A successful plea in bar of trial does not bar the Crown from bringing criminal proceedings if the accused is subsequently found to be fit to face trial.

---

[1] *HM Adv v Wilson* 1942 JC 75, 1942 SLT 194.

[2] *Russell v HM Adv* 1946 JC 37, 1946 SLT 93.

[3] English law adopts the same rule as does Scots law: *R v Podola* [1960] 1 QB 325; discussed by J Bradford and SM Smith 'Amnesia and homicide: *Podola* case and a study of 30 cases' (1979) 7 Bulletin of the American Academy of Psychiatry and Law 219. The Butler Committee Report 'Report of the Committee on Mentally Abnormal Offenders' (1975, HMSO Cmnd 6244) did not propose any significant reform of this rule.

[4] 18 CMR 391 (1954).

[5] 391 F 2d 460 (1968). For discussion of the American amnesia cases, see D H Hermann 'Criminal defences and pleas in mitigation based on amnesia' (1986) 4 Behavioural Sciences and the Law 5.

[6] Discussed by the Thomson Committee (1975), which recommended that there be a trial of the facts in plea in bar of trial cases. In England this reform has now been achieved: Criminal Procedure (Insanity and Unfitness to Plead) Act 1991.

(c) The insanity defence. The defence of insanity is a special defence, requiring prior notice to the Crown which, if successfully raised, results in the special verdict of not guilty on the grounds of insanity. An inevitable consequence of this verdict is the detention of the accused as a restricted patient in a secure psychiatric hospital under s 174 of the Criminal Procedure (Scotland) Act 1975.[1] The discharge of such a patient requires the assent of the Secretary of State, although a patient may appeal against a decision of the Secretary of State in this respect.[2]

The burden of proof in respect of an insanity plea rests upon the defence. This is in contrast to the normal requirement that the burden of proof in a criminal trial rests upon the prosecution.

The criteria of insanity in Scots criminal law

Hume states that the defence of insanity requires that there should be an

'absolute alienation of reason[3] ... such a disease as deprives the patient of the knowledge of the true aspect and portion of things about him – hinders him from distinguishing friend or foe, and gives him up to the impulse of his own distempered fancy.'[4]

This wording is echoed in the modern cases, the most important of which are *HM Adv v Kidd*[5] and *Brennan v HM Adv*[6]. In *Kidd*, Lord Strachan said in his instructions to the jury:

'First, in order to excuse a person from responsibility for his acts on the grounds of insanity, there must have been an alienation of the reason in relation to the act committed. There must have been some mental defect, to use a broad neutral word, a mental defect by which his reason was overpowered and he was thereby rendered incapable of exerting his reason to control his conduct and reactions. If his reason

---

[1] For procedure, see J Blackie and H Patrick *Mental Health: A Guide to the Law in Scotland* (1990) ch 5.

[2] Appeal is to the sheriff court in the sheriffdom in which the patient is detained: Mental Health (Scotland) Act 1984, s 63 (2).

[3] The role played by concepts of reason in the plea of insanity in Scotland dates back to at least the sixteenth century: H Arnot *A Collection and Abridgement of Celebrated Criminal Trials in Scotland 1536 – 1784* II (1833 edn) Part 2, p 363: trial of *Jaspar Lauder*: '...the said Jasper has been furious and wanted the use of resoune...' Discussed by N Walker *Crime and Insanity in England* (1968) 1, p 138.

[4] I, 37.

[5] 1960 JC 61, 1960 SLT 82.

[6] 1977 SLT 151.

was alienated in relation to the act committed, he was not responsible for that act, even though otherwise he may have been apparently quite rational.'

In *Brennan*, in which the accused's plea of insanity was based upon his extreme degree of intoxication at the time of the offence, a Full Bench of the High Court approved *Hume*'s conception of insanity, explaining that

'insanity in our law requires proof of total alienation of reason in relation to the act charged as the result of mental illness, mental disease, or defect or unsoundness of mind and does not comprehend the malfunctioning of the mind of transitory effect . . .'[1]

The direction in *Kidd* resolved the uncertainties which had crept into this area of the law since *Hume*. The McNaghten Rules (discussed below) were rejected by the court and thus their chequered career in Scotland was brought to an end. Yet the definition of insanity proposed in *Kidd* and *Brennan* still raises a number of significant problems. What is meant by an 'alienation of reason' or a 'complete alienation of reason'? Is it merely an old-fashioned way of referring to what would now be considered substantial impairment of cognitive ability?

Is it appropriate to describe a person who suffers from a specific delusion, but who is capable of understanding cause and effect and of acting in a calculating fashion, as suffering from a complete alienation of reason? Then there is the difficulty of those who suffer from volitional disabilities: the reasoning abilities of such persons might be intact in spite of an inability on their part to conform to the rules of society.

The attraction of the alienation of reason criterion is that it does not unduly confuse members of the jury in whose mind the predominant question is likely to be: **is the accused sufficiently mentally abnormal to be blamed for what he did?** In so far as the concept of alienation of reason is an opaque one, particularly to a layman, it may be taken as a mere cypher for the simple question described above. This means though that the real issue of responsibility is effectively left to the jury's intuitions as to culpability, and intuitions it could be argued, provide a hazardous basis for so crucial a matter as criminal guilt or innocence.[2]

---

[1] At 154.
[2] In one view, it makes little difference to a jury what test of insanity is proposed: RA Pasewark 'A review of research on the insanity defense' (1986) 484 Annals of the American Academy of Political and Social Science 100.

The alternatives

(1) The McNaghten Rules. The McNaghten Rules which were applied in Scotland for a period during the nineteenth and earlier part of the twentieth century, have provided one of the most tenacious tests of legal insanity and continue to constitute the basis of the defence in many common law countries. Their unequivocal rejection in both *Kidd* and *Brennan* mean that they are no longer relevant in Scots law, but their widespread influence elsewhere merits attention.

The McNaghten Rules stem from the trial in 1843 of a paranoid schizophrenic Glaswegian, Daniel McNaghten, who suffered from the delusion that he was being persecuted by the Tories. Prompted by this delusion, McNaghten shot the secretary of the Prime Minister of the time, Sir Robert Peel, under the impression that his victim was the Prime Minister himself. McNaghten was found by the jury to be insane, an event which caused general public disquiet. Invited to clarify the law before the House of Lords, the judges stated that:

'to establish a defence on the ground of insanity, it must clearly be proved that, at the time of the committing of the act, the party accused was labouring under such a defect of reason, from disease of the mind, as not to know the nature and quality of the act he was doing; or, if he did know it, that he did not know he was doing what was wrong.'

The McNaghten Rules have stood the test of time and constitute, in one form or another, the core of the insanity test in modern English law as well as in many Commonwealth countries and in a number of United States jurisdictions. They have been widely and persistently criticised on the grounds, inter alia, that they are solely concerned with cognitive defects and pay no attention to volitional questions.[1]

---

[1] In recent decades, this limitation implicit in the Rules has been remedied in some jurisdictions by statutory reform of codified versions of the Rules, or through creative interpretation by the courts. In the Australian appeal of *A-G for South Australia v Brown* [1960] AC 432, [1960] 1 All ER 734 the Privy Council acknowledged that inability to control oneself may be indicative of an inability to distinguish between right and wrong. This allows some role for the concept of 'irresistible impulse', a notion rejected in English law: *R v Rivett* (1950) 34 Crim App Rep 87. Earlier its recognition had been espoused by Fitzjames Stephens (see N Walker *Crime and Insanity in England* (1968) I, 105) and by the Atkin Committee reporting in 1924 (Report of the Committee on Insanity and Crime (Cmnd 2005)). In Canadian law irresistible impulse was rejected in *R v Borg* [1969] SCR 551, but now see *Abbey* (1982) 68 CCC (2d) 394. In the United States irresistible

There is also the issue of the term 'disease of the mind'. This term is an outdated one; modern psychiatry thinks more in terms of mental abnormality or mental impairment. Is a 'disease of the mind' any different from a 'disease of the brain'?[1] Do conditions such as epilepsy[2], or more controversially, premenstrual tension,[3] qualify as a disease of the mind, or are they bodily conditions which give rise to behaviourial disturbance?

Then, what is to 'know' the 'nature and quality' of an act? A person might 'know' something without either understanding or appreciating it; if knowledge only of this superficial sort is required then a person who has little real comprehension of the full significance of his action may be held to know what he is doing.[4] The term 'quality' might itself be taken to require a broad or mature understanding of one's actions, but this was not the view taken by the Court of Criminal Appeal in England in *Codere*[5].

(2) Product and control tests. Dissatisfaction with the narrowness of the McNaghten Rules led to the development in the United States of alternative tests, such as that proposed in *Durham v United States*[6]. *Durham*, which was initially welcomed by both lawyers and psychiatrists, soon became unpopular, as was observed in *Washington v United States*[7]:

'The term "product" has no clinical significance for psychiatrists. Thus, there is no justification for permitting psychiatrists to testify on the ultimate issue. Psychiatrists should explain how the defendant's disease or defect relates to his alleged offence, that is, how the development, adaptation and functioning of the defendant's behavioural processes may have influenced his conduct. But psychiatrists should not speak directly in terms of "product" or even "result" or "cause".'

---

impulse was accepted in a number of jurisdictions, alongside the McNaghten Rules, in the late nineteenth century: *Parsons v State* 81 Ala 577, 2 So 854 (1887). Irresistible impulse has yet to have its day in a Scottish court.

[1] An issue discussed in *Kemp* [1957] 1 QB 399, [1956] 3 All ER 249 (arteriosclerosis leading to a diminished supply of blood to the brain).

[2] Particularly relevant in automatism cases: discussed supra.

[3] *R v Smith* [1982] Crim L R 531: the Court of Appeal in England held that automatism is not applicable where premenstrual tension is involved.

[4] There have been attempts to expand the scope of the Rules by reading the knowledge requirement as a requirement of 'appreciation' or 'feeling' of the effect of action on others: *Willgoss* (1960) 105 Crim L R 295.

[5] (1916) 12 Crim App Rep 21.

[6] 214 F 2d 862 (1954).

[7] 390 F 2d 444 (1967).

The next major development in the American test was the drafting in 1962 of the American Law Institute's Model Penal Code test.[1] This test made the defence available where, 'as a result of mental disease or defect [the defendant] lacks substantial capacity either to appreciate the criminality (wrongfulness) of his conduct or to conform his conduct to the requirements of law'.[2] The ALI test was widely adopted, either through legislation or by the courts themselves, and for a considerable period this test, in one form or another, represented the American consensus on the issue. Political opinion was to change, however, and in response to one particularly controversial insanity acquittal,[3] federal legislation returned to a modified version of the McNaghten Rules, providing that the defence of insanity is available 'at the time of the commission of the acts constituting the offence, the defendant, as a result of a severe mental disease or defect, was unable to appreciate the nature or quality or the wrongfulness of his acts'.[4] This represented a victory for those who argued that there were no means of assessing capacity to conform to norms of behaviour; volition, therefore, which had been so criticised over the years, returned to the centre of the stage.

At state level the dissatisfaction with what was seen as an easy escape for those who could afford to pay impressive psychiatric witnesses, led in a number of states to the total abolition of the defence of insanity,[5] leaving the issue to be determined according to the ordinary rules of *mens rea*.[6] The main objection to this approach is that it could be unduly restrictive: the *mens rea* requirement of intention might well be absent in a person whose understanding of reality is grossly distorted, but could still be satisfied in the case of a person who has a clear idea of what he is doing but whose motivation is grossly affected by mental illness.

The American experience indicates the difficulty of effecting satisfactory reform in this area of criminal law. The McNaghten Rules are undoubtedly limiting, but it is clearly no simple matter to find alternatives once a system is committed to stating specific criteria for non-responsibility on the grounds of mental abnormality. The English Law Commission's proposed code of

---

[1] Section 4.01, ALI Model Penal Code.
[2] Section 4.02, ALI Model Penal Code specifically excludes psychopathy from the category of 'mental disease or defect'.
[3] That of John Hinkley, who attempted the assassination of President Reagan.
[4] Insanity Defence Reform Act 1984. 18 USC, s 20(a).
[5] Brooks 'The merits of abolishing the insanity defence' (1985) 477 Annals of the American Academy of Political and Social Science 125.
[6] For a survey of American developments, see RD Mackay 'Post-Hinkley insanity in the USA' [1984] Crim LR 88.

criminal law abandons the search for those aspects of mental illness which are exculpatory, stating that the defence will be available when it is proved on a balance of probabilities that the defendant was suffering from severe mental illness or severe subnormality.[1] This test requires no causal connection between the illness and the criminal behaviour, in line with the Butler Commission's view that such a connection may be assumed.[2] The Scottish test, although couched in language that has not changed in 200 years, at least has the merit of not tying the court to any but the broadest criteria. As a test of responsibility, however, it is a blunt instrument and will almost always deny a defence to those whose mental illness may not deprive them of reason (whatever that might mean) but whose responsibility could well be questionable. Currently such persons are to be found in prisons in large numbers.[3] It is at least arguable that they would not have offended had they not suffered from a psychiatric condition. We are therefore confronted with the objection that such people are being punished for something they could not help. There may, of course, be no alternative; perhaps prisons are the appropriate place for those who cannot otherwise be treated.

Diminished responsibility

The effect of diminished responsibility in Scots law is restricted to a reduction of a charge of murder to one of culpable homicide.[4] It is therefore not a defence but a mitigating plea, akin in its effect to the plea of provocation.

   The origins of the doctrine precede its recognition in the important case of *Dingwall*[5], a decision which is commonly regarded as its foundation in modern practice. *Mackenzie* argues for the moderation of the punishment for those who are not 'absolutely mad yet

---

[1] Law Commission, Draft Criminal Code Bill (1989) (Law Commission No 177) Clause 35.

[2] But see E Griew 'Let's implement Butler on mental disorder and crime!' (1984) 31 Current Legal Problems 47.

[3] See discussion by A Ashworth and J Shapland 'Psychopaths in the Criminal Process' [1980] Crim L R 628.

[4] There has been some disagreement as to whether it was available in other cases: T B Smith 'Diminished responsibility in Scots law' [1957] Crim LR 354, reproduced in *Studies Critical and Comparative*, p 241. See, however, N Walker *Crime and Insanity in England* I, 144. Lord Clyde put the matter beyond doubt, at least for modern law, in *HM Adv v Cunningham* 1963 JC 80, 1963 SLT 345, when he said '[diminished responsibility] is not open in the case of a lesser crime such as culpable homicide'.

[5] (1867) 5 Irv 466.

are hypochondrick and melancholy to such a degree that it clouds their reason ...'[1] *Hume*, however, was less enthusiastic:

'As to the inferior degrees of derangement, or natural weakness of intellect, which do not amount to madness and for which there can be no rule in law: the relief of these must be sought either in the discretion of the prosecutor, who may restrict his libel to an ordinary pain, or in the course of application to the King for mercy ...'[2]

In a number of nineteenth-century cases the accused's mental state was accepted as grounds for recommendations for mercy,[3] but it was not until the decision in *Dingwall*[4] that the practice was established of returning a verdict of culpable homicide rather than murder in those cases in which responsibility was thought to be diminished. Although the courts were generally sympathetic to the concept of diminished responsibility, by the beginning of the twentieth century a degree of judicial scepticism had set in.[5] In *HM Adv v Savage*[6] the High Court gave a direction on the nature of diminished responsibility which has come to be regarded as the authoritative statement of the modern law:

'... it has been put in this way: there must be aberration or weakness of mind; that there must be some form of mental unsoundness; that there must be a state of mind bordering on, though not amounting to, insanity; that there must be a mind so affected that responsibility is diminished from full responsibility to partial responsibility – in other words, the prisoner in question must only be partially accountable for his actions. And I think one can see running through the cases that there is implied ... that there must be some form of mental disease.'[7]

Subsequent cases have confirmed the *Savage* definition. In *HM Adv v Blake*[8] Lord Brand said in his instructions to the jury:

'A man may suffer from some infirmity or aberration of mind or impairment of the intellect to such an extent as to render him not fully accountable in law for his actions. Such a man is described as being a man of diminished responsibility. If he has not been fully responsible for what he has done, he is guilty not of attempted murder but of assault ...

A man is not of diminished responsibility unless there is aberration or

---

[1] *The Laws and Customs of Scotland in Matters Criminal* I, 1–8.
[2] I, 44.
[3] For example *Jas Scott* (1853) 1 Irv 132; *Alex Carr* (1854) 1 Irv 464. For further instances, and comment, see *Gordon* paras 11–11, 11–12.
[4] (1867) 5 Irv 466.
[5] For example *HM Adv v Aitken* (1902) 4 Adam 88.
[6] 1923 JC 49, 1923 SLT 659.
[7] 1923 JC 49 at 51.
[8] 1986 SLT 661.

weakness of mind. There must be some unsoundness of mind bordering on but not amounting to insanity. There must be some sort of mental illness.

Any slight departure from the normal make-up of a man will not do. One must distinguish between something in the nature of a mental disease and a vicious tendency, between the mentally sick and the morally bad.'[1]

The requirement that there must be some form of mental illness before diminished responsibility can be established was considered at length in *Connelly v HM Adv.*[2] None of the psychiatrists who gave evidence in this case were able to diagnose any form of mental illness, although one called for the defence was of the view that the accused suffered from a personality disorder. It was agreed for the defence, however, that the criteria suggested in the instruction of Lord Alness in *Savage* (excerpted above) should be read as alternatives rather than cumulatively. This would have the effect of allowing diminished responsibility when it could be established that there is 'a mind so affected that responsibility is diminished from full responsibility to partial responsibility'. Evidence from a defence psychiatrist was rejected by the court as worthless, on the grounds that he was expressing himself on precisely the matter which it was for the jury to decide.

It will not therefore be enough for an accused to be described as immature, inadequate, or lacking in self control. In the absence of clear evidence of a mental disorder or mental disease, the criteria stated in *Savage* will not be met. Although this clarifies the situation, in that it indicates what is the minimum that psychiatric witnesses will be required to assert, it leaves the boundaries of the defence unclear in so far as it does not define mental disorder or disease. The court in *Connelly* cited with approval the observation of Lord Justice-Clerk Cooper in *HM Adv v Braithwaite*[3] to the effect that in cases of diminished responsibility stress has been laid upon 'weakness of intellect, aberration of mind, mental unsoundness, partial insanity, great peculiarity of mind, and the like'.

Non-age

There is an irrebutable presumption that a child under the age of eight cannot be guilty of a criminal offence.[4] This age seems re-

---

[1] At 662.
[2] 1990 SCCR 504.
[3] 1945 JC 55, 1945 SLT 209.
[4] Criminal Procedure (Scotland) Act 1975, ss 170, 369. *Merrin v S* 1987 SLT 193.

markably low,[1] but the apparent severity of the law is at least mitigated by the requirement that the Lord Advocate should consent to the prosecution of any child who has reached the age of eight but who is not yet sixteen. Offenders under the age of sixteen are normally dealt with under the children's hearing system.[2]

If an offender under the age of sixteen is prosecuted, his youth should be taken into account in determining *mens rea* questions.[3] This might have a bearing not only on whether he was capable of forming the necessary intention for the commission of the crime, but also on matters such as error.

SELF-DEFENCE

The special defence of self-defence is available for acts which are done in defence of self, of others,[4] and, in some cases, of property. The basic principle here is that a person is entitled to use force to prevent harm to interests and that the use of force, if it falls within the boundaries of the defence, is justified. Self-defence is therefore a matter of justification rather than excuse. The defence is broad in its scope. Most of the cases are concerned with homicide, but the plea has been recognised as a defence to a charge of assault and, recently, to one of breach of the peace.[5] The effect of a successful defence of this nature will be the complete acquittal of the accused.

For a long period Scots law was plagued by confusion between provocation and self-defence, and it was necessary for the courts to spell out the distinction, first in *Crawford v HM Adv*[6], and again in *Fenning v HM Adv*.[7] The origins of this confusion are to be found in *Hume*'s division of self-defence into those situations where the

---

[1] In England the age of criminal responsibility is ten: Children and Young Persons Act 1933, s 50 as amended by the Act of the same name of 1963. In English law, a child aged ten but under fourteen is rebuttably incapable of the *mens rea* necessary for any offence: *J M (A Minor) v Runeckles* [1984] Crim App Rep 255. In Germany the age of criminal responsibility is fourteen; in France, thirteen.

[2] Established under the Social Work (Scotland) Act 1968, Part III. These proceedings are not criminal prosecutions.

[3] As suggested by *Gane and Stoddart* p 284.

[4] *Jones v HM Adv* 1989 SCCR 726, 1990 SLT 517 at 524 per Lord Justice-Clerk Ross: 'Self-defence covers the situation where a man acts in order to defend his own person from or in defence of persons other than himself'.

[5] *Derrett v Lockhart* 1991 SCCR 109.

[6] 1950 JC 67, 1950 SLT 279.

[7] 1985 JC 76, 1985 SCCR 219.

accused was responding to an unprovoked attack and those situations where the accused was involved in a quarrel.[1] In many cases, of course, counsel may wish to advance both provocation and self-defence as alternative pleas. This might be desirable where the accused has responded to an attack on himself with excessive force. Self-defence may be ruled out in such a case on the grounds of, for instance, the accused's ability to retreat from the threat, but the original attack may still constitute the basis of a successful provocation plea. In such a case, however, the issues of self-defence and provocation must be considered by the jury as separate matters.

Killing in self-defence: the requirements of the defence

The defence will be available in a charge of murder or culpable homicide provided the following requirements are met:

(1) There must be an imminent danger to life

The courts have consistently stressed that if self-defence is to be allowed the accused must have been faced with a threat to his life or, in the case of a woman, a threat of rape.[2] The requirement that life be threatened will mean that the defence will not be available where the accused has taken life in the belief that he is physically threatened but that he is not in danger of death.[3]

There are obvious policy reasons why self-defence should be excluded where the accused has intentionally taken his attacker's life merely to avoid some relatively slight harm to himself, but these reasons do not apply with the same force to one who intentionally kills in order to avoid serious physical harm. The current formula, of course, may allow this by permitting any serious injury to be considered a threat to life. Any use of a weapon, for example, is potentially life-threatening, and an accused would normally be justified in thinking his life to be in danger if an attack involved the use of a knife.[4]

It is clear that the requirement that there should have been a

---

[1] I, 217. For discussion, see PW Ferguson *Crimes Against the Person* (1990) p 48.

[2] *Crawford v HM Adv*, supra; *Jones v HM Adv*, supra.

[3] Lord Clyde was adamant on this point in *McCluskey v HM Adv* 1959 JC 39, 1959 SLT 215 where he stated: '...I can see no justification at all for extending this defence to a case where there is no apprehension of danger to the accused's life.'

[4] *Owens v HM Adv* 1946 JC 119 at 125, 1946 SLT 227; cf *Jones v HM Adv* 1989 SCCR 726, 1990 SLT 517 at 524.

threat to the accused's life cannot apply in cases of culpable homicide. If **A** is attacked by **B** and strikes him to ward off what is obviously no more than a minor attack, and if **B** then falls and strikes his head on the concrete (with fatal results), it would be unacceptable to deny **A** the defence.

The threat must be an immediate one rather than one which is to be put into effect at some vague point in the future. The notion of a pre-emptive blow is probably inapplicable in this context, as in such situations the person under threat will normally be able to avoid the danger by retreating or by reporting the threat to the authorities.

(2) An erroneous belief that life is threatened

A person who is subjected to an attack may reach the conclusion that life is threatened although, in reality, it is not. The issue arose in *Owens v HM Adv*[1] in which the appellant had been convicted of the murder of an attacker whom he mistakenly believed to be armed with a knife. The court held that the essential question in such a case was not whether the attacker was really armed with a knife but whether the appellant genuinely believed that he was so armed. The belief, although mistaken, must be based on reasonable grounds. In *Crawford*[2] the court reiterated the requirement of reasonableness, pointing out that 'when self-defence is supported by a mistaken belief rested on reasonable grounds, that mistaken belief must have an objective background and must not be purely subjective or of the nature of an hallucination'.[3] A similar endorsement of the subjective requirement is made in *Jones*[4], where self-defence was held to be justifiable if 'reasonably apprehended'.[5] The test is therefore whether a reasonable person in the position of the accused would have concluded that his life was in danger. An erroneous conclusion that the attacker is concealing a weapon, or an erroneous conclusion of homicidal intent will not preclude the defence, provided that there are reasonable grounds for the reaching of these conclusions.

The decision in *Meek and Ors v HM Adv*[6], which allowed a defence of unreasonable error in rape, might have been taken as allowing unreasonable error in this context too, but *Jones*, with its

[1] 1946 JC 119, 1946 SLT 227.
[2] 1950 JC 67, 1950 SLT 279.
[3] 1950 JC 67 at 71.
[4] 1989 SCCR 726.
[5] At 525 per Lord Wylie.
[6] 1982 SCCR 613, 1983 SLT 280.

insistence on reasonableness, appears to preclude this. There is certainly a case for abandoning the requirement that the accused's belief in the danger to his life should be reasonable, as the person who acts under genuine, though unreasonable, error is as morally blameless as one who draws an erroneous, but still resonable conclusion. English law now prefers this approach,[1] and the Privy Council accepted it in *Beckford v R*.[2] There has been some support for this view in Australia, although reasonableness was still required by the High Court in *Zecevic v DPP of Victoria*.[3]

Scots law allows self-defence where a woman kills in defence against rape. This appears in *Hume*[4], in *Alison*,[5] and was endorsed by Lord Clyde in *McCluskey v HM Adv*.[6] The exception does not extend to threatened sodomy – the point at issue in *McCluskey* – even if it appears outdated and illogical to allow killing to prevent one form of non-consensual penetration but not another.[7]

(3) The danger must have been inescapable

Hume states that self-defence is available where 'the party has other ways of escape from the assault, or some sure and easy means of putting an end to it; but where, out of pride, or humour, or some false notion of dishonour in the thing, he chooses rather to stand and repel the violence'.[8] This possibility of retreat was discussed in *HM Adv v Doherty*[9]; there the accused had an open door and stairs behind him but made no effort to use them. The means of escape, of course, must be reasonably available and not involve the accused in exposing himself to undue danger.[10]

(4) The force used must not be excessive

A person who comes under attack from another is entitled to use only that degree of force which is reasonably necessary to repel the

---

[1] *Gladstone Williams* (1984) 78 Crim App Rep 276, [1987] 3 All ER 411; *Asbury* [1986] Crim LR 258.

[2] [1987] 3 All ER 425, [1988] AC 130.

[3] (1987) 71 ALR 641.

[4] I, 218.

[5] I, 132

[6] 1959 JC 39, 1959 SLT 215.

[7] The decision in *McCluskey* was followed in *Elliott v HM Adv* 1987 SCCR 278, where the accused alleged that he killed his victim to protect himself against a homosexual assault.

[8] I, 226.

[9] 1954 JC 1, 1954 SLT 169.

[10] A duty to retreat is not required in English law: *R v McInnes* [1971] 1 WLR 1600, [1971] 3 All ER 295; *R v Bird* (1985) 81 Crim App Rep 110, [1985] 1 WLR 816 Australia; *Zecevic v DPP* (1987) 71 ALR 641; *R v Howe* (1958) 100 CLR 448.

attack.[1] A person who is the victim of an attack will not be able to judge to a nicety the degree of violence that is used, and the courts will take into account the exigencies of the situation when assessing the reaction of an attack. In *HM Adv v Doherty*[2] for example, Lord Keith instructed the jury: 'You do not need an exact proportion of injury and retaliation; it is not a matter that you must weigh in too fine scales ...'[3] An accused person may therefore use excessive force not because he wishes to do undue harm to his assailant but because he has, in his excitement, miscalculated the amount of force required to protect himself.

The use of grossly excessive force, or a 'cruel excess of force' will exclude self-defence.[4] The proposition advanced in *HM Adv v Kizileviczius*[5] that the use of excessive force will result in the reduction of the offence from murder to culpable homicide is not supported by recent authority.[6] It may be that in such a case provocation will be found which has this effect, but the issue of provocation is to be judged separately from that of self-defence.

For some decades the Australian courts applied a doctrine of excessive defence, the effect of which was to reduce murder to manslaughter when the accused used excessive force to defend himself. The decision of the Australian High Court in *R v Howe*[7], which established this rule, was not well received abroad,[8] and was eventually abandoned in Australia itself.[9]

Self-defence and lawful force

A person is not entitled to defend himself against lawful force. The defence is therefore not available to one who defends himself against lawful arrest or against any other application of lawful force by officers of the law.

The fact that the accused started a quarrel will not mean that the defence is not available to him. For example, if **A** insults **B**, who

---

[1] *Moore v MacDougall* 1989 SCCR 659: the accused stabbed the victim in the buttocks with a pair of scissors after he (the victim) had assaulted her. It was held that this was excessive, given the moderate nature of the assault.
[2] 1954 JC 1, 1954 SLT 169.
[3] See, too, *Fenning v HM Adv* 1985 SCCR 219, 1985 JC 76.
[4] Ibid
[5] 1938 JC 60, 1938 SLT 245.
[6] See *Fenning*, supra.
[7] (1958) 100 CLR 448.
[8] *Palmer v R* [1971] 1 All ER 1077 (PC), [1971] AC 814.
[9] For discussion see: S Yeo 'The demise of excessive self-defence in Australia' (1988) 37 Int Comp L Q 348.

then picks up a weapon and threatens **A** with it, **A** is entitled to defend himself against **B** although he has brought the attack upon himself. The same would apply if **A** struck **B**, provoking him to retaliate. The situation is different, however, if **A** assaults **B**, who then uses force to defend himself against **A**'s attack. **A** is not entitled to defend himself against **B**'s act of self-defence unless **B**'s response is excessive, in which case **B** is no longer acting in self-defence.

One might think that such situations rarely come before the courts, but one did so in *R v Lawson and Forsyth*[1]. Here **L** and **F** were convicted of shooting **V** after **L** had approached **V**, carrying a shotgun. **V**, who had good reason to fear that **L** intended to kill him, drew a revolver and fired a number of shots. **L** argued that he had killed **V** in self-defence, having abandoned any homicidal intention towards **V**. This argument was rejected on the grounds that a change of mind on **L**'s part would need to have been unambiguously signalled to **V** before **L** would be entitled to act in self-defence; at the time of the killing of **V**, **L** was still the aggressor.

Defence of property

There is scant Scottish authority on the legitimacy or otherwise of the use of force in defence of property.[2] In principle, the use of moderate force to prevent damage to one's property or to prevent it being stolen, should be acceptable. It is difficult to imagine a court convicting of assault one who pushes away a thief who tries to steal his wallet. Similarly, a person who hits out at a robber who attempts to snatch his watch off his wrist should not be held to have committed assault. Such cases must be distinguished, however, from a situation where a householder, on surprising a housebreaker in his house, assaults him severely with a golf club or other weapon. This is immoderate force, more than is required to defend property, and should rightly be treated as assault.

Killing in defence of property is implicitly excluded by the judgment in *HM Adv v McCluskey*[3], which limits homicide in self-defence to those cases where life is threatened. The setting of a

---

[1] [1986] VR 515. See also *Viro v R* (1978) 141 Crim LR 88.
[2] *Donald Kennedy* (1838) 2 Swin 213 at 231–232. Bell's *Principles*, p 2032. For English law, see *Smith and Hogan*, p 246. Some writers suggest that the use of force is particularly justified if the aggressor enters one's home: A Ashworth *Principles of Criminal Law*, (1991) p 118. For general discussion, see D Lanham 'Defence of property in the criminal law' [1966] Crim LR, 368 426.
[3] 1959 JC 39, 1959 SLT 215.

man-trap for housebreakers would therefore not be permissible, no matter what the frequency of housebreakings suffered by the householder has been. It is submitted, though, that it should not be culpable homicide if the accused has caused the death of another as a result of the moderate use of force in the defence of property.

NECESSITY AND COERCION

Necessity is a matter of justification: one who raises a successful defence of necessity does not commit an *actus reus* – what he did was a lawful thing to do. The defence is recognised in many legal systems in one form or another,[1] but it has only been directly addressed by the Scottish courts comparatively recently. There are now three recent decisions in which the question of necessity is raised. In *Tudhope v Grubb*[2], a sheriff court decision, the accused drove a vehicle with an excess of alcohol in his blood and argued, successfully, that necessity justified his doing this in order to escape a threat of physical violence. A similar threat was made in *MacLeod v MacDougall*[3] and *McNab v Guild*[4]. In the former case the accused, who was threatened by an aggressive group outside an hotel in which he proposed to spend the night, drove off to escape the threat. He drove past a police car parked further down the road and the court held that even if a defence of necessity was available to the charge of driving with an excess of alcohol (which it did not decide) the necessity had passed once the accused encountered a police car. In *McNab* the accused reversed his car out of a car park at speed in order to escape a threat. Necessity was argued as a defence to a charge of reckless driving but the court held that even if such a defence were available (a point which was not argued) these were not circumstances in which it would apply.

The fact that the High Court declined to settle the matter of whether a defence of necessity is available in Scots law means that the question remains unresolved. The institutional writers do not discuss the matter (other than as a ground for mitigation of punish-

---

[1] There is some controversy as to its status in English law: Glanville Williams is confident that the defence exists: *Criminal Law: The General Part* (2nd edn, 1961), p 724, but cf PR Glazebrook, 'The necessity plea in English criminal law' [1972] Camb L J 87. See also EB Arnolds and NM Garland 'The defence of necessity in criminal law: the right to choose the lesser evil' (1974) 65 J Crim Law and Criminology 259.

[2] 1983 SCCR 350.

[3] 1988 SCCR 519, 1989 SLT 151.

[4] 1989 SCCR 138.

ment) but the overwhelming weight of modern opinion in other jursidictions is that such a defence exists. Principle, too, requires the recognition of necessity: it would be remarkable if a modern system of criminal jurisprudence were to convict of a criminal offence one who, say, destroyed property in order to prevent the spread of fire to a heavily-occupied building. Conviction in such a case would be an example of legal formalism at its worst, would serve no purpose, and would undoubtedly bring the criminal law into disrepute. It is proposed, therefore, to assume in the following discussion that a defence of necessity exists in Scots law even if the authority for this proposition may be reduced to a single sheriff court decision.[1]

The nature of the necessity defence

The defence of necessity is available where the accused acts in a way which is prima facie criminal in order to avoid the occurrence of a greater evil. The driver who drives at a high speed in order to deliver a seriously-ill person to hospital commits a road traffic offence but does so only to save the life of his passenger. An obsessively law-abiding person may refuse to drive in excess of the speed limit even in such circumstances, but that would not be reasonable conduct on his part. A more balanced assessment of the situation would be that necessity justified driving at speed in such a case. Similarly, a miner who has to chop off the finger of a trapped workmate in order to remove him from a tunnel which is about to collapse does not commit assault but is justified in what he does by necessity.

The wrongful act committed by the accused must be more than the evil which it seeks to avoid. This means that a person who feels that he is facing a situation of necessity will have to weigh for himself the relative merits of his avoiding action on the one hand and the evil which is threatened on the other. The standard to be applied here is that of the reasonable man.

The making of such a judgment will not always be simple. There may be little doubt that damaging property in order to save human life is justified by necessity, but the same may not be said about those cases where there is an apparent equivalence of values. A doctor who is responsible for a dementing patient may be of the view that necessity justifies the treatment of the patient even in the absence of the patient's consent and in the face of possible opposition to treatment on the patient's part; but is the value of ensuring the patient's comfort or health necessarily preferable to the value of

---

[1] For further discussion see W Ferguson 'Necessity and duress in Scots law' [1986] Crim L R 103.

protecting people from non-consensual treatment ? This question is not easily answered.

Necessity must be urgent and pressing. Necessity does not justify unlawful action to prevent an occurrence which may be avoided by other means. In *R v Loughnan*[1] the accused argued that his escape from prison was justified by necessity, as he feared that he was to be murdered in prison. This was not accepted, as it would have been possible for him to seek the protection of the authorities through transfer to another part of the prison or otherwise.

The question of whether necessity justifies the taking of life has long been a textbook problem which has attracted more attention than it in reality merits. The issue has arisen, however, in one or two well-known cases, most notably in *R v Dudley and Stephens*[2]. This case, which was a Victorian cause célèbre involved the prosecution for murder of two shipwrecked sailors who, in desperation, killed and ate the cabin boy. They were convicted of murder on the grounds that necessity did not justify the taking of life in such circumstances, although the court did recognise that in so deciding, it was imposing a standard of forebearance which even a judge may find difficulty in meeting. Behind the refusal to allow the defence in this case was a concern on the part of the court that to admit the defence might be to open the way to 'unbridled passion and atrocious crime', though this policy-based objection is really not as weighty as the objection that nobody has the right to take the life of another for whatever reason, even a well-motivated one. A similar view had been taken by an American court in another shipwreck case, *US v Holmes*[3] in which the court took the view that sailors in an overloaded lifeboat should not have thrown passengers overboard to prevent the boat sinking but should have sacrificed themselves first. In modern times, the debate as to whether a defence of coercion or duress should be available where murder has been committed raises precisely the same issues, and is discussed below.

Coercion

The defence of coercion is more clearly established in Scots law than is the defence of necessity. In many respects the defences are similar, the only real differences being the source of the threat (in coercion it comes from another person; in necessity it usually

---

[1] [1981] VR 443.
[2] (1884) 14 QBD 273. The case, and its background, is discussed by AWB Simpson *Cannabalism and the common law* (1984).
[3] 26 Fed Cases 360 (1841).

comes from events) and the fact that in coercion the threat is always to the life or physical integrity of the accused.

The defence of coercion may be raised by one who commits a criminal act in order to save himself (and possibly others) from physical violence. The defence was recognised by *Hume*[1], and receives its modern definition in *Thomson v HM Adv*.[2] In this case the accused contended that he had taken part in an armed robbery only because he feared for his safety should he refuse to do so. The court emphasised that the threat must be an immediate one, and it took the opportunity to endorse the other three qualifications stated by *Hume*: that there must be an inability to resist the violence; that the accused must take a secondary part in the crime (described by *Hume* as a 'backward and inferior part'); and that the accused must do his best to disclose the offence and make amends when it first becomes safe to do so. These requirements were not said to be absolutes, but they were held to be guidelines as to what was required to make the defence a live issue.

It is likely that the courts would not allow the defence where the accused's reaction to the threat was an unreasonable one. The threat should be one which would cause fear in a person of reasonable firmness, and an excessively cowardly reaction to a threat would not justify the defence.[3] The accused should therefore have good reason to believe that the person making the threat will do as he says he will do.[4] The fact that the accused is responsible for putting himself in a position where he will be subject to coercion to commit criminal acts will probably deprive him of the right to the defence. In *R v Sharp*[5] the Court of Appeal in England said that 'where a person has voluntarily, and with knowledge of its nature, joined a criminal organisation or gang which he knew might bring pressure on him to commit an offence and was an active member when he was put under such pressure, he cannot avail himself of the defence of duress'.[6] It would seem reasonable to suggest in such cases that the accused should have known of the gang's violent nature; a person who joins a gang of pickpockets may not expect suddenly to be coerced into committing armed robbery.

The defence of coercion would probably be denied to an accused who kills under threat to himself. Apart from *obiter* remarks, there

---

[1] I, 52.

[2] 1983 SCCR 368; 1983 JC 69.

[3] For dicussion, see P Alldridge, 'Duress and the reasonable person' (1983) 34 N I L Q 125

[4] *R v Graham* [1982] 1 All ER 801, [1982] 1 WLR 294.

[5] [1987] 1 QB 853, [1987] 3 All ER 103.

[6] [1987] 1 QB 853 at 861. Also see *R v Shepherd* (1987) 86 Crim App Rep 47.

is no modern Scottish authority on the matter; *Hume* does not appear to exclude it.[1] The House of Lords considered the matter in *DPP v Lynch*[2], and the Privy Council in *R v Abbott*[3] ruled that the defence was not available in cases of murder. It was not until the decision in *R v Howe and Oths*[4] that the position in English law was made clear by the House of Lords that those who take the life of others under duress will have no defence. A Scottish court might well follow this, although *Howe* has been the subject of some criticism.[5]

[1] PW Ferguson takes the view that *Hume* denies that the defence will be available where the crime committed is an 'atrocious' one: *Crimes against the Person* (1989), p 77. The opposite reading of the relevant passage of *Hume* is possible, however: 1, 52. In his directions to the jury in *Collins v HM Adv* 1991 SCCR 898, Lord Allanbridge stated that '. . .it is repugnant that the law should recognise in any individual in any circumstances however extreme the right to choose that one innocent person should be killed rather than any other person including himself' (at 902).

[2] [1975] AC 653, [1975] 1 All ER 913.

[3] [1977] AC 755, [1976] 3 All ER 140 (an appeal from Trinidad and Tobago).

[4] [1987] AC 417, [1987] 1 All ER 771.

[5] See, for example, P Alldridge, 'Duress, murder and the House of Lords' (1988) 52 JCL 186; L Walters, 'Murder and duress and judicial decision-making in the House of Lords' (1988) 8 Legal Studies 61.

II. OFFENCES AGAINST THE PERSON

9. Assault

The crime of assault consists of an attack on the person of another. An attack is an application of force which may involve (i) a direct physical onslaught, involving the use of the body or a weapon; or (ii) the use of indirect means; or (iii) the use of physically-threatening gestures.

Most assaults fall into the first category. Examples would be administering blows with the fists, beating with a weapon of some sort, kicking, stabbing etc.[1] The degree of violence used may be slight, and it is not necessary that any appreciable degree of injury be caused. Assault may even be by liquid or gas: spitting at a person is an assault,[2] as would the directing at another of a high pressure air hose.

Indirect assaults occur when events are deliberately set in motion with the intention of causing harm or fear of harm. In *David Keay*[3] the accused whipped a pony being ridden by the victim, causing the pony to rear up and throw its rider. This was considered an assault. If injury is caused by the victim's response to some wrongful action on the part of the accused, then that is assault. A person who seeks to escape from a situation which he considers threatening, and who causes himself injury in the course of the escape, may be considered to have been assaulted by the person who caused the attempt at escape.[4]

The use of physically-threatening gestures is an assault. The victim must anticipate harm to himself, and this anticipation must be reasonable. The shaking of a finger at another is unlikely to cause fear or alarm in a reasonable person, and is therefore not an assault.[5] The

---

[1] *Hume* refers to the various colourful terms used in his time, including: invasion, beating and bruising, blooding and wounding, stabbing, mutilation, and demembration (I, 328).

[2] *Jas Cairns & Ors* (1837) 1 Swin 597 at 610.

[3] (1837) 1 Swin 543.

[4] *R v Roberts* (1971) 56 Crim App Rep 95; *People v Goodman* (1943) 44 NYS 2d 715 – discussed by HLA Hart and AM Honore *Causation in the Law* (2nd edn, 1985) pp 330–331.

[5] It may be different if the accused knew of the undue timorousness of the victim: *Macpherson v Beath* (1975) 12 SASR 174 at 177.

pointing of a gun will, however, have precisely that effect,[1] unless the victim knows that the weapon is unloaded or is an imitation firearm. Even then an unloaded weapon or imitation firearm can cause some apprehension, and it is possible to imagine circumstances in which the brandishing of an unloaded firearm is alarming.

In *Atkinson v HM Adv*[2] the appellant had been found guilty of jumping over the counter in a shop, wearing a face mask. Lord Justice-Clerk Ross held that this was sufficient to constitute an assault:

'assault may be constituted by threatening gestures sufficient to produce alarm. For someone with his face masked to come into a shop and jump over a counter towards the cashier in the shop, in our opinion, could constitute assault according to the law of Scotland . . .'[3]

It is not clear whether the victim has to be aware of the threatening gesture. It has been suggested that pointing a gun at another's back should be assault;[4] this is not, however, a 'threatening gesture sufficient to produce alarm', at least not at the time at which the gun is pointed. Is subsequently experienced, or delayed alarm, experienced later, sufficient? If the victim learns ten minutes afterwards that **A** pointed a gun at his back, he may well experience fear or alarm, even though the danger has passed. Certainly the impact to his psyche may be as great as if he had witnessed it personally. The same question arises in relation to threatening gestures directed towards a sleeping person.

The use of threatening words is not in itself sufficient to constitute an assault. Threats are discussed further below.[5]

LAWFUL FORCE

Not all applications of physical force amount to an assault. Force will be lawful in the following circumstances, provided always that it is reasonable and not excessive.

---

[1] *Hume* I, 443.
[2] 1987 SCCR 534.
[3] At 535.
[4] *Gane and Stoddart* p 385.
[5] At p 150.

(1) Lawful chastisement

Parents are entitled to apply reasonable force[1] to their minor children in order to control and discipline them.[2] This power may be delegated to a teacher[3] or other person having temporary control of the child.

A school teacher has a common law right, indeed part of the parent's right,[4] to chastise children within a school. As a result of the decision in *Campbell and Cosans v United Kingdom*[5] corporal punishment is in practice no longer used in local authority schools.

A parent or teacher must not be motivated by malice or ill will in the use of force. Corporal punishment of a child for the purpose of sexual gratification will constitute an assault, as will excessive punishment. In *Gray v Hawthorn*[6] a teacher was convicted of assault after a series of slaps with a tawse administered to a young boy over the course of a school day in circumstances redolent of what the court described as 'unjust persecution'.

(2) Force in restraint of others

Reasonable force may be used on others by those whose position requires them to use such force for the securing of a necessary degree of compliance. The prison officer who uses force to prevent a recalcitrant prisoner from blocking a gangway does not thereby commit an assault, and force may be required to be used by staff of psychiatric hospitals to protect patients or secure compliance with treatment.[7] The latter case poses particularly difficult issues. In general, it is clearly undesirable for nurses in psychiatric hospitals to use force on their patients, and yet there may be circumstances in

---

[1] A parent has no right to use excessive force: *Peebles v McPhail* 1989 SCCR 410, 1990 SLT 245: child of two slapped on face and knocked over – excessive. The fact that the mother acted in anger was taken into account in inferring evil intent. Also *B v Harris* 1990 SLT 208.

[2] A right which has survived the European Court of Human Rights decision in *Campbell and Cosans v United Kingdom* (1982) 4 EHRR 293.

[3] *Stewart v Thain* 1981 JC 13, 1981 SLT (Notes) 2.

[4] *McShane v Paton* 1922 JC 26, 1922 SLT 251.

[5] (1982) 4 EHRR 293. This decision of the ECHR provided that parental rights under the European Convention of Human Rights are violated by the infliction of corporal punishment on their children against their (the parent's) wishes. See also Education (No 2) Act 1986, s 48, enacting a new s 48A of the Education (Scotland) Act 1980.

[6] 1964 JC 69.

[7] *Skinner v Robertson* 1980 SLT (Sh Ct) 43; *Norman v Smith* 1983 SCCR 100.

which a slight degree of force may be needed to break a cycle of hysterical behaviour or to prevent further disruption.[1] This was recognised in *Skinner v Robertson*[2], although it is clear that the court was concerned strictly to limit the extent of this right. In that case the justification for allowing such force was held to be s 107 of the Mental Health (Scotland) Act 1960 (now s 122 of the Mental Health (Scotland) Act 1984). The principle of necessity might be involved in these cases; this principle has recently been given significant endorsement by the House of Lords in *F v West Berkshire Health Authority*[3], a case concerned with the circumstances in which mentally-handicapped patients may be treated without their consent.[4] It is likely that force cannot be used on an informally admitted patient in a psychiatric hospital, the proper response to disruptive behaviour being to ask him or her to leave the hospital.[5] This remedy is clearly unavailable in the case of patients detained under the provisions of the Mental Health (Scotland) Act 1984.

(3) Defence of self, others, or of property

Force used to protect one's own person or the person of another is not assault.[6] The force must not be excessive, and there must be no alternative means of avoiding the danger.[7] The use of force to protect property may be lawful, but only within very narrow limits. The owner or occupier of property is entitled to use reasonable force to eject a trespasser from the property, although there is little modern authority on this issue.

(4) The prevention of crime

Police officers may use force to effect an arrest or prevent the commission of a crime. The amount of force used must be reasonable in the circumstances.[8] Persons other than police officers are entitled to use reasonable force to detain those whom they see committing serious crimes. There must be good grounds for the making of a

---

[1] *Poutney v Griffiths* [1976] AC 314, [1975] 2 All ER 881.
[2] 1980 SLT (Sh Ct) 43.
[3] [1989] 2 All ER 545, [1990] 2 AC 1.
[4] For further discussion, see p 146 below.
[5] B Hoggett *Mental Health Law* (3rd edn, 1990) p 217.
[6] *H M Adv v Carson* 1964 SLT 21.
[7] The matter is discussed at greater length above at p 128.
[8] *Marchbank v Annan* 1987 SCCR 718; *Bonar v McLeod* 1983 SCCR 161.

so-called 'citizens arrest'[1] and mere suspicion that another has committed an offence will not be sufficient.

THE *MENS REA* OF ASSAULT

The accidental application of force to another is not assault. Conviction for assault requires that the accused should have been motivated by 'evil intent'[2] towards the victim. 'Evil intent' has been described as an 'intention to do bodily injury'[3] or an 'intent to injure and do bodily harm'.[4] It used to be clear that assault could not be committed negligently or recklessly,[5] although the reckless causing of harm to others might be prosecuted as culpable and reckless conduct or as causing real injury.[6] A recent decision of the High Court, however, *Connor v Jessop*[7], now appears to allow conviction for assault where there is no intention to injure the particular victim, but where recklessness was present. In this case the accused was charged with assaulting his victim by throwing a tumbler at her. The tumbler had, in fact, been thrown at another person, but had missed the intended victim and hit a bystander. The accused's conviction for assault was upheld on the grounds that the outcome was something which was 'likely to occur' as a result of the accused's action. This may amount to an adoption of recklessness, or it may be an endorsement of the doctrine of transferred intent. In *Roberts v Hamilton*[8] the accused was charged with assaulting **A** by hitting him with a stick. She had, in fact, intended to

---

[1] *Codona v Cardle* 1989 SCCR 287, 1989 SLT 791. The court in this case approved of the statement in Renton and Brown *Criminal Procedure According to the Law of Scotland* (5th edn, 1983) para 5–19: 'A private citizen is entitled to arrest without warrant for a serious crime he has witnessed, or perhaps where, being the victim of the crime, he has information equivalent to personal observation, as when the fleeing criminal is pointed out to him by an eye-witness.' See also, *Bryans v Guild* 1989 SCCR 569, 1990 JC 51, in which the appellant twisted the arm of a youth he mistakenly took to have been a member of a group throwing objects at his house.

[2] *Macdonald* p 115.

[3] *HM Adv v Phipps* (1905) 4 Adam 616.

[4] *HM Adv v Smart* 1975 SLT 65.

[5] Reckless assault was recognised in English law in *DPP v K (a minor)* [1990] 1 All ER 331, [1990] 1 WLR 1067: the accused poured acid into a hot air drier, not with the intention of causing harm to any person but in order to hide the acid. See, however, *R v Spratt* [1990] 1 WLR 1073, (1990) 91 Crim App Rep 362.

[6] Discussed below at p 148.

[7] 1988 SCCR 624.

[8] 1989 SCCR 240, 1989 SLT 399.

hit **B**, but missed. This was therefore another classic case of *aberratio ictus*, or deflection of the blow. In upholding the conviction for assault, the High Court referred to Hume's comments on *aberratio ictus* in murder: 'If John make a thrust at James, meaning to kill, and George, throwing himself between, receive the thrust, and die, who doubts that John shall answer for it, as if his mortal purpose had fallen on James.' This could be applied equally, the court said, to assault,[1] the doctrine of transferred intent being applicable even in respect of crimes which can only be committed intentionally. The court also endorsed the approach taken by Lord Ross in *Connor*, which, on one reading, amounts to an alternative recklessness approach.

The doctrine of transferred intent has been the subject of some criticism. The principle objection is to the fact that it involves convicting the accused of something which he did not intend to do: if **A** is convicted of assaulting **X** (his blow having been directed at **Y**) then the inference is that he bore evil intent towards **X** (which is not the case). This may indeed be misleading, but at the same time **A** is not being convicted of a crime any greater than that which he intended to commit.

CONSENT

Subject to certain limitations, consent to the application of force will normally be a defence to assault. Thus, an arm-wrestling contest over a table will not be an assault, nor will a physical embrace between two consenting partners. Consent to the infliction of significant harm, however, is a different matter, as demonstrated in the decision in *Smart v HM Adv*[2]. The appellant and his victim agreed to fight one another (to have a 'square-go'), and during the course of the fight the victim was severely punched, beaten, kicked and bitten. The court rejected the contention that a person may consent to the infliction of a certain degree of violence, holding that there is no justification for distinguishing between serious assaults and minor assaults. The real test is whether there is evil intent; once

---

[1] For criticism see 'Assault and recklessness' (contributed) 1989 SLT 357. The author points out that it is not apparent that the relevant passage from *Hume* applies to crimes requiring intention: transferred intent in relation to murder may be unobjectionable on the grounds that recklessness may be a sufficient *mens rea* for murder anyway.

[2] 1975 SLT 65.

there is intent to injure and do bodily harm then the consent of the victim is irrelevant.

The court accepted that there will be circumstances in which the application of force will be legitimate:

If **A** touches **B** in a sexual manner and **B** consents to him doing so (and there is nothing else involved which would constitute a crime under statute or at common law) there is no assault because there is no intention to attack the person of **B**. So, too, if persons engage in sporting activities governed by rules, then, although some form of violence may be involved within the rules, there is no assault because the intention is to engage in the sporting activity and not evilly to do harm to the opponent. But where the whole purpose of the exercise is to inflict physical damage on the opponent in the pursuance of a quarrel, then the evil intent is present, and consent is elided.'

Smart is a problematic decision in that its scope is potentially very wide.[1] It would seem that in Scotland consent will be irrelevant, even where a very minor degree of force is employed, as long as there is an intention to harm.[2] The reference to the context of a quarrel, though, could be restrictive. Does this limit the principle to those situations where the parties have quarrelled, or are quarrels merely illustrative of the sort of circumstances in which an intent to cause harm may arise? The latter interpretation is more likely, in which case any violence, other than in recognised sports amounts to assault. Sado-masochists, who deliver and receive pain for purposes of sexual gratification, commit assault according to the decision in *Smart*, although, in practice, prosecutions in Scotland would be unlikely except when the degree of pain inflicted is excessive and involved a severe beating, mutilation, or wounding.[3]

Sporting violence is acceptable – within the rules. In most sports, violence will be incidental to the main aim of the game but boxing and wrestling are anomalies. The main point of boxing is to inflict pain, though presumably not real harm or damage. There is no suggestion, however, that the boxer assaults his opponent under the *Smart* principle.[4] By contrast, a football player who punches a

---

[1] See GH Gordon 'Consent in assault' (1976) 21 JLSS 168.

[2] In the Canadian case of *R v Dix* (1972) 10 CCC (2d) 324 a 'fair fight' consented to by the participants was held not to involve assault.

[3] In the English case of *Donovan* [1934] 2 KB 498, [1934] All ER Rep 207 the accused was convicted of assault after caning a 17-year-old girl. *R v Brown (Anthony)* [1992] 2 WLR 441 concerned sado-masochistic violence of an extreme sort, which resulted in conviction. The consent of the participants was irrelevant.

[4] The issue was discussed in Australia in *Pallante Stadiums Pty Ltd (No 1)* [1976] VR 331. See also *Attorney General's Ref (No 6 of 1980)* [1981] 1 QB 715, [1981] 2 All ER 1057; *Jones* (1986) 83 Crim App Rep 375.

member of the opposing team during the course of a game, commits an assault on the grounds that such an assault is quite outside the rules of the game.

CONSENT TO MEDICAL TREATMENT

Non-consensual medical treatment is normally a matter for civil action but may, exceptionally, be considered to be an assault. A successful prosecution would require there to have been evil intent on the part of the doctor, and it is difficult to imagine circumstances in which such an intention would be present. In fact, a doctor who proceeds to operate on, say, an unconscious patient whom he knows to be non-consenting would likely be motivated by an excess of paternalistic well-meaning zeal rather than by evil intent. Yet the law should protect the bodily integrity of those who do not wish to be treated, and the Jehovah's Witness who receives blood against his or her will may well feel as wronged as one who is assaulted in a conventional fashion. For this reason, in the unlikely event of a court's considering a charge of this nature, it may decide that intent to perform a procedure on a person in the knowledge that it will cause them distress amounts to evil intent, even if the doctor has therapeutic motives.[1]

AGGRAVATED ASSAULTS

Assaults may be rendered more serious by the presence of an aggravating factor. Aggravation of assault may occur as a result of:

(1) The way in which the assault is committed

An assault with a weapon is more serious than an assault with bare hands. The nature of the weapon may make a difference to the severity of the sentence; assaults with firearms are particularly serious.

---

[1] Civil courts have treated the rights of Jehovah's Witnesses as deserving a high degree of protection. In the Canadian case of *Malette v Shulman* (1990) 67 DLR (4th) 321 damages were awarded against a doctor who infused blood into a Jehovah's Witness: a defence of necessity was unsuccessful.

(2) The consequences of the assault for the victim

It is an aggravation to assault the victim to his severe injury, or to his permanent disfigurement or impairment, or to the danger of his life.[1]

(3) The nature of the victim

Assaults on elderly or infirm victims or on children are aggravated by the victim's nature, as are assaults on the Sovereign, judges, sheriffs, and justices of the peace. It is aggravated assault to assault officers of the law in the execution of their duty.[2] The assault will be aggravated only if the accused knew of the nature of his victim.[3]

(4) Breach of trust

An assault is aggravated by a person who is in a position of trust over his victim.[4]

(5) The place of the assault

The fact that an assault is committed in the High Court or Court of Session may be an aggravating factor. Assaults committed within the victim's own home are known as hamesucken, and treated as aggravated. The term hamesucken has been said to have fallen into disuse, but it is still mentioned from time to time in the courts.

(6) An intention to commit another crime following upon the assault

Assault with intent to commit rape or assault with intent to rob are examples of aggravated assaults in this category.

---

[1] Conviction of assault to the danger of life is competent even if the victim's life was not, in fact, in danger: *Kerr v HM Adv* 1986 SCCR 91. See also, *HM Adv v Thom* (1876) 3 Coup 332.

[2] *Monk v Strathern* 1921 JC 4, 1920 2 SLT 364; *Twycross v Farrell* 1973 SLT (Notes) 85. See also s 41 of the Police (Scotland) Act 1967.

[3] *HM Adv v Martin* (1886) 1 White 297.

[4] *Brown v Hilson* 1924 JC 1, 1924 SLT 35 (teacher); *Alex Findlater and Jas McDougall* (1841) 2 Swin 527 (officer of law on prisoner).

MITIGATION OF ASSAULT

The seriousness with which an assault is viewed may be mitigated by the fact that the accused was provoked. *Hume* suggests that provocation can be a complete defence to a charge of assault,[1] and this view of the matter was endorsed in *Hillan v HM Adv* 1937 JC 53: '... where the provocation is of such a kind as to justify the retaliation, the panel is entitled to be acquitted ...', per Lord Justice-Clerk Aitchison. *Hillan* has attracted no subsequent judicial support, and was criticised in *Crawford v HM Adv*[2]. The safer view is that provocation will not therefore be accepted as a complete defence to a charge of assault,[3] but may serve to mitigate sentence.

As to what constitutes provocation in this context, the courts are unlikely to depart from the standard adopted in homicide cases. The provocation would therefore have to be recent and to have been of a nature which would have caused a reasonable person in the position of the accused to have lost control.

CAUSING OR RISKING INJURY TO OTHERS

Culpable and reckless acts which cause injury to others, or which threaten to do so, are punishable as criminal offences. The *mens rea* requirement is that the accused manifested 'an utter disregard of what the consequences of the act in question may be so far as the public are concerned'.[4] In *RHW v HM Adv*[5] the reckless behaviour consisted of the throwing of a bottle from the fifteenth floor of a block of flats, causing severe injury to a person on the ground below. The accused was aware of the risk, and had been

---

[1] I, 334. Yet he contradicts himself on this point: see discussion of *Hume's* views in *Gordon* para 29–44.

[2] 1950 JC 67, 1950 SLT 279.

[3] Cf R Scott 'The defence of provocation' 1965 SLT (News) 193, supporting *Hillan*. *Gordon* para 29–45. *Gane and Stoddart* p 440: '...it is not immediately clear why provocation ought not to provide a complete defence to minor assaults – apart from difficulties of categorising assaults as "minor" or "serious".'

[4] At 24 per Lord Clyde in *Quinn v Cunningham* 1956 JC 22, 1956 SLT 55; approved in *RHW v HM Adv* 1982 SCCR 152, 1988 SLT 42.

[5] 1982 SCCR 152, 1988 SLT 42. See also: *Macphail v Clark* 1982 SCCR 395, 1983 SLT (Sh Ct) 37: farmer culpably and recklessly endangering the lieges by setting fire to straw in a field, thereby causing smoke to drift over and obscure a public road.

warned not to throw the bottle; in *Gizzi v Tudhope*[1], the risk of injury to others may not have been so self-evident, but it satisfied the test laid down in *Allan v Patterson*[2], which is an objective one. The test must therefore be whether the risk would have been apparent to the reasonable person in the position of the accused. This means that there may be liability for recklessly endangering others even if the accused was subjectively unaware of the risk created by his conduct.

The implications of this are significant. If **A** leaves a garden rake lying upside down on his path and this rake is then stepped on by the postman, to his injury, **A** may be liable for recklessly causing injury if the reasonable person would have been aware of the risk posed to others by leaving the rake lying on the path. If **A** was not aware of this obvious risk, he is subjectively innocent and should not be punished for an offence of this seriousness. This is subject, of course, to the 'utter disregard' test, and it is possible that the threshold of recklessness in this context will be kept sufficiently high to prevent inappropriate convictions.

Ulhaq v HM Adv[3] demonstrates the possible use of this form of offence in order to control behaviour which, while admittedly callously anti-social, has missed legislative control. The accused in this case was charged with culpably and recklessly endangering life or health after he sold solvents to adults, over a long period, in the knowledge that these were being abused. The court held that the supply of these substances was the equivalent of their direct administration by the accused and the conviction was upheld.

In another controversial case of a similar nature, *Khaliq v HM Adv*,[4] the accused was convicted of 'culpably, wilfully and recklessly' supplying glue-sniffing kits to children to the danger of their lives. This offence was treated as a variety of the criminal offence identified by *Hume* as that of causing real injury. The accused does not need to inflict the injury himself; this can be done by the victim, to whom the means of inflicting the injury are supplied.

The decision in *Khaliq* has been criticised on the grounds that it offends the principle of legality, namely, *nullum crimen sine lege*. It has not been used to extend criminal liability beyond the confines of solvent abuse, although in theory it might provide authority for the prosecution of one, say, who recklessly sells a carving knife to an

---

[1] 1982 SCCR 442, 1983 SLT 214.
[2] 1980 JC 57, 1980 SLT 77.
[3] 1990 SCCR 593, 1991 SLT 614.
[4] 1983 SCCR 483, 1984 JC 23.

unbalanced person expressing homicidal sentiments. It could also be used as authority for the prosecution of one who recklessly provides a depressed and suicidal person with the means of ending his or her life.[1]

THREATS

The making of threats to another, oral or written, constitutes a criminal offence. The threat may be to do violence to the recipient, to destroy his property, or indeed in any way to menace or intimidate him. It is not criminal, of course, to threaten to do something which one is entitled to do, unless such a threat is made in an improper context (such as threatening an officer of the law with an adverse consequence should he discharge his duties).

[1] Should the criminal law be used to discourage people from recklessly exposing others to the risk of infection, particularly to the risk of HIV infection? Such conduct could be prosecuted in Scotland as culpably risking injury to others, or arguably as assault. For a full discussion of the implications of this issue see KJM Smith 'Sexual etiquette, public interest and the criminal law' (1991) 42 NI LQ 309.

10. Homicide

Human life is afforded protection by the criminal law from the moment of conception to the moment of death. The protection given to the human fetus in its very earliest stages will be theoretical rather than real, given the difficulties of proving pregnancy at that stage, but once pregnancy is established the fetus is protected by the criminal law relating to abortion. This protection is qualified of course: medically-authorised abortion is not an offence and the incipient human being may therefore legally be destroyed until the 24th week of pregnancy or, in the case of abnormal fetuses, where the life of the mother is at risk, until birth.

Abortion, however, is not homicide, and the law of homicide only applies once the child is born. *Macdonald* defines homicide as the destruction of 'self-existent human life',[1] a state which he regards as coming into existence once breath has been drawn. It is difficult to see why the drawing of breath should be considered significant; a child which is extruded from the body of the mother but which has not yet drawn breath is surely as deserving of the protection of the law as is one which has drawn breath. Both have visibly entered the human community, which would seem to be the only real grounds for distinguishing between the fetus which is, say, one day away from birth, and the newly-born infant.

Injuries inflicted on children *in utero* may cause the death of the fetus and subsequent miscarriage. This is not homicide, as self-existent life has not been destroyed. But what is the position if a child is born alive but then dies from injuries sustained *in utero*? *Hume* did not rule out the possibility of homicide being committed in such circumstances,[2] but the matter has not been settled by the

---

[1] Page 87.
[2] I, 187.

Scottish courts.[1] In *McCluskey v HM Adv*[2] the accused was convicted of the statutory offence of causing death by reckless driving[3] in respect of injuries caused to a child *in utero* who was born prematurely and died as a result of those injuries.

SUICIDE

Suicide is not a crime in Scots law and it is therefore not a criminal offence to attempt suicide.[4] Encouraging or assisting another to take his own life is another matter, as the sympathy which the law has for the suicide does not necessarily extend to those who facilitate suicide. There is no Scottish authority on this issue; in other jurisdictions it is not unusual to find statutory provisions which penalise the provision of any assistance to the would-be suicide.[5]

The giving of advice on the best methods of taking one's life raises interesting issues of criminal liability. In the English case of *Attorney General v Able*[6] the court held that the provision of a booklet detailing means of committing suicide could amount to aiding and abetting suicide, provided that the connection between the provision of the booklet and the suicide or attempt at suicide was close enough.[7] In the absence of legislation making it an offence to assist suicide, the issue would have to be determined according to common law principles, and it is submitted that in

---

[1] For general discussion, see J Temkin 'Prenatal injury and the draft criminal code' (1986) 45 Camb L J 414. L Waller 'Any reasonable creature in being' (1987) 13 Monash Law Review 37. Cases include *R v West* (1848) 2 Cox CC 500: homicide committed where prenatal injuries cause death of child; *Kwok Chak Minh (No 1) v The Queen* [1963] HKLR 226; endorsed in *McCluskey v HM Adv* 1988 SCCR 629, 1989 SLT 175.

[2] 1988 SCCR 629, 1989 SLT 175.

[3] Under s1 of the Road Traffic Act 1972 (now Road Traffic Act 1988).

[4] *Gordon* para 23-01 suggests that attempted suicide may be prosecuted as breach of the peace. Suicide was said to be a crime by *Alison* (I, 1) and also by Mackenzie *Laws and Customs of Scotland in Matters Criminal* (1678–99) (I, 13).

[5] In England the Suicide Act 1961 decriminalised suicide but preserved the offence of aiding and abetting a suicide. For a survey of United States provisions, see CD Shaffer 'Criminal liability for assisting suicide' (1986) 86 Columbia Law Review, 348. Cf French law: it is not a crime to assist another to commit suicide as suicide itself is legal, and it is thought that it cannot be criminal to assist another to do a legal act; however, the possibility exists of prosecution in such circumstances under art 63 of the Penal Code, which provides for criminal liability for failure to rescue one in peril: ML Rassat *Droit Penal* (1987) p 427.

[6] [1984] QB 795, [1984] 1 All ER 277.

[7] The court stressed temporal closeness; see criticism in KJM Smith *A Modern Treatise on the Law of Criminal Complicity* (1991) p 57.

Scotland the following possibilities exist:

(1) The giving of advice on suicide, or indeed the provision of means to commit suicide would not give rise to criminal liability on the grounds that the act of the suicide or would-be suicide constituted a *novus actus interveniens* interrupting the causal link between the accused's act and the final result.[1]

(2) The act of the providing of advice or practical means for the commission of suicide constitutes the offence of recklessly endangering life. A strong case for conviction of this offence would be where **A** gives **B** a gun, knowing him to be depressed and knowing him to be contemplating suicide.

(3) The provision of advice on suicide or the practical means of committing suicide amounts to the offence of recklessly endangering life and this, if acted upon and resulting in death, constitutes the basis of culpable homicide. There has been an unlawful act (recklessly endangering life) followed by death, and this is sufficient for conviction of culpable homicide. This option would require the act of the deceased to be disregarded as a *novus actus interveniens*.

(4) The provision of advice on suicide or the practical means of committing suicide amounts to murder on the grounds that the person assisting manifests wicked recklessness, one of the forms of the *mens rea* of murder.

Of the above possibilities, the most appropriate one, should the prosecution authorities wish to proceed in these circumstances, would be the second one. This would avoid any difficulties that might be posed by the *novus actus interveniens* doctrine.

THE DEFINITION OF DEATH

It hardly needs saying that homicide requires a live victim to be killed; the dead are protected against physical insult or indignity,[2] but they are beyond the protection of the criminal law of homicide.

[1] *R v Peverett* 1940 AD 213 (SA): act not a *novus actus*; cf *R v Nbakwa* 1956 (2) SA 557 (Southern Rhodesia): accused had suggested to his mother that she kill herself and upbraided her for not doing so: deceased's act was held to be a *novus actus interveniens*.

[2] Interference with dead bodies after burial, or other storage, is the common law crime of violation of sepulchres: *Hume* I, 85; *Gordon* para 42–01. It might also be the offence of shameless indecency to subject a dead body to disrespectful treatment prior to the stage of burial or consignment for cremation. The implications of the Anatomy Act 1984 and the Human Tissue Act 1961 are discussed by PDG Skegg 'Criminal liability for the unauthorised use of corpses for medical education and research' (1992) 32 Med Sci Law 51.

Death is undefined in Scots criminal law, but requires, beyond doubt, the cessation of cardio-respiratory functions. Developments in medical technology enable respiration and circulation to be maintained beyond the point at which brain death occurs, but persons in this position must still be considered alive. It is submitted, then, that any unlawful act directed towards the stopping of cardio-respiratory activity in such a person would amount to homicide, at least in terms of *Macdonald*'s definition as the destruction of human life. Human life is still present in a brain-dead person, even if it is life of a purely somatic, as opposed to mental variety.[1] The intentional switching-off of an artificial ventilator by one not medically authorised to do so would amount to murder; medically-indicated cessation of ventilation is on a par with other medical cessation of treatment in such circumstances and does not constitute a *novus actus interveniens*.[2]

Spontaneous heartbeat and respiration may survive the death of the higher parts of the brain, resulting in a person being irreversibly comatose. Such persons may present no signs of cortical activity, but are still given the full protection of the criminal law. It would undoubtedly be homicide to kill such a person[3] (for the reasons stated above in relation to the killing of an artificially-ventilated person).

The fact that a person is on his death bed when he is killed in no way mitigates the seriousness of killing him. If **A** is about to die of natural causes, and **B**, wishing to spare him the last few moments of suffering, smothers him, this is homicide.[4] In practice, so-called 'mercy killing' may be treated relatively sympathetically, and grounds may be found for reducing a charge of murder to one of culpable homicide in such a case, but the law continues to set its face against euthanasia.

---

[1] There is a growing literature on the legal implications of the concept of brain death. See, for example, J K Mason and R A A McCall-Smith *Law and Medical Ethics* (3rd edn, 1991), p 259 et seq; I Kennedy and A Grubb *Medical Law: Text and Materials* (1991) p 1156 et seq. For a useful overall survey, see D Lamb *Death, Brain Death and Ethics* (1985). Note that the proposition stated in the text above appears to be in direct conflict with the conclusions reached by the 1976 Conference of Royal Colleges and their Faculties: '...the identification of brain death means that the patient is dead, whether or not the function of some organs, such as a heartbeat, is still maintained by artificial means'.

[2] *Finlayson v HM Adv* 1979 JC 33, 1978 SLT(Notes) 60.

[3] The position of the irreversibly comatose person is discussed by P Skegg 'Irreversibly comatose individuals: alive or dead' (1974) 33 Camb L J 130.

[4] *Gordon* para 23–08.

THE CATEGORIES OF HOMICIDE

There are three categories of homicide: non-criminal homicide, murder, and culpable homicide.

NON-CRIMINAL HOMICIDE

Non-criminal homicide may be **casual** or **justifiable**. Casual homicide is accidental homicide committed by a person who is not engaged at the time in unlawful activity. The category of casual homicide does not include those cases where death has been caused by culpable negligence.

Justifiable homicide consists of killing in circumstances where, in the eyes of the law, the taking of life is a right and proper thing to do. Killing in self-defence is justifiable homicide, as is a soldier's killing of the enemy in battle. *Hume* states that a magistrate is entitled to order life to be taken to suppress a riot, but different considerations may apply to such a situation today.[1] The question of whether necessity justifies homicide is unresolved in Scots law, although it is submitted that it should.[2] If a security guard discovers an un-exploded bomb in a room full of people and, unable to evacuate the room, he throws the bomb out of the window, he should not be punished for the killing of the person whom he sees in the street outside and whom he knows may be killed by the explosion. The choice he made was justified: it was the right thing to have done.

MURDER

Murder consists of the unlawful killing of another by a person who either (i) intends to kill, or who (ii) acts in a way which manifests 'wicked recklessness' as to whether or not his victim lives or dies.

(i) Intentional killing

There is intention to kill where the accused directs his action to the attainment of the desired goal, namely the death of the victim. A clear example of intentional killing is the pointing of a rifle at the

---

[1] *Gordon* para 23–33. Cf PW Ferguson *Crimes Against the Person* (1990) p 13.
[2] The defence of necessity is discussed at greater length at p 134.

victim and the pulling of the trigger in the knowledge that the gun is loaded, and with the desire that death should result. The victim's death may not be wanted as an end in itself, rather as a means to another end; this, of course, is still intentional killing.

The intention of the accused may be gathered from his actings; in most cases there will be no other direct evidence of intention. In assessing what a person intended, the jury will take into account its own experience of human behaviour and motivation.

English law has experienced considerable difficulties in defining intention in this context,[1] a situation which has been avoided in Scotland because of the Scots doctrine of wicked recklessness.[2] The Scots courts have therefore not been exercised over the question as to whether acts done in the knowledge that there is a high degree of probability that a particular consequence will ensue will amount to an intention to achieve that consequence.

(ii) Wicked recklessness

This is the second form of possible *mens rea* for murder and it enables the Scots courts to convict of murder those who kill in morally-reprehensible circumstances but who do not necessarily have any intention to kill. *Alison* states that murder is an act which flows from 'a deliberate intention to kill, or to inflict minor injury of such a kind as indicates an utter recklessness as to the life of the sufferer, whether he live or die'.[3] *Macdonald*'s statement, which has provided the basis of modern judicial instructions on this matter, is as follows: 'Murder is constituted by any wilful act causing the destruction of life, whether intended to kill, or displaying such wicked recklessness as to imply a disposition depraved enough to be regardless of the consequences ...'[4]

In one view wicked recklessness itself is not sufficient justification for conviction of murder; all that it does is to point to the presence of intention to kill. This interpretation was supported in some of the judgments in *Cawthorne v HM Adv*,[5] but is at odds with the view espoused by *Alison*, for example, that wicked recklessness is the

---

[1] The English cases are reviewed by R A Duff *Intention, Agency and Criminal Liability* (1990).
[2] See comments by Lord Goff, p 159, fn 1 below.
[3] I, 1. *Gordon* para 23–16, points out that 'minor injury' in this context means 'non-fatal injury'.
[4] Page 89.
[5] 1968 JC 32, 1968 SLT 330.

equivalent of intention to kill.[1] The modern consensus, however, is clear: wicked recklessness stands on its own as sufficient *mens rea* for murder.

There has been a current of support in the past for a third form of *mens rea* for murder, that of an intent to do serious bodily harm. This suggestion was made at both trial and appeal stages of *Cawthorne* and it appeared, too, in Lord Justice-General Emslie's judgment in *Brennan v HM Adv*[2] and in Lord Sutherland's direction to the jury in *HM Adv v Hartley*.[3] In *Brennan* Lord Emslie said 'Our definition of murder includes the taking of human life by a person who has intent to kill or to do serious injury or whose act is shown to be wickedly reckless as to the consequences'.[4] Then, in *Hartley*, Lord Sutherland said 'If you declare your intention to maim somebody seriously and go out and do so and unfortunately go too far and he dies, that is murder, because you had the intent to cause serious bodily harm'.

The tide of opinion would now appear to be in favour of rejecting an intention to do serious bodily harm as a third, distinct form of *mens rea* for murder. Indeed this view was the conclusion of the House of Lords Select Committee on Murder and Life Imprisonment,[5] before which Lord Emslie had expressed reservations as to the instruction in *Hartley* and had cast doubt on the interpretation of his dictum in *Brennan*.[6]

What constitutes wicked recklessness

The presence of wicked recklessness will be inferred from all the circumstances of a case. Usually it will be the severity of the assault which will entitle the jury to conclude that the accused was indifferent as to the fate of his victim, although the condition of his victim (his age, evident infirmity, etc) may render a moderate assault wickedly reckless. In *HM Adv v Robertson and Donoghue*[7] it

---

[1] *Alison* I, 163: 'In judging of the intention of an accused who has committed an aggravated assault, the same rules are to be followed as in judging of the intent in actual murder, viz, that a ruthless intent, and an obvious indifference to the sufferer, whether he live or die, is to be held as equivalent to an actual attempt to inflict death'. Endorsed by Lord Cameron in *Cawthorne* 1968 JC 32 at 39. Discussion: GH Gordon '*Cawthorne* and the *mens rea* of murder' 1969 SLT(News) 41.

[2] 1977 SLT 151.

[3] 1989 SLT 135.

[4] 1977 SLT 151 at 156.

[5] H L Paper 78–1 (1988–89) no 16.

[6] H L Paper 78–111, Q 2020. Discussion: T Jones and S Griffin 'Serious bodily harm and murder' 1990 SLT 305.

[7] (August 1945, unreported), High Court; *Gane and Stoddart* p 497.

was pointed out by Lord Justice-Clerk Cooper that 'much less violence if applied to a feeble, old man, to a person whom the assailant must have known was a feeble, old man – if you think he must have known it – may suffice to justify an inference of wicked recklessness to consequences'.

The fact that a weapon was used in an attack has been taken as conclusive of wicked recklessness. This was so in *HM Adv v McGuinness*[1] where Lord Justice-Clerk Aitchison said:

'People who use knives and pokers and hatchets against a fellow citizen are not entitled to say 'we did not mean to kill', if death results. If people resort to the use of deadly weapons of this kind, they are guilty of murder, whether or not they intended to kill.'

A similar view was expressed by Lord Carmont in *Kennedy v HM Adv*,[2] but it probably goes too far to hold that the use of weapons will inevitably point to wicked recklessness: the fact that a weapon was used will be one of the factors to be taken into account, but will not of itself settle the matter.[3]

Wicked recklessness: subjective or objective?

Can conduct be described as reckless if the accused had no knowledge of the risks it entailed? Theoretically, it cannot; nor *a fortiori* may conduct be described as 'wickedly reckless' if there was ignorance of the risks – the terms 'wicked' or 'wickedly' imply a cast of mind which, in the absence of such knowledge, simply is not there. A subjective test of recklessness in this context would therefore require an awareness of a risk of death, and if a jury were to be satisfied that the accused genuinely did not appreciate the risk, even if it would have been apparent to the reasonable person in his position, it would be entitled to acquit. The test in Scots law, however, is in practice objective. The issue is whether the conduct of the accused manifested wicked recklessness, and this will be decided according to objective criteria. Conduct which, on its externals, is wickedly reckless, justifies an inference of wicked recklessness on the part of the accused. Not caring whether one's victim lives or dies, then, would seem not to require any awareness of the risk of death. For those purposes, a person may be said not

---

[1]   1937 JC 37 at 40.
[2]   1944 JC 171 at 174.
[3]   *Murder* (Scot Law Com Consultative Memorandum no 61) (1984), p 18. PW Ferguson *Crimes Against the Person* (1990) p 20.

to care even if he has not addressed his mind to the risks entailed in his conduct.[1]

Yet subjective factors cannot be entirely irrelevant. The accused's assessment of his victim, for example, would appear to be relevant; at least this would appear to be so according to Lord Cooper's instruction in *Robertson v Donoghue*, quoted above.[2] It would be open to a future court to introduce further subjective considerations to take into account the rare case where objectively reckless conduct does not reflect subjective recklessness. Certainly there is nothing in such an approach which contradicts accepted statements of the law, including *Macdonald*'s widely used definition, and this would mean that an assailant of limited intelligence, who just does not understand the risks of his conduct, might be convicted of culpable homicide rather than murder.

Wicked recklessness and intention to inflict harm

An act may be wickedly reckless and may lead to loss of life, but may nonetheless involve no intention to cause harm to any person. *Gordon* suggests that such an act will not amount to murder,[3] and cites in support of this proposition Lord Wheatley's direction to the jury in *HM Adv v McCarron*[4] that if the accused had fired a shot at his victim 'not intending to kill or injure her but merely to frighten her, but acted with gross and wicked negligence that he in fact killed her, the crime could be culpable homicide and not murder'. It should be noted that Lord Wheatley referred to gross and wicked **negligence** rather than recklessness; negligence does not require acceptance of risk to life which is of the essence of recklessness.

Gordon's contention is not supported by *Hume*, who states that murder may be committed even when there is no animus directed

---

[1] Cf Lord Goff's comment on wicked recklessness in Scots law 'I think it important to observe that the principle so stated does not necessarily involve a conscious apprehension of the risk of death at the relevant time. This is of importance, because we can think of many cases in which it can be said that the accused acted regardless of the consequences, not caring whether the victim lived or died, and yet did not consciously appreciate the risk of death in his mind at the time – for example when a man acts in the heat of the moment, as when he lashes out with a knife in the heat of a fight . . .I cannot see that the fact that, in consequence, he did not have the risk of death in his mind at the time should prevent him from being held guilty of murder'. 'The mental element in the crime of murder' (1989) 104 LQR 30 at 55.

[2] *Gane and Stoddart* p 497.

[3] *Gordon* para 23–15.

[4] (Feb 1964, unreported), Perth High Court; approved on appeal, March 1964.

towards any particular person:

'It is not even indispensable, that the malice be directed against any one in particular. If a man fire at random among a multitude, or if he wilfully turn loose a mad dog into the street, at a time when it is full of passengers, and a person perish in consequence of this brutality; surely any difference between such a case of indiscriminate malice, and one of special hatred to an individual, is all to the disadvantage of this offender . . . Of this sort, in some measure, was the charge brought against James Niven, 21st December 1795, in that having loaded a small cannon with powder, and a bit of iron, and having pointed it up a lane or street of common passage, he then fired it off, at a time when two persons were standing in the direction of the piece, and several others were passing along the lane; whereby one of the persons first mentioned was killed . . . It was held on the Bench, that . . . he was guilty of no lower crime than murder . . .'[1]

In *R v Hancock and Shankland*[2] two striking miners who wished to frighten and prevent other miners from reporting for work pushed a lump of concrete from a bridge onto cars below, not intending, they claimed, to cause injury to anybody below but hoping to block the road. They were initially convicted of murder, and although this case involved considerations of English criminal law which are not directly relevant in Scotland, the facts of the case provide an interesting example against which to test the require- ment of an intention to harm. Had this incident occurred in Scot- land, the issue would have been whether what the miners did amounted to wicked recklessness. On the authority of *Hume* it would. The pouring of petrol into a letter box of a house, for example, and its subsequent setting alight is wicked recklessness, even if the accused's desire is to harm property rather than an individual. If somebody is killed in the resultant blaze, even if it is somebody whom the accused did not know was there, this may be murder rather than culpable homicide. To hold otherwise would be to exclude potential liability for murder in the case of a terrorist who places a bomb outside premises he wishes to destroy and who then telephones an evacuation warning. If somebody dies as a result of the blast, it would be inconceivable that the resultant charge should be culpable homicide rather than murder.

Homicide and robbery

Homicide committed during the course of a robbery is murder rather than culpable homicide, even if there is no intention to kill and no wicked recklessness. Thus if **A**, while robbing his victim, gives him no more than a moderate blow, he may be held to have

[1] I, 23.
[2] [1986] AC 455 (HL), [1986] 1 All ER 641.

murdered him should the victim die as a result of this assault. Modern support for this rule may be found in *HM Adv v Miller and Denovan*,[1] and more recently in *Melvin v HM Adv*.[2] It would appear that there must be at least moderate force, and that the rule will not apply if death results from some form of mischance (such as pushing the victim backwards, causing him to slip and strike his head on a rock).[3]

It is difficult to see any justification for treating as murder any homicide committed in the course of a robbery, and there has been persistent criticism of similar rules elsewhere. It might be argued that the mere fact of carrying out a robbery amounts to wicked recklessness, on the grounds that robberies can, and do, lead to unexpected deaths, but this extends the concept of wicked reckless-ness unduly. A more likely rationale for the rule – that it deters the use of weapons during the course of a robbery – may have been persuasive in days of capital punishment for murder but current penalties for a serious armed robbery are not necessarily so much lower in real terms than the period of imprisonment involved in a life sentence. English law abandoned the felony-murder rule (as it is known in common law jurisdictions) in the Homicide Act 1957, and the Supreme Court of Canada has ruled that equivalent pro-visions in the Canadian Criminal Code violate provisions of the Charter of Rights and Freedoms.[4]

CULPABLE HOMICIDE

There are two forms of culpable homicide: involuntary culpable homicide and voluntary culpable homicide. The first category encompasses those cases where an unintended death occurs as a

---

[1] (Dec 1960, unreported), High Court; *Gordon*, para 23–26 et seq; *Gane and Stod-dart*, p 500. Cf *HM Adv v Fraser and Rollins* 1920 JC 60, 1920 2 SLT 77.

[2] 1984 SCCR 113, 1984 SLT 365.

[3] Lord Sands in *HM Adv v Fraser and Rollins*, supra: 'I might take the illustration of a thief who tries to snatch somebody's watch. He tries to pull it away and in doing so upsets the man's balance and the man falls on the kerb and has the misfortune to strike his head against the stone and is killed. That would not be murder because there is a certain mischance in the matter ...' (at 63).

[4] *R v Martineau* [1990] 79 CR (3d) 129. For an example of the application of the rule in Australia, see *R v Butcher* [1986] VR 43. (The Law Commission of Victoria has recommended the rule's abolition: *Homicide* (Law Reform Commission of Victoria, Report No 40) 65.) For general discussion, see: D Lanham 'Felony mur-der – ancient and modern' (1983) 7 Crim L J 90; J L Edwards 'Constructive murder in Canadian and English law' (1961) 3 Cr L Q 481.

result of an assault or other criminal act or as a result of culpable negligence; in the second category are those cases where death results from an intentional or reckless act but where, because of provocation or diminished responsibility, the offence is reduced from murder to culpable homicide.

Involuntary culpable homicide

Involuntary culpable homicide usually entails the commission of an assault on the victim. The assault need not be a serious one: all that is required is that the act causing death should satisfy the legal definition of assault. The pointing of a firearm at another may amount to an assault,[1] as may a push, shove, or light slap. In such a case, if the victim were to stumble and strike his head on the ground, the assailant could be liable for culpable homicide.[2] Causing death by fright may be culpable homicide, even if there has been no physical contact between assailant and victim. In *HM Adv v Lourie*[3] there was no challenge to the relevance of an indictment for culpable homicide in a case in which two youths caused the death by shock of a householder from whom they were committing a theft. The fact that there was no allegation of physical contact between the accused and the deceased did not deter the bringing of the charge.

The fact that death is caused by some particular weakness or peculiarity on the part of the victim is irrelevant. The rule that you take your victim as you find him means that it is culpable homicide to cause death by a minor punch to the abdomen of one who, unknown to you, has a misplaced spleen. As Lord Clyde said in *HM Adv v Rutherford*:[4] 'It is no answer for an assailant who causes death by violence to say that his victim had a weak heart or was excitable or emotional . . . He must take his victim as he finds him'.[5]

Unlawful acts other than assault

Although the courts have stressed that deaths which result from any unlawful act is culpable homicide, the reported cases are almost

---

[1] In *Mowles v HM Adv* 1986 SCCR 117 the accused pointed a firearm at another believing that it was unloaded. The gun was grabbed and fired as a result, killing a person other than the person at whom it had been pointed. It was held that the initial unlawful act of assault justified a finding of culpable homicide.

[2] *HM Adv v Hartley* 1989 SLT 135.

[3] 1988 SCCR 634. See also *Bird v HM Adv* 1952 JC 23.

[4] 1947 JC 1 at 3, 1947 SLT 3.

[5] For criticism of this rule, see *Gordon*, para 26–17 et seq.

exclusively concerned with situations in which there has been an intention to cause harm to the person. *Lourie*[1] is a possible exception to this, as is *Mathieson v HM Adv*.[2] In the latter case the accused was convicted of culpable homicide after he had unlawfully started a fire which subsequently caused the death of a number of victims. It is clear then, that any unlawful act directed against property which is capable of causing physical injury, could be culpable homicide. Interference with the mechanism of a lift would be an example, as might be vandalism which impedes the use of fire-fighting apparatus.

It is more doubtful whether culpable homicide is committed where the unlawful act is not one normally associated with the risk of injury. In *HM Adv v Finlayson*[3] the prosecution argued that any act 'tainted' by illegality will be sufficient, but the point did not require to be decided. There is no authority in Scots law for the proposition that the unlawful act requires to be dangerous,[4] but it is submitted that such a limitation is desirable. If there is no such requirement, then there could be liability for culpable homicide when death is quite 'incidental' to the unlawful activity. For example, if a person stealing a bicycle knocks over a child who suddenly appears in the path before him, this death would be culpable homicide, even if entirely fortuitous.

A court would have to decide on the degree of dangerousness required. Differing standards have been applied in those systems recognising such a test, with some courts requiring a risk of serious injury[5] and others being satisfied with even a slight risk of harm.[6] There is a strong argument for requiring a risk of serious injury, and for requiring, too, that the injury should have been foreseeable by the accused; this is on a par with the standard required for conviction for culpable homicide on the grounds of negligence. Any lower standard might extend the boundaries of liability too far: virtually any conduct is statistically capable of causing a slight degree of harm. It is technically dangerous to drink alcohol, for example, as there is a remote risk that one might cause injury to oneself while

---

[1] 1988 SCCR 634.
[2] 1981 SCCR 196.
[3] 1979 JC 33, 1978 SLT (Notes) 18.
[4] English law requires an 'unlawful and dangerous' act for commission of manslaughter: *DPP v Newbury* [1977] AC 500, [1976] 3 All ER 365. For discussion, see R J Buxton 'By any unlawful act' (1966) 82 L Q R 174; G Peiris 'Involuntary manslaughter in Commonwealth law' (1985) 5 Legal Studies 21.
[5] For example, *R v Wills* [1983] 2 VR 201.
[6] *Church* [1966] 1 QB 59, [1965] 2 All ER 72; *DPP v Daley* [1980] AC 237, (1979) 69 Crim App Rep 39.

intoxicated. Should it be culpable homicide if a person who irresponsibly laces another's drink with a small amount of alcohol thereby causes the other to trip over and fall downstairs, with fatal results?

Omissions

If an omission to perform a legal duty leads to death, this is usually culpable homicide rather than murder. The neglect of a dependant and vulnerable person provide examples of such liability;[1] if a person fails to provide food or medical support for a person in his care who needs them, then the omission amounts to an unlawful act.

There is no general duty to rescue in Scots law. This means that a person who fails to take steps to help another in obvious peril commits no offence, unless, of course, he has a legal duty to act. Such a legal duty would exist only where there is a relationship between the parties; where the accused is obliged to act by virtue of the position he occupies; or where the peril has been created by the accused's own actings.

Involuntary lawful act homicide

During the nineteenth century culpable homicide was frequently charged where negligence in the course of employment led to death.[2] This has virtually disappeared in the twentieth century, owing to the fact that statutory controls exist to police dangerous practices in the workplace. Twentieth-century cases of lawful act culpable homicide are therefore rare, and almost entirely concerned with causing death on the roads. At the same time, there is a growing view that homicide prosecutions should follow upon certain acts of negligence, particularly where companies are alleged to have been negligent in relation to safety matters.[3]

The *mens rea* of involuntary culpable homicide in this context is negligence of a particularly high degree. Ordinary negligence, of

[1] *R v Instan* [1893] 1 QB 450; *R v Gibbins and Proctor* (1918) 13 Crim App Rep 134.
[2] The cases are surveyed by *Gordon* para 26–05 et seq. See, for example, *HM Adv v Paton and McNab* (1845) 2 Broun 525.
[3] The question of corporate liability for homicide is one which has attracted considerable attention. See, for example, HJ Glasbeek and S Rowland 'Are injuring and killing at work crimes?' (1979) 17 Osgoode Hall Law Journal 506; GL Mangum 'Murder in the workplace: criminal prosecution and regulatory enforcement' (1988) 39 Labor Law Journal 220; B Fisse *Howard's Criminal Law* (5th edn, 1990) p 608 et seq.

the sort which gives rise to civil liability, will not be enough: there must be negligence which meets the standard set out in *Paton v HM Adv*,[1] that is, 'gross, or wicked, or criminal negligence, something amounting to, or at any rate analogous, to a criminal indifference to consequences'. There is clearly no distinction here between recklessness and criminal negligence – in both cases there is indifference towards the risks involved. Yet criminal negligence is not quite wicked recklessness, and therefore falls short of the *mens rea* of murder.

In deciding whether conduct is negligent for these purposes, a jury will probably be guided by its sense of outrage. If the conduct is outrageous, and deserving of criminal punishment, then it might be considered criminally negligent. If, however, it is the sort of negligence 'which occurs' and which does not demonstrate a cavalier attitude towards human safety, then it might not satisfy what is, after all, a fairly rigorous test.

Causing death through dangerous driving is normally prosecuted under section 1 of the Road Traffic Act 1988. Particularly serious cases may be culpable homicide,[2] however, especially if drunkenness is involved. This enables the courts to impose a sentence higher than the maximum of ten years imprisonment provided for in the Act.

Medical negligence may frequently be the cause of death. The volume of civil litigation in this area has grown considerably, but this has not been matched by an increase in culpable homicide prosecutions, which appear to be unknown in modern Scots law. Courts elsewhere have been generally reluctant to convict doctors of culpable homicide,[3] although recent English cases have shown a greater readiness to do so.[4] Practical jokes or pranks which go wrong may amount to culpable homicide if the victim is killed and if the conduct

---

[1] 1936 JC 19 at 22. In English law, the standard is set out in *R v Bateman* (1925) 19 Crim App Rep 8 where the requirement is stated that the 'negligence or incompetence of the accused went beyond a mere matter of compensation and showed such disregard for the life and safety of others as to amount to a crime against the state and conduct deserving punishment'. For Commonwealth cases generally, see G Peiris 'Involuntary manslaughter in Commonwealth law' (1985) 5 Legal Studies 21.

[2] *Dunn v H M Adv* 1960 JC 55, 1961 SLT 106. See PW Ferguson, *Crimes Against the Person* (1990) p 26 et seq.

[3] *R v Akerele* [1943] AC 255. The Privy Council warned in this case that 'care should be taken before imputing criminal negligence to a professional man acting in the course of his profession'. The comparative immunity of a professional man is perhaps less secure today.

[4] *R v Adamako* [1991] 2 Med LR 277: anaesthetist convicted of manslaughter after he had left the operating theatre for a brief period. See also C Dyer 'Doctors convicted of manslaughter' (1991) 303 Br Med J 1157.

of the accused is considered to be so risky as to amount to gross negligence.[1]

Voluntary culpable homicide

Intentional or reckless killing may be reduced from murder to culpable homicide if there is either diminished responsibility or provocation.[2]

Provocation

Provocation exists where, in response to conduct on the part of the deceased the accused loses his self-control and takes life.[3] Provocation is frequently plead alongside self-defence, but is to be distinguished from self-defence, which is a complete defence which leads to acquittal.[4] The effect of a successful plea of provocation being to reduce murder to culpable homicide, provocation only has a mitigating effect.

The theory underlying provocation is that allowance should be made for the effect of anger and that people are not to be held fully accountable for what they do in 'a blind rage'.[5] Although this accords with our intuitive understanding of human behaviour, the reluctance of the courts to apply the plea in anything but the most limited circumstances is understandable. The criminal law expects self-control, and indeed is based on notions of individual responsibility and self-restraint. Concessions made to ill-temper and anger are concessions to human frailty, are potentially anarchic, and can result in unacceptable notions of the non-punishability of the

---

[1]   In the Australian case of *Jackson and Hodgetts* (1989) 44 A Crim R 320 the putting of meat preservative in a can of soft drink was held to be a 'classic example' of conduct amounting to criminal negligence. In *Streatfield* (1991) 53 A Crim R the accused's act of pointing a gun (which he thought to be unloaded) at his wife and pulling the trigger was described by the court as an 'act of monumental stupidity', justifying conviction of negligent manslaughter and (on appeal) a sentence of five years imprisonment.

[2]   Diminished responsibility is discussed in conjunction with the insanity defence, supra, p 125.

[3]   *Macdonald* defines provocation as follows: 'Being agitated and excited, and alarmed by violence, I lost control over myself and took life, when my presence of mind had left me, and without thought of what I was doing.' (Page 94)

[4]   The difference between provocation and self-defence was stressed in *Fenning v HM Adv* 1985 SCCR 219 at 225.

[5]   Provocation should not be viewed as being based on the notion that the deceased 'deserved it'. This idea sometimes creeps into jury directions: see, for example, the trial judge's instructions in *Lennon v HM Adv* 1991 SCCR 611: 'A man has perhaps the right to revenge himself against an aggressor who attacks him, when the retaliating blow is struck in the heat of the moment, in the heat of blood ...'

'crimes of passion'. For this reason the courts maintain a delicate balance between sympathy for those who have been pushed to the limit of human forbearance, and concern at the potentially anarchic implications of allowing passionate action to go unpunished. As a number of the cases discussed below indicate, this balance is frequently difficult to achieve.

The requirements of provocation

There must have been an assault. Scots law is unlike English law and related systems in that it requires that there should have been a serious assault committed by the victim on the accused. (There is one exception, that of a confession of adultery or unfaithfulness, discussed below.) The rejection of verbal provocation is well-established and consistent. *Hume* said that 'no provocation of words, the most foul and abusive, or of signs or gestures, however contemptuous or derisive soever, is of sufficient weight in the scale',[1] and *Macdonald* is similarly unambiguous: 'Words of insult, however strong, or mere insulting or disgusting conduct, such a jostling or tossing filth in the face, do not serve to reduce the crime from murder to culpable homicide'.[2]

Conduct can, of course, be highly provocative (in the non-legal sense of the word) even if it entails no physical violence. Sexual taunts,[3] drawing attention to and mocking physical infirmities, and racial insults can all be extremely provocative, and it is not difficult to imagine loss of self-control when a particular raw nerve is touched by the insult. Such forms of provocation will be accepted in many other countries as grounds for the plea, but are more or less entirely excluded in Scotland. Their exclusion is not total, however, as the most recent judicial pronouncements on the subject have indicated a willingness to allow the relaxation of the traditional requirements in appropriate cases. At the same time, however, the court in *Cosgrove v HM Adv*[4] ruled that the classic definition put forward by *Macdonald* constituted a proper jury instruction on the matter and that it will not amount to a misdirection if the judge excludes verbal provocation. Whether or not conduct short of an assault can be considered to be provocation depends entirely upon the trial judge's view as to its seriousness.

Conduct not amounting to an assault was accepted as potentially

---

[1] I, 247.
[2] Page 93.
[3] *DPP v Bedder* (1954) 38 Crim App Rep 133.
[4] 1990 SCCR 358.

provocative in *Stobbs v HM Adv*,[1] but a background of business arguments and minor assault was considered not to amount to provocation in *Thomson v HM Adv*,[2] and in *Cosgrove* a confession of indecency was similarly rejected.

The unfaithfulness exception. A confession of adultery by a spouse has long been accepted as an exception to the assault requirement. The rule was originally restricted to cases in which the spouse is discovered in the act of committing adultery,[3] but it later came to be extended to cover confession of adultery.[4] In *HM Adv v Callander*[5] the court allowed provocation to be raised when the sexual unfaithfulness involved a wife and a lesbian lover, and the courts have recently accepted that the principle applies equally when the relationship between the parties is not based on marriage but is an informal equivalent.[6] A discovery of unfaithfulness, or its confession, must still occur in such circumstances as to give rise to a loss of self-control. In *McKay v HM Adv*[7] the confession came at a time when the couple had already been separated and after a lengthy period during which the accused had known that the deceased had been associating with other men. In this context provocation was not accepted.

The response must follow upon the provocation. The accused's act must follow immediately upon the provocation offered by the deceased; a lengthy delay between the provocative act and the response will preclude provocation.[8] As to what constitutes an unacceptable delay will depend on the circumstances, but it is probably the case that a delay of more than a few minutes will be considered sufficient time for the accused to have recovered his self-control.[9] As *Alison* puts it:

'The defence of provocation will not avail the accused, if the fatal acts are done at such a distance of time after the injury received as should have allowed the mortal resentment to subside, or with such weapons, or in such a manner, as indicates a desire of unmeasured revenge.'[10]

[1] 1983 SCCR 190.
[2] 1985 SCCR 448, 1986 SLT 281.
[3] *Hume* I, 245.
[4] *HM Adv v Hill* 1941 JC 59, 1941 SLT 401.
[5] 1958 SLT 24.
[6] *McDermott v HM Adv* 1973 JC 8, 1974 SLT 206; *McKay v HM Adv* 1991 SCCR 364.
[7] 1991 SCCR 364.
[8] *Thomson v HM Adv* 1985 SCCR 448, 1986 SLT 281; *HM Adv v Hill* 1941 JC 59, 1941 SLT 401; *Parr v HM Adv* 1991 SCCR 180.
[9] Cf P Brett 'The physiology of provocation' [1970] Crim L R 634.
[10] Page 8; *Macdonald*, p 94.

There has been some judicial support in the past for the doctrine of cumulative provocation, which would allow the plea where the response is not to recent assault but occurs after a long history of unreasonable and violent behaviour. In *HM Adv v Greig*[1] the accused killed her husband while he was sitting asleep in his chair, but the court accepted that his past violent behaviour towards her could amount to provocation. This decision was welcomed by those who considered the criminal law to be insufficiently sympathetic towards the plight of 'battered women', but more recent decisions have been considerably stricter on the immediacy requirement and the chances of establishing cumulative provocation are slender indeed. In *Parr v HM Adv*[2] provocation was excluded when the accused had killed his mother by whom he had in the past been slapped on the face and with whom he had endured arguments. The court pointed out that there was no evidence of provocative conduct on the deceased's part on the day of the killing; and indeed the court observed that there was no compulsion on him to go on living with his mother and to endure the arguments they had with one another.

Parr is a very weak case of cumulative provocation. It may be possible that future cases of severe domestic provocation will incline the courts to relax the immediacy standards, but the climate of judicial opinion seems against this.[3] A severely-abused woman, who has endured frequent assaults by a bullying husband, may therefore be denied the plea of provocation unless she loses her self-control immediately after a bout of violence. This result demonstrates the potential harshness of having an undifferentiated crime of murder, with a fixed penalty. Such women are not morally guilty to the same extent as those who kill for gain or for some other base motive. The doctrine of provocation, like that of diminished responsibility, provides a means of curtailing the rigours of the law in this area but its efficacy is questionable.

The proportionality requirement. The accused's response to the provocation must be in proportion to the seriousness of the deceased's provocative act. This effectively means that a serious assault will always be required for murder, the only circumstances in which a minor assault will justify homicidal retaliation are where the

---

[1] (May 1979, unreported), High Court; *Gane and Stoddart*, p 526.
[2] 1991 SCCR 180.
[3] For earlier discussion of the English approach, see M Wasik 'Cumulative provocation and domestic killing' [1982] Crim L R 29. In *R v Thornton* [1991] NLJ 1223 the Court of Appeal ruled that prolonged domestic violence did not amount to provocation in the absence of an immediate provocative act.

accused has made a reasonable mistake as to the nature of the deceased's attack on him.[1]

If, in the light of the deceased's conduct, the response of the accused amounts to a 'cruel excess', the plea of provocation is excluded. This rule was endorsed in *Lennon v HM Adv*,[2] an assault case, in which the accused made use of an iron bar in his assault on the victim.

There is no Scottish authority on the question of whether subjective factors may be taken into account in assessing proportionality. The issue may arise where the accused suffers, for example, from some deformity or weakness which makes him more easily provoked. If the test is whether a reasonable person on the position of the accused would have been provoked by what was done, then the fact that the accused was more susceptible to the insult implicit in assault will be irrelevant. As a practical illustration; **A**, a cripple, is struck a mild blow by **B**, who laughs at **A**'s deformity. If **A** then goes into a rage and assaults **B** severely, will he be able to plead provocation even if the slight assault by **B** would not have provoked the average person (who would, by definition, not have suffered from **A**'s disabilities)? In some jurisdictions which have addressed this issue, the response has been to take into account individual characteristics (age, disability, etc) but to require nonetheless a single, objective standard of self-control.[3] Thus the test becomes that of the reasonably self-controlled disabled person, or the reasonably self-controlled 15-year-old, or the reasonably self-controlled person with the relevant characteristic.

[1] *Jones v HM Adv* 1989 SCCR 726, 1990 SLT 517. In *R v Voukeltos* [1990] VR 1 the Supreme Court of Victoria (Australia) held that provocation should go to the jury even when the accused's belief that his wife was having an affair with a neighbour was a delusion on his part.

[2] 1991 SCCR 611.

[3] New Zealand was one of the first jurisdictions to take account of subjective factors in provocation cases: *R v McGregor* [1962] NZLR 1069; *R v Tai* [1976] 1 NZLR 102. For discussion see: W Brookbanks 'Provocation – defining the limits of characteristics' (1968) 10 Crim L J 411.

11. Sexual offences

CRIMINAL LAW AND SEXUAL FREEDOM

The extent to which the criminal law attempts to interfere in the sexual conduct of consenting adults is strictly limited. The libertarian ideal – that the law should intervene only if conduct causes unwanted harm to another – is now largely realised in this area, allowing adults to lead the sexual life of their choice. Most sexual offences arise therefore where there is a victim – one who either does not consent to the conduct in question or who does not have the capacity to give a proper consent. There remain, however, certain significant restraints which have nothing to do with consent. Consensual adult incest is still illegal, as are homosexual acts involving more than two persons or those which take part other than in private. The possession of child pornography is illegal, as is the importation or distribution of obscene material in general. There are also prohibitions against indecent displays and other forms of conduct which the public might find sexually shocking. Sexual freedom is therefore conditional upon the recognition of certain social limits, the contours of which may not always be clear.

Sexual offences in Scots law are both statutory and non-statutory, and there is a degree of overlap between the two categories. For the puposes of this chapter, the following informal classification is adopted: (1) offences against public morality; (2) sexual assaults; (3) offences against young persons; (4) homosexual offences; (5) incest; (6) sundry offences (including prostitution offences).

OFFENCES AGAINST PUBLIC MORALITY

Public morality offences are those offences which might not involve a victim in the normal sense of the term, but which nonetheless entail criminal liability on the grounds that they cause offence to the community at large. This is obviously a controversial area, and it is in respect of these offences that the greatest disagreement is likely to occur between the advocates of legal moralism and those who disfavour any regulation of consensual adult sexual behaviour. As the law stands at present in Scotland, prosecutors have a range of weapons to use against public indecency of various sorts, but the potential of these weapons is considerably limited by increased public tolerance and by changing notions of what is indecent.

Obscene material

Subject to the exception of child pornography, it is not an offence to possess obscene material (for example, an obscene book, magazine, or video cassette). It is an offence, however, to display such items in such a position that it can be seen by a member of the public, or to publish, sell or distribute obscene material.[1] The publication or distribution of obscene material is also a common law offence, although there are no modern instances of common law prosecution of this sort.[2] There are no modern Scottish precedents involving the prosecution of publishers of the written word on grounds of obscenity, although this may be more the result of the traditional preoccupations of Scottish publishing firms (theology) than any legal inadequacy. As a result, the causes célèbres of English law, such as the *Lady Chatterley's Lover* trial, have not had their counterpart in Scotland.

Although the individual may possess and privately relish with impunity almost all forms of pornography, his access to it is legally restricted. The importation of obscene articles is an offence under customs legislation,[3] and it is also an offence to send obscene matter through the post.[4]

The growing use of children in pornography is a social evil which is widely regarded with particular abhorrence, and this category of pornography is now totally illicit. Under the Civic Government (Scotland) Act 1982 it is an offence to take or permit to be taken an indecent photograph of any child under the age of 16, to distribute such a photograph, or to publish an advertisement for it. Section 161 of the Criminal Justice Act 1988 inserts a new section 52A in the Civic Government (Scotland) Act 1982 to create the offence of

---

[1] Civic Government (Scotland) Act 1982, s 51. See also, Indecent Displays (Control) Act 1981.
[2] *Gordon* para 41–16.
[3] Customs and Excise Consolidation Act 1976, s 42; Customs and Excise Act 1952, s 320, Sch 12, Part 1.
[4] Post Office Act 1953, s 11(1).

having in one's possession an indecent photograph of a child under 16. It is a defence if the accused proves that he had a legitimate reason for having the photograph in his possession, or that he was unaware of the nature of the photograph, or that the photograph had been sent to him without his prior request and, once received, had not been kept for an unreasonable time. This section may therefore give rise to omission liability. It will not be enough for a person who receives unsolicited child pornography to leave it lying about the house; he must take steps to destroy it, throw it away, or hand it to the police.

The legislation does not define indecency, and this will therefore be determined by the court. A photograph of the unclothed body of a child is not necessarily indecent, although such a photograph may be erotically stimulating to some. The positioning of the subject in such a way as to draw attention to the sexual parts is likely to render a photograph indecent, as even more clearly will the photographing of a child in the context of sexual activity.

Shameless indency

The proposition that 'all shamelessly indecent conduct is criminal' appears in *Macdonald*,[1] and has been repeated with approval by judges in a number of cases.[2] The scope of the offence is potentially extremely wide, leaving a great deal to the discretion of the court in the indivdual case. Clearly, standards of decency change, and the courts are unlikely to attempt to enforce outdated notions of propriety, and yet the imprecise nature of this offence may cause understandable concern amongst civil libertarians, who argue that the only proper test of criminality in this context should be whether any person has been involuntarily harmed by the conduct in question.

Shameless indecency may take the form of the provision of some sort of sexually-stimulating spectacle or article, or the performance of an indecent act with another person. Charges of shameless indecency of the first sort used to aver that the indecent act was 'liable or likely to deprave and corrupt the morals of the lieges and to create in their minds inordinate and lustful desires'. This no longer needs to be specifically averred, as it has been held that this tendency to corrupt is a necessary implication of indecent conduct.[3]

[1] Page 150.
[2] For example, by Lord Clyde in *McLaughlan v Boyd* 1933 SLT 629; *R v HM Adv* 1988 SCCR 254, 1988 SLT 623.
[3] *Ingram v Macari* 1981 SCCR 184, 1982 JC 1.

As Lord Cameron observed in *Dean v John Menzies Holdings*,[1] '...
it is of the essence of this offence that the conduct be directed
towards some person or persons with an intention or in the knowledge that it should corrupt or be calculated to be liable to corrupt or
deprave in the manner libelled, those towards whom the conduct is
directed. It is this which determines the shameless quality of the
act...' Some form of corruption is required, and this means that
mere erotic titilation will not suffice. Lord Justice-General Cooper
acknowledged this in *Gellatly v Laird*,[2] where he held that some
form of 'pernicious influence' on others was required. This, he said,
amounted to more than the mere stimulation of normal sexual
desires in adults, and required, for example, the encouragement of
perverted or violent conduct.

In *Lockhart v Stephen*[3] the accused had organised erotic perfor-
mances in his bar, employing dancers who made highly suggestive
gestures and movements and who performed acts of simulated
sexual intercourse on the stage. The sheriff held that the shows in
question had been likely only to encourage normal heterosexual
activity (of a sort acceptable according to the standards of the day)
and that, while undoubtedly vulgar, they did not amount to
shameless indecency. By contrast, in the earlier case of *Watt v
Annan*[4] a conviction for shameless indecency was upheld in respect
of the showing of a pornographic film, which included acts of sexual
perversion.

Even if a performance is intended to encourage adult heterosexual behaviour, it may still amount to shameless indecency. The
performance, on stage, of real rather than simulated sexual intercourse would presumably not be tolerated, and would be likely to
be prosecuted as shameless indecency. Is this because such a performance is more likely to corrupt those who witness it (which is
unlikely), or is it because public acts of sexual intercourse are more
shocking to the community ? If the latter explanation is more likely,
the degree of shamelessness is increased by the heightened tendency of the act in question to shock. The portrayal of perversion
which is, by defintion, more capable of shocking, is therefore more
likely to be considered an act of shameless indecency than the
portrayal of conventional sexual activity.

The fact that conduct takes place in private does not preclude

---

[1] 1981 JC 23, 1981 SLT 50.
[2] 1953 JC 16, 1953 SLT 67.
[3] 1987 SCCR 642.
[4] 1978 JC 84, 1978 SLT 198.

shameless indecency. In *Watt v Annan* the spectators of the pornographic film were all members of a social club, and the film was shown only to members. Access to it, however, was fairly readily available, as anybody could become a member of the club by paying small dues on the spot. There was therefore little control over indeterminate access to the entertainment. Yet this issue was not central to the criminality of the conduct, which Lord Cameron held was not necessarily affected by the privacy or publicity of the locus of the indecency. It would appear to be open to a court, then, to convict of shameless indecency in circumstances where a group of adults have, for purely private pleasure, shown an obscene film in a locked room. It could be argued that the standards of the day do not regard such conduct as amounting to shameless indecency, and such a view is suggested by the decision in *Lockhart v Stephen*, but a different outcome might be expected if the film depicted acts of particularly sickening perversion (such as necrophilia).

Material which is not likely to corrupt an adult may nonetheless be regarded as potentially corrupting of a child or adolescent. In *Tudhope v Barlow*[1] magazines displayed in the shop of which the accused was the temporary manageress were held to be likely to corrupt children although they would not have corrupted an adult reader. The fact that the magazines were so stacked as to be able to be seen by children was enough to constitute the offence, although the accused was acquitted on the grounds that she had not been aware of the content of the magazines and their potentially corrupting effect on children. A similar *mens rea* requirement is stressed in *Tudhope v Taylor*.[2]

The other form of shameless indecency offence occurs where an act is performed which may not amount to an indecent assault or any other nominate sexual offence but which may nonetheless be thought to merit prosecution. In *McLaughlan v Boyd*[3] the accused had seized the hand of another man and placed it over his own private parts, an act which the court considered amounted to shameless indecency. Sexual conduct between consenting adult males, if committed in public, if it is prosecuted at all, may be prosecuted as shameless indecency, as indeed may heterosexual conduct performed in public. A sexual act committed by a male on a male under the age of 21 amounts to shameless indecency even if it takes place with consent.

[1] 1981 SLT (Sh Ct) 94.
[2] 1980 SLT (Notes) 54.
[3] 1934 JC 19, 1933 SLT 629.

SEXUAL ASSAULTS

The category of sexual assaults is a not a formal one, but it usefully groups together those offences in which there is a non-consensual intrusion into the sexual integrity of another. A sexual assault may involve considerable violence or very little; the assault element is to be found in the wrongful sexual touching rather than in incidental force used by the perpetrator.

Rape

Rape is generally considered to be one of the most serious sexual offences. It is committed when a man has sexual intercourse with a woman by means of the overcoming of her will. In most jurisdictions it is defined as being sexual intercourse with a woman who does not consent, but this definition, although it has crept into Scots usage, is not strictly accurate for Scots law in view of the fact that a sleeping or unconscious woman is not raped if a man has intercourse with her without her consent.

Rape requires penetration of the woman per vaginam. Penetration must be by the male organ; digital penetration, or penetration by an object of any sort, does not amount to rape, although the affront to the woman's sexual integrity in such cases may be as great. Oral or anal penetration amount to indecent assault but are not rape. Emission is not required, although evidence of emission may help to establish that intercourse took place.

Who is capable of committing rape? Any male over the age of eight may be guilty of rape. A woman cannot commit rape herself but may be art and part guilty of rape, as in a case where she assists a man to commit rape on another woman. The rule that a husband cannot be guilty of the rape of his wife, other than by being guilty art and part of such a rape by a third party, was stated by *Hume* and accepted by later commentators. The basis of this rule – that by marrying a man, a woman gives irrevocable consent to sexual intercourse (at least while the marriage persists) has been widely criticised as being out of step with modern notions of the relationship between spouses. In 1983, and again in 1984, husbands were convicted of the rape of their wives,[1] although in both of these cases the spouses were not living together at the time of the incident. Finally, in *Stallard v HM Adv*,[2] the High Court

[1] *HM Adv v Duffy* 1982 SCCR 182, 1983 SLT 7; *HM Adv v Paxton* 1984 SCCR 311, 1984 JC 105.
[2] 1989 SCCR 248, 1989 SLT 469.

upheld the relevancy of a charge of rape where the husband was co-habiting with the wife at the time. In this case the court observed that attitudes had changed considerably since Hume's time, and that wives are no longer bound to suffer excessive sexual demands on the part of their husbands. The court acknowledged that it may be harder to prove that there is no revocation of consent where the parties are still living together, but the principle that the wife need not have intercourse forced upon her remained applicable in such a case. It is significant, though, that the accused in *Stallard v HM Adv* used very considerable violence, and that in such circumstances it will be difficult for a husband to convince the court that he believed that his wife was consenting.

The *actus reus* of rape. Rape is committed where a man has intercourse with a woman through the overcoming of her will. This requirement is stated by *Hume* in the following terms: 'The knowledge of the woman must...be against her will, and by force'.[1] This emphasis on force has had unfortunate implications in the past in that it has been interpreted as requiring spirited resistance on the part of women, which has been translated in due course into an emphasis on injury sustained in the course of this resistance. In *Barbour v HM Adv*,[2] however, the court stressed that the amount of resistance put up is not the important matter; what really counts is that the woman remained an unwilling party throughout. Resistance, therefore, is significant only in that it is evidence of unwillingness. The use of threats to secure the victim's compliance amounts to rape.[3] These threats may be of any nature; all that is required is that they are sufficient to overcome the woman's resistance. Threats will usually be threats of physical violence, but there is no reason in principle why a threat of another nature, if serious enough, should not have the effect of overcoming the victim's will. For example, a threat to dismiss an employee who relies on her job to support a large family, and who faces financial ruin if dismissed, could have the effect of overcoming her will to resist.[4]

It is rape to administer drink or drugs to a woman with a view to overcoming her resistance and to having sexual intercourse as a result.[5] The nature of the drink or drugs must be concealed from

[1] 1, 302.
[2] 1982 SCCR 195.
[3] *Hume* I, 302; *Alison* I, 212; *Macdonald*, p 121.
[4] See also Sexual Offences (Scotland) Act 1976, s 2(1) (a): procuring or attempting to procure unlawful sexual intercourse through the use of threats or intimidation.
[5] *HM Adv v Logan* 1936 JC 100, 1937 SLT 104.

her if it is to be rape; a man who gives drink to a woman, who knows that what she is taking is intoxicating drink, and who then has sexual intercourse with her when she is so drunk as to be unable to form the inclination to resist, does not commit rape. Similarly, a man who encounters a woman who is intoxicated and who has intercourse with her in the knowledge that the only reason she is doing so is because she is too drunk to know what she is doing, does not commit rape. It is possible, though unlikely, that such a man might be charged with the offence of clandestine injury to woman.

The offence of clandestine injury to woman is committed by a man who has sexual intercourse with a sleeping or unconscious woman.[1] A man does not commit rape in such circumstances because a woman in this state is held to have no will to be overcome. This rule is open to criticism, as the wrong done to a woman who is raped while conscious and one who has non-consensual sexual intercourse inflicted on her while she is asleep or unconscious is, surely, very similar.

Inducing a woman to have sexual intercourse on the basis of a fraudulent misrepresentation does not amount to rape.[2] A possible exception to this is where the man deceives the woman as to the nature of the act of sexual intercourse, an unlikely situation which, nonetheless, arose in *R v Williams*,[3] a case in which a singing teacher convinced his female pupil that intercourse was, in fact, treatment designed to improve her singing voice. A difficulty here for Scots law would be the requirement of the overpowering of the will: if the woman is deceived as to the nature of the act, can her will be said to have been overpowered?

It is not rape if a man obtains intercourse on the basis of a false promise to marry,[4] nor will misrepresentations as to a man's circumstances negate consent. Intercourse obtained on the basis of a fraudulent misrepresentation as to identity will not amount to rape, at least on the authority of the decision in *Fraser*.[5] Thus if **A** agrees to sexual intercourse with **B**, in the belief that **B** is **C**, the fact that **B** has fostered this false belief will not make him guilty of rape. The impersonation of a woman's husband, however, for the purpose of

[1] *Sweenie* (1858) 3 Irv 109; *HM Adv v Grainger and Rae* 1932 JC 40, 1932 SLT 28; *Sweeney and Another v X* 1982 SCCR 509.

[2] *Fraser* (1847) Ark 280.

[3] [1923] 1 KB 340.

[4] This point was considered in the well-known Australian case of *R v Papadimitropolous* (1957) 98 CLR 249. The accused misrepresented to a woman that he and she had gone through a marriage ceremony. Sexual intercourse based on her belief that she was married did not amount to rape.

[5] (1847) Ark 280.

obtaining intercourse is an offence under the Sexual Offences (Scotland) Act 1976.[1]

Rape is committed if a man has sexual intercourse with a girl under the age of 12 years. This is termed constructive rape, and the offence is committed irrespective of whether the girl is a willing party or not. It is submitted that a mistaken belief that a girl is 12 years of age or over should be a defence, as this is a common law offence to which the normal requirements of *mens rea* apply. It is a common law offence to have sexual intercourse with a woman suffering from such a degree of mental abnormality as not to be able to understand the nature of the sexual act, but this matter is now also the subject of statutory regulation.[2]

The *mens rea* requirement in rape. No area of the law relating to sexual offences has been so controversial as the question of the *mens rea* requirement. The fundamental legal proposition is clear enough: the *mens rea* of rape is the intention to have sexual intercourse through the overpowering of the will, or recklessness as to the possibility that the act is performed against the woman's will.[3] If, therefore, a man believes that the woman consents to intercourse, then the *mens rea* of rape is absent.

The difficulty with this otherwise simple proposition is that of misinterpretation on the part of the man of the woman's attitude. In the controversial English case of *DPP v Morgan*[4] the House of Lords affirmed that an error on the man's part is a defence to a charge of rape, even if the error is one which no reasonable man would have made. In this case the accused alleged that they were told by a woman's husband that any attempt on her part to resist sexual intercourse would not signify real resistance but was merely an aspect of sexual enjoyment on her part. The fact that no reasonable man would have believed this was relevant in deciding whether the accused really believed the woman was consenting, but was not, in itself, grounds for excluding the defence. In *Meek v HM Adv*[5] the High Court endorsed this view of unreasonable error, although earlier authorities had consistently required that an error be reasonable before it is capable of being accepted as a

---

[1] Section 2(2).

[2] Mental Health (Scotland) Act 1984, s 102.

[3] 'The crime of rape consists in the carnal knowledge of a woman forcibly and against her will. It involves that the act of the accused is consciously and intentionally or recklessly done against the woman's will' per Lord President Emslie in *Meek v HM Adv* 1982 SCCR 613, 1983 SLT 280.

[4] [1975] 2 All ER 347, [1976] AC 182.

[5] 1982 SCCR 613, 1983 SLT 280.

defence.[1] In practice juries will be unlikely to believe that a man really made an error as to consent if the error is one which no reasonable man would have made, and therefore the significance of the decision in *Meek* is somewhat limited.

There are no Scottish decisions dealing directly with recklessness in rape, but it is likely that the Scottish courts would apply an objective criterion of recklessness (as is done in other contexts) and convict of rape if a reasonable man in the position of the accused would have been aware of a risk that the woman did not consent. Obviously such a possibility may exist in any case in which the woman does not expressly signify consent; it cannot be recklessness, however, for a man to proceed with intercourse in such a case. Recklessness should be inferred only where the woman does something which would raise a real doubt in the mind of the reasonable man that she does not consent to intercourse.

Indecent assault

An indecent assault is an assault which is committed in circumstances of indecency. The normal requirements of assault must be present, namely, physical touching or the threat of physical touching, and there must also be the necessary evil intent (which constitutes the *mens rea* of assault). An indecent assault may be committed by either sex on a member of the same or opposite sex. Consent to the touching is a defence, and it may be defence for the accused to show that he believed that the other person consented. Such a belief would probably require to be based on reasonable grounds.[2]

An assault is indecent if the part of the body touched is a sexual part or a part contiguous to a sexual part. The touching of buttocks, breasts, or sexual organs is indecent, but other parts may be involved if the surrounding circumstances are indecent. Thus the touching of a woman's arm accompanied by the use of suggestive language may be an indecent assault. The conduct in question must be objectively indecent; the fact that the accused has an indecent motive will not render his conduct indecent unless the sexual context is outwardly discernible. It is not an indecent assault to

---

[1] For example, *Crawford v HM Adv* 1950 JC 67, 1950 SLT 279.

[2] In *Young v McGlennan* 1991 SCCR 738 the accused was convicted of indecently assaulting a woman by lightly touching her breasts. It was argued on his behalf that there was no evil intent, but he was nonetheless convicted. The question of whether his belief in consent would require to be based on reasonable grounds was not addressed.

touch the clothing of another for purposes of sexual gratification if the sexual nature of the touching would not be apparent to the observer of such conduct.[1]

Outwardly indecent contact might be rendered innocent by virtue of the circumstances in which it occurs. In *Stewart v Thain*[2] the accused, a schoolmaster, disciplined a partly-naked boy, requiring him to expose his buttocks for chastisement. The court held that this did not amount to an indecent assault, given the right of the schoolmaster to punish the boy: no indecent motive was proved.

OFFENCES AGAINST YOUNG PERSONS

(1) Girls

As stated above, sexual intercourse with a girl under the age of 12 may be charged as rape. Sexual intercourse with a girl who is not yet 13 is an offence under s 31(1) of the Sexual Offences (Scotland) Act 1976. This is an offence of absolute liability, and it does not have to be proved that the man was aware of the girl's age. Sexual intercourse, or attempted sexual intercourse, with a girl aged between 13 and 15 is an offence under s 4 of the same Act. It is a defence if a man charged with an offence under this section either had reasonable cause to believe that the girl was his wife or, being a man under the age of 24 years, and who has not previously been charged with a like offence, had reasonable cause to believe that the girl was aged at least 16 years. Section 4 applies only to 'unlawful' sexual intercourse, which means that no offence is committed if the parties are married.

Sexual acts falling short of intercourse are criminal if committed with a girl under the age 16. It is a common law offence for a man to engage in any indecent practice with a girl under the age of 12 years, and a statutory offence is committed if a man uses towards a girl aged at least 12 but under 16 any lewd, indecent or libidinous practice or behaviour which would have constituted an offence at common law.[3] The consent of the girl is no defence, and there need not be physical contact with the girl.

---

[1] In *R v Court* [1987] 1 All ER 120, [1987] QB 156 the question of a concealed motive was considered. Conduct was held to be indecent where the accused confessed to sexual motives, thus throwing a sexual light on what he had done.
[2] 1981 JC 13, 1981 SLT (Notes) 2.
[3] Sexual Offences (Scotland) Act 1976, s 5.

(2) Boys

Any homosexual act committed with a male under the age of 21 years is a criminal offence, subject to the provisions of the Criminal Justice (Scotland) Act 1980, discussed below. It is a common law offence to commit an act of indecency with a boy under the age of 14. Indecent conduct with a male aged under 21 may be prosecuted as shameless indecency or as lewd and indecent practices.

A woman who engages in sexual practices with a boy under the age of 14 may be prosecuted for the common law offences of shameless indecency or lewd and indecent practices. The position of heterosexual acts with boys aged 14 and over is not clear. It might be considered shameless indecency for a mature woman to engage in sexual practices with a boy aged 14, but prosecution is unlikely, and becomes less likely if the boy is even older.

HOMOSEXUAL OFFENCES

It is the common law offence of gross and shameless indecency for a male to commit a sexual act with another male.[1] The common law offence of sodomy, which consists of the insertion of the penis into the anus of another male, is committed by both parties involved, provided that the patient is consenting.

Homosexual conduct was legalised by section 80 of the Criminal Justice (Scotland) Act 1980, which provides that homosexual conduct is not criminal provided that: the act takes place in private[2] (a lavatory to which the public has access is not a private place); that both parties consent; and that both parties have reached the age of 21 years. A man who wrongly believes a partner to be 21 years of age or over has a defence if he (the accused) is under the age of 24 years, has not been charged with a like offence before, and has reasonable grounds for believing the other man to be at least 21 years old.

Homosexual conduct in the armed services and among members of the merchant navy (on board ship) remains a criminal offence. The Criminal Justice (Scotland) Act 1980 also provides that a male

[1] *McLaughlan v Boyd* 1934 JC 19, 1933 SLT 629.
[2] For discussion as to what is 'in private' (in the context of the similarly worded English legislation), see *R v Reakes* (1974) Crim LR 296. In this case the Court of Appeal endorsed the following approach to the concept of privacy: 'You look at all the surrounding circumstances, the time of night, the nature of the place including such matters as lighting and you consider further the likelihood of a third person coming upon the scene'.

person cannot give a valid consent to homosexual conduct if he suffers from mental handicap 'of such a nature or degree that he is incapable of living an independent life or guarding himself against serious exploitation'.[1]

INCEST AND RELATED OFFENCES

The statutory offence of incest is committed by any person who has sexual intercourse with another person who is related to him or her within the prohibited degrees. Until the passage of the Incest and Related Offences (Scotland) Act 1986, this offence was regulated by the Incest Act 1567. This Act embodied the biblical prohibitions set out in Leviticus 18, and the law was supplemented by additional statutory marriage prohibitions.[2] The extent of the prohibited degrees under the former law was the subject of criticism, particularly in so far as sexual intercourse was prohibited between persons related by affinity, and there was also criticism of the exclusion of adoptive relationship from the ambit of the crime.

Under the Incest and Related Offences (Scotland) Act 1986, the offence of incest is committed by any person, male or female, who has sexual intercourse with a person with whom he or she has a relationship listed in the statutory table.[3] The relationships, which are all ones of consanguinity or adoption are: a man's mother, daughter, grandmother, grand-daughter, sister, aunt, niece, great-grandmother, great-grand-daughter, adoptive mother or former adoptive mother, and adopted daughter or former adopted daughter. The equivalent relationships apply in the case of a woman. Relationships of the half blood are included: it is therefore incest for a man to have intercourse with a woman who shares one parent with him.

The prosecution does not have to prove that the accused knew of the relationship existing between him and the other person; the onus of proving that he did not know that he was related within the prohibited degrees therefore rests upon the accused person. It is also a defence if intercourse took place without consent or if the parties were married at the time of the offence (as might be the case if a marriage recognised in Scotland as valid had taken place abroad).

---

[1] Section 80(3).
[2] Marriage (Prohibited Degrees of Relationship) Acts 1907–1931, applied in a criminal context by the Criminal Procedure (Scotland) Act 1938, s 13.
[3] The Incest and Related Offences (Scotland) Act 1986 inserts a new s 2A in the Sexual Offences (Scotland) Act 1976, in which the table of relationships is set out.

The offence of incest is restricted to those cases where sexual intercourse takes place. Sexual activity between persons within the prohibited degrees may also be prosecuted as shameless indecency, as demonstrated by the decision in *R v HM Adv.*[1] This case involved sexual activity between a father and daughter, which excites particular social disapproval. It is possible that attitudes towards sexual activity between, say, adult consenting siblings would not be regarded as amounting to shameless indecency.

Sexual intercourse between step-parent and step-child is an offence if the child is under the age of 21 at the time at which intercourse takes place, or had at any time before reaching the age of 18 years lived in the same household as the step-parent and had been treated by him as a child of the family. Defences to this offence are listed in s1. The Incest and Related Offences (Scotland) Act 1986 also introduced a new offence of sexual abuse of trust.[2] This offence is committed by a person over the age of 16 years who enters into a sexual relationship with a child under the age of 16 years of age in respect of whom he occupies a position of trust and who is a member of the same household. Such persons are already protected by other provisions of the criminal law; this offence, however, provides for a potentially more severe penalty than would otherwise be available.

SUNDRY OFFENCES

In addition to the crimes described above, the following forms of conduct constitute sexual offences:

(1) Indecent exposure. It is a crime to expose sexual parts in indecent circumstances.[3] The exposure of the body to those who consent to witness is not a criminal offence, and this would probably exclude stage nudity from the scope of the offence. It might, however, be the offence of shameless indecency to appear nude on the stage in inappropriate circumstances, such as in a show attended by children or others who might not expect to witness nudity. The test must be whether the exposure causes shock and distaste on the part of those present.

(2) Bestiality. The having of sexual intercourse with an animal is the common law offence of bestiality.[4] The commission with

---

[1] 1988 SCCR 254, 1988 SLT 623.
[2] Sexual Offences (Scotland) Act 1976, s 2C.
[3] *Niven v Tudhope* 1982 SCCR 365; *Macdonald v Cardle* 1985 SCCR 195.
[4] *Hume* I, 469.

an animal of a sexual act falling short of intercourse might be charged as shameless indecency.

(3) Abduction. It is a common law offence to abduct a female person for the purposes of rape or marriage, a crime which has to all intents and purposes fallen into disuse. It is a statutory offence to abduct a girl under the age of 18 years from her parents or those having care or charge of her for the purpose of unlawful (that is extra-marital) sexual intercourse.[1]

(4) Prostitution offences. The act of prostitution, that is, the selling of sexual services, is not a criminal offence. This applies to both homosexual and heterosexual prostitution, provided, of course, in the case of homosexual prostitution, the act takes place in private and involves consenting persons over the age of 21 years. The fundamental legality of the transaction, however, does not make it possible for a prostitute to ply her trade with impunity. Soliciting in public is an offence under the Civic Government (Scotland) Act 1982, and the Sexual Offences (Scotland) Act 1976 also makes it an offence for any male person to persistently importune or solicit in public for immoral purposes.[2] A man who walks down the street approaching women for sexual purposes commits an offence under this provision. The making of a single sexual suggestion in such circumstances would not be persistent importuning, although it might be prosecuted as a breach of the peace.

The procuring of women for prostitution is an offence,[3] as is the running of a brothel or the allowing of one's premises to be used as a brothel.[4] It is an offence for a man to live wholly or partly on the proceeds of prostitution,[5] and an offence is also committed by a woman who exercises 'control, direction or influence over the movements of a prostitute in such a manner as to show that she is aiding, abetting or compelling her prostitution'.[6]

---

[1] Sexual Offences (Scotland) Act 1976, s 8.

[2] Section 12(1)(b).

[3] Sexual Offences (Scotland) Act 1976, s 1.

[4] Ibid, s 13.

[5] Ibid, s 12. The question of proof of the fact that a man is living on the proceeds of prostitution is dealt with in s 12(3), which in certain circumstances places the burden of proving the contrary on the man.

[6] Sexual Offences (Scotland) Act 1976, s 12(4).

III. SOCIAL PROTECTION OFFENCES

12. Social Offences

MISUSE OF DRUGS

The use of drugs for recreational purposes was not illegal in the nineteenth century, and it is only in the earlier years of the twentieth century that many countries began to introduce criminal sanctions directed against the marketing and possession of certain abused drugs. In the case of the United Kingdom, the first important piece of legislation was the Dangerous Drugs Act 1920. This formed the model for subsequent legislation, of which the Misuse of Drugs Act 1971, referred to below as the MDA, is the current representative. This legislation now regulates the importation, production, possession and supply of a wide range of controlled drugs. In addition, there is a large body of subsidiary legislation, in the form of statutory instruments made under the authority of the MDA, which specifies controlled drugs and regulates incidental matters such as secure storage. There are two other important acts in this area: the Customs and Excise Management Act 1979, under which importation offences may be prosecuted, and the Drug Trafficking Offences Act 1986 which provides, inter alia, for the confiscation of the profits of drug trafficking.

Controlled drugs

The MDA divides controlled drugs into three categories: class A, class B, and class C.[1] Class A encompasses the following commonly abused drugs:

(1) The opiates (heroin, morphine, methadone etc). These may be naturally derived from the opium poppy or produced artificially. A feature of their use is both psychological and physical dependence.

[1] MDA, Sch 2.

(2) Cocaine and its derivatives (principally 'crack'). Cocaine comes from the coca leaf and is a stimulant. Cocaine itself causes mainly psychological dependence, although its derivate, 'crack', produces an intense physical craving for further use.
(3) Hallucinogens. The most notorious of these in common use is LSD, although other forms are widely used. These drugs have a profound psychological effect, and their impact on the chemistry of the brain can be significant.

Class B drugs include amphetamines (stimulants) and cannabis and its derivatives. This latter drug, which is taken in the form of dried leaves or resin, is very widely used. Its effect is to create a feeling of well-being, and there is no substantial evidence of serious medical side-effects. It is not physically addictive, but its psychological effect, particularly when heavily used over a long period, may be deleterious. Certain derivatives of cannabis fall into class A.

Class C drugs include minor stimulants, such as methaqualone. Other drugs which may be abused, and which are regulated to the extent that they are available only on prescription, fall outwith the scope of the MDA. Tranquillisers and certain strong pain killers are widely abused, but their possession is not an offence under the MDA.

Controlled drug offences

Offences connected with controlled drugs fall into three main categories: importation and exportation offences; production and supply offences; and possession offences. The seriousness of the penalty in each case will depend on the nature of the drug involved. The supply of a class A drug, for example, will attract a more severe penalty than the supply of a class B or C drug.

Importation and exportation. Most offences in this category will in practice be concerned with the importation of drugs. This offence is created by the combined effect of section 3(1) of the MDA (which prohibits the importation of controlled drugs) and section 170(2) of the Customs and Excise Management Act 1979 which creates the specific offence of being 'knowingly concerned in the fraudulent evasion of the prohibition on the importation of controlled drugs'.

A person is knowingly concerned with the importation of a controlled drug when he is aware of the fact that a substance with the importation of which he is concerned is, in fact, a controlled drug. If **A** thinks that he is bringing currency into the country, and believes (wrongly) that this is a criminal offence, he does not commit the offence of being knowingly concerned in the importation of a controlled drug even if it transpires that the package he is carrying contains heroin.[1] If, however, **A** believes that he is importing a controlled drug, whereas he is in fact bringing in a harmless powder, he commits the offence of attempting to breach the provisions of section 170(2) of the Customs and Excise Management Act 1979.[2]

The courts have interpreted this provision widely, enabling a person to be convicted of such an offence even if the part he plays in importation comes well before, or well after, the actual importation.[3] Liability may be imposed even where the accused's part in importation has been performed entirely abroad.[4] Similarly, the performance in Scotland of any act intended to breach the provisions of corresponding law abroad is an offence punishable in Scotland.[5]

Production and supply. It is an offence under section 4 of the MDA to produce or supply a controlled drug. Production is defined in section 37(1) and includes cultivation and laboratory production. Cultivation embraces any act which is intended to encourage the growth of a plant in which a controlled drug occurs. In *Tudhope v Robertson and Another*[6] a cannabis plant was found in a bedroom, placed near a window, and the court held that the placing of the plant near the window (in order to encourage photosynthesis) amounted to cultivation. It is not cultivation to leave untouched a plant found growing in one's garden, but cultivation would occur if the plant were to be watered or moved.

Supply offences include actual supply and offering to supply. Intention to supply may be inferred from the actings of the accused in general or from the quantity of the drug which is found in his possession.[7] The presence of scales, and other instruments for measuring and parcelling out drugs, will be evidence of possession with intent to supply.

The offence of offering to supply is committed even if the

---

[1] *R v Taaffe* [1983] 1 WLR 627, [1983] 2 All ER 625.
[2] *R v Shivpuri* 1987 AC 1, [1986] 2 All ER 334.
[3] *R v Wall* (1974) 59 Crim App Rep 58, [1974] 2 All ER 245; *R v Jakeman* (1982) 76 Crim App Rep 223.
[4] *R v Wall*, supra.
[5] MDA, s 20; *R v Evans* (1976) 64 Crim App Rep 237.
[6] 1980 JC 62, 1980 SLT 60.
[7] *Morrison v Smith* 1983 SCCR 171.

accused does not have in his possession the drugs offered and even if he has no means of obtaining them.[1] A person who offers to supply a harmless substance to another, erroneously believing it to be a controlled drug, commits an offence under section 4 of the MDA in spite of his error as to the nature of the substance.[2]

Possession. It is an offence under section 5 of the MDA to be in possession of a controlled drug, and it is under this section that the vast majority of drug prosecutions are brought. Possession for these purposes requires both a mental and physical element: the physical element is that of control, yet even if there is control, a person is not in possession of a substance unless he knows that he has it in his control and unless he knows the general nature of the substance. A person who does not know that what he has in his possession is a controlled drug does not commit an offence under section 5,[3] but conviction does not require that he know the exact nature of the drug. If **A** has in his possession a substance which he believes to be heroin, but which is in reality cocaine, he may be convicted of possession under section 5 irrespective of his error as to the nature of the drug.

Knowledge of the existence of a drug will not be enough to secure a conviction where the accused did not have control over it. A number of cases in this area involve the issue of the presence of controlled drugs in shared accommodation: if drugs are found in a shared house or flat are all the occupants deemed to be in possession of them ? The courts have indicated that something more than knowledge will be required in such a case. Access to the drug will be a factor, as indicated in *Allan and Ors v Milne*[4]. In this case, four persons shared a flat in which cannabis was found, together with drug apparatus. The sheriff stated: '. . .in the absence of any evidence to the contrary, the only reasonable inference from these circumstances was that all the appellants had knowledge of the presence of the cannabis and of its whereabouts. I was further satisfied that any of the appellants had access to the cannabis and could use it as he or she chose'. A somewhat more restrictive view was taken by Lord Cameron in *Mingay v Mackinnon*,[5] in which he stated that even though cannabis smoking clearly took place on a large scale in a shared flat, the prosecution still had to prove in

---

[1] *HM Adv v Ferreira and Ors*, (April 1976, unreported), Glasgow Sheriff Court; discussed by K Bovey *Misuse of Drugs* (1986) p 22.

[2] *Haggard v Mason* [1976] 1 WLR 187, [1976] 1 All ER 337.

[3] *Mckenzie v Skeen* 1983 SLT (Notes) 121.

[4] 1974 SLT (Notes) 76.

[5] 1980 JC 33.

relation to the appellant that 'cannabis resin, or some of it, was in the possession and control of the appellant'.[1]

The question of whether a person can be said to be in possession of the contents of a container which he possesses was addressed in the much-discussed case of *Warner v Metropolitan Police Commissioner*.[2] The thrust of this decision is that in such a case the prosecution must still prove that the accused knew that there was something in the container over which he had actual control, but that once this was done an evidential burden falls on the accused to show that he had no opportunity or authority to open the container, that he had no reason to suspect it contained an unlawful substance, and that he believed that the contents of the conatiner differed from what they actually transpired to be. There is no Scottish authority on the point, but it is likely that a Scottish court would find the decision in *Warner* persuasive.

Further problems in possession include the question of whether the possession of a minute quantity of a drug amounts to possession. The smoking of cannabis, for example, may leave traces of the drug in a pipe used for this purpose, as may the storage of a drug in a receptacle. The taking of a scraping from the pipe or receptacle may permit analysis to reveal traces of the drug, even if these traces amount to little more than a few micrograms. In *Bocking v Roberts*[3] it was held that the test in such a case should be that of usability, and that there would be no possession where the quantity was so small that it could not be used by the accused. This test was disapproved, however, in *Keane v Gallacher*[4] where the court opted for the test of whether the drug could be identified in an acceptable manner. The only limitations, therefore, are those inherent in the scientific tests available, and it becomes possible for a person to be in possession of a controlled drug long after he had thought that the drugs had been disposed of or consumed.

The main objection to this is that it makes it difficult for a person to abandon the use of a drug. A person may experiment with cannabis on one or two occasions, think better of it, and resolve not to have the drug in his possession in the future. But if minute traces of the drug remain in the pocket of his jacket or in his drawer, then his attempts to distance himself from past possession and use are obstructed. This may involve no injustice in the technical sense, in

---

[1] At 35.
[2] [1968] 2 All ER 356.
[3] [1973] 3 All ER 962, [1974] QB 307. Also: *R v Carver* [1978] QB 472, [1978] 3 All ER 60.
[4] 1980 JC 77, 1980 SLT 144.

that it is true that he did at one point have the drug in his possession (in the meaningful sense of the term) and it is therefore permissible to convict him, but the law should encourage a change of heart, and this rule certainly does not do that.

A similar harsh result may be achieved in a case where the accused has forgotten that he has a controlled drug in his possession. In *Gill v Lockhart*[1] cannabis was found in the accused's golf bag, having allegedly been placed there some years previously and forgotten. It was argued on the accused's behalf that the fact that he had forgotten the presence of the cannabis meant that he could no longer be said to be in possession of it, but this argument was rejected. Possession, the court said, did not require constant awareness of an object, otherwise one would not be in possession of those items of one's property which one does not have in mind at any particular time. This is undoubtedly the case, and yet a case may be be made out for stating that a point will come at which it will seem counter-intuitive to say that forgotten property is still in one's possession. This might be so with property which has been forgotten for a period of, say, ten years or more.

It will be a defence to a charge of possession to prove that controlled drugs were taken from another in order to prevent the commission of an offence and that all reasonable steps have been taken to ensure that the drugs were destroyed or handed over to a person lawfully entitled to take custody of them, or to prove that the drugs were received solely for the purposes of handing them over to the authorities.[2] Possession of a controlled drug for a very brief period of time will not amount to an offence provided that the contact is no more than fleeting.[3]

BREACH OF THE PEACE

Breach of the peace is one of the most commonly charged criminal offences and is capable of covering a wide range of conduct which may be considered socially disruptive or offensive. A breach of the peace may actually have caused a disturbance, as in a case where the accused shouted or brawled in the street, or it may just be likely to do so, as in a case where a person shouts a slogan which could cause a fracas but which does not do so, owing to the self-restraint

---

[1] 1987 SCCR 599, 1988 SLT 189.

[2] MDA, s 5(4).

[3] *R v Wright* [1976] Crim L R 248; *Mackay v Hogg* (11 May 1973, unreported) High Court, discussed by K Bovey *Misuse of Drugs* (1986) p 78.

of others. A clear statement of both of these aspects of the offence was provided by Lord Dunpark in *Wilson v Brown*[1] in which he observed:

'It is well settled that a test which may be applied in charges of breach of the peace is whether the proved conduct may reasonably be expected to cause any person to be alarmed, upset or annoyed or to provoke a disturbance of the peace. Positive evidence of actual alarm, upset, annoyance or disturbance created by reprisal is not a prerequisite of conviction.'

The circumstances in which the conduct occurs will determine whether or not a breach of the peace has been committed. Behaviour which is harmless in one context may be inflammatory in another, as is demonstrated by the decision in *McAvoy v Jessop*.[2] In this case the accused was in charge of a marching Orange band which he ordered to strike up when it approached a Catholic church in front of which a priest was greeting parishioners. This was held to constitute a breach of the peace, although the playing of sectarian tunes out of sight and earshot of the church might have been quite innocent conduct.

The essence of the offence is the causing of alarm in the minds of the lieges. This alarm has been variously defined by courts. In *Ferguson v Carnochan*[3] it was said not necessarily to be 'alarm in the sense of personal fear, but alarm lest if what is going on is allowed to continue it will lead to the breaking of the social peace'. Alarm may now be too strong a term: in *Macmillan v Normand*[4] the offence was committed when abusive language caused 'concern' on the part of policemen at whom it was directed.

Can private conduct amount to a breach of the peace? A requirement that alarm be caused to members of the public would appear to exclude this, but in a small number of cases the courts have held that a breach of the peace is committed even when only one or two persons (apart from the accused) are present. In *Young v Heatly*[5] the accused, a schoolmaster, was convicted of a breach of the peace in respect of improper suggestions he had made to boys. The suggestions were made in the presence of only one boy at a time but the court held that this was a special case in which it was justified in holding that a breach of the peace had occurred. In

---

[1] 1982 SCCR 49 at 51, 1982 SLT 361. For a full discussion of the offence see M Christie *Breach of the Peace* (1990).
[2] 1989 SCCR 301.
[3] (1889) 16 R 93, 2 White 278.
[4] 1989 SCCR 269.
[5] 1959 JC 66, 1959 SLT 250.

Thompson v Macphail[1] the accused had injected himself with drugs in a locked toilet. Access was eventually gained to the toilet and blood was found in the walls and a syringe was seen. The court declined to convict of breach of the peace, but observed, nonetheless, that circumstances such as these could lead to conviction of the offence.

The use of abusive language to the police may be a breach of the peace even if no members of the public hear it. In *Logan v Jessop*[2] a conviction of breach of the peace was quashed where the accused had sworn at the police in private, but in *Norris v Macleod*[3] the accused was convicted of a breach of the peace when he swore at the police in a sustained fashion.

In addition to the common law offence of breach of the peace, which has shown remarkable flexibility, minor breaches of public order are covered by the provisions of the Civic Government (Scotland) Act, 1982.[4]

The carrying of weapons in public is dealt with by the Prevention of Crime Act 1953 which makes it an offence to carry on one's person, in public, an offensive weapon without lawful authority or reasonable excuse. Offensive weapons are divided into three categories: (1) weapons made for the purposes of causing injury to others (bayonets, guns[5] etc); (2) weapons which are adapted for such a purpose (a sharpened steel comb, for example); and (3) weapons such as hunting knives, shotguns etc, which may have an innocent purpose. In the case of weapons in classes (1) and (2) the onus is upon the accused to prove that he had the weapon under lawful authority or with a reasonable excuse. In the case of weapons in class (3), the Crown must show that the accused had the weapon on him with the intention of causing personal injury to another.

A fear of crime does not justify the carrying of an offensive weapon. Thus, a taxi driver who carried with him in his taxi a piece of rubber hose with metal in the end of it was convicted of an offence under the Act in spite of his contention that the risk which a taxi driver runs at night justified the carrying of such a weapon.[6]

---

[1] 1989 SCCR 266, 1989 SLT 637.

[2] 1987 SCCR 604.

[3] 1988 SCCR 572.

[4] Particularly ss 46–56.

[5] These are offensive weapons *per se*. Compare *Tudhope v O'Neill* 1982 SCCR 45 (flick knife) with *Woods v Heywood* 1988 SCCR 434 (machete, which also has an innocent use). See also the Firearms Act 1968, s 16; the offence of carrying a firearm with intent to endanger life or cause serious injury to property.

[6] *Grieve v Macleod* 1967 JC 32, 1967 SLT 70. On reasonable excuse, see also *Hemming v Annan* 1982 SCCR 432 (Nunchaca sticks).

The position of security guards is questionable: such guards may have a reasonable excuse for the carrying of a weapon for their personal protection, provided that the weapon is a reasonably appropriate one. If might be permissible for a guard making a delivery of valuables to carry a truncheon on his belt, given the real risk of robbery. The carrying of such a weapon is reasonable in the circumstances, particularly since it is carried by a uniformed man who makes no attempt at concealment. The matter is undecided, however. In the English case of *Spanner*[1] the Court of Appeal held that it was an offence under the Act for a security guard at a dance hall to be armed with a truncheon, the court stressing that weapons should not be carried as a matter of routine or as 'part of the uniform'. Yet in *Grieve v Macleod*[2] the court accepted that there may be circumstances in which the carrying of a wooden truncheon was legitimate, although it did not say what these circumstances would be. Members of the public who run no more than the normal risks of violence common to all have no reasonable excuse for the carrying of a weapon. It would not be legal for a person fearing sexual or other attack to carry a cannister of tear gas spray.

[1] [1973] Crim L R 704.
[2] 1967 JC 32, 1967 SLT 70.

13. Road Traffic Offences

Road traffic law in Scotland is now primarily based on two statutes: the Road Traffic Act 1988 (RTA) (as amended), and the Road Traffic Offenders Act 1988 (RTO). These Acts replace much, although not all, of the previously existing legislation, including the whole of the Road Traffic Act 1972, which contained the bulk of road traffic provisions. This chapter deals only with the main offences contained in sections 1 to 5 of the 1988 Act, and includes consideration of the changes introduced by the Road Traffic Act 1991. The Acts apply both to England and Scotland, and while English decisions are generally regarded as being relevant in Scottish cases, and occasionally vice versa, the two jurisdictions have sometimes differed in their approach to the legislation in more or less identical situations.

The interpretation of the word 'driving' provides a good example. **A** pushes his car along the street, controlling the steering wheel through an open window. Is he 'driving' the car, for the purposes of the RTA? In Scotland the answer appears to be 'yes'. In *Ames v McLeod*[1] it was held that when one is 'in a substantial sense controlling the movement and direction of the car',[2] one is 'driving' for the purposes of the Road Traffic Acts. It is not essential in Scotland that the engine be running, or the accused actually sitting in the car. The opposite conclusion was reached in the English case of *R v McDonagh*,[3] in which the Court of Appeal approved the *Ames v McLeod* test, but added to it the rider that 'it is still necessary to consider whether the activity in question can fall within the ordinary meaning of the word "driving"',[4] in order to prevent absurdities. There was an unsuccessful attempt in *McArthur v Valentine*[5] to import this further requirement into Scots law. In that case

---

[1] 1969 JC 1.
[2] At 3 per Lord Justice-General Clyde.
[3] (1974) 59 Crim App Rep 55, [1974] QB 448.
[4] [1974] QB 448 at 452 per Lord Widgery CJ.
[5] 1989 SCCR 704, 1990 JC 146.

the court said that absurdity was avoided by giving due weight to the words 'in a substantial sense', and on the facts, followed *Ames v McLeod*.

The 'substantial control' criterion means that it is possible for two people to be 'driving' a car at one time, for example where a driving instructor uses dual controls to assist a learner driver. There is some doubt as to the situation where a person merely steers a vehicle which is being towed – such a person has only limited control over the movement and direction of the vehicle, and cannot, it seems, be convicted of reckless driving.[1]

DRIVING AND AUTOMATISM

Following the decision of the High Court in *Ross v HM Adv*,[2] there is now a limited defence of non-insane automatism in Scots law. However, the decision in *Ross* is in terms that automatism negates *mens rea*. Many driving offences are offences of strict liability for which proof of *mens rea* is unnecessary. It is, however, arguable that unconscious 'actings' are not actings at all, since involuntary.

'A person is entitled to be acquitted if if he is in such a state, and the evidence shows that the movement of his hands, body and legs in 'driving' were involuntary and wholly uncontrolled by any conscious effort of will on his part.'[3]

Thus, provided the accused's automatic state was due to some external cause, such as a blow to the head, or the ingestion of drugs, for which the accused was not himself responsible, and the effect of which he was not bound to foresee,[4] automatism may be a defence even to absolute driving offences.

Attempting to drive

Whether there has been an attempt to drive is largely a question of fact, but one which looks primarily to the actions and intentions of the driver. It is, for example, irrelevant that the attempt was

---

[1]   *Wallace v Major* [1946] KB 473. Doubts have been expressed about this case, eg in *R v McDonagh* (1974) 59 Crim App Rep 55; and a person in this situation can be convicted of driving while disqualified – *McQuade v Anderton* [1980] 1 WLR 154, [1980] 3 All ER 540.

[2]   1991 SCCR 823, 1991 SLT 564.

[3]   *Farrell v Stirling* 1975 SLT (Sh Ct) 71. Cf *Hill v Baxter* [1958] 1 QB 277 at 283 per Lord Goddard CJ, [1958] 1 All ER 193.

[4]   See *Ross v HM Adv* 1991 SCCR 823, 1991 SLT 564.

doomed to failure, because the vehicle had broken down, had been clamped, or because the driver was using the wrong key.[1]

SOME FURTHER DEFINITIONS

i. Mechanically propelled vehicle

'A mechanically propelled vehicle intended or adapted for use on the roads'.[2] Thus, if a vehicle is not intended for use on the public highway, it may fall outwith the definition. This may lead to anomalous results. In *McLean v McCabe*,[3] for example, it was held that 'dumper trucks' used in the construction industry are not motor vehicles, since not intended for use on the roads, while in *Woodward v James Young (Contractors) Ltd*,[4] the opposite conclusion was reached in respect of agricultural tractors since they are intended for occasional use on the highways. The definition emphasises the construction of the vehicle, rather than the way in which it is used. A vehicle remains a mechanically propelled vehicle even if it is being pedalled or pushed along a road.[5] A vehicle will not fall within the definition if it has reached 'such a state of mechanical or structural decrepitude' that it would be nonsense to describe it as a mechanically propelled vehicle.[6] However, a vehicle which has broken down is still a mechanically propelled vehicle and depending on its condition, may still fall within the definition.[7] In *Newbury v Simmonds*[8] it was even held that a car remains a 'motor vehicle' when its engine has been removed, although it would be different if there was evidence that the engine had been permanently removed or could not easily be replaced.

ii. Road or other public place

The term 'road' is defined in the Roads (Scotland) Act 1984, s 151, as being any way over which there is a public right of passage, and includes verges, bridges and tunnels. The road need not be a public

---

[1] See eg *Kelly v Hogan* [1982] RTR 352; *R v Farrance* [1978] RTR 225, [1978] 67 Crim App Rep 136.
[2] RTA, s 185(1).
[3] 1964 SLT (Sh Ct) 39.
[4] 1958 JC 28, 1958 SLT 289.
[5] See eg *McEachran v Hurst* [1978] RTR 462.
[6] *Tudhope v Every* 1976 JC 42.
[7] *McEachran v Hurst*, supra.
[8] [1961] 2 QB 345, [1961] 2 All ER 318.

road, but the extent to which private roads fall within the definition is unclear. In *Hogg v Nicholson*,[1] it was held that a road on a private estate, and marked 'Private Road' was nevertheless a road within the statutory definition, since some members of the public, such as traders and the police, had access to it. That case was however decided under a definition of 'road' couched only in terms of 'access'[2] rather than 'public right of passage', and it may be that the courts will now take a different view of this type of situation.[3]

Brown v Braid[4] defined 'road or other public place' as a place 'on which members of the public might be found, and over which they might be expected to be passing, or over which they are in use to have access'. Fields and other pieces of ground used for parking,[5] hotel driveways,[6] lay-bys,[7] and garage forecourts,[8] have all been held to be public places under the definition. In *Young v Carmichael*,[9] however, it was pointed out that a place is not a public place merely because some members of the public have access to it. There must be evidence to show that members of the public in general had access to the place in the sense that they 'normally resorted to it and so might be expected to be there'. Thus, if signs make it clear that only residents are permitted in a car park, it is probably not a public place.

iii. Accident

Whether or not an accident has occurred may be of importance in a number of situations, for example where a driver fails to stop after an accident.[10] It is very much a question of fact in each case whether an accident has occurred, and rather than formulating a precise definition, the courts have preferred to apply a 'common sense' approach. In particular, it seems that the term is not to be confined to cases where there has been an 'adverse physical result'. In *Pryde v Brown*,[11] for example, it was held that where pedestrians walking on

---

[1] 1968 SLT 265.
[2] Road Traffic Act 1960, s 257(1).
[3] See *Young v Carmichael* 1991 SCCR 332, discussed below, and cf *Wheatley* at para 1.8:1.
[4] 1984 SCCR 286, 1985 SLT 37 at 38.
[5] *Paterson v Ogilvy* 1957 JC 42, 1957 SLT 354; *McDonald v McEwen* 1953 SLT (Sh Ct) 26.
[6] *Dunne v Keane* 1976 JC 39.
[7] *MacNeill v Dunbar* 1965 SLT (Notes) 79.
[8] *Brown v Braid* 1985 SLT 37, 1984 SCCR 286.
[9] 1991 SCCR 332.
[10] An offence under s170 of the RTA.
[11] 1982 SCCR 26, 1982 SLT 314.

a main road had been forced to jump out of the way of a speeding car, an accident had occurred. Furthermore, an incident may be described as an 'accident' even where it results from a deliberate act.[1]

iv. Using, causing and permitting

This phrase is encountered in relation to contraventions of the licensing requirements, and construction and use regulations. Liability for 'use' offences seems to be strict, and knowledge of the contravention is irrelevant.[2] Offences involving the 'causing' or 'permitting' of some contravention, on the other hand, require some degree of knowledge of the circumstances giving rise to the contravention.[3] Wilful blindness may suffice however.[4]

THE MAIN OFFENCES

These are contained in sections 1 to 5 of the RTA.

Section 1: Causing death by dangerous driving

In a prosecution under section 1, it is necessary to show that the accused drove in a dangerous manner, and thus caused the death of some person. 'Dangerous driving' is defined in section 2A of the Act[5] which states:

'(1) . . . a person is to be regarded as driving dangerously if (and, subject to subsection 2 below, only if):
    (a) the way he drives falls far below what would be expected of a competent and careful driver, and
    (b) it would be obvious to a competent and careful driver that driving in that way would be dangerous.
(2) A person is also to be regarded as driving dangerously for the purposes of sections 1 and 2 above if it would be obvious to a competent and careful driver that driving the vehicle in its current state would be dangerous.'

The danger in question is danger to any person or serious damage to property. Awareness of danger is assessed objectively, but it is significant that section 2A allows a court to take into consideration any circumstances shown to have been within the knowledge of the accused.[6] Thus special knowledge (such as knowledge that young

---

[1] *Chief Constable of Staffordshire v Lees* [1981] RTR 506.
[2] See *Valentine v MacBrayne Haulage Ltd* 1986 SCCR 692 for a review of the authorities.
[3] *Smith of Maddiston v Macnab* 1975 JC 48, 1975 SLT 86. Cf *Lockhart v MCB* 1981 SLT 161.
[4] See eg *Carmichael v Hannaway* 1987 SCCR 236.
[5] Inserted into the RTA 1988 by the RTA 1991, s1.
[6] RTA, s2A (3).

children are apt to be in a particular part of a road) may impose a duty to take particular care.

Causation. Where an accused is charged under section 1 it is vital to establish a causal link between the dangerous driving and the victim's death. In doing so, it is enough that the accused's driving was a 'material' or operative cause of the death. Thus, there may be a conviction under section 1 even if the victim is contributorily negligent. In *Watson v HM Adv*,[1] for example, the victim drove through a junction without waiting for a filter signal. The accused was also adjudged to have been reckless however, and was convicted of the section 1 offence.

For the purposes of section 1, it seems that the 'person' killed as a result of the driving need not be in life at the time of the accident. There was a conviction under the section in *McCluskey v HM Adv*,[2] where a fetus was in utero at the time the accident occurred, was born alive by caesarian section, but died shortly thereafter as a result of the injuries sustained by its mother.[3] In reaching this conclusion, the court followed the English view that there is manslaughter where a child who has been born alive, dies as a result of injuries sustained while in utero.[4] Scots law on this point is unsettled.[5]

Section 2: Dangerous driving

Dangerous driving is an offence per se, even if no fatality, or indeed any other adverse consequence, results from the driving.[6] The test to be applied is the statutory one outlined above.

---

[1] (1978) SCCR Supp 192. See also *R v Hennigan* [1971] 3 All ER 133, (1971) 55 Crim App Rep 262.
[2] 1989 SLT 175, 1988 SCCR 629.
[3] Cf *Hamilton v Fife Health Board* 1992 GWD 4–193, in which it was held that for the purposes of the Damages (Scotland) Act 1976, a 'person' does not include a fetus in utero at the time injuries are sustained.
[4] See *West* (1848) 2 Cox CC 500; *Kwok Chak Ming* (No1) [1963] HKLR 226, 349.
[5] See discussion at p 151.
[6] See *O'Toole V McDougall* 1986 SCCR 56.

Whether or not driving can be described as dangerous is very much a matter of fact in each case. In *Fraser v Lockhart*,[1] there was a conviction for the former offence of reckless driving where the accused drove at speed while being pursued by the police, and, without signalling, skidded into a farm road in an attempt to escape. Again, in *Rattray v Colley*,[2] a champion go-kart racer performed a 'display manoeuvre' in a public street. In spite of the accused's prowess as a driver, he was convicted of reckless driving since it could be inferred that he had disregarded the danger to himself, his passenger, and to vehicles entering the street from either direction. So objective was the test for reckless driving that it might be inferred purely from the abnormal behaviour of the vehicle in question.[3]

Section 3: Careless and inconsiderate driving

This section contains two separate offences – driving without due care and attention, and driving without reasonable consideration for other road users.

i. Driving without due care and attention. As in sections 1 and 2, the test for careless driving is an objective one, based on the standard of the competent and careful driver.[4] It seems that the driving must also be judged with reference to the reasonably experienced driver – no concession is made to the learner driver whose driving falls below the required standard.[5] The emergency services likewise have no immunity in this regard.[6] As with the previous sections, sub-standard driving may be inferred from the facts and circumstances proved, and it is unnecessary to have any eyewitness to the driving in question:

Looking to the stark facts that this car, for no reason that has been explained, left the road on a perfectly straight stretch, travelled 120 feet along the verge, and then collided with a rock face, is in itself sufficient to raise a prima facie inference of negligence'.[7]

---

[1] 1992 GWD 5–260.
[2] 1991 GWD 1–71; cf *O'Toole v McDougall*, supra, at 59 per Lord Justice-General Emslie.
[3] *Wheatley* para 2.3:4, and cf *Pagan v Fergusson* 1976 SLT (Notes) 44.
[4] See *Simpson v Peat* [1952] 2 QB 24, [1952] 1 All ER 447.
[5] *McCrane v Riding* [1938] 1 All ER 157.
[6] See eg *Marshall v Osmond* [1983] QB 1034, [1983] 2 All ER 225.
[7] *Pagan v Fergusson* 1976 SLT (Notes) 44 per Lord Justice-Clerk Wheatley.

The court must, however, take all the circumstances into account, in deciding whether or not the driving has fallen below the required standard. Thus, a finding of careless driving is not inevitable merely because the driver made a mistake. If, for example, a driver is confronted with an emergency, his driving will be judged in the light of the situation, and will not necessarily be adjudged careless (or dangerous) merely because, with hindsight, it is obvious that he did the wrong thing.[1] There must, however, be a genuine emergency. There was, for example, no emergency in *Stebbings v Westwater*,[2] where the accused, without stopping, attempted to swat a fly on his windscreen. Failure to observe the highway code, while not conclusive of the question, may be one factor tending to establish that driving was careless or dangerous.[3]

Driving 'without due care and attention' covers a very wide range of conduct, from the everyday error of the person who turns without signalling, to the seriously negligent driving of one who, perhaps, causes a major accident, but which falls short of the test for dangerous driving. A charge under section 3 may therefore be appropriate even if someone dies as a result of the accused's carelessness. In such cases, the complaint should not contain any reference to the death, since that would amount to a charge of 'causing death by careless driving' which is not an offence.[4] Nor should the fatal consequences of careless driving be taken into account when sentence is passed.[5] It is not the case, however, that the consequences of an accident are always irrelevant to a charge under section 3. The fact that a collision occurred might be an indication that the accused's driving fell below the standard expected of a careful and competent driver.[6] As with dangerous driving, there may be a conviction of careless driving where an accident has occurred partly as a result of another's carelessness.[7]

ii. Driving without reasonable consideration for others. The offence of driving without reasonable consideration is similarly wide in scope, and no list of possible examples can hope to be exhaustive.

---

[1] At 28 per Lord Goddard CJ.
[2] 1991 GWD 1–55.
[3] See RTA, s38 (7), and *McCrone v Normand* 1989 SLT 332.
[4] See *McCallum v Hamilton* 1986 JC 1, 1985 SCCR 368.
[5] *Sharp v HM Adv* 1987 SCCR 179.
[6] See *McCallum v Hamilton* at 158 per Lord Ross, and cf *Mundie v Cardle* 1991 SCCR 118.
[7] *Tait v Lees* 1991 GWD 2–122.

'Typical cases of driving without reasonable consideration for other persons using the road may include ... the driving of a vehicle too close to the driver in front ...; driving with full beam headlights at night ...; driving needlessly in the outside lane of a motorway or dual-carriageway, or overtaking in the inside lane ...'[1]

There is some doubt, however, as to whether in such cases it is necessary to prove that the driving complained of resulted in any actual inconvenience or hazard to other road users. Such a requirement would seem inconsistent with the objective approach to dangerous and careless driving which looks only to the quality of the driving itself, and does not require proof of danger or inconvenience to others. There is, however, English authority to the effect that in the absence of evidence of inconvenience to others, there could be no conviction under this leg of section 3.[2]

The common law. The RTAs did not abolish the common law offence of 'recklessly or furiously driving a vehicle (or riding a cycle) to the danger of the lieges'.[3] While this offence is uncommon in practice,[4] the common law remains available to the prosecutor in unusual situations. In *Macphail v Clark*,[5] for example, a farmer burned straw in a field next to the A9. The smoke drastically reduced visibility on the road, and a serious accident occurred. The farmer was tried and convicted of recklessly endangering the lives and safety of the lieges.

Section 3A: Causing death by careless driving when under influence of drink or drugs

This offence, created by section 3 of the 1991 Act, is committed by a person who causes death while driving without due care and attention or without reasonable consideration for other persons, and who is, at the time, unfit to drive through drink or drugs or who has more than the prescribed limit of alcohol in his system.[6]

---

[1] *Wheatley* para 2.10:3.
[2] *Dilks v Bowman-Shaw* [1981] RTR 4, described by Ormrod LJ as a 'very unusual' case, and doubted by *Wheatley* at para 2.10:3 who submits that it might not be followed in Scotland.
[3] See *Quinn v Cunningham* 1956 JC 22, 1956 SLT 55.
[4] It may be resorted to where the driving did not take place on a 'road' – see *Wheatley* para 2.4.
[5] 1983 SLT (Sh Ct) 37, 1982 SCCR 395.
[6] Refusal to provide a specimen may also be a ground for conviction of this offence.

Section 4(1): Driving or attempting to drive while unfit through drink or drugs

This offence is committed only if the driving, or the attempt to drive, takes place on a 'road or other public place'.[1] 'Drink' means alcoholic drink,[2] and 'drugs' includes 'any intoxicant other than alcohol'.[3] By far the most common intoxicant is alcohol, and for the purposes of this section the actual amount of alcohol found in the accused's body is irrelevant. The test, set out by section 4(5) of the RTA, is whether the accused's ability to drive was for the time being impaired, and medical evidence will usually be decisive in making out that test.[4] Where the accused is medically examined, for example by a police surgeon, and provided he has 'sufficient command of his faculties to appreciate his position and to behave with reasonable intelligence',[5] the procedural guidelines laid down in *Reid v Nixon*[6] should be followed. Failure to do so must be justified.[7]

Because it is the accused's fitness to drive which is relevant under this section, and not the amount of alcohol he has consumed, it is possible for an accused to be pronounced fit to drive for the purposes of section 4(1), in spite of having more than the prescribed limit of alcohol in his blood.[8] Conversely, an accused might have consumed less than the prescribed maximum, and yet still be found unfit to drive. The fact that the accused has in fact driven a vehicle in a straight line does not necessarily mean that he is fit to drive. But if the accused does drive 'sufficiently far and under such conditions as to demonstrate that his skill, alertness and judgement as a driver were unaffected, that would be a factor to be weighed along with the other evidence as to his condition'.[9]

Section 4(2): Being in charge of a motor vehicle while unfit

Where a person was neither driving nor attempting to drive a motor vehicle, that person may nevertheless be convicted under section

---

[1] As to which, see above.

[2] *Armstrong v Clark* [1957] 2 QB 391 at 394 per Lord Goddard CJ, [1957] 1 All ER 433.

[3] RTA, s11 (2). This definition will include medicines taken for both therapeutic and non-therapeutic reasons.

[4] Lay evidence, usually from police officers, may be enough however, and if need be, the courts will look at all the circumstances to find evidence of unfitness – see eg *Kenny v Tudhope* [1984] SCCR 290; *Wallace v McLeod* 1986 SCCR 678.

[5] *Reid v Nixon* 1948 JC 68 at 72 per Lord Justice-General Cooper.

[6] 1948 JC 68.

[7] At 73. For a commentary on the guidelines, and a review of subsequent cases, see *Wheatley* para 3.5:1.

[8] See eg *McNeill v Fletcher* 1966 JC 18.

[9] *Murray v Muir* 1950 SLT 41 at 43 per Lord Justice-General Cooper.

4(2) of being 'in charge' of a motor vehicle while unfit through drink or drugs. Whether or not someone was 'in charge' of a vehicle is a question of fact, and, at least in Scotland, the test applicable is whether the accused was 'responsible for the control or driving of the car'.[1] The requirement of de facto control links the offence under section 4(2) with that in the preceding subsection.

'We know quite well what is meant by referring to a person who is driving or attempting to drive a car, and when the section goes on to refer also to a person 'in charge of' a car, the reference must be to a person in de facto control, even though he may not be at the time actually driving or attempting to drive. Any other reading or any attempt to include the owner merely because he was present, or because he had possession of [the] ignition key of a car which he had arranged should be driven by [another] would lead to extravagant results.'[2]

In *Crichton v Burrell*,[3] the case from which this statement comes, the accused had arranged for someone to drive him home, and was waiting beside his car with the ignition keys in his pocket for that person to arrive. He was found not to be 'in charge' of his car. The result of this case might well have been different in England. The facts of *Haines v Roberts*[4] were essentially similar to those in *Crichton v Burrell*. In the English case however, Lord Goddard CJ said:

'How can it be said that in those circumstances the respondent was not in charge of the [vehicle]. He had not put it into anybody else's charge. It may be that if a man goes to a public house and leaves his car outside or in the car park and, getting drunk, asks a friend to look after the car for him or take the car home, he has put it in somebody else's charge, but if he had not put it in charge of somebody else he is in charge of it until he does so. His car is away from home on the road or in the car park – it matters not which – and he is in charge.[5]

So in England the driver is in charge of his vehicle until he hands it over to someone else's charge, or abandons it completely. Abandonment is not easy to establish. In *Woodage v Jones (No 2)*[6] the accused left his car in a garage forecourt (a public place), and walked away. He was arrested when about half a mile from the car, and was found still to be in charge of it. His counsel tried to persuade the court to follow *Crichton v Burrell* but the court declined to do so.[7]

[1] *Crichton v Burrell* 1951 JC 107 at 111 per Lord Keith, 1951 SLT 365.
[2] At 111 per Lord Justice-General Cooper.
[3] Ibid.
[4] [1953] 1 All ER 344, [1953] 1 WLR 309.
[5] At 345 per Lord Goddard CJ.
[6] [1975] RTR 119, (1975) 60 Crim App Rep 260.
[7] See James LJ, [1975] RTR 119 at 124/5.

The English approach implies just what the Lord Justice-General in *Crichton v Burrell* thought should not be implied: that the owner of a vehicle may be convicted 'because he might in strict legal theory have taken action which he is not proved to have intended to take, much less to have put into practice'.[1] Thus, it is unlikely in Scotland that a driver will be convicted under the subsection if he was not in the car at the relevant time,[2] unless there is clear evidence of control.[3] A person need not be in the driving seat to be in control of a vehicle however. A driving instructor, for example, may be 'in charge' of a vehicle even though a learner is driving.[4]

It should be noted that this section may decrease in importance in the wake of increased police powers to administer breath tests to those suspected of driving while intoxicated.[5] If it can be shown by scientific means that the accused has consumed more than the prescribed limit of alcohol, then the appropriate charge is under section 5, and it is unnecessary to enter into difficult questions of fact, such as the meaning of being 'in charge' of a vehicle.[6]

Section 4(3) – Defence

Section 4(3) provides a defence for the accused who can prove that 'at the material time the circumstances were such that there was no likelihood of his driving [the vehicle] so long as he remained unfit to drive through drink or drugs'. This is a question of fact in all the circumstances, including the accused's intentions. The court must be satisfied, on a balance of probabilities,[7] not only that the accused did not intend to drive the car while unfit, but also that there was no likelihood that his intentions would be departed from.[8]

In *Neish v Stevenson*[9] the accused and a companion missed the last bus to their lodgings after an evening's drinking. Since it was raining heavily, they decided to spend the night in the cab of the

---

[1] *Crichton v Burrell* 1951 JC 107 at 111 per Lord-Justice General Cooper.
[2] See eg *Adair v McKenna* 1951 SLT (Sh Ct) 40.
[3] Cf the English case of *Leach v Evans* [1952] 2 All ER 264, which may in any event be a product of the stricter English approach.
[4] *Clark v Clark* 1940 SLT (Sh Ct) 68. This seems consistent with the view that more than one person can be driving at the same time – *Langman v Valentine* [1952] 2 All ER 803, [1952] 2 TLR 713. Cf *Winter v Morrison* 1954 JC 7 which came to the opposite conclusion in similar circumstances.
[5] See *Wheatley* para 3.3:4.
[6] See *Wheatley* para 3.3:4 for further examples.
[7] See *Neish v Stevenson* 1969 SLT 229.
[8] *Morton v Confer* [1963] 1 WLR 763, [1963] 2 All ER 765.
[9] 1969 SLT 229.

accused's lorry. The ignition keys were sitting on the dashboard when they were found by the police. It was held that the court was entitled to be satisfied on a balance of probabilities that the exception had been made out.

Section 5: Driving or being in charge of a motor vehicle with more than the prescribed concentration of alcohol in the body

A person who drives, or is in charge of a motor vehicle on a road or other public place, having consumed so much alcohol that the proportion of it in his breath, blood or urine exceeds the prescribed amounts is guilty of an offence.[1] The normal method of determining the proportion of alcohol in the body of the accused is by means of a breath test, administered where a uniformed constable has reasonable cause to suspect the accused of a section 5 offence.[2] Where a specimen is provided, it is presumed that the proportion of alcohol in the accused's breath, blood or urine at the time of the alleged offence was not less than the reading given by the specimen.[3] The Crown Office has renounced the right to prosecute in cases where the breath test reading does not exceed 40 microgrammes of alcohol.[4]

DEFENCES

i. No likelihood of driving

As with the offence of being in charge of a vehicle while unfit through drink or drugs under section 4(1), it is a defence for a person charged under section 5(1)(b)[5] to show that there was no likelihood of his driving whilst the proportion of alcohol in his body remained likely to exceed the prescribed amount.[6]

[1] Section 5(1) RTA – at present the prescribed limits, set out in s 11(2) of RTA are: breath – 35 microgrammes of alcohol per 100 millilitres; blood – 180 milligrammes per 100 millilitres; urine – 107 milligrammes per 100 millilitres.
[2] Sections 6(1), (2) RTA. This preliminary breath test is not essential to a conviction under s 5, and testing may be carried out at a police station under powers given by s 7. The rules and procedures governing this complex area of the law are fully discussed in *Wheatley* ch 4.
[3] Section 15(2).
[4] See *Benton v Cardle* 1987 SCCR 738, 1988 SLT 310; *McConnachie v Scott* 1988 SCCR 176, 1988 SLT 480. The latter case may be authority for the view that where the lower of two breath specimens shows less than 40 microgrammes, it is incompetent for the police to proceed on the basis of a blood sample, under s 8(2).
[5] Being in charge of a vehicle while the proportion of alcohol in one's body exceeds the prescribed amounts.
[6] Section 5(2).

The rules applicable to the section 4(3) defence apply with equal force to that under section 5(2).

ii. Post incident drinking – the 'hip flask' defence

This defence applies to proceedings under both sections 4 and 5 of RTA. As we saw above, where a specimen is provided for analysis, it is presumed that the proportion of alcohol in the accused's blood, breath or urine at the time of the offence was the same as that given by the specimen. However, this presumption can be rebutted if the accused can show, first, that he consumed alcohol after he ceased to drive and before he provided the specimen, and second, that but for this post-incident consumption of alcohol, he would not have been over the limit.[1] Until recently, the courts had held that in order to rebut the presumption set up by an analyst's certificate, the accused had to establish two things:

'(1) that an ascertainable and definite amount of alcohol was consumed subsequent to the event, and between the event and the test, and (2) that that definite and ascertained amount was such as to affect the evidential value of the certificate by reducing the quantity taken before the moving offence below the permissible limit.'[2]

Thus, in *Campbell v Mackenzie*[3] it was held that where it was proved that the accused had taken two drinks from a bottle of whisky and consumed two cans of stout after ceasing to drive, he had failed to establish a sufficiently definite amount to cast a reasonable doubt on the reading given by certificate. However, this line of authority has now been superceded by the case of *Hassan v Scott*[4] in which it was held that in relation to a defence of post-incident drinking it is now possible for the court to proceed on the basis of an approximation as to the amount consumed, provided that the approximation is capable of raising a reasonable doubt as to the amount of alcohol in the accused's body at the time of the incident. This change came about because of amendments made to the defence by Schedule 8 of the Transport Act 1981, which removed all reference to ascertainable or definite amounts of alcohol.

Accordingly, cases such as *Ritchie v Pirie*,[5] *Sutherland v Aitchison*,[6] and *Campbell v Mackenzie*,[7] must be taken to be overruled, at

---

[1] Section 15(3).
[2] *Sutherland v Aitchison* 1975 JC 1 at 5 per Lord Justice-Clerk Wheatley.
[3] 1981 SCCR 341, 1982 JC 20.
[4] 1989 SCCR 49, 1989 SLT 380.
[5] 1972 JC 7.
[6] 1975 JC 1.
[7] 1981 SCCR 341, 1982 JC 20.

least in so far as they govern the 'definite and ascertainable amount' point. However, the last of these cases, *Campbell v Mackenzie*, itself altered the law as it was previously understood. Prior to *Campbell* it was thought that the accused had the persuasive or legal burden of proof in relation to this defence, and was obliged to satisfy the court as to the conditions of the defence on a balance of probabilities.[1] *Campbell* made it clear that if any burden lies on the accused in relation to this defence it was an evidential one only.[2] Some of the dicta in *Hassan* suggest that it is for the accused to satisfy the court on a balance of probabilities of the conditions required by the statutory defence.[3] Such suggestions are inconsistent with *Campbell*, and it is submitted that on this point *Campbell* remains a good authority.

iii. Necessity

There is some doubt as to whether a defence of necessity at common law may be open to a person charged with an offence under section 5, or indeed any of the offences discussed here. These are offences of more or less strict liability, and it may be doubted whether a defence of necessity can affect not merely *mens rea*, but also *actus reus*.[4] In *Tudhope v Grubb*[5] a sheriff court decision, it was held that the defence was available where the accused had driven while over the limit of alcohol in order to escape from a threatened assault. The necessity to escape from the violence rendered the accused's actions involuntary, and meant that there was indeed no *actus reus*. The High Court has since cast some doubt on the soundness of the decision in *Grubb*. In *McLeod v McDougall*[6] the court refused to approve that case, holding that in the circumstances there was no need to rule on the question of whether the defence of necessity is available in Scots law, since at the material time, there was clearly no necessity for the accused to drive. They did hold, however, that in the circumstances there were special reasons for not disqualifying the accused from driving.[7] In *McNab*

---

[1] Cf *Neish v Stevenson* 1969 SLT 229, supra.

[2] That is, the burden of producing enough evidence to allow the court to consider the matter, and to determine on all the evidence whether the Crown have proved their case beyond reasonable doubt.

[3] See opinion of Lord Justice-Clerk, 1989 SCCR 49 at 54E.

[4] See the discussion of driving and automatism, above, and of *Farrell v Stirling* 1975 SLT (Sh Ct) 71.

[5] 1983 SCCR 350.

[6] 1988 SCCR 519, 1989 SLT 151.

[7] Section 34 of the RTO – see *Wheatley* ch 8.

v Guild[1] the court was again asked to consider the defence of necessity, and again made no decision as to its availability. If the defence is available, it will be necessary for the accused to show that he acted under threat of death of serious injury to himself or some other person.[2]

---

[1] 1989 SCCR 138.
[2] See also *Morrison v Valentine* 1991 SLT 413, and cf *R v Conway* [1989] RTR 35, [1989] QB 290, a case on 'duress of circumstances'.

IV. PROPERTY OFFENCES

14. Theft/Reset

THEFT

The popular view of the crime of theft generally involves the clandestine removal of goods from their owner's possession, but it is not confined to that situation. There is theft whenever someone wrongfully appropriates the property of another, with the intention permanently to deprive that other of possession. This was not always the case. Hume confined theft to the popular idea of 'the felonious taking and carrying away of the property of another, for lucre'.[1] Since theft was at that time a capital offence, it is perhaps unsurprising that Hume wished to define the crime as narrowly as possible. His definition excluded from the scope of the crime those who appropriated property with which they had been entrusted. Hume characterised their offence as one of breach of trust, a crime akin to embezzlement.[2] For Hume, a lawful possessor of goods could not be guilty of theft.

The courts found Hume's definition unduly restrictive, and soon began to modify it. In *George Brown*[3] a watchmaker was charged with the theft of nine watches, which he had undertaken to repair. The charge was held relevant, even although the accused had not taken the watches but had been entrusted with them by their owners. In *John Smith*,[4] Lord Meadowbank said: 'It is of no consequence of what character the original possession of the property is. The moment the intention of appropriating the property of another is formed, then the theft is committed'.

Theft thus came to be based on the idea not of removal, but of appropriation – the application of another's property to the appropriator's own use. The crime could be committed as soon as the intention to appropriate was formed.

---

[1] *Hume* I, 57.
[2] See section on *Embezzlement* in ch 17 below.
[3] (1839) 2 Swin 394.
[4] (1838) 2 Swin 28.

In *Herron v Diack & Newlands*,[1] for example, a large and 'very grand' steel coffin, containing the remains of an American writer, was committed to the care of the two accused, who were funeral directors. The accused removed the deceased from the coffin and placed him in a chipboard container for burial at sea. There were difficulties with the burial and Newlands later had the body replaced in the original casket, which was successfully committed. The pair were duly charged with the theft of the steel casket. Diack was convicted, even although he was quite properly in possession of the casket at the time of the 'theft', and even although the casket was eventually used for its intended purpose. Their possession of the coffin, originally lawful, became theftuous when the decision was made to appropriate it to their own use. At that moment, the crime was committed, and could not be 'undone' by their eventual decision to use the original casket.

In cases where the accused has had lawful possession of the goods, it may be difficult to prove the presence of an intention to appropriate them. The law tends, therefore, to rely on the conduct of the accused to show that theftuous intent was present. In *Diack and Newlands*, the use of the chipboard coffin for burial in the face of clear instructions to use the steel casket was strong evidence of appropriation.

What sort of property can be stolen?

Anything which is both corporeal and moveable may be stolen. This includes money, and, as *Gordon* points out,[2] 'theft of notes to the value of £x . . . is theft of £x and not merely a number of pieces of paper'.

Corporeal property

Generally, the prosecution must be able to point to some physical or tangible object which the accused has stolen. Incorporeal property, such as information or a legal right cannot form the subject of a theft charge. A person may be charged with the theft of a thing containing the information or right, such as a file, or a contract, but not with the theft of the incorporeal contents of the document. In *HM Adv v Mackenzies*[3] a man was accused of stealing a

---

[1] 1973 SLT (Sh Ct) 27.
[2] At para 14–28.
[3] 1913 SC (J) 107, 1913 SLT 48.

book containing secret recipes. This was a relevant charge of theft, but an additional charge of copying the secret recipes was not. Two points may be made about this case: firstly, there could probably have been a relevant charge of theft, even if it were alleged that the accused had simply taken the book for the purpose of copying the secrets it contained, and with the intention of returning it later.[1] Secondly, while the accused was relevantly charged only with the theft of the book, and not the information it contained, the court took the contents of the book into account in assessing the seriousness of the charge. 'It is quite evident', said Lord Justice-Clerk Macdonald, 'that a book of no real value in itself may be of great value because of what is written in it.'[2]

An accused person may therefore be charged with the theft of a document which is valuable because of the information it contains. But it is not theft (or any other crime) to memorise secret information, or to make copies of documents containing such information. This is so even where information is 'taken' with the intention of selling it 'for lucre'. The accused in *Grant v Allan*,[3] made copies of print-outs from his employers' computer, 'detained' these copies, and offered to sell the information they contained to rivals of his employers. He was charged with an innominate offence on the basis of this conduct. The High Court held that the charge disclosed no crime known to the law of Scotland, and the court declined to exercise its declaratory power to make it so. Lord Justice-Clerk Ross said:

'For the appellant clandestinely to make copies of computer print-outs belonging to his employers may well have breached an express or implied obligation owed to his employers by him not to disclose confidential information obtained in the course of his employment, but it is quite another thing to proceed to categorise such behaviour as criminal.'[4]

Whether or not energy may be classified as corporeal or tangible, charges of theft of electricity are common.[5] Similarly, non-solid things, such as water or oxygen may be stolen.[6]

---

[1] See *Milne v Tudhope* 1981 JC 53, 1981 SLT (Notes) 42 discussed below and cf *HM Adv v Dewar* (1777); *Burnett* 115; *Hume* I, 75. *Gordon* expresses a contrary view (footnote 84 at para 14–32), but this probably cannot be reconciled with *Milne v Tudhope*.

[2] 1913 SC (J) 107 at 110, 1913 SLT 48. See also *Gordon* para 14–29.

[3] 1987 SCCR 402, 1988 SLT 11.

[4] 1988 SLT 11 at 14.

[5] See *Gordon* para 14–34.

[6] *Gordon* para 14–33.

Moveable property

Property must be moveable in order to be stolen. But 'moveable' is not to be understood in the technical sense known to Scots lawyers. It simply means 'capable of being moved'.[1] Thus, many items of heritable property may be stolen – fruit growing on a tree, turnips in a field,[2] or slates from a roof.

Another's property

One cannot steal one's own property.[3] Nor can one steal ownerless property, although the scope of this category is very limited. Wild animals are considered to be *res nullius*, and ownership is acquired by the first person to capture or confine them.[4] Once captured or confined however, wild animals may be stolen. A person who removed salmon from beach nets, for example, would be guilty of theft. Living, adult human beings cannot be 'stolen', but children under the age of puberty are considered in law to be the property of their parents, and as such can form the subject of a theft charge. This type of theft is known as *plagium*.[5] Human remains may be stolen prior to burial – thereafter the relevant crime is that of violation of sepulchres.[6]

Property which has been abandoned falls to the Crown, and appropriation of such property is probably theft.[7] Lost property may be stolen, but it is unclear whether appropriation of such property is always theft.[8]

In some situations, it may be unclear who owns an item of property. The question of ownership is determined by the civil law. For example, a firm of builders are constructing a house on land owned by **A**. They supply double glazing and central heating, and these are duly incorporated into the house. Payment for the construction of the house is by instalment, and when defects in the

---

[1] See *Gordon* para 14–38.

[2] *Alex Robertson and Ors* (1867) 5 Irv 480.

[3] *Hume* I, 77. But note the difficulties which may arise.

[4] Poaching is a separate offence based on incorporeal rights of the Crown or the landowner – but a poacher becomes the owner of the game he traps or kills. See eg *Scott v Everitt* (1853) 15 D 288.

[5] See *Downie v HM Adv* 1984 SCCR 365; *Hamilton v Mooney* 1990 SLT (Sh Ct) 105 and J M Fotheringham 'Plagium' 1990 35 JLS 506.

[6] *HM Adv v Dewar* 1945 JC 5.

[7] See *Lord Advocate v University of Aberdeen* 1963 SC 533, 1963 SLT 361 and *Gordon* para 14–41.

[8] *Gordon* para 14–22.

construction emerge, **A** withholds further instalments. To force **A** to resume payments, the builders remove the double glazing and central heating from the house, and take it back to their premises. When these items were incorporated into the house, they became the property of **A**. The builders may well be guilty of theft.[1]

Difficulties may arise where, for example, a buyer removes goods from a shop without paying for them, but at a time when ownership had passed to him.[2] If this was a credit sale, clearly there was no theft. If not, then a charge of theft might relevantly be brought, provided the necessary theftuous intent could be proved.[3] A charge of fraud might also be possible.[4]

The *actus reus* of theft

Although theft is now defined in terms of appropriation, most cases of theft involve the straightforward taking of another's property. As we noted above, the appropriation of lost property may also form the basis of a theft charge. This mode of theft is considered under the heading of theft by finding. No matter which of these three possible modes of theft is in issue, problems of distinguishing *actus reus* from *mens rea* loom large. If property can be stolen while in the thief's possession, it may be difficult to point to any act which might constitute the *actus reus*.

Theft by taking

'Any amotion of the goods from what is considered as their proper place of keeping, and which clearly evinces the purpose of the taker, is a carrying away, and a sufficient completion of the act.'[5]

Amotio is the term used to describe the physical taking away of a thing. According to *Burnett*, there must be amotio, and this 'removal' or 'carrying away'[6] must be such as to demonstrate the intentions of the taker. Simply to take hold of goods, or even to move them around within their 'proper place of keeping' would

---

[1] See eg *Milne v Tudhope* 1981 JC 53, 1981 SLT (Notes) 42.
[2] *Gordon* paras 14–47 and 14–48.
[3] See eg *Clyne v Keith* (1887) 1 White 356, 14 R (J) 22.
[4] But note the problems which arise if the purchaser decides not to pay after the goods have been obtained – see *DPP v Ray* [1974] AC 370, [1973] 3 All ER 131, discussed below.
[5] *Burnett* 121. It has recently been held that actual movement of the goods is unnecessary, provided that there is appropriation. See *Black and Penrice v Carmichael* 1992 GWD 25–1415, a case involving the use of a wheel clamp to immobilise a car.
[6] See *Gordon* para 14–42.

hardly be enough to constitute the *actus reus* of theft, since it would be difficult to interpret such actions as showing theftuous intent. In *Cornelius O'Neil*,[1] however, where the accused stood outside an open window, and used a hook to pull towards him objects inside the room, it was held that there was sufficient amotion to justify a theft charge.[2] Thus, the question of sufficient amotion will depend on the particular circumstances. While any degree of movement may demonstrate an intent to steal a car parked on the street, it would probably be necessary to show that goods in a shop were taken beyond the check-out point before an intent to steal could be demonstrated.[3]

Theft by appropriation

As we noted above, Hume did not regard as theft the appropriation of goods by their lawful possessor. Hume required an actual taking of possession before a charge of theft could be made.[4] Thus, where an owner of goods voluntarily handed over possession to another, that other could not steal the goods since there could be no physical removal of the goods from their owner's possession. This led to the growth of an artificial distinction between a possessor of goods, and a mere custodier.[5] A custodier could be found guilty of theft, but a possessor could not. As the modern law developed however, it became clear that a lawful possessor of goods could quite competently be charged with their theft.[6] Thus, in *O'Brien v Strathern*,[7] in which it was held that a soldier could steal his kilt, Lord Justice-General Clyde said that 'looking to the course which the law has taken ... I think there is no doubt ... that the appropriation of goods by the person to whom they have been entrusted for a limited and specified purpose constitutes theft.'[8]

In *Dewar v HM Adv*,[9] the manager of Aberdeen crematorium was charged with the theft of more than 600 coffin lids. On receipt of the coffins for cremation, Dewar saved the lids and retained them for

---

[1] (1845) 2 Broun 394.

[2] This type of conduct would probably now be charged as attempted theft.

[3] See *Gordon* paras 14–15, 14–16. Cf also *Black and Penrice v Carmichael* 1992 GWD 25–1415.

[4] *Hume* I, 57.

[5] *Hume* I, 63–65. A custodier was defined as one who holds goods only for a 'limited and specified purpose', while a possessor was one who had some right to use the goods on his own behalf. See also *Gordon* para 14–03.

[6] See *George Brown* (1839) 2 Swin 394 and *John Smith* (1838) 2 Swin 28.

[7] 1922 JC 55, 1922 SLT 440.

[8] 1922 JC at 57.

[9] 1945 JC 5.

use in other cremations, for firewood, or for use in some other 'economic way'. There was no evidence that he made a profit from this practice. Dewar claimed that coffins sent for cremation had been abandoned by their owners, and that accordingly they were 'completely under his jurisdiction for disposal'. It was held however, that the coffins were sent to him for the sole purpose of destruction, and that by preserving and re-using the coffins, he was appropriating them to his own use. He was therefore guilty of theft.

In such cases, it is difficult, if not impossible, to distinguish *mens rea* and *actus reus*, since the prosecution can point to no physical act removing the property from the owner's possession. Indeed the thief in such cases is authorised to possess and to carry out certain acts using the property. It may be necessary therefore to examine carefully the conduct of the accused to determine the moment of appropriation[1] – the point at which the *mens* became *rea*, and at which the crime was committed.[2] Thus in *Dewar*, the moment of appropriation and theft was the moment when Dewar saved the coffin lids from destruction, and in *Diack & Newlands*, when the two accused removed Mr Groom from his princely casket, and placed him in the chipboard cut-price coffin. O'Brien's act of appropriation was the sale of his kilt to a fellow soldier, and at that moment he committed theft. To constitute appropriation, the accused's conduct must therefore amount to an assertion of an unlimited right of disposal – of the rights of the owner, in other words. Sale or destruction of goods are the main examples of such conduct,[3] but any unauthorised act inconsistent with the rights of the true owner may amount to appropriation.[4]

Theft by finding

Theft by finding may be considered as a type of theft by appropriation. A person does not steal goods merely by finding them, even if he retains the goods for some time after the discovery. Such a person may, for a reasonable time, be presumed to possess the goods with the intention of returning them to their true owner.[5]

---

[1] Cf *Morris (David)* [1983] QB 587, [1983] 2 All ER 448 (CA), [1984] AC 320, [1983] 3 All ER 288 (HL).
[2] See Lord Meadowbank's dictum from *John Smith* (1838) 2 Swin 28.
[3] See *Gordon* para 14–25 for further examples.
[4] See *Smith and Hogan* p 493.
[5] Cf *Hume* I, 62.

Once that reasonable time has elapsed, however, it may be presumed that the finder has appropriated the goods to his own use, and at that point, theft has occurred.

In *MacMillan v Lowe*,[1] a man claimed to have found a cheque book and card in a telephone box. These items clearly bore the owner's name and that of his bank. The accused retained the items for at least four hours without making any attempt to return them to the owner, and when initially apprehended and searched by the police, he attempted to conceal the items. It was held that there was enough evidence to justify a conviction for theft.[2]

Once again, the conduct of the accused is vital to the question of whether there has been appropriation. A finder may be found guilty of theft if he pawns the goods shortly after finding them and without attempting to trace the owner.[3] Similarly, there may be theft if a farmer puts his own brand on sheep which he has found straying.[4]

There is, however, some doubt as to whether every appropriation of found goods is theft. For example, a rich lawyer finds a £5 note in the street and puts it into a tin rattled by a passing collector for charity. Is he guilty of theft?

In theory, the answer must be yes, since there is clearly appropriation of property belonging to someone else. In *Campbell v MacLennan*,[5] however, the accused was acquitted in circumstances very similar to those in the example above. Lord Young said:[6] 'A man of large property may find money in the street, and may give it in the way of alms to the next beggar; that is undoubtedly appropriation. Yet who would call it theft, even if the finder had denied having found it?' In *Angus MacKinnon*,[7] Lord Justice-Clerk Inglis took the view that a finder might innocently retain property while he tried to locate the owner, and that any subsequent appropriation would not be a 'grievous violation of moral right'. This view certainly accords with common sense, but it is hardly consistent with cases such as *John Smith*,[8] and *MacMillan v Lowe*.[9] *Gordon* argues that it may be a defence to a charge of theft to show that the finder took all reasonable steps to locate the owner before making the decision to retain

---

[1] 1991 SCCR 113.
[2] Cf *Angus MacKinnon* (1863) 4 Irv 398 at 405 per Lord Ardmillan.
[3] *McLaughlin v Stewart* (1865) Macq 32.
[4] *Paterson v HM Adv* (1901)3 Adam 490, 4 F (J) 7.
[5] (1888)1 White 604, 15 R (J) 55.
[6] (1888) 1 White 604 at 608.
[7] (1863) 4 Irv 398.
[8] (1838) 2 Swin 28.
[9] 1991 SCCR 113.

the goods.[1] The argument would be the stronger if the goods in question are of 'no great value'.[2]

This argument does some violence to the idea that finding coupled with appropriation amounts to theft,[3] and it may be better to regard the appropriation of articles in such circumstances as a matter for prosecutorial (and personal) discretion, rather than as an exception to the substantive law. In any event, a person who finds any article is obliged by the Civic Government (Scotland) Act 1982[4] to take reasonable care of it, and within a reasonable time to deliver or report its finding to a police officer or to the owner or occupier of the premises on which the article is found. Failure to do so constitutes an offence in itself,[5] and might well demonstrate an intention to appropriate the article such as to form the basis of a theft charge.[6]

The owner's consent

Appropriation occurs when a person acts in such a way as to assert a right of ownership over property in fact owned by another. Theft is committed only if the property is appropriated without the owner's consent. Since appropriation is an act assertive of ownership, any consent must be to the transfer of ownership of the property – if the owner has consented only to the transfer of possession, any subsequent appropriation will amount to theft.

A steals a cheque book belonging to **B**. He represents to **C**, who is selling his car, that he is **B**, and forges **B**'s signature on a cheque from the stolen cheque-book. **C** accepts the cheque and gives **A** the keys to his car. He drives away. In this case **C** has consented to the transfer of ownership in his car to **A**. His consent was induced by **A**'s fraudulent use of **B**'s cheque-book. But there is no theft in this situation. Consent induced by fraud is consent nevertheless.[7] Indeed, the absence of the owner's consent is what distinguishes theft from fraud.[8] The significance for the criminal law of this distinction has been greatly reduced by section 60 of the Criminal Procedure (Scotland) Act 1975, which provides inter alia that a person charged with theft may be convicted of fraud, and vice-versa. The

---

[1] Para 14–22.
[2] See Lord Justice-Clerk Inglis in *MacKinnon* (1863) 4 Irv 398 at 402.
[3] See *John Smith* (1838) 2 Swin 28 at 51–52 per Lord Meadowbank.
[4] Sections 67–75.
[5] Section 67 (6).
[6] See *Gordon* para 14–24.
[7] *Hume* I, 57.
[8] See *Alison* I, 259.

distinction retains considerable importance in the civil law of property however. A person who has obtained goods from their true owner by fraud may competently pass ownership to a third person – a person who has stolen goods can never do this. This means that a victim of theft is entitled to recover his property even from innocent third party purchasers of stolen property;[1] the victim of a fraud is entitled only to damages.[2]

The *mens rea* of theft

At the start of this chapter theft was defined as the appropriation of the property of another, with the intention permanently to deprive that other of possession. Until recently, that represented a complete definition. In his second edition, *Gordon* stated that 'it is clear that Scots law requires an intention to deprive the owner permanently of his goods'.[3] What was required was an intention to detain the goods from the owner on a permanent basis, whether or not the thief kept the goods for himself,[4] and whether or not the goods were in fact returned to their owner.[5] If goods were appropriated with the intention permanently to deprive the owner, the crime is complete, and cannot be 'undone' by any subsequent event.[6]

Following the case of *Milne v Tudhope*,[7] however, the above definition must be modified. In *Milne v Tudhope*, the High Court accepted that theft generally requires an appropriation of property with the intention permanently to deprive the owner of possession. But in exceptional circumstances, the court held that an intention to deprive the owner of the property on a temporary basis might suffice: '...A clandestine taking, aimed at achieving a nefarious purpose, constitutes theft, even if the taker intends all along to return the thing taken when his purpose has been achieved.[8]

This statement,[9] has 'effected a radical alteration in the law of

---

[1] See eg *Macdonald v Provan Ltd* 1960 SLT 231.
[2] See *Macleod v Kerr* 1965 SC 253, 1965 SLT 358, and cf *Wm Wilson* (1882) 5 Couper 48.
[3] *Gordon* para 14–65.
[4] See *Hume* I, 75, and *Gordon* para 14–63. The goods are 'detained' even if they are destroyed, given away or merely abandoned.
[5] *Hume* I, 79.
[6] Cf *Herron v Diack & Newlands* 1973 SLT (Sh Ct) 27. Dicta in *Cameron v HM Adv* 1971 JC 50 at 53 per Lord Cameron, 1971 SLT 202, 333, to the effect that 'Whether the intent be permanent or only temporary appropriation, the clandestine or felonious taking of the article constitutes the crime', seem to be based on a misunderstanding of this rule – see *Gordon* para 14–65, note 67.
[7] 1981 JC 53, 1981 SLT (Notes) 42.
[8] Sheriff Fiddes adopted by Lord Justice-Clerk Wheatley at 56 in *Milne* 1981 JC 53.
[9] Referred to hereafter as the *Milne v Tudhope* rule.

theft'.[1] It is based largely on a passage in *Macdonald*[2] to the effect that there is is theft 'if the owner of property is clandestinely deprived of possession of it even although the deprivation be temporary'. *Gordon* argues that this statement was not warranted by the authorities cited in support of it.[3] Be that as it may, the decision in *Milne v Tudhope* appears to have been accepted as part of Scots criminal law – the real difficulty lies in the interpretation of the new rule.

Milne carried on business as a builder, and in 1978 entered into a contract to renovate and modernise a cottage in Newarthill. The work was nearing completion and the contract price had been paid when a dispute arose about the quality of the work. The owner of the cottage delivered to Milne a list of defects which required to be put right. Milne refused to carry out the remedial work unless he received further payment. The owner refused to make such payment, and Milne and three others went to the cottage while the owner was out, and removed 24 doors, 10 radiators, 11 windows, a boiler, and a quantity of tiles. The owner was informed that the items would be returned if Milne was allowed to complete the contract, and receive additional payment. Milne and his accomplices were convicted of theft and appealed to the High Court.

The High Court accepted without amplification the sheriff's view that temporary appropriation was sufficient to form the basis of a theft charge, and disapproved sheriff's MacPhail's decision in *Herron v Best*,[4] that 'an intention to deprive permanently' is essential. Applying the law to the instant facts, they held that the conviction was good.

(i) The taking had been 'clandestine'.[5] Milne's counsel argued that to satisfy this requirement, the taking had to be accomplished in secret – Milne had removed the items in broad daylight. The court held that the taking was sufficiently clandestine if it was done without the owner's knowledge, and so the requirement of 'clandestinity' adds little to the definition of the new rule.

(ii) The purpose of the taking was 'nefarious'. The High Court was clearly of the opinion that Milne's scheme to obtain payment was unlawful, but added that for the purposes of the appeal it was irrelevant whether 'nefarious' meant 'criminal' or merely 'unlawful'. Sheriff Fiddes commented that Milne was in effect

[1] Gordon's commentary to *Sandlan v HM Adv* 1983 SCCR 71 at 96.
[2] Page 20.
[3] Para 14–72. See also his commentary to *Sandlan*, supra.
[4] 1976 SLT(Sh Ct) 80.
[5] *Macdonald* p 20.

'holding the articles to ransom'. This may have been an echo of Gordon's earlier comment[1] that 'where **A** takes **B**'s property with the intention of returning it if and only if he is paid a ransom for it', there is clearly extortion,[2] and probably theft.[3] In such a case, **A** does have an intention to return the article, but it is a conditional intention, based on an unlawful (because extortionate) condition.

It may therefore be possible to argue that the *Milne v Tudhope* rule is confined to cases in which the temporary appropriation itself forms part of the *actus reus* of another crime. There are only two other reported cases appying the *Milne v Tudhope* rule, and both lend support, albeit very passive support, to this possibility. In *Kidston v Annan*,[4] the accused was asked to give an estimate of the cost of repairing a television. Acting beyond his instructions, he repaired the television and refused to return it unless the owner paid him for the work. In *Sandlan v HM Adv*,[5] the accused was a company director who removed records and stock from company premises to avoid disclosure of stock deficiencies, intending to return the items later. Lord Stewart directed the jury in terms of the rule in *Milne v Tudhope*, that an intention to appropriate goods on a temporary basis will suffice to bring home a charge of theft, if the appropriation is for a 'nefarious' purpose. He referred to the removal of the items as a 'manoeuvre to save Sandlan's face', but it seems clear on the evidence that it formed part of a conspiracy to defraud the auditors and shareholders of the company.[6]

Thus, in the few reported cases which apply the *Milne v Tudhope* rule, the temporary removal of the property formed an element in another crime as well as theft. *Gordon* points out, however, that in *Milne v Tudhope*, the court 'approved a general reference to taking for a nefarious purpose'.[7] Accordingly, any unauthorised 'borrowing' of property may constitute theft whether or not it forms part of the *actus reus* of another offence, if the article is to be used to further a 'nefarious' purpose. That purpose must be an unlawful one, but not necessarily criminal.[8] On this view, it would clearly be

---

[1] *Gordon* para 14–66.
[2] See section on *Extortion* in ch 17 below and especially the case of *Black and Penrice v Carmichael* 1992 GWD 25–1415 in which employees of a security company immobilised a vehicle parked on private ground and refused to release it unless the vehicle's owner paid a sum of money.
[3] Cf *R v Coffey* [1987] Crim LR 498, a case interpreting s6(1) of the Theft Act 1968.
[4] 1984 SCCR 20, 1984 SLT 279.
[5] 1983 SCCR 71.
[6] See Gordon's commentary at 96.
[7] *Gordon* 1st supplement, paras 14–65 to 14–76.
[8] *Milne v Tudhope* 1981 JC 53 at 57 per Lord Justice-Clerk Wheatley.

theft to borrow a house-key in order to commit housebreaking,[1] and, presumably, in order to facilitate the commission of any other offence. It is unclear, however, what other forms of unlawful conduct may be encompassed by the rule. Would it be theft, for example, temporarily to appropriate property for use in conduct which amounted to a deliberate breach of contract? Sheriff Fiddes' view that the rule applies only in 'exceptional cases'[2] makes it seem unlikely, but because *Milne* provides so little guidance as to the meaning of 'nefarious', it is impossible to define the limits of the rule with any precision. A further problem is that *Milne* further obscures the distinction between theft and unauthorised borrowing.[3] If it is accepted that temporary appropriation ought to constitute theft,[4] we need a more satisfactory definition of such appropriations than that contained in *Milne*. One way to do this consistently with the case-law would be to make clear that a 'nefarious' purpose means a criminal purpose.[5]

Theft and borrowing

Prior to the decision in *Milne v Tudhope*, it was thought that mere borrowing of property could never amount to theft. 'If the goods are taken with the intention only of using them for a time this is not theft although it may constitute another crime.'[6] The 'other crime' is that of 'clandestinely taking and using'[7] which is considered later.[8] Following *Milne v Tudhope*, the relationship between theft and borrowing is altogether less clear.

Authorised borrowing. This is relatively safe ground. If property is taken with the owner's consent, there is no theft. It is always a defence to a theft charge to argue that one genuinely believed that the owner was consenting to the removal of the property, or that he

---

[1] See *Gordon* 1st supplement, paras 14–65 to 14–76. See below p 229 on housebreaking.
[2] 1981 JC 53 at 55.
[3] As to which see below p 224.
[4] See Glanville Williams 'Temporary appropriation ought to constitute theft' [1981] Crim LR 129.
[5] Glanville Williams' suggestion that temporary appropriations for a 'dishonest' purpose, ought to be classified as theft, hardly takes the argument any further – see 'Temporary Appropriation ought to constitute theft' cited above, and cf D W Elliot 'Dishonesty in theft: a dispensable concept' [1982] Crim LR 395.
[6] *Gordon* para 14–65. See also *Burnett* p 115, *Hume* I, 73.
[7] See *Strathern v Seaforth* 1926 JC 100, 1926 SLT 445.
[8] see below p 226.

would have consented had he been aware of the circumstances.[1] But borrowing may become theft even if initially authorised by the owner.

A borrows a book from the public library. He reads the book, and places it on his bookshelf, intending to return it later. In fact, he forgets about the book, and the library reports the matter to the police. At this stage, no theft has occurred, since **A** lacks the appropriate *mens rea*. However: **A** borrows a book from the library. He reads it, places it on his bookshelf intending to return it later, and forgets about it. The library sends him a reminder that the book is overdue. He sees that a substantial fine is due on the book, and decides not to return it at all.[2]

A theft has been committed since **A** has now formed the requisite *mens rea*. Appropriation has taken place. **A**'s retention of the book in spite of the reminder would probably provide adequate evidence of this.[3]

Unauthorised borrowing. It is not necessarily theft to take property without the owner's consent. Provided that the property was truly taken with the intention to return it to the owner in due course, and was not done in furtherance of a nefarious purpose, then it appears that there can be no theft.[4] As we saw above, there is no theft if property is borrowed in the genuine belief that the owner would have given consent, had he known the circumstances.[5]

Presumption of intent to steal

These defences are obviously open to abuse, and accordingly the law presumes that where someone takes property from its owner without the owner's consent, there was an intention to steal.[6] *Gordon* argues that this is a rebuttable presumption,[7] and in principle this must surely be right, for otherwise there would be no need for the *Milne v Tudhope* rule,[8] since every taking of property without consent would be theft. In *Kivlin v Milne*,[9] the accused took a car

---

[1] See *Gordon* para 14–71 and cf Road Traffic Act 1988, s178(2)(b).

[2] Cf Glanville Williams, supra, at 132.

[3] Cf *Morris (David)* [1983] QB 587, [1983] 2 All ER 448 (CA), [1984] AC 320, [1983] 3 All ER 288 (HL). *Smith and Hogan* (p 493) suggest that the simplest test for appropriation is to inquire whether what the accused did was authorised by the owner.

[4] *Milne v Tudhope* 1981 JC 53.

[5] See *Gordon* para 14–71.

[6] *Hume* I, 76.

[7] *Gordon* para 14–79.

[8] Although *Mcleod v Mason & Ors* 1981 SCCR 75, 1981 SLT (Notes) 109 casts some doubt on this conclusion – see Gordon's commentary at 78.

[9] 1979 SLT (Notes) 2.

without the owner's consent, drove it around, and then abandoned it in a place where the owner was unlikely to find it. It was held that the sheriff was entitled to infer from the accused's conduct that he intended permanently to deprive the owner, and his theft conviction was upheld. The court did accept, however, that whether or not such an inference could be drawn would depend on the individual circumstances of the case. Accordingly, the conduct of the accused will be very important in determining whether or not theft was committed.

Consumption and destruction. The presumption of theftuous intent will be strengthened if the accused uses the property as if it were his own. In *Kivlin v Milne* the accused 'borrowed' a car for a joyride. However, the fact that he then abandoned the car in an unlikely place gave rise to the inference that he intended to deprive the owner of the car permanently. Similarly, if a person takes property, and consumes it or destroys it, it is clear that appropriation has taken place, whether or not the accused intended to return the property.[1]

In England, theft is a statutory offence requiring a dishonest appropriation with an intention permanently to deprive the owner.[2] Section 6(1) of the Theft Act 1968 provides that a person who takes property ostensibly with the intention to return it to the owner, is nevertheless to be regarded as having an intention to deprive the owner permanently if 'his intention is to treat the thing as his own to dispose of regardless of the other's rights'. Section 6 has been described as a statutory provision which 'sprouts obscurities at every phrase',[3] and it is by no means clear what sort of conduct is struck at by the section. In *Lloyd*,[4] it was said that: '...a mere borrowing is never enough to constitute the necessary guilty mind unless the intention is to return the thing in such a changed state that it can truly be said that all its goodness or virtue has gone.'[5] Doubts have been expressed about this view,[6] and it seems that section 6 may be wide enough to cover the type of 'ransom' situations now caught by the *Milne v Tudhope* rule in Scotland.[7] In Scotland, it would certainly be theft to 'borrow' an article and

[1] See *Gordon* para 14–68.
[2] Theft Act 1968, s1(1).
[3] By J R Spencer in 'The metamorphosis of s6 of the Theft Act' [1977] Crim LR 653.
[4] (1985) 81 Crim App Rep 182, [1985] 2 All ER 661.
[5] [1985] 2 All ER 661 at 667 per Lord Lane.
[6] See J C Smith's commentary to *R v Bagshaw* [1988] Crim LR 321.
[7] *R v Coffey* [1987] Crim LR 498.

return it having 'used-up' its usefulness, since 'consumption or destruction constitutes appropriation'.[1] A person who 'borrows' a season ticket for the opera, uses it until the end of the season, and then returns it, is certainly guilty of theft. He has 'treated the thing as his own to dispose of regardless of the owner's rights'. But it may also be theft to 'borrow' consumable goods, use them, and to replace them with goods of equivalent value. For example, **A** is late for a lunch date, and discovers that he has no cash. He takes the cash from the petty cash box, fully intending to replace the money after lunch once he has visited a cash machine. He knows that he is not entitled to take money for this purpose.

Technically this may amount to a theft, since the money taken has been used up, and the owner deprived of it permanently. In England, there is theft in such a situation if the accused's behaviour can be described as 'dishonest',[2] but 'dishonesty' is a word almost as vague as 'nefarious', and seems an unsatisfactory basis for a rule of law.[3] *Gordon* regards this situation as one best left to the prosecutor's discretion.[4]

Taking and using

If property is 'borrowed' without consent, and used for a 'nefarious' purpose, then according to *Milne v Tudhope*, there is theft, even if the 'borrower' fully intends to return the property when his purpose has been accomplished. But even if the purpose for which the property was taken was not nefarious, the taker may be guilty of the crime of 'clandestinely taking possession and using'. Burnett had long ago suggested that temporarily to appropriate a thing, use it, and then return it to its owner, was not theft, but was nevertheless 'an irregular and punishable act'.[5] It was not until 1926, however, that the High Court clearly adopted this view,[6] in what was arguably an exercise of the declaratory power.[7]

In *Strathern v Seaforth*[8] Seaforth was charged with clandestinely taking possession of, and driving a car, knowing that he had not received permission from the owner, and that permission would

---

[1] *Gordon* para 14–68.
[2] See eg *R v Velumyl* [1989] Crim LR 299.
[3] See *Gordon* para 14–71 and cf D W Elliot 'Dishonesty in theft: a dispensable concept' [1982] Crim LR 395.
[4] *Gordon* para 14–71.
[5] *Burnett* p 115.
[6] Cf *Dewar* (1777); *Burnett* p 115.
[7] See above ch 1.
[8] 1926 JC 100, 1926 SLT 445.

have been refused had he requested it. The sheriff-substitute upheld a plea to the relevancy of this charge, and the prosecutor
appealed to the High Court. Lord Alness said that although he was
convinced that the authorities supported the relevance of the
charge, he would have held Seaforth's conduct to be criminal even
without such authority:

'The matter may be tested by considering what the contention for the
respondent involves. It plainly involves that a motor car, or for that matter
any other article, may be taken from its owner, and may be retained for an
indefinite time by the person who abstracts it and who may make a profit
out of the adventure, but that if he intends ultimately to return it, no
offence against the law of Scotland has been committed.'[1]

Lord Alness thought this an 'absurd' argument, and sustained the
relevancy of the complaint. It is interesting to compare his reasoning with that in the English unauthorised borrowing cases, decided
under section 6(1) of the Theft Act. In *R v Lloyd*,[2] for example, two
film projectionists removed films from the cinema where they
worked, copied them for a 'pirate' company, and returned them to
the cinema before they were missed. It was held that this was not
theft, in spite of the fact that huge profits were being made by pirate
companies from such copying, because the films had not lost any of
their value.

The crime created in *Strathern v Seaforth* has not proved popular
with prosecutors however. The only other reported example of the
offence is the case of *Murray v Robertson*,[3] in which an Ardrossan
fish merchant was charged with clandestinely taking possession of
some fish boxes, and using them to transport fish to Glasgow. His
conviction was quashed, because there was no evidence that he had
taken possession of the boxes 'clandestinely' – Lord Justice-Clerk
Alness regarded 'clandestine possession as an essential element in
the charge'.[4] As in *Milne v Tudhope* however, it may be that
'clandestinely' means no more than 'without the owner's knowledge'.[5]

In *Strathern*, the court placed much emphasis on the mischief
which would result if the conduct complained of was not declared
criminal.[6] It is arguable, therefore, that the offence created in

---

[1] *Strathern v Seaforth* at 102 per Lord Justice-Clerk Alness.
[2] (1985) 81 Crim App Rep 182, [1985] 2 All ER 661 – although note the doubts
which have been expressed about this case – see JC Smith's commentary to *R v
Bagshaw* [1988] Crim LR 321.
[3] 1927 JC 1, 1927 SLT 74.
[4] 1927 JC 1 at 4–5.
[5] See *Gordon* para 15–32.
[6] See Lord Justice-Clerk Alness at 102 in *Strathern*.

Strathern was largely the result of the pressing need to protect car owners from joyriders, and can be regarded as a legal museum piece. If, as *Gordon* argues, 'the effect of *Murray v Robertson* has been to discourage any extension of *Strathern v Seaforth* beyond vehicles like boats or cycles',[1] then the scope of the crime is certainly very narrow, since there are now statutory provisions forbidding the unauthorised borrowing of motor cars.[2] In any case, where it is unclear whether the accused had the intention to steal a car, or merely to take it and drive it away, it seems that an intention to steal will be presumed.[3]

Error

Identity and consent. '. . .If the [accused] takes, believing that what he is taking is his own, or that he has the owner's concurrence, he is not guilty of theft.'[4]

A takes **B**'s umbrella in the belief that it is his own. This is not theft. **A** asks **B** if he can have some item of property. **B** says 'no' but **A** mishears and thinks that he has said 'yes'. **A** takes the item of property. This is not theft.

If in the examples above, however, **A** realises that the umbrella may belong to **B**, or that **B** may have said 'no', and takes the items nevertheless, he is probably guilty of theft.[5] Furthermore, it seems likely that in the first example at least, **A**'s mistaken belief would have to be an 'honest and reasonable [one], based on colourable grounds', before it could be accepted as a defence[6]. Doubt in the case of the second example arises from the decision of the High Court in *Meek & Ors v HM Adv*.[7] In *Meek* the court indicated that an unreasonable though honest belief in a woman's consent to intercourse is a defence to a rape charge. Since lack of consent is an essential element in theft as well as rape,[8] it may be that an honest but unreasonable belief in the consent of the owner to the removal of his property constitutes a defence to a theft charge.[9]

---

[1] *Gordon* para 15–31.
[2] Road Traffic Act 1988, s 178 – considered more fully in ch 13.
[3] Indeed must be presumed – see *McLeod v Mason & Ors* 1981 SCCR 75, 1981 SLT (Notes) 109.
[4] *Macdonald* p 18.
[5] See *Gordon* paras 14–81, 14–82.
[6] *Dewar v HM Adv* 1945 JC 5 at 8 per Lord Justice-Clerk Cooper.
[7] 1982 SCCR 613, 1983 SLT 280.
[8] See Lord Hailsham in *R v Morgan* [1976] AC 182 at 214 E-G, [1975] 2 All ER 347.
[9] See ch 11 for a full discussion of *Meek*.

Claim of right. An error as to legal entitlement to property is probably a good defence. There is very little authority on the question, but the question typically arises because of erroneous interpretations of the law of succession.[1] For example, **A** has been cohabiting with **B**, who has just died intestate. In the mistaken belief that one cohabitant's property falls to the other on death, he pawns **B**'s diamond ring. This probably is not theft.

Aggravated thefts

Theft by housebreaking

Certain modes of theft are considered to aggravate the offence. The most common of these modes is theft by housebreaking. This is something of a misnomer however, since 'Scots law does not distinguish among different types of building, and housebreaking can take place against any roofed building'.[2] Since housebreaking is the mode by which the theft is accomplished, it must precede the theft. **X** enters a house through an open window on the ground floor, steals a valuable painting, and then breaks out through a locked door. There is clearly theft, but not theft by housebreaking.

'Housebreaking' is to be interpreted loosely – while it is clearly housebreaking to force open locked doors or windows, it is also housebreaking to enter a house using a stolen[3] or even a found key to unlock doors or windows.[4] It may be housebreaking to use a key which is lawfully in one's possession to gain unauthorised entry to premises. In *Farquarson*,[5] an employee was given the keys of business premises to take to the owner after the premises were locked for the night. Instead of doing so, he returned to the premises, and used the key to gain entry. This was held to be housebreaking. Note, however, that a person authorised to use a key to gain entry to premises would not commit the aggravation if he steals from the premises after using the key to gain entry.[6] Nor is it housebreaking to unlock a door by turning a key found in the lock.[7]

Entering by unexpected or unusual means may also constitute

---

[1] See *Gordon* para 14–83.
[2] *Gordon* para 15–03.
[3] *Hume* I, 98.
[4] *Alex Macdonald* (1826) *Alison* I, 282
[5] (1854) 1 Irv 512.
[6] *Gordon* para 15–10.
[7] *Peter Alston and Alex Forrest* (1837) 1 Swin 433.

the aggravation[1] – entering by a window is probably house-breaking, even if the window is unlocked, or open.[2] Indeed, it may be the case that it is housebreaking to enter premises by any route other than the conventional one. Thus it is housebreaking to enter premises by means of chimneys, sewers, openings in the roof, or trap-doors.[3] It is housebreaking to insert implements, or parts of the body into a house through a window or door, in order to steal things inside – in *O'Neil*,[4] the accused used a hook to 'fish' for property through an open window. If any unusual mode of entry to premises is in fact commonly used by the owner or occupier of the premises, it may not be housebreaking if a thief also enters by that method,[5] but even in such a case, the aggravation may be made out if it is proved that no-one else would be expected to enter by that method.[6]

Finally, gaining entry by means of trickery might be regarded as housebreaking:[7] **A** induces **B** to open his door by pretending to be a representative of an electricity company. He then pushes past **B** and steals a number of items. In this situation, **A** might well be charged with robbery, however, since the theft was accomplished by the use of force.[8]

Opening lockfast places

Opening a locked room in a building does not constitute house-breaking,[9] but it does constitute the separate aggravation of opening lockfast places. For example **X** and **Y** have separate bed-rooms in a shared flat. When **Y** is out, **X** picks the lock on his door and steals his hi-fi. **X** can be charged with theft by opening lockfast places.

Rooms within buildings, safes, drawers, cupboards, motor cars and boxes may all be 'lockfast places', and to open any of them by breaking, picking locks, or using stolen or found keys constitutes

---

[1] *Alison* I, 282.
[2] See *Wm Anderson* (1840) Bell's Notes 199.
[3] See eg *Rendal Courtney* (1743) *Hume* I, 99; *John Carrigan and Thos Robinson* (1853) 1 Irv 303; *Angus Sutherland* (1874) 3 Couper 74.
[4] (1845) 2 Broun 394.
[5] *Jas Davidson* (1841) 2 Swin 630.
[6] *Angus Sutherland*, supra.
[7] See *Hume* I, 100; *Macdonald* p 25; *Alston and Forrest* (1837) 1 Swin 433 at 470 per Lord Moncreiff.
[8] See *Alison* I, 287, and *O'Neill v HM Adv* 1934 JC 98, 1934 SLT 432.
[9] See *Alison* I, 287, and eg *Gilchrist and Hislop* Bell's Notes 34.

the aggravation.[1] Again, it must be shown that the theft was achieved by the opening of a lockfast place. The aggravation is not invoked where a box or safe is stolen and opened elsewhere.[2]

The use of explosives to open lockfast places acts as an aggravation of the aggravation, and is regarded by the courts as particularly serious.

Theft by drugging – and other aggravations

Theft by drugging the victim and then stealing from him is in theory an aggravation of theft.[3] In modern practice, housebreaking and opening lockfast places are the only commonly libelled aggravations of theft.[4] Other aggravations, such as stealing articles of high value, theft by a known thief, and theft by those in a position of trust, will probably now be regarded as relevant only to the question of sentence.

Preventive offences

Housebreaking with intent to steal, and opening lockfast places with intent to steal are distinct offences, and in spite of early doubts,[5] are commonly encountered in modern practice.[6] Housebreaking and attempts to open lockfast places are not criminal per se;[7] they must be done with intent to steal. That intention will usually be inferred from the circumstances however.

COMMON LAW RESET

Reset is in essence the handling of ill-gotten goods or gains. The crime is committed when a person retains possession of goods obtained by theft, robbery, fraud, or embezzlement, with the intention of keeping the goods from their true owner. It is probably the

[1] See *Gordon* para 15–15.
[2] *Gordon* para 15–17.
[3] *Macdonald* p 31. This situation is regarded as theft and not robbery – see eg *Stuart* (1829) Bell's Notes 22 and ch 14.
[4] See *Gordon* paras 15–20 to 15–25.
[5] See eg *Allan Lawrie* (1837) 2 Swin 101 and cf *Macdonald* p 51.
[6] See eg *McLeod v Mason* 1981 SCCR 75, 1981 SLT (Notes) 109.
[7] Although they may amount to malicious mischief – see below ch 18.

case that reset can be committed only in respect of the dishonestly acquired goods themselves. On this view[1] receipt of the proceeds of stolen goods is not reset.

It is important to distinguish between a thief or an accomplice to a theft on the one hand, and a resetter on the other, since a person involved in the theft of goods, actor or art and part, cannot be convicted of their reset.[2] It may not be easy to determine which is which however. In *Robert v Agnes Black*[3] Mrs B found a pocket book and took it home to her husband. Both were convicted of theft on the ground that the intention to appropriate the book had been formed in concert after Mrs B had taken it home. Had she appropriated it herself and then brought it home that would have been a completed theft, and Mr B could have been guilty only of reset.[4] Thus, in this type of situation a conviction for reset will depend largely on the question of when and by whom appropriation took place.[5]

The *actus reus* of reset

'It is the fundamental circumstance in the description of this crime that the stolen goods are received into the offender's possession.'[6] Hume took the view that possession of the goods, in the broad sense of having control of them, should be a requirement for conviction of reset. Thus, a person who keeps stolen goods in his warehouse, or in a safety deposit box in a bank to which he has the key, has sufficient 'possession' for the purposes of this offence. This is so even if the goods are put there by some other person. Macdonald extended this idea somewhat, saying that 'If the [thief] with [the resetter's] knowledge hide the property, even in a hole in a wall, and [the resetter] connive at this, he is guilty'.[7] Gordon agrees 'provided the goods are hidden there for [the resetter] and not for the thief'.[8] For Gordon it is crucial that the resetter have some degree of control over the goods. The problem with Macdonald's state-

---

[1] As to which see *Gordon* para 20–07.
[2] *Hume* I, 116; *Gordon* para 20–15 and see eg *Backhurst v McNaughton* 1981 SCCR 6.
[3] (1841) Bell's Notes 46.
[4] *Gordon* para 20–15. It may be that Mr B could not be convicted even of reset. See discussion of *Smith v Watson* 1982 JC 34, below.
[5] As to which see above on theft. Note also that where an accused is charged with theft, he can be convicted of reset, but not vice versa – Criminal Procedure (Scotland) Act 1975, ss60(1), 312(m).
[6] *Hume* I, 110.
[7] *Macdonald* p 68.
[8] *Gordon* para 20–02.

ment lies in its use of the word 'connive', which seems to imply that a person is guilty of reset who merely knows the whereabouts of stolen goods.

In *HM Adv v Browne*,[1] Macdonald, who at the time was Lord Justice-Clerk, developed this idea, holding that 'reset consists of being privy to the retaining of property that has been dishonestly come by'.[2] Thus, in Macdonald's view, reset is possible where the accused has had neither actual nor constructive possession of stolen property, but where he has simply 'connived' at the retention of the property from its true owner. The precise meaning of this expression continues to exercise the courts. In *Gilbert McCawley*,[3] it was held, following *Browne*, that a passenger who knew that the car in which he was being driven had been stolen, was guilty of reset, while in *McNeil v HM Adv*[4] it was found that a person present when thief was introduced to resetter, is similarly guilty.

In *Clark v HM Adv*,[5] the Criminal Appeal Court expressed doubts about *Browne* and the views of Lord Justice-Clerk Macdonald, which they had difficulty in reconciling with the views of Hume and Alison that 'it is fundamental to the crime of reset that the goods be received into the accused's possession'.[6] They did not overrule the offending case, but were clearly of the opinion that 'mere inactivity' cannot constitute 'connivance' for the purposes of reset.[7]

The accused in *Clark* was present when 1 000 stolen cigarettes were handed over to a resetter in a pub, but apparently took no active part in this transaction or in the accompanying conversation. The court nowhere defines precisely what 'connivance' means, but in quashing the accused's conviction for reset seemed to imply that some 'overt act' on the part of the accused is required.[8] On its facts, *Clark* is clearly inconsistent with *McCawley* and *McNeil*. But the latter case post-dates *Clark*, and in *McNeil* Lord Justice-General Clyde described the observations made by the court in *Clark* as obiter, placed emphasis on the views of the

---

[1] (1903) 6 F(J) 24, 11 SLT 353.
[2] (1903) 6F(J) 24 at 26.
[3] July 1959, unreported, High Court.
[4] 1968 JC 29, 1968 SLT 338.
[5] 1965 SLT 250.
[6] *Hume* I, 110; see Lord Justice-Clerk Grant at 252, Lord Strachan at 253 in *Clark*, supra.
[7] See Lord Justice-Clerk Grant at 252 in *Clark*.
[8] It seems that counsel were agreed that this was the proper interpretation of *Browne* – see Lord Justice-Clerk Grant at 252 in *Clark*.

court in *McCawley*, and re-iterated the view expressed in *Browne* that reset can be committed by one who is merely privy to the retention of the stolen goods. Again no further assistance was given as to the meaning of connivance.

In *McNeil*, the accused was in a car when the thief of certain goods, which were also in the car at the time, was introduced to the resetter. In *Hipson v Tudhope*,[1] the accused was a passenger in a stolen car. His conviction for reset was quashed since, when stopped by the police, he made no attempt to get away, and said nothing to the investigating officers. Again, the implication of the case is that silence or inactivity in the presence of stolen goods is insufficient to justify a conviction for reset, since there is no 'connivance' with the thief. However, the grounds for the decision were purely evidential – on the evidence, the court were simply unconvinced that the accused knew that the car was stolen. On the one hand the case refers with approval to *Clark*, while on the other, it suggests, consistently with *McNeil*, that a person may be 'privy to the retention' of stolen goods provided only that he knows the origin of the goods. Lord Wheatley said that: 'the situation falls clearly into the category that was recognised in *Clark v HM Adv* as being a situation where an inference of guilty knowledge could not be garnered from the mere silence of the accused.'[2]

This decision appears to confuse *actus reus* and *mens rea* in reset. There is no doubt that knowledge of the theftuous origin of the goods is required for a conviction. But more is required than mere knowledge. In *Clark* Lord Strachan said that 'I cannot hold that the crime of reset may be committed by merely refraining from reporting to the police that stolen property is being disposed of'.[3] Hume did use the words 'privity and connivance'[4] in relation to reset, but he was referring to the situation where stolen goods are placed in the accused's house with his knowledge and approval. For Hume, the accused's knowledge of the presence of the goods is necessary in order to show his possession of them. In consciously allowing the goods to be brought into his house, the accused has performed an 'overt act' showing his connivance with the thief, and his intention to retain the goods from the true owner.[5] Active connivance with the thief is required, not because

[1] 1983 SCCR 247, 1983 SLT 659.
[2] 1983 SLT 659 at 660.
[3] 1965 SLT 250 at 253.
[4] *Hume* I, 114.
[5] See Lord Justice-Clerk Grant at 252 in *Clark*, supra.

it demonstrates that the accused knew that the goods were stolen, but because it shows that the accused had a sufficient degree of control over the goods to allow an inference of possession to be drawn. In so far as *Browne* is inconsistent with this analysis, and this is by no means clear, it is submitted that that case was wrongly decided and now requires to be overruled. The older authorities are adamant that possession is required before a conviction for reset can follow,[1] and that view seems to be in accordance with principle – knowledge that a crime has been committed does not infer complicity.

The *mens rea* of reset

There are two essential elements in the *mens rea* of reset – guilty knowledge that the goods are stolen, and an intention to retain the goods from their true owner.

Guilty knowledge

To bring home a conviction for reset it is necessary for the prosecutor to prove that the accused knew that the goods were stolen. 'Bare suspicion' is not enough. In *Shannon v HM Adv*[2] the accused concealed his possession of a 'sawed-off' shotgun, and made off when the police came to search his home. However, the accused's possession of an illegal weapon was not enough to justify the inference that the accused knew that the weapon was stolen.

If on the evidence it is clear that the accused must have known the origins of the goods,[3] a conviction will be possible, and for this purpose 'wilful blindness' as to the facts is probably sufficient.[4] Where there is evidence that the accused knew the goods to be stolen, very little in the way of corroboration will be required. In *Nisbet v HM Adv* the thief testified that the accused had such knowledge. For corroboration, the Crown successfully relied on the fact that Nisbet had told an 'awkward story of the way of getting the goods' – in effect that the goods had fallen off the back of a lorry!

---

[1] *Hume*, I 110; *Alison* I, 328; *Burnett* p 155.
[2] 1985 SCCR 14.
[3] See *Alison* I, 330.
[4] See *Herron v Latta* (1968) 32 JCL 51, (1967) SCCR Supp 18.

Intention to retain the goods from their true owner

Provided there is an intention to 'conceal and withhold' the goods from their true owner,[1] it is not necessary to show that the goods were retained for a lengthy period, or that the resetter intended to keep the goods for himself. If someone hides goods, perhaps only for a matter of minutes while the police search the thief's house, there is reset. There can be no conviction in the absence of such an intention, for example where someone finds stolen goods and is apprehended when conveying them back to the owner or to a police station.

The husband and wife rule

'A wife is not in the ordinary case held guilty of reset if she conceal property to screen her husband, without proof of active participation.'[2] Thus, a woman will not be convicted of reset solely by reason of her receipt of stolen goods from her husband.[3] There are limits to this rule however: it must be shown (a) that the property was brought into the house by the husband and (b) that the wife's only purpose in retaining the goods was to protect her husband.

In *Smith v Watson*[4] it was said that 'the doctrine is a relic of an age when wives were expected as a matter of course to submit to their husbands and could therefore be presumed to have done wrong *ex reverentia mariti*'.[5] In modern conditions the rule seems somewhat archaic, particularly in view of the number of cohabiting couples who, if unmarried, presumably do not enjoy its protection to any extent. While accepting that the doctrine is 'firmly rooted' in our law, the court insisted that the conditions set out above must be strictly complied with. In the circumstances it was clear that someone other than the husband had brought the goods into the house, and that the wife was simply retaining them until her husband's release from prison.

---

[1] *Hume* I, 113.
[2] *Macdonald* p 68.
[3] *Gordon* states that the rule would also be held nowadays to apply to a husband who received stolen property from his wife – para 20–05. Cf *Alison* I, 339.
[4] 1982 SCCR 15, 1982 JC 34.
[5] See opinion of the court at 35.

15. Robbery

Robbery may be regarded as a form of aggravated theft, involving the use of personal violence or threatening behaviour.[1] However, in robbery the taking is achieved by violence or threats, and accordingly there can be no robbery by appropriation of property lawfully obtained, as in theft. This difference apart, the rules regarding *actus reus* and *mens rea* in theft are applicable, and defences to a theft charge, such as error or claim of right, are likewise defences to a charge of robbery.[2]

PERSONAL VIOLENCE

Robbery is in essence the taking of goods by force. When goods are forcibly taken from their owner, there may be a preceding assault, or the act of taking may itself be of such violence as to constitute robbery – in *O'Neill v HM Adv*[3] for example, the accused knocked the victim's head against a wall and grabbed her handbag. However, robbery must be distinguished from theft by surprise, as when goods are simply snatched from their owner in the street, or filched by a pick-pocket. This may not be an easy distinction to draw, since it is unnecessary to prove an assault in order to obtain a conviction. In *O'Neill* Lord Justice-Clerk Aitchison said that 'It is well settled that in robbery there must be violence. On the other hand, it is not necessary to robbery that there should be actual physical assault. It is enough if the degree of force used can reasonably be described as violence'.[4] The accused in *O'Neill* was charged with assault and robbery. The jury found the assault not proven, but it was held that it was competent nevertheless to find the accused guilty of robbery.

[1] Although technically it is a separate offence – see *Gordon* para 16–02.
[2] Although not, of course, to any charge of assault arising out of the incident.
[3] 1934 JC 34, 1934 SLT 432.
[4] At 101.

Thus, it is a question of circumstances in each case whether there has been violence sufficient to constitute robbery. The cases suggest that the degree of violence required is minimal.

In *Cromar v HM Adv*,[1] the robber approached the victim from behind, took hold of a bag which the victim was holding, and tried to pull it away. The victim held onto the bag, but its handle snapped and the robber made off. The jury were directed in terms of *O'Neill* and found the accused guilty of robbery.

It is essential that the taking be achieved by means of violence. Thus, if a thief uses force to escape having once removed the goods, there is no robbery, but only a theft followed perhaps by an assault.[2] It should be noted, however, that even though the thief uses no violence initially, it is robbery if he later resorts to force to overcome resistance from the victim.[3]

Where the taking is preceded by an assault, the assault is usually subsumed by the robbery, since it is regarded simply as the mode by which the robbery is committed. But not every taking preceded by an assault will constitute robbery. If the assault is not connected with the taking, because either the two acts were performed by different, unconnected people, or because the original motive for the attack was not theft, then there is no robbery.[4] The second of these possibilities would of course be very difficult to establish and it is probably the case that in these circumstances it would be presumed that the attack was made with intent to rob.[5]

THREATS

The classic case of armed robbery is where the robber points a gun at the victim and threatens, expressly or by clear implication, to shoot the victim should he fail to hand over the loot. Thus, actual violence is unnecessary to constitute robbery – it is enough that there is 'such behaviour as justly alarms for the personal and immediate consequences of resistance or refusal'.[6] *Gordon* says

---

[1]   1987 SCCR 635.

[2]   See *Gordon* para 16–07.

[3]   See eg *Cromar*, supra, and *Hume* I, 105.

[4]   See *Gordon* para 16–08. Cf *Burnett* p 150, and *Alison* I, 238, who both take the view that there can be robbery even though the intention to steal arises after the assault has taken place.

[5]   *Gordon* para 16–08.

[6]   *Hume* I, 107.

that:

'The development from violence to intimidation is clear – it is robbery
to shoot **B** and steal from him; it is also robbery, because it is technically
an assault, to present a weapon at **B** and intimidate him into handing
over his goods; and from there it is but a short step to say that it is
robbery to threaten to shoot **B** without actually producing a weapon.'[1]

However, where the threat does not constitute an assault (that is
where neither gun, knife nor fist is presented at the victim), it
becomes very difficult to distinguish robbery from extortion.[2]
According to *Gordon*, 'robbery by threats is distinguished from
extortion by the immediacy of the threat and the obtaining of the
money'.[3] Insofar as *Gordon*'s reference to 'threats' relates to
threats of immediate violence, his statement is unobjectionable.
However, he then proceeds to give as an example of robbery the
case of a person who telephones another and threatens to report
him to the police immediately, unless a certain sum of money is
paid. To allow threats other than those of immediate injury or
violence to form the basis of a robbery charge seems to move
unacceptably far from the idea of a taking by force.[4] The older
authorities suggest that violence, actual or threatened, is of the
essence in robbery,[5] and while it is unnecessary to establish that
any menaces used themselves constituted an assault, a requirement for 'threats of present injury and not merely of some future
wrong'[6] seems necessary to distinguish robbery from extortion.
Thus, menaces which 'appear in the weapons shown, in the
number and combination of the assailants, or in their words, gestures and carriage, if in the whole circumstances of the situation
they may reasonably intimidate and overawe, are therefore a
proper description of violence, to found a charge of robbery'.[7]
There is little authority on the point, but in the old English case
of *Knewland and Wood*, for example, it was held not to be
robbery to 'extort' money from a 'young and ignorant country
girl' by threatening to carry her before a magistrate and thereafter to Newgate prison.[8]

---

[1] *Gordon* para 16–12.
[2] As to which see section on *Extortion* in ch 17 below.
[3] *Gordon* para 16–14.
[4] See eg *Burnett* p 147, where he refers to threats which operate as 'an act of force
sufficient to constitute robbery'. Burnett doubted whether any threat other than
one of bodily injury would suffice for robbery.
[5] See *Hume* I, 107; *Macdonald* p 41.
[6] *Macdonald* p 41.
[7] *Hume* I, 107.
[8] *Hume* I, 108.

PIRACY

'Piracy is a crime nowadays of rare occurrence ...and has over the years acquired certain picturesque and picaresque associations. But the crime itself, stripped of the highly coloured detail with which storybook romance has clothed the concept, is in essentials of sordid and squalid simplicity.'[1]

In *Cameron v HM Adv*,[2] it was held that piracy is in essence the robbery of a ship. Thus, where a vessel is taken out of the possession of its owner or master, by the use of violence or threats of violence, the crime committed is piracy *iure gentium*. Possession may be seized by members of the crew,[3] or by others,[4] and it is probably enough to constitute piracy that there is a frustrated attempt to take possession of the ship.[5] A similar offence is created in respect of aircraft by the Hijacking Act 1971.[6]

---

[1] *Cameron v HM Adv* 1971 JC 50 at 52, 1971 SLT 202, 333.
[2] Supra.
[3] As in *Cameron*.
[4] See *re Piracy Jure Gentium* [1934] AC 586.
[5] No firm conclusion was reached in *Cameron* on this matter.
[6] Section 1.

16. Fraud/uttering

In England, the Theft Acts provide that anyone who 'by deception dishonestly obtains' goods or services, is guilty of an offence.[1] In Scotland, fraud remains largely a common law offence,[2] and one with a rather different emphasis from, and a wider scope than, the English offences involving deception.

COMMON LAW FRAUD (SIMPLE FRAUD)

It is of the essence of the crime of fraud that a false impression should be conveyed to the victim, with the deliberate aim of achieving some practical, and to the victim, usually prejudicial, result. It is also essential that the false pretence should have brought about this desired result.[3] As we shall see however, it is not necessary that the accused should have gained any item of property through his false pretence. There may indeed be fraud where the victim has not lost any item of property.

The false pretence

The false pretence may take a variety of forms. It has been said that it is enough that there is '. . .any deception by which one man makes another believe to the latter's injury, something that really does not

---

[1] Theft Act 1968, s15(1); Theft Act 1978, s 1(1).
[2] Although there are numerous statutory frauds, such as – bankruptcy frauds; weights and measures frauds; company frauds; trades descriptions frauds; food and drugs frauds and so on. These are beyond the scope of a work of this nature, but are dealt with in some detail by *Gordon* in ch 19. Note that some such frauds may also be frauds at common law – eg bankruptcy frauds. Cf *HM Adv v Livingston* (1888) 1 White 587, 15 R (J) 48.
[3] *Gordon* para 18–02.

exist. It may be done by direct assertion or by a suggestion, not amounting to a direct assertion, of something which was untrue'.[1]

However, the emphasis in Scots law is not so much on the idea of deception – the active creation of a false belief in the mind of the victim[2] – as on the facts that a false pretence has been made, and that some practical result is brought about by the pretence.[3] This approach avoids some of the problems inherent in the English offences involving deception. Thus, it is not necessary in Scotland to show that anyone was in fact deceived, provided that the causal link between false pretence and result is proved.[4]

The pretence may be about any relevant matter, the only proviso being that the pretence must bring about the practical result. Thus, for example **A** falsely represents to **B** that she is the daughter of **C**, a person known by **B** to be of good credit. **B** hands over goods to **A** in the belief that **C** will pay him later. **A**, who is never seen again, commits fraud.[5]

A says to **B** that he can sell him a fragment of Burns' original handwritten manuscript of 'Tam O'Shanter'. The manuscript is a clever but worthless forgery, a fact well known to **A**, but not to **B** who pays a very large sum for the manuscript. **A** commits fraud.[6]

A wishes to purchase **B**'s large house. He wishes to convert the house for office use, but is aware that **B** will not sell the house except for residential purposes. He tells **B** that he intends to use the house as a residence for himself and his family, and **B** sells him the house on that basis. **A** commits fraud.[7]

Implied representations

It is not necessary that the accused should have made a false statement however. It is enough that he has acted in such a way as to create a false impression about any of the matters referred to above. In the English case of *Barnard*,[8] for example, a townsman walked into an Oxford shop dressed as an undergraduate and obtained

[1] *HM Adv v Livingstone* (1888) 1 White 587 at 592 per Lord Fraser.
[2] See re *London and Globe Finance Corporation* [1903] 1 Ch 728 at 732 per Buckley J, and cf Lord Denning in *Welham v DPP* [1961] AC 103 at 133.
[3] See *Macdonald* p 52.
[4] See eg *DPP v Ray* [1974] AC 370, [1973] 3 All ER 131, considered below, and see A T H Smith 'The idea of criminal deception' [1982] Crim LR 721.
[5] Cf *Morrison v Robertson* 1908 SC 332, (1908) 15 SLT 697.
[6] Cf *Frank v HM Adv* 1938 JC 17, 1938 SLT 109.
[7] See eg *Richards v HM Adv* 1971 JC 29; *Steuart v Macpherson* 1918 JC 96, 1918 2 SLT 125.
[8] (1837) 7 Car & P 784.

goods on credit thanks to the false impression he had thus created. At no time did Barnard explicitly claim to be an undergraduate: he was nevertheless convicted of fraud.

In the extraordinary case of *James Paton*,[1] the accused inflated the skins of his cattle to make them look fatter, and fixed false horns on to them. He wanted to win a prize at a cattle show, but instead was charged with fraud. Although he was acquitted on other grounds, it was held that the false impression created by his 'window dressing' was sufficient to form the basis of a fraud charge.

Cheques. Cheque-book and credit card frauds, by which goods are obtained using stolen cheques or cards, are increasingly common. There is little Scottish authority on the implied representations made by the drawer of a cheque. If the representation is that the cheque will be honoured, it is a representation about the future, which cannot found a fraud charge.[2] If the representation is that the drawer has money in his account, then 'many very respectable persons are in danger daily of having a criminal charge laid against them'.[3] Without more, no fraud charge can be laid since the drawer may be authorised to overdraw his account, or may know that funds will be paid into his account in time to meet the cheque. In England it has been held that the drawer represents:

(a) That he has an account at the bank issuing the cheque – thus anyone using a stolen cheque-book to 'purchase' goods is clearly guilty of fraud;
(b) that he had authority to draw on that account for the amount of the cheque; and that consequently,
(c) 'the present state of affairs is such that, in the ordinary course of events, the cheque will on its future presentment be duly honoured'.[4]

These are all statements about the present, and a false representation as to any of these matters would be relevant to a charge of fraud. There is English authority to the effect that the use of a cheque or credit card involves an implied representation that the holder has authority to use the card, and that their unauthorised

---

[1] (1858) 3 Irv 208.
[2] *Gordon* para 18–06. Representations of present intentions as to future conduct may ground such a charge however – see *Richards v HM Adv*, supra.
[3] *Rae v Linton* (1874) 3 Couper 67 at 72 per Lord Neaves, 2 R (J) 17.
[4] *R v Page* [1971] 2 QB 330, [1971] 2 All ER 870.

use may constitute fraud. It may be doubted whether these cases would be followed in Scotland.[1]

Silence as a false pretence

In some circumstances, a false impression may be created by remaining silent about the true facts. Thus, where a person has a contractual or statutory duty to disclose certain facts to another, and fails to do so, that person may commit common law fraud.[2] Gill expresses the view[3] that where (a) disclosure of the undisclosed fact would have caused the victim to act otherwise than he did, and (b) the accused intended that the victim should not have acted otherwise than he did, fraud is committed. He derives some support for this view from the case of *HM Adv v Livingston*,[4] a prosecution under the Bankruptcy Acts, in which the accused obtained a loan without revealing his status as an undischarged bankrupt. Lord Fraser directed the jury that the accused's failure to reveal his state of bankruptcy constituted a relevant false pretence – the accused 'knew perfectly well that if he had told that fact he would not have got credit for a single sixpence'.[5] With respect to Dr Gill, his seems too wide a view. Unless there is a duty to reveal a particular fact, there can be no fraud. To hold otherwise would be to render liable to prosecution those who withhold, for example, commercial information when they are perfectly entitled to do so. Thus, while it has been held that there is a duty to reveal the fact that one is an undischarged bankrupt when seeking credit,[6] or to correct inaccuracies in a company prospectus which one has published,[7] it seems that there may be no duty to correct a mistake, provided the mistake was not induced by anything the accused said or did.

In the English case of *Dip Kaur v Chief Constable of Hampshire*,[8]

---

[1] See *R v Charles* [1977] AC 177, [1976] 3 All ER 112; *R v Lambie* [1982] AC 449, [1981] 2 All ER 776. Glanville Williams has expressed doubts about the legitimacy of implying such representations. See his *Textbook of Criminal Law* (2nd edn, 1983) pp 778–780. These cases also give rise to acute problems of causation and are considered further below.

[2] See eg *Strathern v Fogal* 1922 JC 73, 1922 SLT 543; *HM Adv v City of Glasgow Bank Directors* (1879) 4 Couper 161, 6 R (J) 19.

[3] In 'The crime of fraud: a comparative study' – unpublished PhD thesis, Edinburgh University 1975, at p69n.

[4] (1888) 1 White 587, 15 R (J) 48. See also *Patterson v Landsberg* (1905) 7 F 675, 13 SLT 62; *HM Adv v Pattisons* (1901) 3 Adam 420.

[5] *HM Adv v Livingstone* at 592.

[6] *HM Adv v Livingstone*, supra.

[7] *HM Adv v Pattisons* (1901) 3 Adam 420.

[8] [1981] 1 WLR 578 CA, [1981] 2 All ER 430.

goods in a supermarket were mispriced. The accused, who clearly realised what had happened, presented the goods at the cash desk and obtained them at the lower price. Lord Lane CJ held that the accused had practised no deception, nor made any false pretence.[1]

Had the shop-assistant known the truth, no doubt he would have acted differently; nevertheless, there was no fraud.[2] Similarly, sellers of goods have no general duty to reveal defects,[3] although someone selling reconditioned goods which appear to be new, has a duty to reveal their true nature.[4] Whether or not there is a duty to disclose may depend on the relationship of the parties. Although the accused in *Kaur* clearly knew that the goods were mispriced, she was entitled to rely on the cashier's authority to sell the goods at a lower price.[5] But where a customer expresses a mistaken view of the price, nature or quality of certain goods the seller is probably obliged to correct that view.[6] Again, the position is different if the accused has taken active steps to conceal the truth – if Kaur had herself placed the wrong price on the goods for example – and then remains silent, her conduct would have amounted to a misrepresentation.[7]

Of course, the distinction between conduct amounting to a misrepresentation, and non-fraudulent silence is not an easy one to draw. In *HM Adv v Pattisons*,[8] the accused published a company prospectus containing accounts which had been prepared from the company books. Those books contained material omissions which the accused failed to disclose. It was held that the presentation of the books to the accountants without explanation amounted to a misrepresentation that they were accurate and complete.[9] But unless the accused had a duty to make full disclosure of their

---

[1] See Lord Lane CJ at 583D. Kaur was charged with theft, so Lord Lane's dictum was obiter, and the crucial question in the case was whether Kaur's dishonesty over the price had vitiated the contract. If it had, then ownership remained with the shop, and her removal of the goods from the shop would have amounted to theft. *Kaur* has since been doubted (on the theft point), by Lord Roskill in *Morris (David)* [1984] AC 320 at 334, and that doubt has itself been doubted, by *Smith and Hogan* p 494.

[2] But cf J C Smith *The Law of Theft* (4th edn, 1979) p88, and compare the cases of *Charles* and *Lambie*, which seem inconsistent with *Kaur*.

[3] See eg *Smith and Hogan* p 547.

[4] See *Gibson v NCR* 1925 SC 50, 1925 SLT 377, and cf *Patterson v Landsberg* (1905) 7 F 675, 13 SLT 62. The appearance of the goods is said to constitute an implied representation as to their nature.

[5] See *Kaur* [1981] 1 WLR 578 at 583C, [1981] 2 All ER 430.

[6] Cf *With v O'Flanagan* [1936] Ch 575; *Incledon v Watson* (1862) 2 F&F 841.

[7] *Kaur* [1981] 1 WLR 578 at 581D and 583F.

[8] (1901) 3 Adam 420.

[9] Ibid at 470.

company's finances to potential investors, their presentation of the books to the accountants could not amount to such a misrepresentation.

Representations of intention

There was for many years considerable doubt in Scots law as to whether a statement of intention, and in particular, a statement of intention to pay,[1] could form the basis of a fraud charge.[2] Such statements present problems for the criminal law, since people frequently break promises, or fail to pay their debts. In such cases, the promisor or debtor has failed to carry out his intention,[3] but not all such people ought to be treated as criminals. There are some promises with which the law ought not to become involved, and business people who genuinely intend to meet their obligations may become unable to do so. Even wilful failure to pay a debt is not necessarily treated as criminal, as a visit to any small claims court will demonstrate.

Although the older cases[4] suggest that only a misrepresentation of past or present fact is relevant to a fraud charge, there can now be no doubt, following the case of *Richards v HM Adv*,[5] that a false statement of intention can ground such a charge. Richards wished to buy a property in Edinburgh from the local authority. He was aware that the authority would sell the property only if it was to be used as a private residence, and accordingly he represented to the authority that he intended to use the property as his family home. In fact he had no such intention, and he was convicted of fraud. The court refused to recognise the distinction drawn in the nineteenth century case of *John Hall*[6] between misrepresentations of fact, and misrepresentations of intention, saying that '. . .a man's present intention is just as much a fact as his name or his occupation, or the size of his bank balance'.[7]

Particular problems have arisen where a person orders goods or services with the initial intention of paying for them, but later changes his mind, and defaults on his obligation.

In *DPP v Ray*[8] a group of young men ordered a meal in a Chinese

---

[1] See *John Hall* (1881) 4 Couper 438, 8 R (J) 28.
[2] See *Gordon* para 18–13.
[3] Note the problems of classification here – see *Gordon* para 18–13.
[4] Such as *John Hall*, supra.
[5] 1971 JC 29.
[6] (1881) 4 Couper 438, 8 R (J) 28.
[7] *Richards v HM Adv* 1971 JC 29 at 32 per Lord Justice-Clerk Grant.
[8] [1974] AC 370, [1973] 3 All ER 131.

restaurant, fully intending to pay for it. After they had consumed the meal they changed their minds and left the restaurant without paying. The House of Lords treated their initial representation of intention to pay as a continuing one,[1] which was falsified by their later change of mind.

Ray gave rise to a number of problems,[2] not the least of which was that by treating representations of intention to pay as continuing ones, the House of Lords seemed to imply that there is a duty to disclose that the representation has become false. Such an approach is to run the risk of 'treating every defaulting debtor as guilty of fraud where it can be shown that but for his non-disclosure of his change of mind the creditor would have taken steps to try to secure payment'.[3] In Scotland, following *Richards*,[4] a charge of obtaining goods or services 'without paying and without intending to pay' is clearly relevant.[5] However, if it is accepted, as it was in *Ray*, that the initial intention of the fraudster was to pay for the goods, and that only at some later stage, after the goods were handed over, did he form the intention to withhold payment, it would in Scotland be very difficult to frame an appropriate charge, since the goods were not obtained by any false pretence.[6]

Statements of opinion

Statements of opinion generally cannot form the basis of a fraud charge, since such statements cannot easily be shown to be 'true' or 'false'. It might be shown, however, that the maker of the statement did not really hold the opinion claimed, or that he knew of facts tending to negate the opinion, and on that basis a fraud charge might be held relevant.[7]

Manufacturers and retailers of goods frequently make extravagant or even false claims about their products. Such claims are sometimes called advertiser's 'puffs'. Provided, however, that such

---

[1] Or possibly as containing a further implied representation that they would not later change their minds – see Lord Morris at 386A.
[2] As to which see GH Gordon 'Two recent developments in English criminal law' (1975) 20 JLS 4.
[3] *Gordon* para 18–12.
[4] 1971 JC 29.
[5] See also *Gordon* para 18–13, n78. It should be noted, however, that in the particular circumstances of *Ray*, there might well have been an acquittal in Scotland because of problems of causation.
[6] Cf GH Gordon 'Two recent developments' (1975) 20 JLS 4 at 7.
[7] See *Smith and Hogan* pp 510–511.

claims amount only to statements of opinion about the goods, and are not false statements of fact, there is no fraud.[1] In *Tapsell v Prentice*,[2] Lord Ardwall referred to statements which were 'just the ordinary lies which people tell when they want to induce credulous members of the public to purchase goods, or to do something for them'.[3] In drawing the line between statements of fact and statements of opinion, advertisers are given considerable freedom. Few people believe the grandiloquent claims which some manufacturers make for their products in their advertising campaigns. Nevertheless, such statements are not generally regarded as fraudulent.[4] It is likely to be regarded as a matter of fact and degree whether more outrageous examples of such statements represent relevant false pretences.[5] Where goods are advertised or sold in the course of a business, the application of a false description to the goods would in any event render the advertiser or seller liable to prosecution under the Trade Descriptions Act 1968.[6]

The result

Fraud is popularly perceived as an offence by which the perpetrator gains possession of some item of the victim's property, or makes some gain at the victim's expense. In England, for example, an offence is committed by any person who 'by any deception dishonestly obtains property belonging to another'.[7] Hume seems to have regarded fraud in this light – he defines fraud as a false pretence made 'for the purpose of obtaining goods or money, or other valuable thing, to the offender's profit',[8] and Alison refers to 'All those falsehoods and frauds by which another is deprived of his property'.[9] During the nineteenth century, however, fraud seems to have lost the requirement of economic loss to the victim, or indeed gain for the accused. This extension of the offence seems to

---

[1] See *Gordon* para 18–09.
[2] (1910) 6 Adam 354, 1911 SC (J) 67.
[3] (1910) 6 Adam 354 at 357.
[4] Some advertisements may, however, give rise to complaints to the Advertising Standards Authority.
[5] See *Gordon* para 18–09.
[6] Section 1(1). See *Gordon* paras 19–25 to 19–50.
[7] If he has the intention permanently to deprive the other of his property – see the Theft Act 1968, s 15(1).
[8] *Hume* I, 172.
[9] *Alison* I, 362.

have been due to the incompetency at that time of a charge of attempted fraud, and acts came to be regarded as fraudulent which involved little or no actual economic prejudice to the victim, but which merely exposed the victim to a risk of such prejudice. Thus, in *Jas Paton*,[1] in which the accused inflated the skins of his cattle beasts in order to win a prize at an agricultural show, it was enough that the accused won the competition, and thus obtained a right to a prize. The lack of any averment that the prize was actually paid was not fatal to the relevancy of the indictment.[2]

The classic modern statement of the result requirement in fraud is to be found in the case of *Adcock v Archibald*.[3] In that case, Lord Justice-General Clyde said that 'It is . . .a mistake to suppose that to the commission of a fraud it is necessary to prove an actual gain by the accused, or an actual loss on the part of the person alleged to be defrauded. Any definite practical result achieved by the fraud is enough.'.[4] This statement was approved in *HM Adv v Wishart*.[5] Wishart was a solicitor who entered into a complex scheme with a stockbroker whereby the latter's accounts were made to appear healthier than was in fact the case. There was no averment that anyone had suffered loss because of the scheme, and the only result was that the stockbroker's auditors were induced to report to the Stock Exchange as genuine, accounts which were inaccurate and misleading.[6] Lord Macdonald held that economic loss is unnecessary in fraud, and found the charge to be relevant.

Fraud in Scots law is therefore a crime remarkably wide in scope. It does not even appear from the opinions delivered in *Adcock* that the result must be prejudicial to the victim. While it may be accepted that prejudice does not necessarily imply economic loss,[7] to do away altogether with the requirement of prejudice to the victim would lead to absurd results – on this view, there would be fraud if a person was induced by false pretences to accept some benefit.[8] What does seem clear is that the victim must have been induced actually to do some act, rather than simply to believe a

---

[1] (1858) 3 Irv 208.
[2] See also *Hood v Young* (1853) 1 Irv 236.
[3] 1925 JC 58, 1925 SLT 258.
[4] 1925 JC 58 at 61.
[5] 1975 SCCR Supp 78.
[6] Cf *HM Adv v Pattisons* (1901) 3 Adam 420.
[7] See the examples given by *Gordon* at para 18–21.
[8] *Gordon* para 18–19.

lie. Mere deception is not enough.[1] Gordon submits that the result must not only be prejudicial but that the prejudice must be more than merely trivial.[2] In support of that contention he cites the case of *HM Adv v Camerons*.[3]

The Camerons wrote a letter to their insurance firm in which they fabricated a claim in respect of some jewellery, which they claimed was stolen from them. The insurers sent the accused a claim form but the matter went no further than that. Although the insurers had been induced to part with a sheet of paper, and the cost of posting the form to the accused, the charge was one of attempted fraud only.

The result, although definite and practical, was clearly considered too minor to warrant a fraud charge. But although the Crown saw fit to charge the Camerons only with the inchoate offence, there is no legal reason to suppose that a charge libelling the completed crime would not have been held relevant. As Gordon recognises,[4] there is no *de minimis* rule in Scotland, and the 'practical result' accepted in *Adcock v Archibald* was of no more significance than the result of the Camerons' false pretence.[5]

In *Adcock*, the accused was a miner who put his own marker on a hutch of coal mined by another. His employers were thus induced to make an entry in their books signifying that it was he who had mined the coal and not his colleague. This book entry was the only practical result however, since Adcock had failed to extract enough coal to qualify for a productivity bonus.

In theory then, it appears that fraud may be committed where the victim is 'induced to do something [he] would not otherwise have done',[6] and that that 'something' may be extremely trivial. Gordon's view that the result must involve some 'legally significant

---

[1] Cf *Welham v DPP* [1961] AC 103. It may be that Scots law's acceptance of any practical result of a false pretence would allow a charge of fraud where the 'victim' was a computer or other machine. Such charges are not possible in England because of the need to show that someone was deceived. See *Computer Crime* (Scots Law Com Consultative Memorandum no 68) paras 3–2 to 3–8; *Report on Computer Crime* (Scot Law Com Consultative Memorandum no 106) (1987); and cf JC Smith 'Some comments on deceiving a machine' (1972) 69 Law Soc Gazette 576.

[2] Cf the pre-Theft Act English law, which did not require economic loss in fraud, but did require that the result of the pretence be prejudicial to the dupe.

[3] (1911) 6 Adam 456, 1911 SC (J) 110.

[4] See *Gordon* para 18–19, note 8.

[5] *Gordon* argues (at para 18–19) that while the dicta expressed in *Adcock v Archibald* may have been sound, their application to the facts of the case was not.

[6] Lord Hunter in *Adcock* 1925 JC 58 at 61.

prejudice' seems, at least in theory, debatable. In practice, how-ever, it appears that the Crown Office is taking a similarly narrow view of the result requirement.

In *McKenzie v HM Adv*,[1] the accused made false statements to solicitors in Edinburgh, and thereby induced them to raise unfounded civil actions against Caley Fisheries of Peterhead. A charge of attempting to defraud the fishing company was found to be relevant, even although the fraudulent scheme was halted at a very early stage in its development.

In this case, the accused were charged only with an attempt to defraud the fishing company of sums of money. The facts of the case support the view that there might have been a completed fraud on the accuseds' solicitors. False representations made by the accused to their solicitors led to a definite practical result – the raising of the actions against Caley Fisheries.[2] Support for the view that this could have been charged as a completed fraud may be found in *Adcock* where Lord Hunter says, somewhat obscurely, that fraud may consist in inducing someone to 'become the medium of some unlawful act'.[3] On the basis of *Adcock*, it might therefore have been averred that the prejudicial result here lay in the fact that the solicitors became the innocent agents of a fraudulent scheme, and that a completed fraud on the solicitors was committed as soon as the spurious actions were raised.[4] Another result which might in theory have formed the basis of a fraud charge was the simple fact that the solicitors were induced to spend valuable time on a fool's errand. In relation to this possibility, however, an analogy may be drawn with cases such as *Kerr v Hill*,[5] and *Robertson v Hamilton*,[6] which indicate that the making of false reports to the police, whereby they are induced to spend time making investigations, is not a form of fraud.

Physical prejudice has on occasion also been regarded as a relevant result in fraud. It is, for example, fraud to induce a woman to consent to intercourse by means of a false pretence to be the woman's husband.[7] There are limits to the relevance of physical injury in a fraud charge however. A person who causes injury by

---

[1] 1988 SCCR 153, 1988 SLT 487.

[2] See opinion of the court at 489H.

[3] *Adcock v Archibald* at 82 – Lord Hunter may also have had in mind the situation in which the dupe renders himself liable to prosecution – see *Gordon* para 18–25.

[4] This was the moment when the scheme became an attempted fraud on the fishing companies – see the opinion of the court at 489H.

[5] 1936 JC 71, 1936 SLT 320.

[6] 1987 SCCR 477, 1988 SLT 70.

[7] *Wm Fraser* (1847) Ark 280.

means of false pretence may well be guilty of a crime involving real injury, rather than fraud,[1] and to allow this as a relevant result in fraud would be to blur the distinction between these two diverse areas of the criminal law.

The causal link

The third requirement of a relevant fraud charge is that there must be a causal connection between the false pretence and the result.[2] The result must have been brought about by the false pretence, and 'it is a defence to a charge of fraud to show that the false pretence did not influence [the victim] in his actings'.[3] Thus, if someone obtains goods from a seller, and later hands to the seller a cheque which is dishonoured, there is no fraud, since the seller did not deliver the goods as a result of any false pretence that the cheque would be honoured in due course.[4] For the same reasons, false statements as to 'collateral' matters cannot form the basis of a fraud charge.

In *Tapsell v Prentice*,[5] a woman falsely represented to a shopkeeper that she was a member of a band of gypsies encamped in the area who would buy provisions from his shop. No doubt in anticipation of future custom from this travelling band, the shopkeeper bought the rug, and the woman was charged with fraud, by inducing the shopkeeper to 'purchase a rug in excess of its proper value'. The court dismissed the charge as irrelevant. In the first place, the sale of an article in excess of its value was 'a thing that is done any day and is not a criminal offence'.[6] Secondly, the representations were 'not directly connected with the rug, which may have been a perfectly good one ... There can be no crime in such a sale as [was] here alleged unless the fraudulent misrepresentations relate directly to the articles to be sold'.[7]

In England, acute problems of causation have arisen in relation to cheque and credit card 'fraud'. It will be recalled that the user of such cards impliedly represents that his use of the cards is

---

[1] See above p 241, and cf CS Kenny *Kenny's Outlines of Criminal Law* (19th edn, 1965) para 377.
[2] See generally *Gordon* paras 18–26 to 18–29.
[3] *Gordon* para 18–26.
[4] *Mather v HM Adv* (1914) 7 Adam 525, 1914 SC (J) 184.
[5] (1910) 6 Adam 356, 1911 SC (J) 67. See also *Strathern v Fogal* 1922 JC 73, 1922 SLT 543.
[6] Lord Justice-Clerk Macdonald, (1910) 6 Adam 356 at 356.
[7] Lord Ardwall at 357.

authorised by the bank or credit card company.[1] Where the user is overdrawn, or has exceeded his credit limit, it has been held[2] that his implied representation of authority is falsified, and that since the person from whom he is purchasing goods would not have completed the transaction had he known the true situation, there is fraud.[3] This view has been much criticised.[4] A shop assistant, runs the argument, generally gives no thought to the question of the card-holder's relationship with his bank or credit card company. The assistant is concerned only to ensure that the shop is paid. He is induced to accept the cheque or credit card not by any misrepresentation, but by his knowledge that provided the card is not on the 'stop list' of stolen cards, and that the correct procedures are followed, the shop will be paid.

The cases which gave rise to these problems, *Charles* and *Lambie*,[5] were concerned with the English offence of obtaining a pecuniary advantage by deception. In Scotland, as we have seen, the result requirement is much wider, and it might be argued that by using a cheque or credit card when unauthorised to do so, the accused has induced the bank or card company to confer a benefit in the form of overdraft or increased credit facilities.[6] But again it may be objected that the bank is induced to grant such facilities not as a result of the card holder's false pretence, but rather because of its contract with the seller, by which the bank guarantees to make payment on presentment of a cheque or credit card voucher in respect of which the proper formalities have been complied with. There is no Scots authority on the question, and it might well be that a Scottish court would take a somewhat stricter view on the question of causation than did the House of Lords in *Charles* and *Lambie*.[7] In any event, it is probable that the decisions in those cases were influenced by 'the opportunities for fraud which were perceived following from the use of cheque cards and credit cards',[8] and will be confined to their own facts.

---

[1] See above p 243 and the cases of *Charles* [1976] 3 All ER 112, [1977] AC 177, and *Lambie* [1981] 1 All ER 332, [1981] 2 All ER 776.

[2] In *Charles* and *Lambie*, supra.

[3] *Charles* and *Lambie* are of course cases concerning the English 'deception' offences under the Theft Acts.

[4] See eg Glanville Williams, *Textbook of Criminal Law* (pp 778–779); *Smith and Hogan* (5th edn), p515.

[5] Supra.

[6] Cf *R v Charles* [1976] 3 All ER 112.

[7] See GH Gordon 'Two recent developments' (1975) 20 JLS 4; but Lord Fraser of Tullybelton concurred with the majority in *Charles*.

[8] *Smith and Hogan* p553.

The *mens rea* of fraud

The *mens rea* requirement in fraud may be split into two elements: the *mens rea* required in relation to the false pretence; and that in relation to the result.

(a) The false pretence

Clearly a representation made in the knowledge of its falsity is enough to satisfy this requirement. However, a reckless belief in the truth of a representation may also suffice, or at least a realisation that the statement may be false.[1] It is however 'unlikely that a situation in which [the accused] does not apply his mind at all to the truth or falsity of the statement would be regarded as fraudulent'.[2]

(b) The result

Whether the accused made the false statement recklessly or knowingly, he must have intended thereby to bring about the result. Fraud cannot be committed by accident.[3]

UTTERING OF FORGED DOCUMENTS

Forgery – the manufacture of falsely authenticated documents – is not in itself a crime.[4] Anyone may while away his or her time perfecting conterfeit signatures without becoming liable to the sanctions of the criminal law. Nor does the forgery become criminal if forged documents are stumbled upon by accident. The crime is committed only when a document is intentionally uttered as genuine,[5] in the knowledge that it is false.[6] Although fraudulent schemes may thereby be arrested at an early stage of their development, the introduction of the crime of attempted fraud,[7] has considerably reduced the scope of this crime. Subject to the *mens rea*

---

[1] *Gordon* para 18–31.
[2] Ibid.
[3] See *Gordon* paras 18–32, 18–33, and 7–12.
[4] See eg *Alison* I, 402.
[5] See eg *Macdonald* p 65; *Jas Devlin* (1828) *Alison* I, 402.
[6] *Hume* I, 154.
[7] In the Criminal Procedure (Scotland) Act 1887, s61.

elements just mentioned, the prerequisites for a charge of uttering are two:

(1) The uttering must be carried out with the intention of deceiving the person to whom the document is uttered.[1]
(2) The uttering must be 'towards' the prejudice of the victim. In *Macdonald v Tudhope*[2] the treasurer of a club forged the signature of a third party on certificates recording the amounts of money withdrawn from the club's gaming machines. He was convicted, and appealed on the grounds that there was no averment that anyone was prejudiced by the uttering, and in particular, no allegation that the certificates were anything other than a true record of the monies withdrawn from the machines. His appeal was dismissed on the grounds that ... 'It was not necessary that actual prejudice should ensue: what was essential was that the uttering should be towards the prejudice of the intended recipient'.[3] The fact that the recipient of the certificates accepted them as genuine documents to be recorded as such in the club's accounts was regarded as sufficiently prejudicial in this case.

If one regards the presentation of a forged document as a false pretence, and looks to the result or potential result which may ensue, it is easy to classify such actions as fraud or attempted fraud, rather than uttering. *Gordon* regards it as a matter of convenience only, whether uttering or fraud is the offence charged in such cases.[4]

The modes of forgery

A forged document is one which falsely purports to be authenticated by a particular person.[5] It is forgery to sign a document with a fictitious name, at least in circumstances where the recipient of the document 'will be led to believe that the document is the document of some person other than its maker'.[6] If it is forgery to sign a fictitious name, it is even more so to imitate the signature of a real person and append it to a document.[7] However, it appears that the

---

[1] See *Gordon* para 18–52.
[2] 1983 SCCR 341, 1984 SLT 23.
[3] At 23 (SLT).
[4] See *Gordon* para 18–35. Cf *HM Adv v Hardy* 1938 JC 144, 1938 SLT 412.
[5] *Hume* I, 140; *Macdonald* p 59.
[6] *Gordon* para 18–40. See also *Macdonald* p 63, and eg *Jas Hall & Ors* (1849) Shaw 254. Cf *Griffen v HM Adv* 1940 JC 1, 1940 SLT 175.
[7] See eg *John Henderson* (1830) 5 D & A 151.

forged signature need not resemble the genuine one[1] – a logical conclusion once it is accepted that fictitious signatures will suffice.

'As there were two ways in which Mahomet and the mountain might be brought together, so there are two ways in which a forged bond may be made, either by signing a false name below the bond, or by writing the bond above the genuine signature without permission ...'[2] Accordingly, there may be forgery where a genuine signature has in some manner been attached to a false deed. Similarly, a deed genuine in all respects may become a forgery by the making of unauthorised additions or alterations to it.[3] The alterations must be such as to affect the essential character of the deed, or significantly to alter its meaning.[4]

It is not forgery merely to make a false statement in a deed, however. In *Simon Fraser*,[5] a sheriff officer persuaded a colleague to subscribe as a witness to an execution of citation. The citation never took place, and the officer was accused of uttering the execution of citation as genuine. The charge was held to be irrelevant. Lord Justice-Clerk Inglis drew a theological analogy:

'In the scientific study of the evidences of Christianity, one becomes familiar with the distinction between the genuineness and the authenticity of the books of the New Testament – the term 'genuineness', as applied to them expressing merely the fact that they were written by the persons whose names they bear, apart altogether from any question as to the truth or credibility of their contents. For a writing, though genuine, may contain nothing but falsehoods.'[6]

But although false documents which are genuinely authenticated are not forgeries, it might well be fraud or attempted fraud to utter such documents as genuine.[7]

The modes of uttering

To utter a forged document is to present it or deliberately to display it as a genuine document. There must therefore be an intention to utter the document – involuntary uttering is not an offence. In *Jas*

---

[1] *Hume* I, 141; *Macdonald* p 59.
[2] *Simon Fraser* (1859) 3 Irv 467 at 494 per Lord Neaves.
[3] *Hume* I, 159–160.
[4] *Wm Mann* (1877) 3 Couper 376; *Thos Mackenzie* (1878) 4 Couper 50.
[5] Supra.
[6] Lord Justice-Clerk Inglis at 475.
[7] See Lord Justice-Clerk Inglis in *Simon Fraser* (1859) 3 Irv 467 at 476.

Devlin,[1] for example, the trial was stopped when it became apparent that the forged document, which Devlin had clearly intended to utter, had fallen from his hand before he could present it.[2]

Uttering may therefore be committed by presenting the document to a particular person, but it is also uttering to 'present' the document to the public at large, as when someone purporting to be a qualified lawyer hangs his forged practicing certificate in the waiting room of his chambers, or simply to place the document beyond the utterer's control.[3] To post a letter is therefore to utter it,[4] as is the presentation of a document to a third party with instructions to utter it. *Alison* takes the view that in these circumstances it is necessary to prove that the third party in turn presented the document to the victim.[5] *Gordon* takes the opposite view, but while the weight of authority appears to be in his favour,[6] it would seem contrary to principle to allow a charge of uttering in circumstances where the accused could still intervene to prevent his agent from presenting the document to the intended victim.[7]

False articles and 'practical cheating'

Occasionally, a clever painter reproduces the style of an Old Master, and presents it to the public, or at least to the art world, as the genuine article. Such conduct is popularly categorised as forgery, and it would seem logical to assume that the presentation of the work is an uttering, and a crime as such. This is particularly so where the painting has been 'signed' by the forger in the name of the original artist.[8] Uttering seems however, to be a crime confined to the presentation as genuine of falsely authenticated documents. An analogy might be drawn between the case of the forged painting and a 'forged' historical or literary work. In *HM Adv v Smith*,[9] the accused sold a number of letters under the pretence that they were written by Burns and Scott. He was charged with fraud and not uttering.[10]

---

[1] (1828) *Alison* I, 402.
[2] *Gordon* states that this might now be charged as attempted uttering.
[3] See *Gordon* para 18–55.
[4] See eg *Daniel Taylor* (1853) 1 Irv 230.
[5] *Alison* I, 403–405.
[6] See eg *Wm Jeffrey* (1842) 1 Broun 337; *John Smith* (1871) 2 Couper 1.
[7] Cf the law of attempt and eg *Samuel Tumbleson* (1863) 4 Irv 426.
[8] See *Gordon* para 18–49.
[9] (1893) 1 Adam 6.
[10] See also *Frank v HM Adv* 1938 JC 17, 1938 SLT 109. According to *Gordon* 'the fact that the successful use of the letters was charged as fraud does not mean that it could not have been charged as uttering'. (Para 18–44.)

The idea that the tendering of false articles may be a form of 'practical cheating' stems from the (rather obscure) case of *Alex Bannatyne*.[1] In that case the accused sold a mixture of oatmeal, barleymeal and bran as pure oatmeal. The account for the supply of this mixture was not paid. Although Bannatyne was charged with and convicted of fraud, 'the delivery of an article which is disconform to contract is not a 'definite practical result', nor is it in itself a crime'.[2] According to *Gordon*, the crime consists in disguising an article to make it appear genuine.[3] Three points may be made about this case, however:

(i) The court in *Bannatyne* did not purport to be creating or dealing with any offence other than fraud.
(ii) To induce a buyer to accept as genuine adulterated or 'disguised' goods which would not otherwise be acceptable, might well be regarded as sufficient to constitute fraud.[4]
(iii) The circumstances of *Bannatyne* would no doubt be treated now as attempted fraud, and it seems unlikely that the Crown would seek to develop a new crime analogous to uttering.[5]

In England, the equivalent crime is limited to the forging of 'instruments',[6] which definition is limited to documents, stamps, and certain recording devices. Thus, it is not forgery to alter car number plates,[7] nor to falsify product wrappers,[8] since such objects are not regarded as documents.

---

[1] (1847) Ark 361.
[2] *Gordon* para 18–50.
[3] Ibid.
[4] See above p 173.
[5] This may indeed be a 'rash assumption' following the revival of shameless indecency in 1978 (see above p 173).
[6] Forgery and Counterfeiting Act 1981, s 8.
[7] *Clayton* (1980) 72 Crim App Rep 135.
[8] *Smith* (1858) Dears & B 566.

17. Embezzlement/extortion

'Perhaps there is no part of our law which is more involved in obscurity, as propounded by our elementary writers, than the distinction between breach of trust and theft.'[1]

EMBEZZLEMENT AND THEFT

Theft is not confined to the situation where property is clandestinely taken and carried away.[2] A person who is lawfully in possession of goods, and holds them of consent, may be guilty of theft if he subsequently appropriates them to his own use. In looking for evidence of such appropriation, the courts must usually have regard to actions of the accused which suggest an assumption of the rights of the owner – the sale or pledge of the goods, for example. But what if the possessor is authorised by the owner to deal with and to dispose of the goods? In such cases, it cannot be said that the goods are appropriated merely because the possessor has assumed some of the rights of the owner. Solicitors, accountants, fund managers and certain types of mercantile agents are frequently entrusted with property which they have no obligation to return to the owner in its original form. It is the function of such agents to deal with the property for the benefit of their principal, and to account to him or her for their intromissions with the property. Where the property thus administered is diverted to the agent's own use, embezzlement may be committed. How then is this crime to be distinguished from that of theft? 'The trespass lies ... in the short accounting, and

---

[1] *Watt v Home* (1851) Shaw 519 at 521 per Lord Colonsay. The term 'embezzlement breach of trust' was the old name for the crime now known simply as 'embezzlement'. There are some suggestions however, that breach of trust may be a distinct offence – see Gordon's commentary to *Grant v Allan* 1987 SCCR 402 at 411.

[2] See above ch 14.

concealment of [the] receipts, not in the withdrawing of the species or corpus.'[1] The crucial point here is not simply that the accused was entrusted with the property, for a person in such a position can clearly be convicted of theft.[2] In *HM Adv v Smith & Wishart*,[3] for example, two bank tellers were relevantly charged with the theft of money which was in their care. Lord Medwyn said that 'a party may undoubtedly steal a subject entrusted to him',[4] but much was made of the limited extent to which the tellers were entrusted with the money, and in particular of the fact that a 'teller has no power of administration, his duties being simply to pay and receive the money of the bank'.[5] Lord Craighill stated in *HM Adv v John Smith*[6] that 'the fact that a man is a manager does not prevent him stealing'. In *Smith* £50 was handed to the accused in payment of an account. He appropriated the money and his conviction for theft was upheld on appeal. The court observed that:

'It depends entirely on the facts as they may arise whether the crime is embezzlement or theft. It is embezzlement if the manager ought to account for money received, and fails to do so; and it is theft if it was his duty to hand over to his employers the very sums he received and instead of doing so he kept them.'[7]

Thus, it seems that the essentials of an embezzlement charge are, first, the accused's power to administer the property of another, and second, his subsequent failure to account for dealings with that property in the exercise of his power of administration. Where, on the other hand, the accused's duty is to hand over a particular thing or sum of money, there will be theft if he fails to do so.

The question of authority

Another possible way to distinguish the two crimes is by looking at the extent of the accused's authority to enter into the transaction in question. *Kent v HM Adv*,[8] concerned the disposal of a large quantity of apple puree, and turned on the question of whether or not the

---

[1] *Hume* I, 60.
[2] See eg *HM Adv v John Smith* (1887) 1 White 413; *Smith & Wishart* (1842) 1 Broun 342.
[3] (1842) 1 Broun 342.
[4] Ibid at 350.
[5] Lord Medwyn at 350; see also Lord Justice-Clerk Hope at 351.
[6] 1 White 413 at 415.
[7] Ibid.
[8] 1950 JC 38, 1950 SLT 130.

disposal was authorised. The accused was convicted of embezzlement on the basis that the sale was authorised, but that conviction was set aside, there being no evidence of authorisation. On the facts, the court held that the appropriate charge was one of theft. But on one view, *Kent* threatens the basis of the working definition set out above. 'It is at least logically possible to disentangle the facts of even the most complicated embezzlement and consider each incident separately, and if this is done it will be clear that in every case the accused dealt with his principal's property in an unauthorised way.'[1] On this view, every appropriation of another's property would amount to theft, since every such appropriation would involve an unauthorised act, such as the paying of another's money into the accused's bank account, and the crime of embezzlement would disappear.[2] In many cases of course, it will be impossible to identify any particular unauthorised act, or any particular thing which has been appropriated, and the only evidence of misappropriation will be a discrepancy in a set of accounts, or a failure to pay over an expected sum at the end of a period of administration.[3] The Scottish courts clearly do recognise the crime of embezzlement. However, in *HM Adv v Wishart*,[4] Lord Macdonald implied that the question of authority is not the decisive one in determining whether or not there has been embezzlement – 'a charge of embezzlement or theft can arise immediately as soon as a solicitor does an unauthorised act concerning the funds of his client'. It is not clear that the case on which Lord McDonald based that dictum will bear the interpretation which he placed on it however.

The case was that of *Wormald*,[5] in which a solicitor was instructed to obtain a heritable security for a client, and a sum of money was placed on deposit-receipt to enable him to do so. Before he obtained a security, and thus when unauthorised to do so, the accused uplifted and appropriated the money. Although no objection was taken to a charge of embezzlement, it seems that the court in *Wormald* regarded the case as one of theft by taking, and not by appropriation, since the accused had not even begun to administer the client's money and had no authority to uplift it.[6]

---

[1] *Gordon* para 17–23. *Gordon* describes *Kent* as an exceptional case in that only one transaction was involved 'so that it was easy to disentangle the facts and point to what had been stolen and to when and where it had been stolen'.

[2] See also *HM Adv v Wormald* (1876) 3 R (J) 24.

[3] See eg *Edgar v McKay* 1926 JC 94, 1926 SLT 446.

[4] 1975 SCCR Supp 78.

[5] (1876) 3 R(J) 24.

[6] Cf *Alex Gilruth Fleming* (1885) 5 Couper 552. Note *Gordon's* comments on this case at para 17–19.

On the assumption that the question of the accused's authority is a relevant factor in embezzlement, there remains the theoretical problem posed by *Kent*. If the accused acts without authority, surely any appropriation by him is theft? A possible means of reconciling these views is to say that there is theft if appropriation takes place during a transaction which is itself unauthorised, but that if the appropriation takes place during the course of an authorised transaction, there will be embezzlement. The fact that the act of appropriation is itself unauthorised does not assist in the making of the distinction, since in any case there is no crime if the appropriation is by consent of the owner. It is by no means clear that the case law supports this view however.

For example, a charge of embezzlement was found to be relevant in *HM Adv v Wishart*[1] in which a solicitor drew cheques on his clients' accounts which he paid to a stockbroker friend in return for a cheque for an identical sum. The purpose of these transactions was not to appropriate the clients' money, but to enhance the stockbroker's balance sheet at the end of the financial year. These payments were clearly not part of any authorised transaction, yet the relevancy of the charge was upheld.[2]

In *Laing*[3] the accused received money from a client in order to discharge a bond, and instead of doing so simply paid some of the money straight into his own bank account. He was convicted of embezzlement, in spite of the fact that he had not yet entered into any authorised transactions.

The decision does however seem a strange one in the light of cases like *HM Adv v Smith*,[4] and both cases highlight what *Gordon* has described as the 'sociological aspect of the distinction between theft and embezzlement'.[5] In practice, juries seem reluctant to convict of theft those 'responsible' people – lawyers, accountants, and company directors, for example – who appropriate property entrusted to them. No such reluctance is apparent in relation to accused persons with more 'menial' occupations, however.

What therefore seems to identify embezzlement is not whether the goods have been entrusted to the accused, nor even the accused's authority to enter any particular transaction, but rather the accused's misappropriation of property over which he has a

---

[1] 1975 SCCR Supp 78.
[2] *Wishart* may not be consistent with the previous case law however. See comments on *Wormald*, supra.
[3] (1891) 2 White 572.
[4] (1887) 1 White 413.
[5] *Gordon* para 17–06.

power of administration[1]. It may be that for this reason, a charge of embezzlement is irrelevant where the accused has not yet begun to administer the property, or where the administration has come to an end,[2] the appropriate charge in such a case being one of theft. It should be noted that the distinction between theft and fraud is not of crucial importance in most cases, since it is competent to convict of embezzlement on a theft charge, and vice versa.[3] There may still be some situations, however, where differentiation will be required. The court in *Kent v HM Adv*,[4] for example, declined to substitute a conviction for theft for the discredited embezzlement conviction, since the jury were never asked to consider the evidence in relation to theft.[5]

The *actus reus* of embezzlement

Thus, where the accused diverts property to his own use while carrying out the instructions of or exercising authority to administer property given to him by his principal, there will be embezzlement. It seems, however, that actual appropriation, still less permanent appropriation, may not be required. Where there is a fiduciary relationship between the accused and the victim, as for example between solicitor and client, it will amount to embezzlement to employ the victim's funds in any way contrary to the trust.[6] In *Wishart*,[7] because the cheques were handed over simultaneously, the clients' funds never left the bank. Nevertheless, the court said that the potential risk to the clients' money created by the transaction was 'appropriation in the sense necessary to found a charge of embezzlement'.[8] In one of the older cases it was said that 'There seems no doubt that if an agent receives money on behalf of a client, and uses it for his own purposes, he is guilty of theft or embezzlement, whether he lodges it in his bank account, or employs it in his business, or pays it on account of other clients.'[9]

---

[1] See eg *Alex Gilruth Fleming* (1885) 5 Couper 552; *Gordon* para 17–22.
[2] *Alex Mitchell* (1874) 3 Couper 77. But cf *Edgar v Mackay* 1926 JC 94, 1926 SLT 446, and *Laing* (1891) 2 White 572.
[3] Criminal Procedure (Scotland) Act 1975, ss60, 312(m).
[4] 1950 JC 38, 1950 SLT 130.
[5] See also *O'Brien v Strathern* 1922 JC 55, 1922 SLT 440, which may imply that a person cannot be convicted of reset of theft when it is shown that the goods were embezzled.
[6] *HM Adv v Lawrence* (1872) 2 Couper 168.
[7] 1975 SCCR Supp 78.
[8] Lord Mcdonald at 84.
[9] *HM Adv v Laing* (1891) 2 White 572 at 574 per Lord Kincairney.

In some circumstances it may be very difficult to prove any specific act of appropriation, because of the degree of the embezzler's control over the property in question. In such cases, it may be that the only evidence of appropriation is a failure to account to the victim within a reasonable time of a demand for such an accounting. In *Edgar v Mackay*,[1] for example, the accused failed to account to the complainer for a sum of money, and only paid it over on the day of his arrest. These facts were sufficient to justify an inference of appropriation.

The *mens rea* of embezzlement

In order to bring home a charge of embezzlement, the Crown must prove a 'dishonest and felonious intention' to appropriate the property.[2] Thus, as in theft, a belief in the consent of the owner to the acts in question is a good defence to an embezzlement charge.

In *Allenby v HM Adv*[3] the accused was a fish salesman who acted for a number of different trawler owners. Proceeds from fish sales were paid into a common fund out of which the various owners were paid their share. Allenby was in the habit of making loans to the various owners out of this fund, and because of this practice he was charged with embezzlement. There was evidence that he kept strict records of all his intromissions, but the sheriff directed the jury that to use the common fund in this way amounted to embezzlement. There was a direction that a belief in entitlement to act in this way might be a defence, but in the absence of a direction that evidence of dishonesty was necessary, his conviction was quashed. In addition to a defence of belief in consent, a defence of claim of right, as opposed to a mere denial of dishonesty, may be relevant in embezzlement cases.[4]

EXTORTION

Where goods are obtained by the use of violence or threats of immediate violence, robbery is committed.[5] If the threat is one of

[1] 1926 JC 94, 1926 SLT 446.
[2] See Lord Kincairney's charge to the jury in *Laing* (1891) 2 White 572.
[3] 1938 JC 55, 1938 SLT 150.
[4] See *Gordon* para 17–33.
[5] See ch 14 above.

future violence, or some other type of threat, the relevant charge is one of extortion or blackmail.[1]

'There is the element of force or fear applied – that is the 'threat'; there is the element of intention, the intention being to overcome the reluctance of the victim, and there is the element of so 'extorting' – forcing out – a benefit to oneself which the victim would otherwise have refused to afford or to pay.'[2]

The threat

The use of certain types of threat is in itself criminal – threats to kill or injure, to do serious damage to property, or seriously to damage someone's 'fortune or reputation' fall into this category.[3] Where such threats are attached to demands for money or for some other advantage, the relevant charge is one of extortion. It is of the essence of extortion that threats are used to back up the demands of the accused.

In *HM Adv v Donoghue*,[4] five paintings were stolen, and the thief sent a letter to the owner explaining that for £1 200 he was in a position to secure their return. A charge of extortion was held to be irrelevant, for lack of any averment that any threat, such as a threat to destroy the paintings, was made to enforce the demand for money.[5]

The paradigm case of extortion is where the gangster offers the shopkeeper or businessman 'protection' against the future destruction of his property, in return for a regular payment. It is not necessary that the threat be one of future violence, however, either to the person or the property of the victim. Another common case is where the blackmailer threatens to make some damaging revelation about the victim. The allegation may be one of dishonesty, crime,[6] or sexual immorality,[7] and a charge of extortion is relevant regardless of whether the facts alleged are true or false.[8]

---

[1] *Hume* I, 108.
[2] *Silverstein v HM Adv* 1949 JC 160 at 165 per Lord Mackay, 1949 SLT 386.
[3] *Jas Miller* (1862) 4 Irv 238. *Gordon* submits (at para 21–05) that the latter category of threats is too widely expressed.
[4] 1971 SLT 2.
[5] What seems to be required is that the threat should be one to alter the victims position for the worse, and in *Donohue*, there was no such threat, only an offer to help. See *Gordon* para 21–14. See also *Kenny and Another v HM Adv* 1951 JC 104, 1951 SLT 363.
[6] See *Alex Crawford* (1850) Shaw 309.
[7] *Marion Macdonald* (1879) 4 Couper 268.
[8] *Alex Crawford*, supra.

Almost any threat will suffice provided it creates 'in the victim fear that unless he yields, his position will be altered for the worse'.[1] It is probably the case, however, that there is no extortion unless the threats used were objectively such as to overbear the will of the victim.[2] If the victim is unduly timid, there will be no extortion where he accedes to threats which are mild or vague. In the English case of *Harry*,[3] for example, it was held that a threat of 'inconvenience' to shopkeepers who failed to buy immunity from the organisers of a student charity campaign was insufficient to overcome the will of an 'ordinary person of normal stability and courage'.[4]

In addition, the accused must have intended that the threat should overcome the reluctance of the victim to confer the required benefit.[5] Extortion cannot be committed carelessly. However, it is almost certainly not, as it is in England,[6] a defence for the accused to show that he believed that the threat was a proper means of enforcing his demand.[7]

There may be extortion even though the threatened conduct would in some circumstances be regarded as perfectly legitimate. In seeking payment of a debt or performance of some obligation, the law regards as permissible certain types of pressure – for example a threat to resile from a contract, raise an action in court, or do diligence on a court decree.[8] However, where such a threat is used to achieve an illegitimate end, extortion is committed. In *Silverstein v HM Adv*,[9] the accused was the managing director of a landlord company. He informed tenants that unless a sum of money was paid to him as an individual, he would arrange to have them evicted. His conviction for extortion was upheld on appeal, in spite of an acceptance by the Crown of the argument that a landlord has the right to use threats to evict his tenants should they fail to agree a higher rent.

'. . .the threat to use one's own position and influence as a lever to alter the position of another to his detriment, unless that other buys immunity, is a relevant ground of charge. What brings about this result is that the payment

---

[1] Lord Justice-Clerk Thomson in *Silverstein v HM Adv* 1949 JC 160, 1949 SLT 386.
[2] *HM Adv v Silverstein* 1949 JC 160 at 163 per Lord Mackay.
[3] [1974] Crim LR 32.
[4] Sellars LJ in *Clear* [1968] 1 All ER at 80, [1968] 1 QB 670.
[5] See Lord Mackay's dictum in *Silverstein* at 165, supra.
[6] Theft Act 1968, s21.
[7] See *Gordon* para 21–15, and cf *Alex Crawford* (1850) Shaw 309 at 324 per Lord Justice-Clerk Hope.
[8] See *Silverstein v HM Adv* 1949 JC 160 at 163 per Lord Justice-Clerk Thomson, 1949 SLT 386. These categories are not exhaustive of the types of pressure the law will regard as legitimate.
[9] 1949 JC 160, 1949 SLT 386.

demanded is not a payment to which the claimant has any right arising out of his legal relationship to the victim.'[1]

Silverstein would have been entitled to make such threats in order to secure a more favourable result for his employers,[2] but not entitled to seek any benefit for himself. For this reason, threats to report someone to the police unless a sum of money is paid would be regarded as extortionate, whether or not the alleged crime has really been committed.[3] Such threats are not, of course, criminal in themselves, and there is some doubt as to whether there will be extortion if the thing demanded of the victim confers no benefit on the accused.

In *Hill v McGrogan*[4] the accused threatened to report a cleaner to the police for theft from her employers unless she quit her job. The charge of extortion was held to be irrelevant, since it was not alleged that the threats were used for an improper purpose, such as the pursuit of personal enrichment or malice. The sheriff-substitute said[5] that he could not 'see that it is wrong in law to do what you are entitled to do without warning or that it makes it worse to add that if the person attacked chooses to put the matter right to your satisfaction you will not pursue her'.

This case suggests that there will be no extortion where the accused gives the 'victim' an opportunity to put right some wrong, provided that the remedy does not involve conferring some benefit on the accused. However, while it is always open to the victim of a theft to refrain from reporting the matter to the police, and perhaps even to make it a condition of that abstention that the thief returns the property,[6] or, where the thief is an employee, that he should resign, it is not, it is submitted, open to others to make such 'bargains'. If the owner of stolen goods has any such rights, they arise out of his legal rights over the goods, or his legal relationship to the employee. In the absence of such a legal framework, any use of the word 'unless' in relation to such threats would be extortionate.[7]

---

[1] *Silverstein* at 163 per Lord Justice-Clerk Thomson.
[2] Where, in addition to rent, a premium is demanded by a landlord in return for the renewal, or assignation of a lease, a crime is committed – ss 101, 102 of the Rent (Scotland) Act 1971. The Rent (Scotland) Act 1984, s22(2) also makes it an offence to harass tenants in such a way as to interfere with their peaceful enjoyment of the lease.
[3] See eg *Alex Crawford* (1850) Shaw 309 at 326 per Lord Justice-Clerk Hope.
[4] 1945 SLT (Sh Ct) 18.
[5] At 19.
[6] See *Gordon* para 21–10.
[7] See *Silverstein* 1949 JC 160 at 165 per Lord Mackay, and compare Lord Justice-Clerk Thomson's dictum at 163.

This would mean that the theft victim could not demand payment for the goods in return for his failure to report the matter to the police. In this situation both threat and demand are legitimate, but there is extortion because there is no legally acceptable link between the two. The only legitimate threat in that case would be one to raise a civil action for the return of the goods, or for damages.[1]

The demand

While threats of legitimate behaviour will be regarded as extortion if they are linked to an illegitimate demand, the converse – that illegal threats render legitimate demands extortionate – is also true. Whether or not a debt is due, a creditor cannot enforce payment by threats of violence to the debtor, his family or his property,[2] and it matters not that the creditor genuinely believes in the justice of his claim.[3] While the demand is usually for money, or for some other benefit to the accused, it seems that any demand will suffice if it is to the 'detriment'[4] of the victim and provided there are accompanying threats which are not linked to the demand in the appropriate way. Thus, a demand that the victim resign from his job would be enough,[5] or even, perhaps, that the victim should donate a sum of money to charity. In *Black and Penrice v Carmichael* (1992 GWD 25–1415) the High Court held that the practice of wheel clamping could result in relevant charges of extortion (or attempted extortion) and theft. In such cases there is an illegitimate threat to the owner of the vehicle that his property will not be returned to him unless he pays the sum demanded. The court stressed that the proper method for the recovery of sums owed was by means of the legal process: resort to other methods was not permissible.

---

[1] Cf the unreported case of *Samuel Smith*, the complaint in which is narrated by *Gordon* at footnote 30 to para 21–10.

[2] *Alex Crawford* (1850) Shaw 309.

[3] Ibid at 324 per Lord Justice-Clerk Hope. Cf the subjective approach taken in England which excuses a blackmailer who believes (a) that there are reasonable grounds for his demand and (b) that the use of menaces is a legitimate way of enforcing the demand – Theft Act 1968, s 21(1). See the contrasting views expressed in [1966] Crim LR 467–480 by Sir Bernard MacKenna and Brian Hogan.

[4] See dictum of Lord Justice-Clerk Thomson in *Silverstein*, supra.

[5] But see the discussion of *Hill v McGrogan* 1945 SLT (Sh Ct) 18, and compare the English position which requires that the demand be one which confers a benefit on the defendant, or causes loss to the victim, and that the benefit or loss must be in money or property – Theft Act 1968, s34.

18. Malicious mischief

Traditionally, malicious mischief was a crime involving physical damage to property, and appears to have been regarded by Hume as one additionally requiring an element of civil disorder:

'It may be affirmed generally, with respect to every act of great and wilful damage to the property of another, and whether done from malice, or misapprehension of right, that it is cognisable with us as a crime at common law; if it is done, as ordinarily happens, with circumstances of tumult and disorder, and of contempt and indignity to the owner.'[1]

Hume then gives a number of examples to illustrate this statement, such as the casting down of houses, the destruction of the sluices or aqueducts of a mill, or the burning of boats and nets at a fishery. As the law developed, the crime retained its character as a crime of violence against property, but lost the element of riot and Gordon describes the crime as consisting 'simply in the destruction or damage of the property of another whether by destroying crops, killing or injuring animals, knocking down walls or fences, or in any other way'.[2]

It now appears, however, that the crime includes actions (and possibly omissions) in respect of property, which result only in patrimonial loss to the owner. Physical damage is no longer required. The authority for this is the case of *Wilson v HM Adv*,[3] in which a disgruntled employee at Hunterston 'B' power station, activated an emergency stop button bringing to a halt one of the turbines, and causing a temporary loss of generating capacity which had to be replaced at a cost of £147 000. In holding that the actions of the accused amounted to malicious mischief, Lord Justice-Clerk Wheatley said[4] that 'it was not suggested, nor could it be, that if the turbine had been stopped not by pressing the emergency stop button by hand, but by hitting the button with a hammer in such a way

---

[1] *Hume* I, 122.
[2] *Gordon* para 22–01.
[3] 1983 SCCR 420, 1984 SLT 117.
[4] 1984 SLT 117 at 119.

as to stop the turbine, the crime of malicious mischief would not have occurred'. The Lord Justice-Clerk then went on to say, having consulted the 'Shorter Oxford English Dictionary', that while the older cases all involved physical damage to property, the word 'damage' had a wider connotation, and could include situations where there was financial loss only. 'To interfere deliberately with the plant so as to sterilise its functioning with a resultant financial loss such as is libelled here is in my view a clear interference with another's property which falls within Hume's classification of malicious mischief . . .'

It seems doubtful whether Hume intended that his definition of the crime should cover this sort of situation however. It is true that Hume talked of 'interference' with property as being a sufficient basis for a charge of malicious mischief, a phrase which taken in isolation might well be capable of supporting the interpretation which the court placed on it in *Wilson*. It is also true that Hume regarded fire-raising as an act intended generally to do patrimonial injury.[1] But the whole context in Hume suggests that 'interference' is to be read as a synonym for violence. Fire-raising obviously results in physical injury to the property involved, as well as financial loss to the proprietor, and the case[2] in which the question of 'interference' arose was one in which a dam-dyke was pulled down. There was additionally a 'tumultous intrusion into the possession of the pursuer's lands', and thus the question arose of the accused's interference with the possessory, as opposed to proprietary, rights of the victim. 'It is grounded in the same reason, namely, the due regard to the order and tranquillity of society, that the pannel shall equally be convicted, whether he interfere with the property of another, or with his state only of peacable and lawful possession.'[3]

The Lord Justice-Clerk appears to have taken this statement out of its context in order to avoid the unpalatable conclusion that:

'no matter how deliberate and malicious the invasion of and interference with the other's property may be, if the positive act which sets in train the real injury to the other's property does not involve physical injury to the property, then irrespective of what the consequences of the invasion and interfence of the other's peacable possession may be, the act is not one of malicious mischief'.[4]

---

[1] *Hume* I, 125. Hume regarded fire-raising as one of the most important, and serious, forms of criminal damage to property. See also *Stewart and Walsh* (1856) 2 Irvine 359.

[2] *Monro of Auchinbowie, Hume* I, 122.

[3] *Hume* I, 123.

[4] *Wilson v HM Adv* 1983 SCCR 420, 1984 SLT 117.

It is not clear that this last statement is a correct summary of the pre-*Wilson* law, however, since it is quite possible to imagine non-violent acts which would cause actual physical damage to property – opening the seacocks of a ship, thus causing it to sink, is one possible example.[1] In any event, while the distinction between acts causing physical damage, and those causing only financial loss 'may seem narrow and artificial, it is nevertheless a distinction which ... the law has made'.[2]

Following *Wilson* it is, of course, no longer a distinction which the law makes, and there is one case, referred to only in passing by Lord McDonald,[3] which might justify the majority conclusion. The case is the unreported one of *David Monro*,[4] in which the accused deliberately removed the bung from a barrel of oil, causing the oil to escape. The analogy seems a close one, particularly if one were to imagine that Wilson had not stopped the generator, but had disconnected it from the grid, thus wasting the electricity generated. The analogy is not exact however, and the indictment in *Monro* avers that the oil ran out, and was 'wasted and lost or otherwise destroyed', while in *Wilson*, although generating capacity was lost, and in that sense 'damaged', there was no physical damage to any corporeal property. The majority, and particularly Lord McDonald, placed some reliance on the case of *Miller*,[5] in which the accused wilfully, maliciously and unlawfully placed a stone on a railway line 'in a manner calculated to and intended to obstruct trains and endanger the lives or safety of the passengers'. The stone was removed before the train arrived, and no damage or injury occurred. This charge, the relevancy of which was not challenged was said to be 'so obviously an example of conduct amounting to malicious mischief, albeit without actual physical damage, as to be beyond dispute'.[6] However, this case does not seem like an example of malicious mischief at all, having more in common with the crime of recklessly endangering the lives or safety of the lieges.[7]

The result of *Wilson* appears to be that whenever there is a deliberate interference with the property of another, and that interference results in financial loss, then a charge of malicious

---

[1] Cf *David Monro*, *Alison* I, 451; *Macdonald* p 84.
[2] Lord Stewart dissenting at 122 in *Wilson v HM Adv* 1984 SLT 117.
[3] At 121.
[4] *Alison* I, 451; *Macdonald* p 84.
[5] (1848) Ark 525.
[6] Lord McDonald in *Wilson* 1984 SLT 117 at 120.
[7] See eg *John Murdoch* (1849) Shaw 229, and the commentary to *Wilson* at 1983 SCCR 429.

mischief can be made out, regardless of the question of physical damage.[1] The case also raises, but does not answer, the question of whether the crime may be committed by an omission to interfere with property – the Lord Justice-Clerk reserved his opinion on 'what the position might be in a case where the initial act [sic] was of a negative and not a positive nature'.[2] The court's use of the word 'interference' may militate against the inclusion of omissions as relevant to the *actus reus* of this offence, since that word seems to imply some positive act on the part of the accused. However, the logic of the court's extension of the law in this area seems to be that where the actions of the accused have 'set in train' damage to property, whether physical or financial, then there is criminal liability for those actions. Logically, omissions to act are equally capable of setting such damage in train, and on this view it would be but a short step to extend the *actus reus* of the crime to include such omissions. There are, after all, situations where a person has a duty to act, whether through contract, or because they have themselves created some danger,[3] and where failure to perform that duty may result in physical damage or economic loss. Strikes are a conspicuous example of this, and it may be felt, at least where only economic loss is involved,[4] that these are situations which would be better dealt with by the civil law.

THE REQUIRED *MENS REA*

The very name of this crime – malicious mischief – seems to imply that there must be a 'deliberate wicked intent to injure another in his property'.[5] This is not the case. It is enough that 'the damage[6] is done by a person who shows a deliberate disregard of, or even indifference to, the property or possessory rights of others'.[7]

The latter statement was made in the case of *Ward v Robertson*,[8]

---

[1] Physical damage to property will of course remain a relevant ground of charge on the basis of the previous law.
[2] Lord Wheatley at 120.
[3] See eg *MacPhail v Clark* 1982 SCCR 395, 1983 SLT (Sh Ct) 37.
[4] Cf the English case of *Miller* [1983] 2 AC 161, [1983] 1 All ER 978, a case involving physical damage.
[5] Lord Justice-Clerk Aitchison in *Ward v Robertson* 1938 JC 32 at 36, 1938 SLT 165. Cf *Gordon* para 22–04 on the older authorities which required proof of spite in order to establish the offence.
[6] Or presumably, in the light of *Wilson*, economic loss.
[7] Lord Justice-Clerk Clerk Aitchison in *Ward v Robertson*, supra, at 36. Cf *Stewart and Walsh* (1856) 2 Irvine 359 on the *mens rea* required for fire-raising.
[8] 1938 JC 32, 1938 SLT 165.

in which the accused and two companions walked across grazing land, trampling the grass, and rendering it unfit for grazing. It was held that in the absence of evidence that the accused knew, or should have known that in crossing the field he was doing or was likely to do damage to the grass, his conviction for malicious mischief could not stand.

The situation might have been different had the accused trampled an ordinary growing crop, or had by walking in circles or taking more steps than necessary deliberately set out to cause damage. In the circumstances, however, his behaviour did not display the type of indifference required to constitute the offence. Such indifference might be present even where the accused believes the property damaged to be his own, if his belief is arrived at recklessly.[1] Where the accused's belief is not that the property is his own, but that he is entitled to damage the property of another, it seems that his belief, however genuine, is not a defence to a charge of malicious mischief. In *Clark v Syme*[2] the accused was a farmer who was in dispute with a neighbour whose sheep were eating his turnips. He shot one of his neighbour's sheep and was convicted of malicious mischief.

'A desire to vindicate [the accused's] rights of property is all very well in its proper place, but, when that involves the deliberate destruction of the property and the invasion of the rights of others, it ceases, in my view, to be excusable.'[3]

VANDALISM

The Criminal Justice (Scotland) Act 1980, section 78 created the new offence of vandalism. Under that section, any person who without reasonable excuse wilfully or recklessly destroys or damages any property belonging to another shall be guilty of the offence of vandalism. The section excludes fire-raising from the ambit of the offence. On the face of it, this statutory offence looks very much like malicious mischief. The High Court has held however, that the offences are distinct.

In *Black v Allan*[4] it was said that:

---

[1] See *Gordon* para 22–06 and cf *R v David Smith* [1974] 1 QB 354, [1974] 1 All ER 632, in which it was held that the accused's honest belief that the property was his was a defence to a charge of causing criminal damage, regardless of whether the belief was justifiable.

[2] 1957 JC 1, 1957 SLT 32.

[3] *Clark v Syme* 1957 JC 1 at 5 per Lord Justice-General defenceClyde, 1957 SLT 32.

[4] 1985 SCCR 11 at 12–13 per Lord Justice-General Emslie.

'the Crown interest in this appeal is simply to guard against the risk that any support should be given for the view that the offence created by section 78(1) [of the 1980 Act] is simply an echo of of the common law crime of malicious mischief. If anyone thought that it was such an echo, then the sooner they disabuse themselves of that notion the better.'

It is difficult to see precisely how the statutory offence differs from the common law crime, however. Both involve damage to property, although it remains to be seen how the courts will interpret the concept of 'damage' in relation to the statutory offence; both can be committed intentionally, and both can be committed with some degree of recklessness. It was on the issue of recklessness that the High Court appears to have rested their distinction, saying that where recklessness was in issue, the Crown had to show recklessness of the type required in *Allan v Patterson*[1] – the conscious and deliberate courting of material risks, or failure to notice obvious risks by reason of gross inattention – in order to bring home a vandalism charge. The implication is that this is a higher standard than that applicable to malicious mischief, but it is by no means clear how it differs from the standard laid down by Lord Justice-Clerk Aitchison in *Ward v Robertson*, quoted above, of a 'deliberate disregard, or even indifference to, the property or possessory rights of others.'

FIRE-RAISING

For long regarded as one of the most serious of criminal damage offences,[2] fire-raising is an offence in its own right,[3] and consists in the setting on fire of another's property.[4] There used to be a distinction between, on the one hand, wilful fire-raising, and on the other, culpable and reckless fire-raising, this distinction based on the division of fire-raising into capital and non-capital fire-raising.[5] However, in *Angus v HM Adv*,[6] it was said that 'the materiality of this distinction ...has now been swept away'.[7] Wilful fire-raising

---

[1] 1980 JC 57, 1980 SLT 77.

[2] See eg *Hume* I, 125.

[3] Although frequently charged as a form of malicious mischief – see *Gordon* para 22–24.

[4] It is a defence to a fire-raising charge for the accused to show that the property was his own – *Gordon* para 22–25. But if an accused set fire to his own property and the fire spreads to another's property, then in presence of the requisite *mens rea*, a charge of fire-raising may be held relevant.

[5] See the opinion of Lord Justice-General Dunedin in *Angus v HM Adv* (1905) 13 SLT 507.

[6] (1905) 13 SLT 507.

[7] At 508 per Lord Justice-General Dunedin.

was a crime which could only be charged where certain objects –
buildings, corn, growing timber, and mine-shafts were set alight.
Angus holds that wilful fire-raising may be charged where other
objects are burned – 'it would really be absurd' said the Lord
Justice- General, 'to say that what would amount to a crime if it
were done culpably and recklessly is not a crime if it is done wilfully'.[1] Conversely, it is competent to charge culpable and reckless
fire-raising where the object set on fire was one which was formerly
reserved for wilful fire-raising charges.[2]

Mens rea

There are some suggestions among the older writers that wilful
fire-raising may be committed recklessly, for example where a person intentionally sets fire to his own property, and the fire spreads to
the property of someone else.[3] Gordon submits, however that the
charge should be brought only where the fire-raising was deliberate.[4] There is very little authority, and in principle, Gordon's view
seems preferable. However, the debate seems rather a sterile one in
view of the decision in *Angus*.[5] Thus, it might be argued that, since
the distinction between wilful and reckless fire-raising is now obso-
lete, there is in Scots law a single crime of fire-raising, which can be
committed intentionally or recklessly.[6] In relation to the recklessness requirement, it seems that as in malicious mischief,[7] there
must be a high degree of indifference or carelessness.[8] Mere negligence is not enough.[9]

---

[1] At 508.
[2] *Geo Macbean* (1847) Ark 262.
[3] See eg *Hume* I, 130; *Alison* I, 433; Anderson *The Criminal Law of Scotland* (2nd edn, 1904) p 212.
[4] *Gordon* para 22–26.
[5] (1905) 13 SLT 507.
[6] Cf Lord Justice-General Dunedin in *Angus* (1905) 13 SLT 507.
[7] See *Ward v Robertson* 1938 JC 32, 1938 SLT 15.
[8] *Hume* I, 128.
[9] See eg *Geo Macbean* (1847) Ark 262.

V. OFFENCES AGAINST THE STATE AND ADMINISTRATION OF JUSTICE

19. Offences against the state

TREASON

The Scots law of treason is based wholly on English law,[1] and there is no recent Scottish case law.

Who may be guilty of treason?

Treason is a breach of allegiance to the Crown, and only a person who owes such allegiance can be guilty of treason in UK law. Thus, British citizens are subject to the law of treason no matter where in the world the treasonable acts take place. Such a person cannot escape liability by changing his nationality – indeed, to become the naturalised citizen of an enemy state is itself a treasonable act.[2] British subjects who are not British citizens can be charged with treason only in respect of acts taking place within the UK,[3] or its non-self-governing colonies. The same rule applies to aliens, the theory being that while in the UK they also owe allegiance to the Crown. An alien who holds a valid British passport and who has not surrendered it, nor taken any other overt step towards withdrawing his allegiance at the time of the relevant acts may also be guilty of treason, even if all the treasonable acts take place outwith the realm.[4]

---

[1] Treason Act 1708, s1. For a fuller treatment of the subject, see *Smith and Hogan* ch 21.
[2] *R v Lynch* [1903] 1 KB 444.
[3] British Nationality Act 1948, s3.
[4] And even if the passport is obtained by false pretences – *Joyce v DPP* [1946] AC 347. The case turned on the notion that while holding the passport, Joyce was entitled to the protection of the Crown. This ground of decision has been strongly criticised – see eg SC Biggs (1947) 7 Univ Tor LJ 162; Glanville Williams (1948) 10 Camb LJ 54.

The forms of treason

The ways in which treason may be committed are still governed by the Treason Act 1351. The prohibited acts which remain of importance are:

(1) Compassing or imagining the death of the sovereign, or of his Queen, or of their eldest son and heir

On the face of it, the first of these provisions is extremely wide, but in practice requires more than mere 'imaginings'. Some overt act is required, which, as well as acts and conspiracies of a violent nature, may include words spoken or written and published which compass the death of the sovereign.[1]

(2) Levying war against the sovereign in her realm

A plot to levy war on the sovereign would not be covered by this provision, but would be regarded as a compassing of the death of the sovereign.[2] The levying of war against the sovereign is said to be of two types – direct and constructive. It would clearly be regarded as levying war to engage in a direct campaign or uprising against the authority of the sovereign, but it is not necessary that acts of violence take place – the mere recruitment and marching of a rebel force would be enough,[3] and for this purpose, the size of the force is irrelevant.[4]

There may be a constructive levying of war where armed force is directed not against the sovereign, but used 'for the purpose of effecting innovations of a public and general nature'.[5] Thus it would be a levying of war to raise an armed force to achieve the repeal of a particular statute, improve the general level of wages, or even, it seems, to attempt to destroy the places of worship of a particular religious group.[6] There is no levying of war where there is a demonstration of force on a purely local issue, and such a case

---

[1] *Smith and Hogan* p 827.

[2] *Hume* I, 515.

[3] *R v Vaughan* (1696) 13 St Tr 485; *John Baird* (1820) *Hume* I, 522. Where no fighting takes place, treason is probably not committed unless the group is armed – *Hume* I, 523.

[4] See 3 Coke's Institutes 9.

[5] *Smith and Hogan* p 828.

[6] See eg *R v Dammaree and Purchase* (1710) 15 St Tr 52.

would be dealt with as one of mobbing and rioting,[1] or perhaps breach of the peace.[2] Cases involving armed mobs, demonstrating even on national issues are generally now treated in a similar way.[3]

(3) Being adherent to the sovereign's enemies in the realm, giving them aid and comfort in the realm, or elsewhere

In recent times, the most common form of treason has been the offence of adhering to the enemies of the sovereign. It is this provision which is used to prosecute acts of assistance to the enemy during wartime.[4] The assistance may be practical, material, or moral, as in the cases where the defendants took part in enemy propaganda broadcasts. In those cases, as in the following one, there was some doubt as to whether, being outwith the realm at the time of the broadcasts, they were subject to the law of treason. In *R v Casement*[5] an officer in a German Prisoner of War camp tried to persuade Irish prisoners to fight for the Irish Brigade against the British. He argued that only acts committed within the realm were relevant to a charge under this provision, and that the words 'or elsewhere' referred not to the acts giving aid and comfort to the enemy, but to the effect of those acts. That argument was rejected, and Casement was convicted. A British citizen will be convicted of giving assistance to an enemy no matter where the assistance is given.[6]

For a conviction under this heading, there must be proof of an 'evil' intention to give aid and comfort to the enemy. Thus, the accused's belief that he was entitled to perform the acts in question may be a relevant defence.[7] Similarly, if the accused was compelled to act by threats,[8] either to himself or his family, it may be impossible to prove the necessary intention.[9]

---

[1] *R v Andrew Hardie* (1820) 1 St Tr (Notes) 609.

[2] See eg *John Duncan and Ors* (1843) 1 Broun 512.

[3] See *Smith and Hogan* p778.

[4] The certificate of the Secretary of State is conclusive evidence that a state of war exists between the UK and the 'enemy' state – *Rv Bottrill, Ex parte Kuechenmeister* [1947] KB 41.

[5] [1917] 1 KB 98.

[6] See also *Joyce v DPP* [1946] AC 347.

[7] See eg *R v Ahlers* [1915] 1 KB 616.

[8] Against his life – *R v MacGrowther* (1746) 18 St Tr 391.

[9] *R v Steane* [1947] KB 997, [1947] 1 All ER 813 – *Steane* was not a case involving the defence of coercion, and it has been strongly argued that *Steane* was wrongly decided. See Glanville Williams *The Mental Element in Crime* (1965) para 21–22; *Gordon* para 7–19.

Misprision of treason remains a separate offence, and consists in the 'concealment or keeping secret of treason',[1] or possibly a treasonable plot,[2] from the authorities.

SEDITION

The crime of sedition consists in words written or spoken which are 'calculated to excite popular disaffection, commotion, and violence and resistance to lawful authority'.[3] In extreme cases, because of its connection with constitutional matters, seditious conduct occurring during a public assembly may be treasonable.[4] In modern conditions, it is thought that the words used would have to be very extreme to justify a sedition charge. What is required is that the accused be

'made out not to be exercising his right of free discussion for legitimate objects, but to be purposely, mischievously, without regard to his allegiance, and to the public danger, scattering burning firebrands, calculated to stimulate and excite such effects as I have mentioned – reckless of all consequences'.[5]

This 'right of free discussion' is now somewhat wider than it was in 1793 when Lord Braxfield described the British constitution as the best in the world, and implied that any proposal for the reform of that constitution was necessarily seditious.[6] It has been said in an English case[7] that 'it is in the highest degree essential that nothing should be done in this court to weaken the liberty of the press', and it seems likely that the same view would prevail in Scotland.[8]

To bring home a sedition charge, there must be proof that the relevant words were published intentionally. Once there is such proof however, it is unnecessary to prove that the accused intended to bring about any of the effects referred to above. Recklessness as

---

[1] *Sykes v DPP* [1962] AC 528 at 555 per Lord Denning.

[2] C S Kenny *Kenny's Outlines of Criminal Law* (1965) para 421.

[3] Indictment in *HM Adv v Aldred* (June 1921, unreported) Glasgow High Court. *Gordon* para 39–01 reported on another point.

[4] See *Chas Sinclair* (1794) 23 St Tr 777 at 800 per Lord Justice-Clerk Braxfield, since it may involve the levying of war against the sovereign.

[5] *John Grant and Ors* (1848) 17 Shaw 50 at 80 per Lord Justice-Clerk Hope.

[6] See his summing-up in *Thomas Muir*'s case (1793) 23 St Tr 118 at 229.

[7] *Caunt* (1947, unreported). See *Smith and Hogan* p786.

[8] See eg Lord Keith in *Lord Advocate v Scotsman Publications* 1989 SLT (HL) 705 at 709, [1990] 1 AC 812.

to the consequences is sufficient, provided that the words were objectively 'calculated' to have seditious effect.[1]

Sedition and treason appear to overlap in the area of conspiracies to alter the constitution by force. There is a constructive levying of war, since there is a conspiracy to effect changes of a 'public and general nature', and there is probably sedition if the conspirators publish their intentions.[2] In recent times, charges of conspiracy to further the aims of terrorist groups, such as the IRA have been brought,[3] but such cases are now likely to be dealt with under the Prevention of Terrorism Acts.[4]

THE OFFICIAL SECRETS ACTS

Spying and sabotage

Section 1 of the Official Secrets Act 1911[5] prohibits the collecting of information from, or being on or around a 'prohibited place',[6] for any purpose prejudicial to the safety or the interests of the state.

The test for conduct prejudicial to the interests of the state is an objective one, and it is not necessary to prove any particular act tending to show a purpose prejudicial to the interests of the state.[7] Motive and the presence or absence of 'evil intention' are irrelevant to a charge under section 1. In *Chandler v DPP*[8] the defendants were campaigners for nuclear disarmament. They were charged with conspiring to gain entry to an American Air Force base in England, and to prevent operations taking place. They argued that far from being a purpose prejudicial to the interests of the state, their purpose was the highly beneficial one of preventing the outbreak of a nuclear war. It was held that no matter what their ultimate intention or desire, the offence was committed, since one of

---

[1] *John Grant and Ors* (1848) 17 Shaw 50. There is no need for the words to produce any actual effect.

[2] See *John Grant and Ors*, supra, especially Lord Wood at 50.

[3] See eg *HM Adv v Walsh* 1922 JC 82, 1922 SLT 443; *HM Adv v MacAlister and Ors* (November 1953, unreported) Edinburgh High Court; *Gordon* para 37–26.

[4] See below.

[5] As amended by the Official Secrets Act 1920.

[6] 'Prohibited place' is comprehensively (and widely) defined in s3 of the 1911 Act (as amended), and includes not only MOD establishments but railways, roads and other public works.

[7] Section 1(2)

[8] [1964] AC 763, [1962] 3 All ER 142.

their subordinate purposes was the obstruction of aircraft operations. 'The accused both intended and desired that the base should be immobilised for a time, and I cannot construe purpose in any sense that does not include that state of mind'.[1] Judged by the policies of the democratically-elected government of the day, that was a prejudicial purpose, and the defendants were convicted.

Although the section is referred to in the sidenote as relating to spying, other 'prejudicial purposes' are covered by section 1. An obvious example is sabotage, as well as the type of conduct encountered in *Chandler*.

Divulging confidential information

Section 2 of the 1911 Act made it an offence to communicate, use, wrongfully to retain, or to fail to take reasonable care of confidential information relating to affairs of state. Again the motive for the disclosure was irrelevant – if information was deliberately disclosed, it mattered not that the accused thought that his action was likely to be beneficial to the interests of the state.[2] The nature and importance of the information was also irrelevant. In *R v Crisp & Homewood*[3] for example, documents relating to contracts between the War Office and the army's clothing suppliers were passed on to the director of a tailoring firm. It was held that the disclosure of this vital information was an offence under section 2. It was also irrelevant that the information would be of no value to an enemy.[4]

Section 2 has now been repealed and replaced by the provisions of the Official Secrets Act 1989. Section 1 of this Act deals with the disclosure of information about the security and intelligence services.[5] Under section 1, the nature and content of the information communicated remains irrelevant where the communicator is or has been a member of the security or intelligence services.[6] Where the communicator is a Crown servant or government contractor, it is necessary to show that the disclosure of the information is, or is

---

[1] Lord Reid at 790.
[2] *R v Fell* [1963] Crim LR 207.
[3] (1919) 83 JP 121.
[4] Cf s1, which prohibits the making of sketches, plans, or models, and the collecting of information which may be of use to an enemy, and for the purposes of the section, 'enemy' includes potential enemies – *R v Parrot* (1913) 8 Crim App Rep 186.
[5] 'Security or intelligence' services are defined in s1(9), and presumably includes MI5, MI6, and intelligence gathering stations such as GCHQ.
[6] Official Secrets Act 1989, s 1(1).

likely to prove, damaging to the security services.[1] It is a defence for a person charged under this section to show that he did not know, nor had reasonable grounds to believe, that the information related to security or intelligence matters, and for a Crown servant[2] to show that he did not realise, nor have reason to believe, that the disclosure would be damaging.[3] The Act contains similar provisions relating to the disclosure of defence information,[4] and information relating to international relations.[5]

The offence of receiving confidential information has been abolished.[6] However, section 5 provides that where information is received by a person who knows, or has reasonable cause to believe, that it is protected by the provisions of the Act, and disclosure of the information would be damaging, then that person commits an offence if he discloses the information.[7]

Other offences under the Acts include the obstruction of the forces of the Crown in the execution of their duties in relation to a prohibited place;[8] the harbouring of a person or persons who have committed or are about to commit an offence under the Acts;[9] gaining admission to a prohibited place by fraud, forgery or impersonation;[10] and attempts to commit, or the aiding and abetting of the commission of offences under the Acts.[11]

TERRORISM

The first Prevention of Terrorism Act was passed in 1974 as a reaction to the IRA's mainland bombing campaign of that year. Since then, the legislation has been re-enacted with modifications from time to time, the latest being the Prevention of Terrorism (Temporary Provisions) Act 1989. The Acts give power to proscribe organisations which promote or encourage terrorism in the UK,[12] and it is an offence to be a member of, solicit support for, or

---

[1] Official Secrets Act 1989, s1 (3), (4).
[2] But not a member of the security services.
[3] Official Secrets Act 1989, s1(5).
[4] Ibid, s2.
[5] Ibid, s3.
[6] Official Secrets Act 1911, s2(2).
[7] Ibid, s5(2).
[8] 1920 Act, s3.
[9] 1911 Act (as amended), s7.
[10] 1920 Act, s1
[11] 1920 Act, s7
[12] 1989 Act, s1(2).

assist in the management of such organisations.[1] The only currently proscribed organisations for the purposes of the Prevention of Terrorism Act are the IRA and the INLA.[2] It is a defence to a charge of being a member of such an organisation for the accused to show (a) that he did not become a member while any of the Prevention of Terrorism Acts were in force, and (b) that he has not been an active member since the passing of the Acts.[3]

Public displays of support for proscribed organisations, such as the wearing of particular items of dress, or the carrying of any particular article are also an offence under the Act.[4] In *O'Moran v DPP*[5] it was held that the wearing of dark glasses, a black beret, and dark clothing at an IRA funeral was the wearing of a uniform, and the wearing of such clothing would almost certainly constitute a public display of support, contrary to the provisions of the Act, as would the wearing or carrying even of single items such as badges or flags.[6]

Funding of terrorism

Persons who contribute money or other property, who enter into funding arrangements, or who accept or solicit such contributions, either for specific acts of terrorism,[7] or for the benefit of a proscribed organisation,[8] are guilty of an offence. Where contributions are solicited or accepted, it is necessary to prove that the accused intended that the contribution be applied to particular terrorist acts, or had reasonable cause to suspect that it might be so used.[9] Where the charge is one of making contributions, the prosecution must show that the contributor knew or had reasonable cause to suspect that his contribution would be used for the prohibited purpose.[10] It is a defence to a charge of contributing to proscribed organisations, or of entering into arrangements for their support, for the accused to show that he did not know nor had reasonable cause to suspect that the money was to be used for the benefit of such an organisation.[11] The 1989 Act also makes it an offence to

---

[1] 1989 Act, s2(1).
[2] Ibid, sch 1.
[3] Ibid, s1(3).
[4] Ibid, s3.
[5] [1975] 1 All ER 473, [1975] QB 864.
[6] *O'Moran* at 480. See also *Smith and Hogan* p795.
[7] 1989 Act, s9.
[8] Ibid, s10.
[9] Ibid, s9(1)(b).
[10] Ibid, s9(2)(b).
[11] Ibid, s10(2).

becomepartytoarrangementswherebyterrorists'fundsareconcealed, removed
from the jurisdiction, or transferred to nominees.[1] The offence is designed to deter the 'laundering' or concealment, by banks or other institutions or dealers, of monies used to fund terrorism. Once again there is a defence where the accused can show that he did not know or suspect that the arrangement related to terrorist funds.[2] No offence is committed under sections 9, 10 or 11 if the person involved in the transaction obtained express consent to his actions from a constable, or if, having entered into a funding arrangement, he discloses to a constable his suspicions that the arrangement was for the benefit of a terrorist act or organisation. The disclosure must be made on his own initiative, and as soon as it was reasonable for him to do so.

Disclosure of information

Where a bank official or other person in a position of financial responsibility suspects or believes that money or other property with which he is dealing is derived from terrorist funds, that official may disclose his suspicions to the police, regardless of any contractual duty of confidentiality.[3] This provision may be contrasted with section 18, which makes it an offence to fail without reasonable excuse to disclose information which the accused knows or believes might be helpful in preventing the commission of a terrorist offence or in securing the apprehension of persons involved in such offences.

Exclusion orders

Where the Secretary of State is satisfied that a person has been concerned in the commission of or preparation for terrorist offences in Great Britain or Northern Ireland, or is attempting or may attempt to enter those jurisdictions for terrorist purposes, he may make an exclusion order against that person, prohibiting him from being in, or entering Northern Ireland[4] or part of the UK.[5] Orders excluding persons from the UK cannot be made in respect of

---

[1] 1989 Act, s11.
[2] Ibid, s11(2).
[3] Ibid, s12(1).
[4] Ibid, s6.
[5] Ibid, s7.

British citizens.[1] It is an offence for anyone to fail to comply with such an order,[2] or knowingly to be concerned in the illegal entry into Great Britain, Northern Ireland or the UK of a person subject to an exclusion order,[3] or the harbouring of such a person in those places.[4]

[1] 1989 Act, s7(4).
[2] Ibid, s8(1).
[3] Ibid, s8(2)(a).
[4] Ibid, s8(2)(b).

20. Offences against the administration of justice

PERJURY

Hume described perjury as 'the judicial affirmation of falshood on oath'.[1] It is of the essence of the crime that an 'absolute falsehood be explicitly and wilfully affirmed'[2] while the accused is giving evidence on oath in some judicial proceeding.[3] Ambiguities in the accused's testimony will be resolved in his favour, and it is only very clear falsehoods which will justify a perjury charge.[4] Accordingly, a failure to tell 'the whole truth' probably does not amount to perjury.[5] In any event, it is necessary to prove that the accused intentionally affirmed the falsehood, in the knowledge of its falsity,[6] and this would be difficult where his evidence was merely ambiguous or incomplete.

The perjured evidence must have been given in the course of evidence both competent and relevant, and provided that it is so given, it does not matter that the falsehood is trivial or seemingly insignificant.[7] Evidence which goes merely to credibility, and not to any specific issue in the case is relevant evidence for the purposes of a perjury charge.[8]

---

[1] *Hume* I, 366. Note that a person who does not take the usual form of oath, because he is an atheist, for example, but merely affirms that he will tell the truth is still liable to a perjury charge – False Oaths (Scotland) Act 1933, s7(1)(b).

[2] *Hume* I, 366.

[3] Provided that the tribunal can and does administer the oath to witnesses – see *Gordon* para 48–03.

[4] Ibid.

[5] But see *Gordon* para 48–11.

[6] *Hume* I, 368.

[7] See *Lord Advocate's Reference No 1 of 1985* 1986 SCCR 329, 1987 SLT 187 in which it was held that Hume's reference to the need for the falsehood to be 'material' (*Hume* I, 368–369), simply meant that the falsehood must relate to relevant evidence. *Gordon's* contrary view, expressed in para 48–14 cannot now be accepted.

[8] See eg *Elizabeth Muir* (1830) Alison I, 469–470; *HM Adv v Smith* 1934 JC 66, 1934 SLT 485.

The competency requirement means that a falsehood affirmed in the course of evidence which should have been disregarded as incompetent, cannot ground a perjury charge, and the matter of competency is one which can be reviewed in subsequent perjury proceedings by the trial judge,[1] or exceptionally, by the jury.[2] A particular aspect of the competency requirement is that the Crown cannot rely on statements made in precognitions in order to establish a perjury charge. Such statements are inadmissible, even for the purpose of attacking a witness's credibility, and cannot be relied upon.[3] Furthermore, it is not enough for the Crown merely to prove that the accused has sworn contradictory oaths on different occasions. 'The Crown must be able to prove that either **x** or not **x** is the case, they cannot merely show that [the accused] must have committed perjury on one or other occasion'.[4] Finally, it is no defence to a perjury charge that the false testimony was given at the witness's own trial on some other charge. In *HM Adv v Cairns*[5] the accused was acquitted of murder, but subsequently convicted of perjury in respect of his evidence at the trial that he did not assault and stab the deceased, the truth being that he did indeed carry out the attack.

Subornation of perjury

A person who induces another to commit perjury is himself guilty of subornation of perjury.[6] It is not necessary that the witness be intimidated or bribed into giving perjured evidence, although intimidation or bribery will suffice. Simple persuasion is enough.[7] It is necessary, however, that the witness should actually give the perjured evidence[8] – if the witness does not in fact give evidence, resists the inducement to commit perjury,[9] or informs on the accused at or before the trial,[10] there can be a conviction only of attempted subornation. An attempt to procure false evidence from

1   *HM Adv v Smith*, supra.
2   *Low v HM Adv* 1988 SLT 97, 1987 SCCR 541.
3   See eg *Low v HM Adv*, supra.
4   *Gordon* para 48–18
5   1967 JC 37, 1967 SLT 165.
6   *Hume* I, 381.
7   *Gordon* para 48–21.
8   *Angus v HM Adv* 1935 JC 1, 1934 SLT 501.
9   See *Hume* I, 382.
10 *Robert Stirling* (1821) *Alison*, 487

a witness may also constitute contempt of court,[1] or an attempt to pervert the course of justice.[2]

CONTEMPT OF COURT

The person accused of contempt of court is in the peculiar position of having committed a punishable offence, but not a crime in Scots law. Contempt of court

'...is the name given to conduct which challenges or affronts the authority of the court or the supremacy of the law itself, whether it takes place in or in connection with civil or criminal proceedings. The offence of contempt of court is an offence *sui generis* and, where it occurs, it is peculiarly within the province of the court itself, civil or criminal as the case may be, to punish it under its power which arises from the inherent and necessary jurisdiction to take effective action to vindicate its authority and preserve the due and impartial administration of justice.'[3]

It is a notable feature of the law in this area that where someone is held to be in contempt of court, the judge may deal with the matter immediately, without the need for formal charge or trial, and the person in contempt may be imprisoned or fined then and there. In relation to some types of contempt, for example where a witness prevaricates in order to avoid answering a competent and relevant question, judges will generally give the witness a chance to purge his contempt before making use of the sanctions available to them.[4] In any case, the person allegedly in contempt should be given an opportunity to explain himself.[5] Furthermore, where a witness is giving evidence for the defence in a criminal trial, it may constitute a miscarriage of justice in relation to the accused if the judge deals with the witness's contempt in open court.[6]

What types of conduct will result in a person being found to be in contempt?

(a) Conduct which challenges or affronts the authority of the court. At common law, the conduct must be such as to demonstrate a neglect of the duty to uphold the dignity of the court, or a wilful or

[1] See below.
[2] See *Gordon* paras 48–40, 51–13.
[3] *HM Adv v Airs* 1975 SLT 177 at 179, 180 per Lord Justice-General Emslie.
[4] See eg *Wylie and Another v HM Adv* 1966 SLT 149.
[5] See eg *Royle v Gray* 1973 SLT 31.
[6] See eg *Hutchison v HM Adv* 1983 SCCR 504, 1984 SLT 233.

reckless interference with the course of justice.[1] Thus, drunken or disorderly conduct in court will almost certainly constitute contempt.[2] Slandering, or murmuring of judges is also contempt of court,[3] as well as being a common law crime.[4] Criticism of judges and the law is not of itself contemptuous, however. In *R v Commissioner of Metropolitan Police, ex parte Blackburn,*[5] Salmon LJ said that '...no criticism of a judgment, however vigorous, can amount to contempt of court, providing it keeps within the limits of reasonable courtesy and good faith'. Even where there is some indication that the criticism falls outwith those limits, the courts have said

'over and over again that the greatest restraint and discretion should be used by the court in dealing with contempt of court, lest a process, the purpose of which is to prevent interference with the administration of justice, should degenerate into an oppressive or vindictive abuse of the court's powers'.[6]

In addition, it may be the case that abusive statements about judges would not be treated as contempt unless they related to a particular case or cases.[7]

Witnesses who prevaricate or refuse to answer competent and relevant questions,[8] or who perjure themselves,[9] may also be held in contempt. Unauthorised or improper absence or lateness from court proceedings by solicitors, jurors, or witnesses may also constitute contempt,[10] provided that there is no reasonable excuse for the absence.[11] Wilful failure to attend may also be charged as an attempt to pervert the course of justice.[12]

(b) Conduct which challenges the supremacy of the law. It has sometimes been argued that certain classes of witness – for example doctors and journalists – may refuse to answer questions on the grounds of professional confidentiality. It is true, of course, that certain witnesses are entitled to refuse to answer questions

---

[1] See eg *Pirie v Hawthorn* 1962 JC 69, 1962 SLT 291; *Mackinnon v Douglas* 1982 SCCR 80, 1982 SLT 375. Cf *Butterworth v Herron* 1975 SLT (Notes) 56.
[2] *Hume* II, 138; *Gordon* para 1–02. See eg *Dawes v Cardel* 1987 SCCR 135.
[3] See eg *Milburn* 1946 SC 301, 1946 SLT 219.
[4] Judges Act 1540; *Hume* I, 406.
[5] [1968] 2 QB 150 at 155, [1968] 2 All ER 319.
[6] *Milburn* 1946 SC 301 at 315 per Lord President Normand.
[7] Cf *Gordon* para 51–03.
[8] *Hume* I, 380.
[9] *Gordon* para 51–04.
[10] See eg *Muirhead v Douglas* 1979 SLT (Notes) 17. Cf *Macara v Macfarlane* 1980 SLT (Notes) 26.
[11] Cf *Mackinnon v Douglas* 1982 SCCR 80, 1982 SLT 375
[12] See *HM Adv v Mannion* 1961 JC 79; *Gordon* para 48–41.

relating to professional communications – the confidentiality attaching to communications between solicitor and client is a good example. Unless the witness falls into one of the recognised exceptions however, it will be contempt if he fails to answer a competent and relevant question, such failure being regarded as challenge to the supremacy of the law itself, whatever the motive for the witness's silence.[1] The court has a residual discretion to excuse a witness from answering such a question on the grounds of conscience, but *HM Adv v Airs*[2] strongly suggests that no such relief will be available to journalists, in criminal proceedings at least.[3] Further, there is no requirement that the question which the witness fails to answer must be 'useful'. If it is competent and relevant it must be answered, and in any event 'it is hard to figure any circumstances in which a relevant question could, in the course of a trial or proof, be judged unnecessary or not useful . . .'.[4]

The Contempt of Court Act 1981

It is a contempt of court to prejudice the possibility of a fair trial, or the administration of justice generally,[5] by publishing information or opinions likely to lead to pre-judgement of the issues.[6] Contempt generally requires some degree of *mens rea*, in the form of a wilful or reckless disregard of the authority of the court.[7] In relation to pre-trial publicity however,[8] the Contempt of Court Act 1981 provides that liability for contempt is strict, and is incur-

[1] *HM Adv v Airs* 1975 SLT 177 at 183 per Lord Justice-General Emslie.
[2] 1975 SLT 177.
[3] The Contempt of Court Act 1981, s10 provides that journalists and others need not disclose the source of information unless disclosure is deemed by the court to be necessary 'in the interests of justice or national security or for the prevention of disorder or crime'. It is not enough however that the information would be relevant to the determination of an issue before the court, since that would mean that disclosure could be required in respect of all admissible evidence. The disclosure must further be 'necessary' in the technical sense of being necessary in the interests of the administration of justice in the course of court proceedings – *Maxwell v Pressdram Ltd* [1987] 1 WLR 298, [1987] 1 All ER 621. This provision probably would not have assisted Mr Airs, who was in possession of information about a terrorist group.
[4] *HM Adv v Airs*, supra, at 180 per Lord Justice-General Emslie.
[5] *Atkins v London Weekend Television Ltd* 1978 JC 48, 1978 SLT 76; *Hall v Associated Newspapers Ltd* 1979 JC 1, 1978 SLT 241.
[6] *Glasgow Corporation v Hedderwick and Sons* 1918 SC 639, 1918 2 SLT 2; *Stirling v Associated Newspapers* 1960 JC 5, 1960 SLT 5.
[7] See *Mackinnon v Douglas* 1982 SCCR 80, 1982 SLT 375.
[8] Contempt of Court Act 1981, s2(1).

red whenever a publication, be it speech, writing, broadcast or any other form of communication addressed to the public at large, creates 'a substantial risk that the course of justice in the proceedings in question will be seriously impeded or prejudiced'.[1] To incur liability under the Act, it is a further requirement that the proceedings be 'active', a requirement which covers not merely the duration of the trial itself, but the entire period when the person concerned is under the 'care of the court and within its protection'.[2] Thus, a case becomes 'active' when a suspect is arrested,[3] or, in a civil case, when the record is closed.[4]

Section 3 of the Act creates a defence for publishers or distributors of contemptuous material who, having taken all reasonable care to avoid liability, do not know or have reason to suspect that the proceedings are active, or that the material is contemptuous. The Act further provides that fair and accurate reports of public legal proceedings, published contemporaneously with those proceedings, and in good faith, do not constitute contempt.[5] However, the court can order the postponement of publication of such reports where the risk of prejudice would be 'substantial'.[6] Publications which in good faith discuss public affairs or matters of general public interest and which incidentally cause a risk of prejudice to particular legal proceedings,[7] are also protected. In the latter case, the onus is on the Crown to prove that the risk of prejudice to the particular legal proceedings was (a) more than merely remote, and (b) that it was not merely incidental to the matter under discussion.[8]

MAKING FALSE REPORTS TO THE POLICE

It has for a long time been a criminal offence to falsely accuse someone of a crime.[9] Simply to waste the time of the police is clearly now a separate crime at common law. The essence of the

---

[1] Contempt of Court Act 1981, s2 (2).
[2] *Hall v Associated Newspapers Ltd* 1979 JC 1 at 12 per Lord Justice-General Emslie.
[3] *Hall v Associated Newspapers Ltd*, supra. Or perhaps even where a suspect has been detained under statutory powers. Cf *Gordon* para 51–11.
[4] See eg *Young v Armour* 1921 1 SLT 211.
[5] Contempt of Court Act 1981, s4.
[6] Ibid, s4 (2). See eg *Keane v HM Adv* 1986 SCCR 491, 1987 SLT 220.
[7] Contempt of Court Act 1981, s5.
[8] *A–G v English* [1983] 1 AC 116, [1982] 2 All ER 903.
[9] *Hume* I, 341–342.

crime consists in the making of false reports to the police, such that they are 'deliberately set in motion by a malicious person by means of an invented story'.[1] In *Kerr v Hill*,[2] the accused was charged that he falsely claimed to have seen a pedal cyclist struck by a bus, thus wasting police time on an unnecessary investigation, and rendering certain bus drivers liable to suspicion and accusations of reckless driving. It would be easy to regard such a charge as one of fraud, particularly in view of the breadth of the result requirement of that crime in Scots law.[3] In the subsequent case of *Robertson v Hamilton*[4] the accused falsely claimed to have been bitten by a police dog during their arrest on other charges, thus rendering the police-dog handler liable to suspicion and possible disciplinary action. At first instance, the sheriff held that the complaint relevantly disclosed a species of fraud. On appeal, however, the High Court expressed no concluded opinion on the question of fraud, and rested their conclusions entirely on *Kerr v Hill*.[5]

Both *Kerr v Hill* and *Robertson v Hamilton* involved specific accusations made against others. However, it seems that specific allegations are unnecessary to the commission of this crime. It is enough that false information is conveyed to the authorities, causing them to embark upon a fruitless investigation. In *Bowers v Tudhope*[6] the accused falsely represented to the police that he had lost his giro cheque. Relying on dicta from *Kerr v Hill*, the High Court rejected the argument that a false accusation is a necessary element in the crime.[7] '[If] a person maliciously makes a statement, known to be false, to the police authorities, with the intention and effect of causing them to make inquiries into it, he commits a criminal offence'.[8] It is not, however, a crime merely to tell lies to the police,[9] or, presumably, to induce another to tell lies to the police.[10]

---

[1] *Kerr v Hill* 1936 JC 71 at 75 per Lord Justice-General Normand, 1936 SLT 320.
[2] 1936 JC 71, 1936 SLT 320.
[3] See ch 16 above on *Fraud* and Gordon's commentary to *Bowers v Tudhope* 1987 SCCR 77 at 79.
[4] 1987 SCCR 477, 1988 SLT 70.
[5] 1936 JC 71, 1936 SLT 320, and in particular Lord Justice-General Normand's dictum quoted above.
[6] 1987 SCCR 77, 1987 SLT 748.
[7] The interpretation of *Kerr v Hill* adopted in *Bowers v Tudhope* has been criticised by 'Forensis' (1987) 32 JLS 353.
[8] *Kerr v Hill* 1936 JC 71 at 76 per Lord Fleming.
[9] See *Curlett v McKechnie* 1938 JC 176 at 179 per Lord Fleming, 1939 SLT 11 and *Gordon* para 48–40.
[10] But see *Dalton v HM Adv* 1951 JC 76, 1951 SLT 294.

ESCAPING FROM LAWFUL CUSTODY

When a person is lawfully confined to prison, under a valid warrant applicable to him, he commits the common law offence of prison-breaking if he escapes.[1] It is not necessary that violence should be used to effect the escape – even if a prisoner simply walks out of a door which has been carelessly or deliberately left open, prison-breaking is committed.[2] The specific offence of prison-breaking only applies where the accused was held in a public prison, and cannot be charged where the accused was held in some place of temporary custody, such as a police cell.[3] If the accused was not in a public prison, or was not in any place of custody at all, though still a prisoner, the relevant charge is one of defeating or attempting to defeat the ends of justice by escaping from lawful custody. Such was the charge in *HM Adv v Martin*,[4] for example, where the accused was a member of a 'chain-gang' working outside the prison where he was being held. A person assisting the escape of another, whether from prison or from any other place, is also likely to be charged with hindering or defeating the ends of justice.[5]

[1] *Hume* I, 401–402; *Gordon* paras 49–01, 49–03.
[2] *Hume* I, 402; *Gordon* para 49–05.
[3] *Hume* I, 404; *Gordon* para 49–02.
[4] 1956 JC 1, 1956 SLT 193.
[5] See eg *HM Adv v Martin*, supra; *Turnbull v HM Adv* 1953 JC 59.

Index